Drunk Before Noon

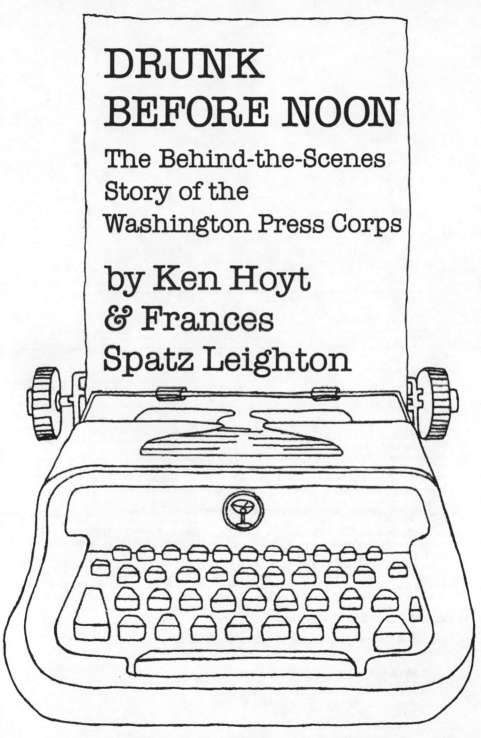

DRUNK BEFORE NOON

The Behind-the-Scenes
Story of the
Washington Press Corps

by Ken Hoyt
& Frances
Spatz Leighton

Prentice-Hall, Inc., Englewood Cliffs, New Jersey

Book design by Joan Ann Jacobus
Art Director: Hal Siegel

Drunk Before Noon: The Behind-the-Scenes Story of the Washington Press Corps, by Ken Hoyt and Frances Spatz Leighton

Printed in the United States of America
Prentice-Hall International, Inc., London/Prentice-Hall of Australia, Pty. Ltd., Sydney/Prentice-Hall of Canada, Ltd., Toronto/Prentice-Hall of India Private Ltd., New Delhi/Prentice-Hall of Japan, Inc., Tokyo/Prentice-Hall of Southeast Asia Pte. Ltd., Singapore/Whitehall Books Limited, Wellington, New Zealand
10 9 8 7 6 5 4 3 2 1

Library of Congress Cataloging in Publication Data
Hoyt, Kendall K
  Drunk before noon.
  Bibliography: p. 409
  Includes index.
  1. Journalists—Washington, D. C.—Biography.
I. Leighton, Frances Spatz, joint author. II. Title.
PN4871.H63 070'.92'2 79-18668
ISBN 0-13-220830-X

＊ ＊ ＊ ＊ ＊ ＊ ＊ ＊ ＊ ＊ ＊ ＊

To the Good Ol' Boys of the National Press Club Tap Room this book is irreverently inscribed....

It is altogether fitting and proper that we do this but in a larger sense *we* cannot congregate; *we* cannot merry make; *we* cannot rally around. Those brave men, living and dead, who guzzled here have swallowed it far beyond our poor power to add or detract. It is for us the living rather to be here rededicated to the great unfinished cask remaining before us, that these spirits fled shall not be drunk in vain; that our potions here, by God, shall give a new mirthful freedom; and that the gentlemen of the P. Club, by the P. Club, for the P. Club shall not perish here from thirst.

* * * * * * * * * * * *

The authors gratefully acknowledge the generous help of many men and women of the Washington press corps. Many are credited in the book while others chose to remain anonymous. We are especially indebted to Felix T. Cotten, Frank Holeman, and other past presidents of the National Press Club for telling it as it was.

Contents

Foreword

We are about to enter the little-known realm of the Washington press corps, the most heard group in the world and—aside from a few superstars—one of the least seen.

How can we tell you what an average newsperson is like? We cannot anymore than we can describe a typical beast of the forest. Fierce lions, shy gazelles, chattering monkeys, slavering hyenas. Like them or not, all have their place in nature.

Roaming in Capital pressdom are some two thousand of varied species involved in newspapers, wire services, magazines, newsletters, photos, radio, and television. We shall see all kinds.

Over them are lion tamers known as editors and circus bosses called publishers. We may glimpse slinking creatures called investigative reporters stalking their prey, able to bring down even a president.

The power of the press has been rated as second only to that of the people. Since people act from what the press tells them, it may stand first as long as it keeps free of curbs and manipulation.

Who are those men and women who shadow the great and put itching powder on the seats of power? Sundry books have dealt with one phase or another— White House reporting, television, muckraking, and ego trips. Lacking is a view of the whole pack. We thank our colleagues for leaving it to us.

If our book were quite serious, then I, Ken Hoyt, would trace the rise of journalism and its role in the future success or failure of our nation.

If it were all fun, my coauthor, Fran Leighton, would weave yarns to interest and amuse and keep you turning the pages. Between us, we try to do both.

There will be more fun than sobriety. Fran has ranged through the Press Club pouncing on anecdotes like a cat in a meadow of mice. For my part, I have looked back to the old days, tried to detect some pattern in it all, and inserted semicolons in Fran's flowing prose.

We intend to stress neither the strength nor weakness of the press but to strike a balance. On the plus side, its people never were better educated or had such marvelous equipment to speed the news. But how well can the system meet the hard times ahead? Think about that as we go along.

Meanwhile let us see how Washington press folks work and live and play. We hope you will find them likable, with the caution that much of the world's trouble comes from good ol' boys who can do no wrong. Ponder also upon that.

Where can we find the varied types who prowl in search of news? To hunt in the wild, the vantage point is at the water hole, where all creatures come to drink. In Washington, the place is the Tap Room of the National Press Club. Let us take you there.

Kendall K. Hoyt
Washington, D.C.

* * * * * * * * * * *

"Woe to the land whose princes drink in the morning..."
—Unknown

part one * * * *

DRUNK
BEFORE NOON

1/Drunk Before Noon

When Art Wiese, stalwart president of the National Press Club and Washington bureau chief of the *Houston Post*, invited President Carter's top aide, Hamilton Jordan, to speak at a Club luncheon in the spring of 1979, Jordan wanted to be sure of what he was getting into. "Is the membership broken down by sex?" he asked.

Wiese mulled that over a moment and replied, "Well, frankly we have a much greater problem with alcohol."

They don't make drunks the way they used to. Heaven and the National Press Club can attest to that. Around the Club, "sober as a judge" took new meaning and meant "sober as Judge Grice."

"Judge" Grice was no more a judge than he was sober. But he *was* a member in good standing, if you could call it standing. As Pat Munroe, an old-timer here, recalls, "The judge was the only man I ever saw who could pass out at the bar and remain upright. He did this by locking his thumbs and fingers around the rim of the bar. One would say pleasantly, 'Good morning, judge.'

"Closer inspection, when he did not answer, revealed his eyes were closed. Wait a few minutes and he would come to life, shake his head, and order, 'Another double.'

"One day his hold slipped and he flopped to the floor. An ambulance was called and he was put on a stretcher. As the attendants were about to roll him away, he held up his hand and called to the barkeep, 'How's about one for the road?'"

As I say, they don't make drunks the way they used to. Judge James Grice considered the morning wasted if he wasn't drunk before noon. He was not alone, though few Club members have quite followed in his footsteps. Some even stay sober all day.

If the time ever comes when the Club bar no longer opens in the morning as a refuge from the world and editors, it will be a sad day. Best that we capture the moment and look back at the glory of "those brave men, living and dead, who guzzled here."

Of all the picturesque topers, Homer Dodge was a standout. Homer, the last at the Club to hang on to his cane and gray spats, could not change; did not care to change. Yet, members always were hoping he would, especially in the matter of tippling.

There was the day it seemed Homer had taken a turn for the better. He was seen drinking sherry instead of the usual hard stuff.

George Dixon, a rewrite man for the *New York Daily News*, and later Hearst humorist, wanted to put in a word of encouragement. So he began, "Oh, I see you're drinking sherry, Homer." He sounded like a pleased schoolteacher as he asked, "Are you tapering off?"

Homer looked at him with scorn. "No, George. I'm tapering *on*."

Once when the Club's board was debating whether to expel a member who, in a drunken moment, struck a waiter, it was said he was a nice guy when not in his cups. Homer, who had been snoozing, woke to mutter, "If he is a son of a bitch when he's drunk, he's a son of a bitch when he's sober."

If old soldiers never die but simply fade away, perhaps old topers just evaporate. A disembodied Homer Dodge must remain in some corner of the Tap Room with a ghostly glass in his hand and an eyebrow cocked in disdain over the ebb in refined chitchat and repartee. We shall see more of Homer and his friends.

We shall meet Paul McGahan, who could drink standing on his head; a marine who thought he was followed by an elephant; and the little man whose hat was glued on. We'll tell you the macabre story of the man who made his mark, and scores of others. On the serious side, we shall find how the news business works in Washington and view its greats and its rank and file on the job.

First let us show you the setting. We will go on a tour of that unique institution, the National Press Club. The building it owns rises fourteen stories, with the Club on the top two floors, at Fourteenth and F streets in northwest Washington. The U.S. Treasury is a block to the west and the White House just beyond. The Capitol is to the east, a short cab ride away, as are most other offices where news is found.

We enter the National Press Building and take the lift to the thirteenth floor. The Club impresses newcomers. Fairly prominent men in business and government who, as my guests, came for the first time, took it as a rare treat. Yet I have never seen a description of the place. This might tell you something about the perceptivity of the writers who run it. We thank them for leaving it to us.

Even in the elevator, one knows this is an unusual place. The car does not whoosh to the top. Usually it makes stops for reporters bound for the Club dining room or bar or a look at the news tickers. You may hear snatches of conversation on what to cover today. The White House? Capitol Hill? The State Department? Some of the talk may be in languages you don't know—French, Swedish, Russian, Japanese.

The elevator doors open.

Helen Brinegar—it rhymes with vinegar—is supervisor of the front desk. She long has been holding the Press Club members at bay.

One day there was a long line trying to pay food checks and cash personal checks, so Vinegar Helen's nerves were a little more frayed than usual. Clark Hoyt, a newspaper man, but no relative, finally got Helen's attention and sought to lighten the atmosphere with a little friendliness.

"Helen," Clark said, "I've been wanting to ask you something for a long time."

Helen continued thumbing through the food checks as she replied, without looking up, "Shoot."

He said, "I keep wondering, why do you wear that rubber on your thumb?"

Now Helen did look at him and said without a moment's hesitation, "To keep from getting pregnant."

The men fell apart at the counter laughing and slapping one another's backs, but Helen and Clark continued to look at each other with utter seriousness. "But does it work?" Clark pursued.

Helen shot back with mock irritation, "Well, it's worked so far."

Past the front desk to the left is the West Lounge, with an abstract painting displayed, a swirl of crimson by artist-author Fran Leighton.

The south window, for those few who pause there, gives a view of the tall shaft of the Washington Monument, the marble dome of the Jefferson Memorial, and planes rising from National Airport across the Potomac River. In April, one can see the famed Japanese cherry blossoms around the Tidal Basin.

It's one of the best views in Washington. The Club had the wall knocked out for a picture window. It may have marred the outside of the building, but members sitting with drinks to enjoy the panorama don't care about that.

Homer Dodge used to look out with binoculars. So he

was called a dirty old man. We'll get to that later. Let's keep to the tour.

Back we go out the West Lounge, skirting the front desk and its guardian angel, and into the long friendly corridor that leads to the hideaways. To the left is the Tap Room, formerly called the Men's Bar or the Members Bar and still mostly a male domain. It opens at 9 A.M. so that some members can have their favorite breakfast. According to member Stan Jennings, "It's called the Breakfast of Champions—bourbon and water." We pass it now, promising to return for a drink.

To the right is the card room, with its dark green tables for those who both drink and gamble, the last male bastion. Though females may enter, they don't. I can't tell you what goes on, not having been there since before World War II. But I can see the heads of players from my window across the court.

The Club keeps a clerk on the desk till 2:00 A.M. for card addicts who frequently come out to cash checks. Some members say they should bloody well bring cash or write checks for their losses.

As we move along, we see that the Club is no soulless shell of metal and plastic but a place given character by the flow of national and world events. The wall of the long corridor we are treading is paneled in rich brown and studded with the front-page mats of many newspapers. Some of the headlines are historic, such as the end of World War II.

Now we reach the main lounge, two floors high, over-looked by a balcony. The furnishings are a bit tacky but cheerful. The room is dominated by a life-size portrait of a recumbent nude, her knee raised to hide this and that. A Club bard once wrote, "I dreamed that Phyrne dropped her knee. It was a wondrous sight to see."

The plaque attests that this lavishly endowed creature was indeed Phyrne, the Grecian beauty who posed for sculptures by Praxiteles, so her measurements are known. When the walls of Thebes were razed, she offered to rebuild them with a sign: "Destroyed by Alexander the Great; Restored by Phyrne the Courtesan." So she invented billboard advertising.

An old-timer told me the picture really is of Maxine Elliott, actress friend of J. P. Morgan, financier. It was the talk of the *Salon de Paris* in 1910. Anyhow, she was a successful whore, an inspiration to all.

Among the Club keepsakes is the grandfather clock with its slow tick, topped by a moth-eaten stuffed owl. The clock was presented by Club wives long ago as a constant reminder to their husbands that they were waiting at home.

Another memento is a hobgoblin figure made of tree trunks and bent branches, brought from Alaska by reporters on President Harding's final trip. They named it irreverently "Princess Alice" after Teddy Roosevelt's darling daughter, then still cutting a wide social swath.

On the mantel of the fireplace, where logs burn in winter, is a plaster reproduction of the Club's old Billiken, the pointy-headed little god of all the best in life.

Beyond the lounge is the main dining room, crowded at lunch time. The diners—of assorted ages, shapes, and sizes—look like average people who would not attract notice for elegance or lack of it.

Few beards or long hair are seen among the men, mostly in conservative business suits. Reasonably attractive dress is worn by the women who range from old biddies and square-jawed lassies to some rare beauties.

Look around, you might find a news celebrity here, a Walter Cronkite or Barbara Walters or Jack Anderson.

Reporters in a hurry rush to the end of the lounge to glance at the news-tickers, tick-a-tacking the news in three versions—AP, UPI, and City. Yards of typed reports of the day's happenings festoon the walls. My office is just under the tickers, one floor down.

At the top of my stairs is the Club's lounge—a stand-up bar, an outpatient ward from the main alcoholic dispensary, called the 64 Bar for the year it was installed. Never will the Club bars fall. Members stand propping them up from their midmorning opening till late at night. The unofficial name of the 64 is the Belly Button Bar. Since drinkers need their hands to hold their glasses, they support the bar with their middles, lacking any other push as some say, in that area.

Next to this bar is the ballroom, high-ceilinged and spacious, with tall windows on each side. The noontime sun streams in. The Club is known throughout the country for its luncheons there and for little else. For more than half a century, the great and near-great of the world have come to speak. Before television, it was unseen. Now you often view the rostrum with the

Club seal on newscasts as celebrities face cameras and barbed questions.

This big room, set with round tables, usually is crowded then. In truth, most of the people seated and more on the balcony are there just for the event and will write nothing about it. But such an audience looks impressive and is part of the show.

Beyond the ballroom is the East Lounge, little used now except for special events. Earlier it was for overflow dining midday. Women, then not admitted to the Club till after 6:00 P.M., could go there. It is a dismal room, with walls of faded blue and nothing to identify it with the press or with what is supposed to be one of the world's most glamorous places.

A pity Fran Leighton was not allowed to beautify it. As cochairman for decoration, she enlivened the corridor that goes to the lounge with photos of notables who have visited. But the project stopped short of the lounge door. Newspeople, with exceptions, seem to have little feel for tradition or elegance.

To complete our tour, we return through the ballroom, past the Belly Button Bar, and mount one flight to the top floor. Here, along the mezzanine that overlooks the main lounge, are several small dining rooms for private meetings.

Then we come to the library, a long, paneled room with shelves of magazines and out-of-town papers read by a few and books unread. Oldsters slumber here. Snoozing downstairs, especially by dodderers who cannot hold their water, is frowned upon.

One might suppose that among press people interested in facts, the library would be busy. In truth, I never have seen anyone open a book. Some kind soul donated a *New York Times* microfilm file and a machine to read the tapes. It gathers dust. There also is a typewriter room, a dingy cubbyhole with out-of-town phone books, unused.

So it does not matter that directories are out-of-date or that there is no world atlas. In World War II, pull down maps were hung near the tickers so one could locate battle areas. When peace came, they were put in a dark corner and then disappeared. A library committee works to upgrade references to no avail.

So little does the Club care that the library three times was made a lunchtime dining room. One year the Board of Governors decided to close the East Lounge and serve in the library just at the hour when members might need to use it. Out went the big chairs and tables; in came smaller ones. Since the library is a symbol of erudition, there were snorts of outrage and the room was restored.

Another spin of the world; another Board. Same thing over again, as if it had not been tried before. There was no indignation then but serving lunch there did not pay. After the heavy oak furniture had been lugged back it was hard to believe this could happen a third time. But a female on the Board wanted it. Out went the big tables. Finally it began to look silly even for the Club, so back came the furniture and the library was a slumber room again. Let us hurry on before they bring back the lunch tables.

Past the library is a billiard room where balls click and members shout when they score or fail to score. One fellow I knew lost his job from spending too much time there. Recently the balls had to be locked up. The eight ball, symbol of frustration, kept getting stolen—a sign of the times.

This completes our tour of the Club. It is really several clubs in one as patrons of the bars, dining room, card room, and billiard room go their separate ways.

Now let us return to the Tap Room. The entrance is set in a wood-paneled alcove off the main lobby. A pair of phones are there so drinkers can tell their employers or wives that they have been detained on business. A swinging door, faced with strips of shiny brass, shields the place from public gaze. A small window prevents collisions between comers and goers.

Beside the door is an inscription in Old English lettering, the rule of a monastic order ascribed to St. Benedict that applies here, if one can stop to read without being trampled by thirsty arrivals.

Bene dictum, benedicte!

If any pilgrim monk come from distant points, if he wish to dwell in the monastery, and will be content with the customs he finds in this place, and do not perchance in his lavishness disturb the monastery, but is simply content with what he finds he shall be received, for as long a time as he desires. If, indeed, he find fault with anything, or expose it, reasonably and with the humility of charity, the Abbot shall discuss it prudently, lest perchance God has sent him for this very thing. But if he has been found gossipy and contumacious in the time of his sojourn as guest, not only ought he not be joined to the body of the monastery, but also it must be said to him, honestly, that he must depart. If he do not go, let two stout monks, in the name of God, explain the matter to him.

Such is the rule, usually unwritten, of any institution in being long enough for inmates to have become set in their ways. This one has been here close to fifty years.

Go through the swinging door and you are in a long, narrow oak-paneled room, dingy as the wood darkened with age and tobacco smoke. Ahead is a stand-up bar some thirty-feet long, with a great array of bottles behind it, a red-coated barkeep or two and members two-deep in rush hours, at lunchtime and late afternoon.

Beyond are heavy oak tables with leather seats along the walls behind them and hard-seated chairs in front. Meals can be ordered.

To most a visit can be a quick in-and-out—"A moment's halt, a momentary taste of being from the well amid the waste." For the regulars it is a way of life. The effect on a man is, as in the land of the Lotus Eaters, described in the *Odyssey:*

Once tasted, no desire felt he to come
With tidings back, or seek his country more,
But rather wished to feed on lotus still
And to renounce all thoughts of home.

Well, life may be an odyssey to all men in their minds, even if they stay in one place. But let us take our drinks and leave this dingy room to sit overlooking that grand view of Washington from the south window. Maybe the spirit of Homer Dodge will be with us.

Homer loved the Club. We are indebted to him for memories that would have been lost had he not helped put them to paper in a little book printed in 1958 for the Club's fiftieth anniversary.

The name of the book was chosen from the jumble of letters that a linotype operator would strike to fill when a mistake was made. Running his fingers down the keys, he would print "etaoin shrdlu."

So the book is called *shrdlu*. It might mean that the moving finger has spotted a mistake so it can be corrected. The world would be safer if that principle could be applied more widely, from Homer's Olympian view of life.

10

Homer, as we have said, used to sit in this room with binoculars. He came at dusk to scan the facade of the Willard Hotel across the street. He was accused of lewdly peeping at goings-on in the hotel but insisted that he was just counting the starlings that came to roost on the sills and ledges.

"Homer, are you still counting them?" a member teasingly inquired.

"Yes," our voyeur answered.

"How many are there?" his friend asked.

Homer replied, "I can't say for sure but two are missing."

The National Press Building which houses the National Press Club is still the place to be, even though there is a brisk traffic in moving men carrying in and carrying out.

It was a black day when the prestigious *Wall Street Journal* picked up and moved elsewhere—Connecticut Avenue. There had been some griping about the slowness of elevators but the Wall Streeters felt it was the last straw when water from the men's room swooshed into the newsroom, and they almost needed boats to get around.

Walk on any floor and a journalism student would get a thrill—so would an old-time reporter. On some floors it's like a tour of the world. On others it's just seeing famous newspaper names.

The National Press Building, as well as the Club, takes pride in the success of *Roots* author Alex Haley and feels that his success is somehow their own.

For two years Haley hung on, not eating too well, while he worked on the final writing and editing of *Roots* in a small office in the National Press Building.

As a matter of fact, the building management wanted to evict Haley for nonpayment of rent after the bill passed three-thousand-dollars. The building's lawyer came to investigate.

Helping to stall the wolf from Haley's door was NPC member Ofield Dukes a public relations man who had faith in Alex and occupied an adjoining office. It was a very special occasion when Alexander Haley came to speak at a Press Club luncheon in February of 1977, soon after he had sent his rent check, plus a check of $328 to Ofield, for repayment of loans. The Club, as a gag, presented the author with a canceled check for over four thousand dollars.

Only when Club members saw Haley stand up to make

his speech did some of them vaguely remember having seen the slim, average-size man in the elevator or entering an office down the hall from the *Milwaukee Journal*'s Washington bureau, where the name on the door said The Kinte Foundation.

Now they knew that Kinte referred to Kunta Kinte, Haley's African ancestor who was kidnapped and brought to America as a slave.

Alex Haley freely admitted that many was the night he had no money for a hotel room and slept on the couch in his office, hoping the management wouldn't notice.

What thrilled every would-be book author in the audience and gave them new hope was learning that his book was something like twelve years overdue at the publishers, before it was finally turned in.

"My publisher and my agent kept asking—and quite rightly—how much longer they would have to wait," Haley confessed.

"People were beginning to say that I would never finish it, and sometimes I almost agreed with them."

Yet, there he was, at age fifty-five, standing as a true Horatio Alger example of rising from—well, not rags exactly—but from poverty to millionaire.

There was hope for everybody.

You always know when company is coming to the National Press Club on the top floor. There is a sudden flash of chauffeur-driven limousines. There are security guards hovering around the building entrance, the lobby, and the hallways—depending on how important the guest is and how controversial.

Once—I believe it was before an Israeli visitor arrived—an explosives-sniffing dog was led through the building. This wonderful beast came into my office. Once, in a bomb scare, all tenants had to be out for an hour or so.

The list of important people who have had offices in the National Press Building, or still do, is endless and amazing. An early ghost writer—Michelson—who did speeches and other writing for Franklin Delano Roosevelt, had an office here.

There are one-man and two-men bureaus, and huge news bureaus like UPI on the third floor, whose flashes are wired to some thirty countries around the world.

There are newsletters by the dozens, public relations firms, and a modeling agency for girls.

Tass, the Russian news agency, makes its home in the National Press Building—at one time on the second floor. It was always pointed out with amusement how the floor was shared by three strange bedfellows—Tass, the *Wall Street Journal* and the USIA.

Then one day someone threw a stink bomb into the second floor window of *Tass* and the agency decided it would be wiser to move to a higher floor.

There is *"The Hartford Courant*, America's Oldest Newspaper—established 1764—Robert Waters, Correspondent."

There are doors marked Dong-A Ilbo [Korean]; Toronto Star Syndicate; Swiss Broadcasting Corporation; Hanh Trinh [Korean]; A.N.S.A. Italian News Agency; Il Popolo; Embassy of Spain, Information Department; Der Spiegel [German]; Washington Farm Letter; Christian Beacon Press, Inc.; Embassy of Japan Press Room; Nippon Television Network; The Capital Spotlight; United Egg Producers; Nuclear Safety Research Association.

There have been some mysterious tenants. Mighty mysterious tenants. One young woman got the nickname Match Girl. She would enter the building and go up in the elevator to the *Paris-Match* office, where she evidently worked, strung with camera gear and holding a rose between her teeth.

The *Paris-Match* office moved and so did the girl with the rose. Fran Leighton once saw her in the elevator and had to bite her tongue to keep from asking why the rose. To my knowledge nobody ever asked. Maybe she was waiting to see if they would.

An even more mysterious tenant is Ralph Nader, who, according to Lou Davis, one of the managers of the building, has had an office in the building since 1966. Where it is Davis cannot say—he is sworn to secrecy.

Nader does not answer knocks on the door, even for those who manage to find the right door. To see Nader, you slip a note under his door and wait for him to contact you. A few years back Nader had a second office in the building which was used for testing the safety of products on the market. "Once," says Davis, "Nader's neighbors almost got smoked out when electric blankets were being tested for safety. The smoke rolled out into the hall all the way to the elevators. It turned out they didn't know any better than to use water to test them."

Many in the Press Building have felt at times that their telephones were being tapped. True, men in telephone uniforms are forever wandering around. An antenna on the roof had one writer convinced he was being spied upon at the same time a foreign news bureau's people were certain they were the target. There are so many messages going out from the Press Building, it's hard to know what is going on.

Member Don Curry recalls when a fellow NPCer returned to his floor in the Press Building after spending a bit of time in the Tap Room.

Unsteady of foot but firm of purpose, this gentleman of the press tried to enter an office other than his own. The sign on the glass read: *London Daily Mirror and London Evening Standard*.

After the Club member vainly tried to open the door with his key, a cleaning woman said, "Sir, your office is over there." Our friend replied, "Don't tell me where my office is. And nobody's going to keep me out of it!"

As Don tells the story, "He picked up one of the cleaning tools, broke the glass, entered the office and took a nap.

"Next day, he received a bill for the damage. Not only did he have to replace the glass, but also all the lettering on the door. At something like $1.50 per letter, it took him two pay periods to get the money for the bill. He later commented: 'Why the hell couldn't I have picked on a simple newspaper like the *Sun!*'"

Drew Pearson's old column partner still has an office in the National Press Building. Robert S. Allen projects the tough guy image but he is much gentler than he used to be.

In World War II, he served in the Army on George Patton's staff and became a lieutenant colonel. He lost an arm but learned to type all over again, maintaining an office in the National Press Building.

He seemed, and still seems, to be a loner, pacing the twelfth floor corridor for exercise. He speaks to no one unless they speak to him first. But if they speak they are rewarded with comments of dry wit.

Chilton Publications has one of the most glamorous offices in the building and its head man is a very special NPC member.

Neil Regeimbal is a whizbang of a public speaker, ready to get up and talk to anyone about anything, any time. And he has a high position—Washington bureau chief of Chilton, which publishes twenty-three business and industrial magazines, two consumer magazines, and several newsletters.

But it wasn't always so. The Club members enjoy hearing Neil tell how the Club cured his "platform palsy" and made him what he is today.

"In 1967," Neil begins, "Club President L. David LeRoy, a transplanted southern gentleman from Georgia, then covering Congress for *U.S. News & World Report*, decided that some of the aspiring Club politicians should have their chance to try the bright sunshine of the president's chief prerogative: presiding at a major speaker's luncheon with radio and television coverage and a chance to poke a little fun at something or someone.

"I was the first he anointed. The luncheon was in honor of NATO and the speaker was its secretary general, Manlio Brosio, a towering Italian who could have stood eye-to-eye with any current basketball star.

"I'm five feet five.

"The Club's lectern is an ingenious device made to accommodate speakers of varying heights by being raised and lowered—but certainly not every minute or so between questions and answers.

"The Club's head porter solved the problem by providing me with an empty wooden soft drink case so I could reach the microphones adjusted to the speaker's towering height. I must have looked like a nervous puppet on an elastic string as I jumped up and down on that damn Coke case on my maiden appearance in the arena of international politics.

"But that wasn't the only problem.

"In addition to the main speaker, all the ambassadors to the United States from the NATO countries were seated at the head table and had to be introduced. Other than the British and French ambassadors, none of the others had easily pronounceable names.

"This I solved by calling the embassy press offices and getting a reasonably good phonetic pronunciation, which I scribbled on the formal cue cards.

"All but one. I was unsuccessful in getting a usable translation from the Turkish embassy in the time I had. I was all set to introduce, in the order of protocol, all of "His Excellencies" except the Turkish ambassador, Turgut Manemencioglu.

"But he was a gentle and skilled diplomat, and at the last

minute, as we were about to mount the head table, I explained my problem.

"'My son,' he said, 'just remember: *Many men chew glue* and you'll do fine.'

"I did fine with the glue, then managed to muff the easiest name of all when British Ambassador Sir Patrick Dean became a Bean.

"But NATO survived.

"After that, a speaker's platform holds little terror."

Regeimbal showed his courage in still another way. He stole a loaded tractor-trailer from a trucking terminal to show how easy cargo theft is accomplished. His article led to various programs in industry and the Department of Transportation (DOT) aimed at curbing cargo theft, and instead of a prison sentence, Neil got a writing award—the Tom Campbell.

One of the most secretive tenants of the National Press Building is Nina Auchincloss Straight, who cringes if anyone discovers that she is the half sister of Jackie Kennedy Onassis.

She is, as well, the ex-wife of a Republican congressman from Maryland, Newton Steers, which she also cringes to remember. The marriage kept her from being a regular around the White House in the Kennedy years but she did, as far back as the 1950s, break into newspaper writing, through working for Charles Bartlett of the *Chattanooga Times*.

In fact, Bartlett's office in the National Press Building is the same one now occupied by Fran Leighton.

These days Nina has an unmarked office near Frannie's, which is also unmarked. But whereas Fran keeps her door open so her friends can find her, Nina stays hidden behind her door, writing books for Random House.

With those she knows, Nina is witty and a lot like her more famous half sister. The other day she commented to Frannie that Texans did not only lift dogs by the ears but they also lifted people by the ears.

She told Frannie how Bartlett had sent her to Capitol Hill to see Speaker Rayburn on one of her first assignments. She was so intimidated by that personage that she could only ask the same question over and over in trying to get him to enlarge on his answer.

Rayburn, not knowing what to make of her, grabbed her by both ears and dragged her to the better light under the chandelier. "Come here, daughter, let me get a look at you," he said.

"He said he wanted to see if I was a Gore." She is indeed a member of the illustrious Gore family—a granddaughter of Senator Thomas Pryor Gore of Oklahoma. If her writing proves as good as some of her writing relatives, including half brother Gore Vidal, she will no longer be able to hide away in the Press Building.

2/National Press Club Confidential

"The early breed of National Press Club members were not the most immaculate housekeepers," Club historian Scott Hart relates. "When they had their quarters over a jewelry store at 1205 F Street someone set fire to the place with a cigarette.

"That was nothing new. They were always setting fire to themselves and their wastebaskets. But this time was different. This time the drunken reporters ran out of seltzer water and had to call the fire department."

Reporters had long talked of having their own place rather than sitting among strangers in taprooms. Their first attempts went broke. In the 1890s, a nearby club with lush Victorian furnishings was for sale and eighty-five newsmen took it over. Soon it was heavily in debt. Though seven thousand dollars was raised from a benefit performance by entertainers from New York, the club had to close. It proved unwise to give newsmen food and drinks except on a strictly cash basis.

At last the National Press Club was founded in 1908. Men from local newspapers played a leading part. The initial spark came from Graham Nichols, tall and red-haired, a police reporter for the *Washington Star*. He had lost a leg and hobbled energetically on crutches. The first president was William P. Spurgeon, managing editor of the *Post*.

The club quarters were makeshift, first over a jewelry store, then over a drugstore on Fifteenth Street, a block west of the present site.

The huge William Howard Taft was the first President to visit the old club quarters above Affleck's Drugstore in 1910, puffing as he trudged up the rickety stairs. Teddy Roosevelt was there in November, when he had just returned from a big-game hunt in Africa. Woodrow Wilson came to the opening of the Club's third home in the Albee Building, lamenting that the duties of President forbade his coming often. This third home was more spacious than the others, including a roof garden, cooler on summer nights than indoors in the days before air conditioning.

One symbol that accompanied the moves was the little fat god Billiken, a nude figure like a plump pointy-headed Buddha, with eyes closed and a smile of contentment, a popular good-luck piece.

In my home, one sat on the mantelpiece on a throne inscribed, "God of things as they ought to be."

In the upheaval of World War I, many a member went in the service and returned. Prohibition came as the aftermath. When Washington went dry, Maryland was still wet. The interurban trolley line to Baltimore, the W. B. & A., was known as the Whiskey, Beer, and Alcohol. Then the whole nation was dry—nothing but bathtub gin and "dago red" wine.

Without bar sales, the Club nearly foundered. Rather than flout the law as some others did, the Board obeyed. In arrears for rent, the Club was threatened with eviction. But its landlord, a bank, was reminded that President Wilson was a member and it would not look well to dispossess him.

The bone-dry rule was relaxed for a visit by Edward, Prince of Wales, in 1919, by which time the Club had moved to its third location, the Albee Building at Fifteenth and G Streets. It was thought His Royal Highness would like Scotch. Jimmie, of the Club staff, was sent to procure same. He acted as royal taster to be sure of the quality; then broke into the receiving line to say in a stage whisper, heard across the room, "Have a little drink, Prince?"

There was a sequel years later. After Edward left the throne to marry the "woman I love," he came to town as Duke of Windsor in 1941. A special bar was set up by Julius Reiner, Club factotum, with everything he thought would be wanted—especially Scotch.

When the Duke was asked to name his poison, he called for gin and ginger ale, then a favorite only in Washington's black belt. Scurrying for the ingredients, Julius muttered, "How could I know he would want a U Street highball!"

I came to the club and to the profession of newswriting when the present building was still new and sparsely settled. After a summer of engineering work on a western river, I was to have gone to Leland Stanford for a graduate business course. But the Washington bureau of the McGraw-Hill papers wanted to hire an engineer. I was chosen, sight unseen.

Paul Wooton, a prominent member of the National Press Club, headed the bureau, a plump little man with horn-rimmed glasses and courtly manners, from New Orleans and

19

Mexico. McGraw-Hill had magazines for sundry industries—electric, chemical, mining, textiles, aviation, and later *Business Week*, for business as a whole. In the boom years, oblivious to the rule that what goes up must go down, the company kept buying more papers till the 1929 crash.

As well as learning overnight, under Paul Wooton's tutelage, what news was and how to pursue it, I was supposed to become an instant expert in all these specialties and in the federal agencies that dealt with such things. Schools of journalism were no big factor. To become a reporter, one got hired as a cub and made it or not, sink or swim.

Joining the National Press Club speeded my initiation into this strange new world as I made friends among the old pros. During Prohibition, there was no bar. A small room called the Paddock had lockers where members could keep bottles. As a neophyte, I did not know about that.

Aside from dances and evening events, the Club was busiest for lunch. A tasty meal cost thirty-five cents, with no tipping for waiters, plus fifteen cents for dessert. During the Depression, I had to forego dessert, except one day when I found a quarter that had fallen out of someone's pocket on a sofa.

The dining room was bigger; it rounded the corner into where the bar lounge now is. Overlooking the scene was the Crow's Nest, on a balcony with a stuffed crow on the railing. The members who ate at the special table up there, I was told, liked to work out their bets on horse races.

Presiding over a round table was a unique character named H. O. Bishop, known as Bish. Also, there was a long table where I sat. Every day a quorum appeared—writers for newspapers, trade papers, and newsletters, plus public relations men. We were close friends after hours too, going to parties and visiting one another's homes.

Bishop looked like a senator of the old school. Rotund in body, he wore his grizzled hair long. A black suit was draped tentlike over his bulk. When he left the building, he wore a black hat with a wide brim and thumped the ground with a heavy walking stick.

Bish's top fan was Kip—Willard M. Kiplinger. Kip was first to make it big in the newsletter business. Solemn warnings of "inflation ahead and what to do about it" held readers enthralled. For table laughs, my translation, freely shared, was "inflated behinds and what to do about them."

Kip was a great friend of Bishop's. In fact, once Kip had statuettes made of notables in Washington, including one of Bish sitting in a chair. The day Bish died, Kiplinger placed it on the round table. It is still in the Club.

Kiplinger had a waggish humor. He used to go with Bish to look for real estate in the Virginia mountains. When they came to a town, the villagers thought Bishop was Senator William E. Borah, the renowned orator. They would tip their hats while Kip would walk a bit to the rear and acknowledge the salutes.

Bish was as fearful of women as an elephant of mice. Kip tricked him into entering the ladies' room one day. Standing outside the door in conversation, he held his hand over the *WO* in *WOMEN*. Bish went in and fast retreated with cries of horror.

Kip told of a partnership he once planned with a Mr. Hurrey and a Mr. Ryder. Since his name could not come last, the firm name would have been some such combination as Kiplinger, Hurrey & Ryder or Ryder, Kiplinger & Hurrey. They called the whole thing off.

Ribaldry then was sent across the country by telegraphers. In off moments, they chatted by Morse dash-dot. Then came the airlines with coast-to-coast communications, so anything choice got relayed. One of our lunch group was an aviation man who later became named top vice-president of Eastern Airlines, Paul Brattain.

Scarcely a day went by without a laugh. For example, this gem at our table was ascribed to the head of the Bank of England!

The sexual drive of the camel
Is greater than anyone thinks.
In moments of sexual passion,
He often makes love to the Sphinx.
But the Sphinx's posterior entry
Is blocked by the sands of the Nile,
Which accounts for the hump on the camel,
And the Sphinx's inscrutable smile.

Well, it was fun in those days. Time went on and here came 1933 and Roosevelt and repeal. First came beer. The suds first flowed at a bar in what is now the cardroom area.

Unforgettable characters abounded. Paul McGahan, who became a colonel in World War II, could stand on his head and drink a glass of booze upside down if you would buy him one, and many did. Otherwise Paul was a very dignified man.

Once a member, standing at the bar rail looking for attention, was anointed by P.R. man Steve Walters with juices from the squirt-top flavorings on the bar. Steve rubbed the syrups on the man's bald head. He purred like a kitten. Then he put on his hat and went home, only to find he had to sleep in the hat, because it was glued tight.

Another fellow was morose as he drank. A Marine captain who served in Haiti, he ascribed his troubles to the loss of a *ounga* (pronounced *wanga*) that a witch doctor had given him: a little bag of horrid ingredients, like bats' wings, to hang around his neck and ward away harm. Eventually he thought an elephant was following him, and walked down 14th Street to the Potomac in hope the beast would keep going into the river.

Out of the hundreds of Club members I knew, dozens remain vivid in memory. The top dog for years was Arthur Krock of the *New York Times*, confidant of presidents but considered a pompous ass by the more down-to-earth press group.

Foreign correspondents were few. Tass, the Soviet news service, was represented by Lawrence Todd, a mild-mannered protagonist whose aims included such heresies as social security long before it became law. Anyone who thought the Reds did not understand what was happening here was wrong. Before the 1948 election, when almost everyone thought Truman would lose, Larry and I went over the situation at supper and agreed that a Truman win was possible or even likely.

The *London Times* was long represented by Sir Willmott Lewis. An affable and distinguished-looking Welshman who came to Washington to cover the Senate debate on the Versailles Treaty after World War I, Sir Willmott was a leading figure in the Club for thirty years.

He served his country well by making himself the unofficial ambassador to the U.S. press. Knighted for it in the King's honors list of 1931, he was in the Club cardroom when he heard the news. His irrepressible wife said, "Now I'm a lady!"

Bill Lewis and a few others did more than will ever be known to swing American opinion toward intervention in World War II to prevent the collapse of Britain. There was a secret project that employed newsmen, including some I knew, for a propaganda blitz.

Lewis was followed by Charles H. Campbell, editor of the *New Orleans Item*, who set up the British Information Service in Washington. He had a heavy mustache, smooth manners, and a knack for making friends.

Campbell once heard it said of someone ungrammatical, "He doesn't know the King's English."

"Well," said he, "the King isn't English. He hasn't been since William the Conquerer."

Not many members got tossed out. One lawyer, who was called the Judge, had an office facing mine in an adjacent building. He would practice speeches, pacing and gesturing with his admiring secretary for an audience. Late in the day, they would discreetly draw the blinds.

After a night of dissipation, he would appear in the Club disheveled and unshaven. When he had not been seen for some time, someone asked what had become of him. "Don't you know?" a waiter replied. "He was dismembered."

One drunken reporter nearly killed another member. When he saw what he had done, he never drank again, and spent his remaining years on a copy desk in New York. "In lonely exile," the Club members would add when talking of it.

An old timer one night relieved himself from the ballroom balcony, like the Britisher in the theater who drew from the pit the plaintive cry, "Shyke it about a bit! Gor blime, I'm getting it all!" In this case, the president of the Club happened to be passing below. His fury was no less eloquent.

The Club through the years tried to keep its family problems out of the newspapers. Anything untowards was hushed if possible.

One fellow jumped thirteen floors from the men's room at the bar to his death. A grating was put on the window afterward, pointless as others still could be opened.

One sad case was the man who took poison. My friend Larry Stafford noticed him in the club library, sweating and obviously in distress. Presently the fellow said he had taken bichloride and was beginning to feel it. Horrified, Larry led him to the men's room. At the urinal the poison ate into the porcelain. The man later died in agony.

The stain lasted for years until new plumbing was installed. Every time I saw it, I had the wry thought that of all who piddled their lives away, this man was the only one who truly left his mark.

My old boss Paul Wooton seemed the opposite of the bold, brash reporter. He did not smoke, drink, or use expletives stronger than "gee whiz," But under a placid-exterior, he had a core of iron.

Once, when he was backing into a parking space, another driver tried to sneak in behind him. Paul stepped on the gas and mashed the front of the car. He jumped out and admonished, "Don't ever do that again. You might get badly hurt." Then he drove away, leaving the other car with water streaming from its broken radiator. Paul told this with chuckles at our morning staff conference.

Paul carved himself a little niche by organizing press groups that put him on the rostrum as master of ceremonies. He set up the White House Correspondents Association for annual dinners with the President, the Overseas Writers Association, and a monthly lunch for trade-paper correspondents. Thus he hobnobbed with the great.

Once I went to a reception for the British writer H. G. Wells. There he stood, heavy-set and mustachioed, drinking, rather bored. Paul propelled me over to him saying, "Don't be bashful. Go right up and talk to him." Of course, with that all the things I wanted to say evaporated and I was tongue-tied.

When Paul was host at a dinner for Queen Elizabeth of England, she had been making schoolgirlish speeches. This had drawn comment. So she, or her speech writer, produced a little gem of a talk. After the applause, Paul beamingly said, "Your Majesty, that was just splendid."

Paul was on the way to becoming Club president in 1930 but lost to an opposing faction. He bided his time, worked his way upward again, and was elected in 1946. As I indicated, he was a bulldog. His spirit remains. There is still a Paul Wooton Foundation.

In the mid-1930s unruly elements in the Club got out of hand. There was heavy drinking, dice games that were later banned and gambling into the small hours. Once when I worked late I went down the elevator with a Club president barely able to walk, with money sticking from all his pockets. I recall he said, "Ken, I think I'm going to die."

I said, "You will if you keep staying here all night."

But mostly the club ran tranquilly enough. Board members were elected vice-president and rose to president without opposition.

Few of us in the prewar years could have realized fully that we were living in a golden age. We made little money compared with now but prices were low. My wife could go to the butcher and ask for a pork roast "about so long," measuring a foot or more with her hands, "and a pound of bottom round for the cats." We had cars and pleasant surburban homes with maids. We had dances and parties and dinners.

Even after the "phony war" in Europe—so called because nothing dramatic happened for months and months— erupted into Hitler's blitz that quickly overran France and isolated Britain, we were not prepared. Ours was a dream world. One evening a friend, who lived near a Japanese national, called to say, "We are going to war."

"How do you know?" I asked.

"Dato is burning his papers. I can smell the smoke."

On the Sunday when Pearl Harbor was attacked, the "day of infamy," I was in my office catching up on work when my wife called to tell me the radio news. When I rushed to the Press Club, a small Japanese man, his face gray with fear, was hurrying on some last desperate errand. In the Club, the newsticker had come alive to tap-tap the scanty details.

Next day at noon the Club lounge was packed. We all stood as the national anthem was played and President Roosevelt, by radio, grimly announced a state of war. With sinking heart I thought of what was to happen to the pleasant lives of all of us.

I cannot tell you much about the war years at the Club as I was not there. The liquor supply was not curtailed. While odd brands of liquids resembling sheep dip were drunk elsewhere, the Club, in its wisdom—due to inside information—had invested forty thousand dollars in a whole boatload of Hanky Bannister Scotch.

Bottles were sold, one each, to members who came for the daily apportionment with the exact change, cash in hand. Charles Stewart of the Central Press, recognized as the Club dean, was given first place in line, Sir Willmott Lewis of the *London Times* was Number Two.

War was war and all of that but the members felt that the high standards of the Club must be maintained, protocol observed, and the dispensary must proceed in an orderly and *sober* fashion.

The tides of history flowed through the Club. The celebrity parade through the years included such fabled names as Winston Churchill, Madame Chiang, Prince Edward, Fidel Castro,

King Hussein, and Golda Meir, to name only a few. Many a leading American has talked here and stood for questions under the bright lights of television.

If any room should be named one of Washington's historic sites, to be preserved for the ages, the Club ballroom is it.

One memorable event was the return of General Mac-Arthur after he had been fired by President Truman from his Asiatic command. After the Chinese attacked in the Korean War, he would have risked a major conflict by invading the mainland.

Howard Hughes met the press here after he flew around the world in 1938. He was a tall, slender young man, modest and soft-spoken. He complained that he almost ran into a mountain because the Russian maps showed it lower than it was.

Soon afterward, he admitted to an error of judgment that almost wrecked the expedition.

Putting the two statements together, I wrote that the Russian contour lines were in meters and Hughes read them in feet so the mountain was three times as high as he thought it was. My editor at the *Journal of Commerce* killed the story. As far as I know, this narrow escape of Hughes is related here for the first time.

Before War II, such appearances in this ballroom made headlines, but readers were not much aware of the Club. Since World War II, as television has become the first source of news, the Club rostrum is seen in every living room. But what the public doesn't see is the picturesque behavior of our gang at their watering holes.

Once a well-known correspondent had a few rounds at the bar with a New England senator. Then, in search of a more interesting atmosphere they went to Trader Vic's for dinner. The newsman ordered one of those exotic Polynesian drinks that come in a goblet slightly smaller than a bird bath. A gardenia floated. The flower was real but the leaves were plastic.

After several swallows, the reporter began to eat the petals. Then he tried a leaf. He chewed and chewed. Finally he took it from his mouth and threw it down. To the waiter he complained, "This artichoke is too tough to eat. Take it back."

Some people are adventure-prone. Such a man was good old Homer Dodge. Once in New York, Homer told a cab driver to take him to the Flatiron Building, long a landmark there. The driver asked where it was.

Homer was indignant. "Where have you been for the past twenty-five years?" The cabbie said, "Sing Sing Prison."

Homer Dodge shut up after telling him where to drive.

26

He waited till he was getting out to ask, "What were you up for?" The cabbie looked at him a moment. "They called it murder."

Dodge is remembered as the star raconteur of the Club. No one has been able to beat him or tried. He was one of a kind, a slight man who kept a serious face when he told a story, his mustache twitching if someone failed to get the point.

Earlier, when he spent less time at the bar, he was a leading financial writer. In monetary matters, he would not bow to the highest officials. Henry Morgenthau, Roosevelt's not-too-bright Secretary of the Treasury, said to Homer at a press conference, "You're new here, aren't you."

Homer replied, "No, Mr. Secretary. You're new."

Sometimes the bitterest and most disappointed men turn into the greatest wits. Maybe this is how it was with Homer. At least it could have accounted for his feeling about women—he was agin 'em. He flew into a rage every time the Club opened its doors an inch to admit female guests.

Though he had a delightful wife and children, according to members who were lucky enough to meet the family, he had absolutely nothing good to say about women. It became almost dangerous to mention the possibility that some day the Club might want to consider letting in a few as members. His response was like a brushfire.

One day Club President John Cosgrove said to him, "Homer, why are you so against women?"

Dodge said, "I'm going to tell you why if you really want to know. It's not a story I spread around. You know, John, I'm from Cleveland, but you don't know that my mother worked as a secretary for John D. Rockefeller in his struggling days.

"At one point, when Mr. Rockefeller couldn't give her a raise, he offered mother stock in his new company. She said she didn't want any stock. She wanted cash."

Homer paused and added with understandable bitterness, "If she had taken that stock I wouldn't have to be working today. And since I have had that to reflect on all my life, can you blame me for questioning the judgment of females?"

On the day that famed Gertrude Ederle swam the English Channel, wives and friends of members were invited to the Club to view the new bar.

Homer sat glumly in a corner waiting for them to go home, pretending he didn't see them.

But one bubbling female, wanting to spread sunshine,

rushed over to him and said, "Oh, Mr. Dodge, isn't it wonderful, here I am, a woman, in this room."

He grumpily told her, it wasn't wonderful; it wasn't their place.

"What is women's place, Mr. Dodge?" the lady persisted. "What do you think is their place?"

"I think," said Homer Dodge coolly, "women's place is in the English Channel."

A compleat Clubman, Homer was happiest sitting in the Tap Room amusing his fellow members. In the dim light—dim both day and night—it was always easy to spot him because of his graying crew cut, always neat and dapper.

Homer was inventive. He led his colleagues at the bar on a hunt for negative words that had lost their positive meanings, such as *inept, inscrutable,* and *unkempt."*

His interest was inspired by a story, then current, about a man who said his wife was impregnable. A friend asked, "Don't you mean inconceivable?" The man said, "Anyhow, she's unbearable."

At the outbreak of World War II, Homer proposed to outfit a privateer to capture enemy vessels, given a letter of marque as provided in the Constitution. A number of members gave him one-thousand-dollar-IOU's for the project.

Jim Hay, a great writer and a great drunk, had his own routine. When in his cups and faced with a deadline—he worked for various papers at various times—he would go to a Turkish bath and sober up.

One winter's day, he trudged through the snow to the bath for its cleansing heat. This time, all the steam in the world couldn't do the trick. So Jim was led into the next room to sleep off his drunk.

Eventually, a buddy came looking for him and was told by the proprietor, "He's in that room sleeping it off."

The buddy went to get him but came back out saying, "No, he's not in there."

The proprietor said, "Of course he's in there. He couldn't be anywhere else."

The loyal friend looked once more and again reported there was no one in there.

Scoffing at the blindness of reporters, the proprietor strode into the room himself. "My God, he's disappeared!" he exclaimed. "I can't understand it." He walked to the bed and let out a whoop. Jim Hay was completely covered with snow. He had opened the window, but so drunk was he that he did not wake up as the snowflakes drifted over him. Once on his feet, it is said that he came to life as fine as ever, walked back to the office, and got on with his story.

The Club has seen some great drinkers. There are arguments about who was the greatest. According to Sam Fogg no one could, or ever will, outshine Bob Considine, the Hearst star, both as a good guy who would help young reporters or as a man who could hold his liquor. "Bob could outdrink anybody in sight." Sam recalls with awe. "I once ran into Bob at the Tap Room and it was a nice reunion. I covered the United Nations with him in New York before I came to Washington.

"We stood drinking at the bar and we went till four in the morning. He was drinking Scotch mists. I was clinging to the bar with my fingernails, and I was only on Ballantine ale.

"Bob told story after story, never missed a word or a sip. Finally, he looked at his watch and said, 'I'm sorry, Sam, but I have to write my column.' And he did, having arranged to use an office somewhere in the Press Building. At that point I collapsed on the rail and moved to a booth where I slept the rest of the night. They don't make men like Bob Considine anymore. The world misses his great reporting and I miss him too."

Famed director Stanley Kramer of Hollywood scoffs at the thought that anyone could outdrink Hollywood's finest, saying the Press Club gang isn't in the same league.

Kramer once told Tom Snyder, NBC's ace interviewer, that the greatest boozer of all time was Spencer Tracy. He would throw chairs and tables through plate-glass windows of gin mills. "Katy Hepburn," he said, "would go after him with a studio ambulance before police could get to him."

The Club has had furniture throwers too, but of a gentler breed. They had the courtesy to open a window before dropping things thirteen stories.

Member Frank Holeman recalls someone once threw an armchair from a window of the ballroom and it crashed down on F Street. There was the time a potted palm flew out of the Club lounge on an "otherwise quiet Sunday." Holeman thinks about that for a moment and adds, "That wouldn't happen now. The Club is closed on Sundays."

29

And then there's the matter of *people* out the window. Various members of the Club, past president Felix Cotten among them, still talk about the night that a huge drunken Swede became annoyed at a puny waiter called Pee Wee. The big hulk picked him up and hung him out a window of the Bar holding him by the heels.

Pee Wee looked thirteen floors straight down and screamed in holy terror: "Help, help!" For about five minutes the members stood helplessly by, wondering what to do while the little waiter's pleadings floated in to them.

If they grabbed the drunken Swede, he just might let go. "Better bring him in," was all they could think of to say and they repeated this nervously, with an occasional "Say, don't you think it's time to haul him back?"

Suddenly the Swede pulled Pee Wee in. The moment he felt the firm floor, he started running. Not stopping for an elevator, he ran down the twelve flights of steps and did not stop till he got safely to Salisbury on the Eastern Shore of Maryland.

Says Felix, "It was said he ran across Chesapeake Bay without waiting for a ferry. He was never seen in the Club again, even to pick up his check. The Swede was suspended, though he protested it was just a little drinking prank and that he never intended to let go."

It took Jim Sloan of the *Chicago Tribune* to finally top that story. It happened at the Chicago Press Club when it was quartered at what was then the Sheraton-Chicago. An argument developed over a poker game.

An aggrieved player grabbed another and held him out the twelfth-story window until, as Jim tells it, "Someone yelled, 'Hold it. I don't want to have to write an obit at this hour.'

"That cut the tension and the guy was hauled back in, never to play poker at that club again. But then, he was hardly missed, because he was only a *radio* man."

Some members didn't need windows to have their fun. As former president Frank Holeman, tells it: "During Prohibition, they frequently swung on the chandelier from the Crow's Nest to the middle of the dining room and back. It was a test of courage, sobriety, and the light fixture."

With such goings on, it was not surprising that the stories of the Press Club spread across town to the staid Metropolitan Club, where one member was reported to have asked another, "Is it true that every day at high noon is as noisy at the Press Club as New Year's Eve here?"

One of the best Press Club stories to come out of the Prohibition era is told by John Hinkel, on the *Washington Post* at the time. He and several other *Post* men, including John Malloney, used to sit around the old Sigma Alpha Epsilon house in 1931 moaning about the terrible bootleg whiskey they were subjected to.

"We were tired of bathtub gin. What made it most galling was that our fraternity was right across the street from the Russian embassy, where we heard they had the finest vodka and wine cellar imaginable.

"We would sit looking at the embassy, which was shuttered and, we were told, had a fine burglar alarm system. Still we dreamed of trying to get in and take a look at that wine cellar; in the interest of good reporting, of course.

"One Sunday night the SAE gang were really excited. Malloney had news, which he had picked up at the *Post*. Police had been asked to keep a close surveillance at the embassy because the burglar alarm system was on the fritz and the watchman was on vacation.

" 'The police will probably never get there,' Malloney said, 'Now is the time for us to investigate.'

"In no time at all, four of us were there trying to rip the boards off the window on the side where we thought the wine cellar might be located. I was the lookout. The others pulled. By the time they got the third board off, we found out Malloney was wrong on two counts.

"The watchman was back and the burglar alarm was fixed. The watchman fired his gun in the air. We flew out the gate. I ran down Sixteenth Street. Malloney ran in a different direction and didn't stop until he had arrived, gasping, at the *Post* and collapsed in a chair in the city room.

"Norman Baxter, a prominent member of the Press Club, was in the editor's chair and didn't seem aware of Malloney's condition. He looked up and saw him and said, 'Malloney, where in the hell have you been! There's been a robbery at the Russian embassy. Get over there.'

"Malloney, alarmed but too frightened to say anything, got up and dragged himself back to the embassy as if he'd never been there. Later Malloney told me how it felt to interview the watchman. 'Can you imagine the nerve of the bastard. He was telling me he had to fight off four toughs. I felt like taking a big poke at him. And I had to quote the damned braggart on everything he'd said.'"

What happened to Malloney? Today he lies buried in Arlington Cemetery near Secretary of the Navy Frank Knox, on whose staff he served in World War II as speech writer.

Hinkel, who tells the story, has come a long way too. He has the rank of colonel and is author of a book, *Arlington— Monument to Heroes*.

What Club members drink is of intense interest to no one in the world except themselves and their buddies. One member is the pride and despair of his friends—pointed out for the greatest show of loyalty in Club history. He has ordered only Virginia Gentleman and water for nigh on twenty-two years.

Now and then members go on long trips to the far corners of the world and return with tall tales to widen the horizons of those who think the ultimate drink is a seven-to-one martini.

Thanks to Helen Thomas, the Press Club learned on her return from Peking, when Nixon went to China in 1972, that there is an equally potent form of firewater there called *Mao Tai*, otherwise known to the press travelers as Chinese White Lightning.

On National Press Club trips abroad, members have had the sobering experience of discovering that martinis in Denmark cost $6.50. As travel chairman of the Club, Bill Whyte commented, on his return, "It made us rediscover other pleasures, such as intense observation of model ships in the hotel lobby and sunset strolls.

"But the Danes are the greatest hosts in the world and had their own way of getting the life-giving martinis to us. Martinis were even put in bottles labeled 'seasickness medicine' on our morning boat tour of the harbor. Perfect guests that we were, no one complained at the prank. Many even pretended that the medication helped them feel much better. Wherever we were invited," Bill Whyte reports, "we ate and drank all that was put before us, whether that be *Gammal Dansk* at morning coffee with the Prime Minister or aquavit and beer with the Lord Mayor of Copenhagen in Tivoli Gardens."

But the most interesting drinking experience on that trip occurred during a luncheon at the world-famous art center, the Carlsberg Foundation. Each member of the group was invited—nay, required—to drink one bottle of each of Carlsberg's Tuborg Brewery's leading beers. Five in all.

And after the "luncheon," so as not to leave the world's largest brewery "smelling of coffee," as their hosts put it, each guest was required to drink yet a sixth bottle of beer. As Bill recalls "Every gentleman, lady, and jackanapes graciously did as required."

Barney Hunter, a retired commodore, is a good and faithful member of the Club and maintains an office on the twelfth floor. His stories of the Press Club gang go back many years. He recalls the time Henry Flynn, a copy editor of the old *Times-Herald* and one of the best tipplers as well as editors, was at the bar, ranting and raving about the Irish Catholics. In view of the fact he was one himself, he felt free to criticize. It was his favorite drinking subject.

Flynn was in such shape that as an act of mercy, Barney decided to take him across the street to the Willard Hotel and put him to bed. Flynn could hardly move, having become almost paralyzed except for his flapping mouth and one hand raising and lowering his glass. Barney half carried him to the elevator, through the lobby, out of the Press Building, across the street, and up to a room at the Willard. Barney assured the room clerk. "He'll pay his bill, but if there's any trouble, I'll take care of it."

After he was sure Flynn was safely tucked away, he went back to the Press Club bar. As he opened the door, there was Flynn, leaning against the bar, one hand clenched around a glass, ranting about his favorite subject—Irish Catholics.

Henry Flynn has gone to his reward but his memory lives on. The moral of the story is that the old drunks were indestructible. They just don't make them with such stamina anymore.

Yet, maybe things haven't changed too much. Just a few months ago, a National Press Club Board member, no less, made the police blotter by going slightly berserk after a long, diligent night at the bar. Leaving the Press Building he gleefully started letting the air out of the tires of parked cars, chortling as he went.

He was on his fourth car when another screeched to a halt. He was unable to do anything about the tires of the fifth car which had dared cross his path because that was the one that hauled him off to the pokey.

The Club has not yet become too staid to applaud its own.

3/Life Around the Club

There's mother's little helper, there's the plumber's helper, and then there is the NPC little helper. Without the NPC's little helper, life would be sheer hell for some.

The helper is a battery of bins kept filled with press releases on every subject, in the lobby of the National Press Club, mercifully near the Tap Room entrance.

Messenger boys who deliver releases to newspaper bureau doors throughout the National Press Building would not dream of leaving without filling a slot in the bin in the Press Club. Thus many a shaky reporter is able to find a suitable press release and work it over at the Tap Room bar before phoning it in or taking it back to his office to file it on the wire or "clean copy" it for mailing.

The story is told about the Club member, a Washington correspondent for a New England newspaper, who got so drunk, however, that he couldn't even do that much and a buddy did it for him.

The only problem was that the buddy was well into the sauce too, and so just for security a second buddy also filed a different version of the story for him by Western Union.

The editor was not pleased about the extra cost and let out a scream heard round the world. Still stories on the same subject kept coming by teletype, by day letter and night letter.

And on the seventh version of the same press release, which was phoned in the next day, the editor was reported to have exclaimed, "Tell them to keep 'em coming. They're getting better."

Such days are not completely in the past, nor are the persons helped always obscure of byline. Frank Aukofer, former National Press Club president and Washington correspondent for the *Milwaukee Journal*, recalled the time, somewhere along the campaign trail, when no less a personage than a certain Pulitzer Prize winner was unable to finish a story due to taking on too great a load of strong waters. And no less a personage than the distinguished columnist of the *Washington Post*, David Broder, displayed his innate nobility by finishing the story.

34

But the next day, was the reporter grateful as Broder was sure he would be? Not at all. As Broder and others waited for the kind words to flow, the ungrateful wretch announced, "Hell, I could have written a better story drunk than Broder sober."

It's hard to know who you'll find around the Club. Big Dan, a former waiter, was so beloved that when he retired recently he was given an honorary membership in the National Press Club. Now he may be found sitting grandly at the watering hole waiting for service, or kibitzing at the stand-up bar.

Stories about him are legion. One concerns his quick service—but not for food. One day when Walter Riley, the Trans-World columnist, was distractedly making notes at a table, Big Dan asked him what he wanted.

Not knowing what he wanted, Walter said, "How about a blonde, sunny side up?"

Big Dan said, "Coming right up," and, in another minute, had escorted a gorgeous blue-eyed blonde to his table and plopped her down. As the wife of a public relations type, she was case-hardened to Press Club gagsters.

Press Club games are like no others.

Sometimes the boys at the bar vie to see who can get the greatest number of middle names right. For example, few people know that Jack Anderson has a middle name, let alone that it is such an unusual name as Northman.

Or that the *C* in Ben Bradlee's name stands for Crowninshield.

Anyone who knows that a Crowninshield ancestor in the eighteenth century was hanged for a botched burglary in which a man was killed gets extra brownie points.

Sometimes the Club members stand around giving word definitions. One day the word under discussion was *gigolo*. The best definition anyone could come up with was "A gigolo is the egg that layed the golden heir."

When the Tap Room was built, it was called the John O'Brien Tap Room in honor of the member who had been president at that time. Since it was a men's bar in a men's club and not even a visiting female was permitted in the bar, the members decided to have a little fun with the sign for the men's room.

Since visiting men would say, "Where is it?," they decided to have a sign made for the door saying, Here. For years when the men would get drunk, they would remove the *E* at the end of the word, hoping to embarrass a new member or guest who would have to go into a rest room marked "Her."

There are endless stories about the club's toilet problems. Unfortunately the Tap Room rest stop had only two urinals, and beer drinkers would come out cursing about having to stand in line.

Once Jim Butler, correspondent for *Editor and Publisher*, became annoyed at the impatience of another man in the pub's rest room. The man was shifting from foot to foot as he waited his turn and cursing about "this goddamn bar—they build a fifty-thousand-dollar bar with only two goddamn urinals."

Butler said, "Hey, fellow, you must be new here."

"I am, I am, said the newcomer, brightening at this show of interest and what he mistook for sympathy. "How did you know?"

Butler's voice turned suddenly cold, "Because, when we built this room, we only had two pricks in the Club."

Famous reporters are sometimes startled while relieving themselves in the bar's men's room, to have some worshipful young reporter ask, "Are you Dan Rather?" or, "Pardon me, sir, but are you Jack Anderson?"

Once the annoyance was brought about when a club member who was at the urinal thought he was being rushed along by the man behind him. What the slightly pixilated man behind him was muttering through thickened tongue was, "Pardon me, sir, are you Drew Pearson?"

The man in front irritably replied, "Hell no, I haven't even started yet."

At the Press Club off beat stories about the famous figures of history are especially cherished and each time one is told by a visiting National Press Club member from a different part of the country, it's added to the lore of the Club.

So it was a red-letter day when Jim Sloan, who had risen from copy editor and war correspondent to assistant Sunday editor at the *Chicago Tribune*, made the bald statement at the bar, "I must be the only living person who said no to Amelia Earhart."

It couldn't have been a better opening and the visitor from Chicago was quickly pressed to tell his story. "I was just a beginning reporter in my hometown of Marion, Indiana, on the

Chronicle-Tribune," Jim began, "when Amelia Earhart came to speak about her solo Atlantic flight."

He paused for dramatic effect, the name Amelia Earhart having stopped all other conversations.

"It was a big deal for the town, an international celebrity, first woman to span the Atlantic, coming to a little place like that to make a talk. I had a buddy who was just out of high school, like me, and about the same age, which was eighteen, and he was the lucky fellow assigned to cover the talk. I went along with him—his name was Bill Oates—because I'd never seen a celebrity before.

"Afterward we rushed back to the newsroom and I hung around while he wrote his story. The city editor, Jack Clarke, looked over Bill's story and felt it merited more coverage, so he told Bill to get on down to the hotel and interview the lady.

"Bill said nervously, 'Jim, you've got to come with me. I can't go see her alone.' He was really nervous, which made me a little uneasy too.

"We thought we were off the hook when the desk clerk in the Spencer House said haughtily, 'Miss Earhart does not wish her room number disclosed.' We stood around in the lobby assuring each other we had done all we could when the elevator boy, who was another school chum, surreptitiously waved us over and whispered that he knew where the lady was. We left the lobby inconspicuously—we hoped—and soon were approaching her door. 'You knock,' said Bill.

" 'No, I won't,' I said. 'It's your story.'

"We were arguing this way when we got to her door and heard her voice asking the desk to send up a bellhop because she was checking out. I said to Bill, 'We're in.'

"He gulped, 'What do you mean?'

" 'We're the bellhop,' I replied, feeling very experienced, very blasé. 'Let's wait a couple of minutes.' Then I knocked on the door and she said, 'Come in.' And almost in the same breath, when we did so, she said, 'Who the hell are you guys?'

"I'll never forget that moment of quick realization that we weren't making it as bellboys. I gulped and explained who we were. She seemed amused and said, 'You guys are pretty sharp,' and did answer a few questions that we hazarded as we stood shuffling our feet. Both of us wished we could think of something really exciting to ask her but all that came out were routine questions like where she was going, how long she'd stay there.

"Suddenly she said, 'I've done you a favor. Now it's your turn to do one for me. Where can I get my car serviced? I have to drive to Cleveland tonight.'

"I told her about a service station next to the newspaper office and she said, 'Come on, I'll drive you back.' I wished we could go with horns blazing. Here we were being chauffeured by the top female flier of the world and nobody was looking.

"When we got there Bill ran in to work on his story but I stayed with her on the excuse of making sure she was being taken care of. Suddenly I realized she was looking me over and out of the blue she said. 'I'd like for you to come along with me. Can you drive to Cleveland with me tonight?'

"My mind reeled with terror as it flashed to my five-dollar bankroll. How would I get back tomorrow. How could I be at work early in the morning?

"These were matters I felt I had to keep to myself and so I said a reluctant no to the famous aviatrix."

Jim's listeners shook their heads sadly, wondering what the story would have been had he gone.

"For years I never spoke of it. I was too embarrassed," Jim confessed, shaking his own head, "but now I'm old enough to kick myself in the behind publicly for the dumbest answer I ever gave. Later I learned of her open marriage life-style."

Everyone at the bar agreed that among the mysteries that still remain concerning Amelia Earhart, perhaps the greatest mystery was her plan for one Jim Sloan, cub reporter.

The Bar Committee has had some prominent names on its roster. When retired Air Force General Carl "Tooey" Spaatz, went to work for *Newsweek*, writing a military affairs column, he was appointed chairman of the Bar Committee.

Someone commented glowingly of this to Lyle Wilson, head of the UPI bureau, saying, "It must be something for the Press Club to have a four-star general on the Bar Committee."

Lyle responded wryly, "Yes, and it's probably the only club that needs one."

One of the several groups within the National Press Club was the Washington chapter of the Chili Appreciation Society. The society was founded by George E. Haddaway, a Texan who long published *Flight* magazine, for which I still write. A legendary figure, George made friends everywhere. But he had his angry moments. Once at the Houston airport, George was served a bowl of alleged chili contaminated by Boston baked beans. He invaded the kitchen and threw it at the chef. The cops were summoned, and, being good Texans, held the act justified.

Not quite so violent was a chili competition among senators from several states. Words sufficed.

In the old tradition of sectional rivalry, the senators roundly derided one another's products. Senator Barry Goldwater, upholding Arizona, said, "If you find a lump in Texas chili, it's a turd."

For years a valiant little group, member Harry Stringer and attorney Al Beitel among them, have met at the Press Club on a regular basis to thresh out, over luncheon, what ball games to bet on. They treat the subject with as much solemnity as if they were trying to balance the national debt.

The Club has its little problems.

Bottle lifting goes without saying. But the Press Club also has been embarrassed by a vast increase in petty thievery.

The worst thing probably was what happened in 1978. Chancellor Helmut Schmidt came to speak. As he rose to give his luncheon address he took off his watch and put it in front of him to be sure he didn't overstay his allocated time.

As he was leaving he realized he didn't have his watch. He sent someone back for it. It was gone, disappeared off the face of the earth and never turned in. The president of the Club was red-faced, offering to replace it with a new watch.

"No, thank you," said Schmidt, "I am able to afford to get my own watches. That watch had great sentimental value to me because it was given to me by my wife."

The only Club president who has managed to make Club thievery jolly is Bob Farrell. When he was sworn in, a special edition of *Business Week*, on which he was cover man, purported to tell why the Club generates such affection among its members.

The major point was that it had a "unique plan, under which members may retain, in their own homes and offices, the Club's silverware, library books, and historical artifacts."

It commented that this practice "has gained wide notice" for the Club.

Let it not be said the Club hasn't had a serious side. There was the time during the Nixon administration, when the

Professional Relations Committee, under the chairmanship of investigative reporter Jim McCartney of Knight-Ridder News-papers, made an all-out effort to drag the National Press Club, kicking and screaming, into what Jim called "a twentieth-century involvement in professional questions."

What they attempted to do was to document from the public record evidence that Nixon had indeed launched an assault on the press that endangered the freedom of this precious American institution—a proposition that is now so widely accepted, as a result of the disclosures of Watergate, that it seems almost ridiculous that there was strong resistance to the effort in the Press Club itself.

There was. The Board of Governors of the Club was split down the middle, with many pro-Nixon members who fought the committee's efforts and sought to undermine them.

As Jim McCartney tells the story, "We had a lot of good people on the Committee trying to do an honest job of improving the conditions for the press—Helen Thomas, Allen Otten, Dan Rather, Jim Srodes, Alan Barth, and Warren Rogers.

"But others made efforts to kill the study of Nixon's record, to bury the committee's report. And at one point a member of the NPC Board played the role of Nixon's spy.

"He asked me if he could sit in on a crucial meeting at which final decisions on the wording of the committee's report on Nixon's White House press operations were to be made. Because he was an elected member of the Board, of course I said yes.

"What I didn't know at the time was that he would later play the role of an informer—giving Ken Clawson, of the White House staff, a full report on what happened at the meeting.

"He didn't tell me, Clawson did, later—laughingly bragging that he had known everything the Committee was doing while the report was being prepared.

"Clawson, of course, was a hatchet man for Charles Colson in the days before Colson went to jail and was born again. As far as I know, Clawson, to this day, has not been born again.

"What is clear in looking back on all this is that the press corps in Washington was involved in a war with the White House—a war in which Nixon himself and his top aides were seeking to destroy the credibility of the press with the public in every dirty way they knew. And they had many allies in the press corps itself.

"I said after this effort as committee chairman that it is

probably better for the Press Club to remain a social and drinking club and not pretend it is something else, and I still believe that. In fact, the National Press Club should probably change its name to the National Public Relations and Political Hangers-On Drinking Society, or some other name that befits its actual membership. I feel I can discuss this with some authority. I've been a member for eighteen years."

He has a point. The Club certainly is at its worst at handling big problems like the future of the National Press Club building or assaults against freedom of the press, and at its best at offbeat humor. Goodness knows the hardworking reporters can use a little nonsense to counteract the tensions of covering an ever-nervous and fitful Washington.

A night that went down in Press Club history occurred several years ago when the Norwegian ambassador was guest of honor at a great Norwegian-American Society party.

Many ladies wore Norwegian costumes. For three weeks preceding the party, ladies had used old family recipes from Norway, baking all manner of delicacies.

The men hadn't been idle either. They had sent to Norway for eight hundred bottles of Norwegian beer and several cases of Norwegian vodka, said to be far superior to the Russian.

The party had just gotten started, an orchestra was playing, and the table was set with a tremendous buffet, when suddenly bells started ringing.

Some thought this was a signal that it was time to eat. But others realized it was the fire alarm. Some had the presence of mind to grab a bottle of vodka or a few bottles of beer.

The ambassador helped bring down a man who was so sorely crippled he was using two canes, almost carrying him.

In the lobby, it was discovered the fire was in the grease pit in the fine restaurant, Costins, which had its own entrance on the first floor. However, since the exhaust ducts go to the roof, the smoke had permeated the building.

The Norwegian partygoers made the best of the bad situation, dancing in the lobby and drinking what little they had rescued.

But what they didn't know was that back in the ballroom they had left a different party was going on. The firemen, after breaking a few holes to make sure there was no fire and accidentally letting a hose cover the floor with some two inches of water, had decided it would be a pity to waste all that good food and liquor.

As Club member John Hinkel, who was there, tells the story, "You know, all food is automatically condemned when there is a fire and even though the fire was not in the Club, their conscience was clear. They milled around in their rubber gear, having the best feast they ever had—a beer in one hand and a big chunk of food in the other."

If the Club has any problems with the membership at night, it's almost bound to be something connected with the drinking of strong waters.

But at least once, the complaint involved a different kind of dalliance.

According to a former president, Frank Holeman, one morning back in the 1950s, a very agitated manager met the Club president and said, "We've got a very serious problem."

"What is it?" asked the president.

"Well, last night about four A.M. the cashier went from the front desk into the west lounge and saw two couples in there making love."

"Were they members?"

"Yes."

"Has anybody complained?"

"Only the night cashier."

"He's not a member," said the president. "Let's do nothing until a member complains. And, by the way, tell the night cashier to stay at the front desk after this. Somebody might steal the cash register."

4/Presidents All

It's to the pride or disgrace of the Club—I'm not sure which—that President Warren Harding frequently popped in to join the nonstop poker game. He came early and stayed late. As former Club President Frank Holeman tells the story, "One night a sportswriter sitting in on the game was bemoaning the plight of former heavyweight champion Jack Johnson. Johnson had just finished a term in Leavenworth Penitentiary on a dubious Mann Act conviction.

"But he didn't have money to pay a heavy fine and was going to stay in jail many extra months. 'Isn't it a shame about old Jack Johnson,' the sportswriter said. 'He's got to stay in jail just because he's black and broke.' Harding didn't answer, just kept playing.

"Every time it came his turn to deal, the sportswriter would hold the cards and complain again about the injustice of it all. 'Deal! Deal!' Harding blurted at last. 'I'll pardon him in the morning.' And he did."

A President of the United States laid the cornerstone of the National Press Building and another saved it from bankruptcy.

It was in 1926 that the National Press Building was being built by the Club on a shoestring, and funds were desperately needed. The Club solved its problem uniquely—it staged the laying of a phony cornerstone. President Cal Coolidge dabbled about with a *real* golden trowel and pictures were taken, one of which is still on exhibit at the Club.

The stunt worked—investment money flowed in. The fourteen-story building, including the Club's quarters on the top two floors, was brought to completion and was opened in 1927.

A few years later, the Club was again hanging on the ropes financially, and bankruptcy seemed inevitable. The Chase Bank, now Chase Manhattan, held the mortgage, which was in default. Bascom Timmons, whose life centered on the Club, charged out like the biblical David, slingshot in hand, to face the Goliaths of Wall Street.

"If you dare to foreclose," he warned them, "the name of Chase and Rockefeller will be anathema to the press forever." It was a bold statement for a lone reporter challenging the banking giant. They promised to wait—but not for long. Bankruptcy was still inevitable.

Texas Tim, as he was called, knew that there was only one real hope—the law would have to be changed. Fortunately Timmons knew Jesse Jones, a close financial adviser of Franklin D. Roosevelt, then running for President. As a matter of fact, Jones owned the *Houston Chronicle*, the leader in Tim's stable of newspaper clients, represented by his news bureau.

Now it was 1932 and Tim was on the Roosevelt campaign tour. As the train choo-chooed and whistle-stopped across the country, he had his own campaign with the President-to-be. Pointing out that many businesses were going under, he asked for a change in the law so a corporation could go through bankruptcy without losing control if the creditors agreed.

FDR, always mindful of the little fellows who have the most votes, said, "I'll see what I can do." The change was included in Roosevelt's first hundred days when he could get anything from Congress. Tim was watching and ready to move the minute the act was signed. As soon as he got word, he rushed to court to be the first to file under Section 77-B that saved so many businesses.

It is said that Bascom Timmons was the best president that Club ever had. I say he was the greatest.

Believe it or not, the National Press Club has a past president with a real "history connection." Robert Ames Alden, its sixty-ninth prez, is an eleventh-generation direct descendant of John Alden, to whom Priscilla said, when he tried to marry her off to his boss, "Why don't you speak for yourself, John?"

A different kind of history was made when Bob, world news editor of the *Washington Post*, was sworn in February 1976. He had two showstoppers. Pearl Bailey officiated in swearing him in while President Ford kibitzed. Alden also received The Order of the Snail, a new award presented him by Dr. Lloyd Elliott, president of George Washington University, for having taken seventeen years to earn his degree—in night classes.

After Alden had been ribbed from all sides, President Ford admitted that he himself had no right to talk either because it had taken him as long to become President of the United States as it had taken Alden to achieve his club presidency. They came to Washington about the same time—Ford from Michigan and Alden from Cleveland.

Arthur S. Curtis, a member of the Club for thirty years, is undoubtedly the only member who taught a present or past president of the United States.

"Jimmy Carter was one of my students at the Naval Academy in 1944 and '45," Curtis recalls. "I taught American government and foreign policy. Obviously he got over it and became President of the United States."

Arthur Curtis's favorite memory of life around the Club, was when Jack Reed, of the *Indianapolis Star*, was running for the Board of Governors of the NPC.

"It was during one of those periods when the Club was undergoing one of its many upheavals over the quality of the food and service in the main dining room. A whole bunch of us were sitting at the round table having lunch and I asked Jack what his platform would be.

"He looked around the table gravely and said, 'My platform is clear and simple. It is this: Food with our meals.'

"We all agreed it was an excellent platform but evidently we were in the minority because, as I recall, he didn't make it."

A favorite story recalls the day some workmen were in the Press Club repairing the fireplace, which always glows with burning logs every winter afternoon and evening.

As Earle Marckres remembers it, the workmen looked at the names of past Club presidents enshrined above the mantel, a new name added every year.

"Hey, what the hell is this?" one of them asked looking at the proud array of presidents. "Are all these guys buried in here?"

It was the greatest put-down the Club presidents had ever suffered.

Installing a new Club prez early each year is a gala event crowded with dignitaries. The president's newspaper or magazine puts out a special issue to spoof him.

No outsider can fully appreciate what goes with becoming a National Press Club president. As the more perceptive fellows there have remarked, "It's a damned good thing they only get to be president one year. Otherwise they'd end up feeling they were somewhere between President of the United States and Christ Almighty."

As proof of how members revere their Club president, there is the case of Stan Jennings. After years of newspaper and magazine work, he now runs a news photo business in the Press Building and takes pictures of notables who visit the Club. Stan often will grab his camera and rush upstairs to photograph the president of the Club with some famous or fatuous guest.

So when Frank Aukofer of the *Milwaukee Journal* became president last year, Stan was there to record it for history. The ceremony was carried out in grand style with Vice-President Mondale administering the oath of office.

Next day Egypt's Anwar Sadat was the Press Club luncheon speaker. Again Stan was there. Famed caricaturist Oscar Berger, a member of the Club, attended both events, including the receptions, and a few days later Berger phoned Jennings and asked, "Did you get my picture with the President?"

Stan assured Oscar that the picture was a good one, whereupon Oscar asked for prints to be sent to New York right away.

A few days later Berger again phoned. "*Mister* Jennings," he said, "when I said, 'My picture with the *President*, I meant President Sadat, *not* President Aukofer.'"

Stan's retort made Club history: "I've been a member of this Club a long time, Whenever anybody uses the word *president* it means just one thing: president *of the National Press Club.*"

Dave LeRoy, Club president in 1967, said it best when he tried to explain what the job means. "You are a hybrid—something of a dignitary, a master of ceremonies, a conciliator, a father confessor, a politician, a business manager, a TV star, a social lion, and if you have time left over, a newsman."

However high and mighty a Club president is, every now and then one takes a tumble. Dave LeRoy doesn't mind remembering his:

"One day we had a high official of India as the speaker. I was all charged up. The TV cameras were all in place as I was preparing to go into my role as master of ceremonies at the head table.

"Suddenly I received a jolt that just about threw me into the pits. A card had been handed me from a Club member in the audience which said, 'What a dumb thing to do! Don't you know better than to serve steak to an audience that includes leaders from India?'

"I was well aware of the Hindu taboo on eating of beef. I was shocked because the Club, from long experience, should have known the intricacies of protocol and national practices and religious beliefs.

"I looked around the big ballroom to see many private conferences going on between waiters and the seated hungry. Later I learned that the repeated query to the waiter was, 'Can I please have a fruit plate instead?'

"Shaken, I went on with my role. There was nothing else to do."

Dave LeRoy was a fairly typical Press Club president. A Capitol Hill staffer for *U.S. News & World Report*, he had been a member of the Club for fourteen years and a resident of Washington for some twenty years when his "elevation" came.

Presidents usually work up from the ranks, and Dave had held various Club positions, including financial secretary, treasurer, chairman of the Board of Governors, and vice-president. Like many other presidents, he had been sworn in at a gag ceremony by Chief Justice of the United States Earl Warren, who enjoyed the Club and came often.

On LeRoy's swearing-in, *U.S. News & World Report* put out a special inaugural issue. On the cover was his picture and the misleading promise: "EXCLUSIVE INTERVIEW WITH THE PRESIDENT." Also headlined was "A Look Ahead—and Backward. Also: A Look Around."

Inside the magazine under a title of "Was Election Rigged? The Inside Story" appears a picture of a rotund pigeon-toed toddler identified as Baby LeRoy. A rhyme tells it all:

> On the night
> That he was born,
> Frightened hound dogs
> Bayed till dawn.

George Stimpson, Club president in 1936, was reputed to have been the greatest scholar the Club has produced. A bachelor, who *almost* got married, he spent most of his spare time at the Library of Congress, finding answers to questions most often asked of *Pathfinder*, a favorite publication of schools throughout the country, of which he was an editor. He also authored question books.

Stimpson lived at the George Washington Inn, on Capitol Hill. He would dream up some outrageous story or quip as he shaved in the morning. Then he would walk over to the Longworth Building and have breakfast with a few congressmen and reporters.

Everyone waited for his story to start the day with a

chuckle and they were seldom disappointed. At the end of the day he would head downtown for the Press Club only to have someone tell his own story back to him. By then it might be somewhat changed and credited to someone else.

George Stimpson became most famous around the Club for his story of three Presidents: "George Washington couldn't tell a lie; FDR couldn't tell the truth, and Harry Truman can't tell the difference."

He told it to Hill friends at breakfast and at the Press Club at dinner time, it was being repeated to everyone—without credit to him. Stimpson was sorry when his quip was used against Truman in the 1948 election. He didn't think that was fair.

Stimpson also is credited with the comment that "Truman is like the fellow who played piano in a whorehouse for two years without knowing what was going on upstairs."

In 1940—in the year of the presidency of Richard Wilson, of the *Des Moines Register* and *Tribune*—the Club held a wonderful party for all the many presidential candidates who would never get a chance to run because, as everyone knew, Franklin Delano Roosevelt was going to be President forever.

It was known as the Candidates Dinner and Wilson invited such big names as socialist Norman Thomas, Senator Arthur Vandenberg, and RFC Chief Jesse Jones.

Jesse Jones, who was said to be lazy in everything except when it came to making money, tried to get out of preparing a speech by asking former President and Club good guy George Stimpson for some help with his speech.

Stimpson was not about to be imposed on and he said, facetiously, "Why don't you tell them the story you told us last night?"

Jesse Jones took him seriously and rose to tell five hundred male guests—many of them puritanical—the Texas story Stimpson had referred to:

"It's about a strike in a whorehouse," Jones said, "if you know what I mean. Some country boys came to town and found the girls picketing. Obligingly, they asked what they could do to help.

"'Well,' said one of the girls, 'you boys can go fuck yourselves.'" Having delivered this message to the distinguished assemblage, Jones sat down.

The next day Senator Vandenberg told some of the reporters, "Did you hear the story Jesse Jones told last night? If I had told it, I would be run out of town today."

He was right. The amazing thing is that as long as a man sticks to his established image he's all right. It's when he tries to change his image that he gets into trouble in Washington.

There are some reporters who hold that if the press had not found out, via the infamous tapes, that President Richard Nixon cussed like a trooper, he would have remained President. What the public could not abide was the change in the sanctimonious image of the man they had elected President.

In May 1952 George Stimpson was very ill from diabetes complications. The Club threw a party in tribute of him and among those present to pay their last respects were Chief Justice Fred Vinson and Speaker of the House Sam Rayburn.

After they had spoken, George got up and said, "As I listen to you, I wonder who the man could be you are talking about."

Four months later Stimpson was dead, and the Club was glad it had let him know how everyone felt about him while he was still living.

The craziest swearing-in ceremony was that of Felix Cotten in 1943. Since he was of the South, and covered the Hill a lot in those days, it was felt that Speaker Sam Rayburn of Texas should participate.

But what do you do with Sam? Well, since he's a politician, why not have him unveil a statue. That will give it political flavor. But Sam had a fatal flaw—though important, he was not glamorous. Glamour was needed. Definitely a feminine touch was in order. What to do? There was that six-foot-seven guy in the *New York Daily News* bureau, Frank Holeman. Why not fling a dress over him and make him play the part of a dainty "little girl" helping Mr. Speaker (barely five feet four or five inches tall) unveil the statue?

It's hard to hold down a six-foot-seven-inch giant to throw a dress over him—let alone a wig. It took a committee of strong men to haul him kicking and flailing out of the National Press Building. They delivered the unhappy giant to Jack's rent-a-costume place, which again took some doing, because Jack had a walkup shop above a store. But shove him up the stairs they did. Even Jack was appalled. He had never transformed a six-foot-seven male into a "little girl" before. Werewolves, yes. Little girls, no. But he coped.

And it came to pass, that the night of the inaugural, a monstrous little girl with long curls skipped on stage and stood towering over the short Rayburn before she flung off the statue's cover, revealing none other than a smothering Felix Cotten.

Poor Cotten's condition was of absolutely no concern to the heartless crowd. They wanted that "winsome" girl, who had flounced off the stage. They roared for more. Sam Rayburn, too, had lost control. It might as well have been Frank Holeman's inaugural. A few years later it was.

What can you do for a six-foot-seven giant who has already been a star and heard the roar of the crowd? Something with pizzazz was in order. The year was 1956. Computers and Univacs were coming into style. The club geniuses built a giant cardboard computer with holes in it. Inaugural night, lights flashed and bells rang from within the computer as Doug Edwards of ABC read the news of an ongoing club election.

Suddenly the moment of truth and the winner of the election stood revealed as the head of Frank Holeman popped through a hole. Then the head of the Chief Justice of the Supreme Court, who would swear him in, popped through another hole.

Frank Holeman, formerly of the *New York Daily News*, is now a public relations man for the tire industry's safety council and the biggest man ever to become Club president. "But I'm only six-feet six these days," says Frank solemnly. "Marriage grinds one down."

As a gag when he took office in 1956, the *News* ran an extra, devoting the whole edition to his ascendancy to the throne. The headline was but one word—HOLEMAN, and his picture. But only half of him could fit on the front page. The rest of him, posed against the Capitol dome was on the wraparound back page and showed his long legs.

Holeman was billed at the Club as being the only man over six feet four ever to attend the University of North Carolina without a basketball scholarship. He got through on no scholarship and started his writing career as copyboy on the *News*. In his election platform, he had pledged to upgrade the game room clientele to match the wallpaper, a very lively print.

Holeman earned the right to talk in terms of game room improvements because he held two trophies: The 1955 James Wingo Trophy for the poker player showing the greatest improvement during the year; and the Leo Farrell Plaque for the player most in need of improvement.

A poem to Holeman was written by Frank's *Daily News* colleague, Lowell Limpus, expressing the hope the Press Club would keep him busy and out of their hair:

It's bad enough when he gets a scoop
And that roaring voice makes the ceiling droop
And he gallops in like a herd stampedes
Full of inserts, adds, and bright new leads.

Frank's story is no longer typical. He stormed New York at the age of twenty-one, applying immediately to the *News*. The famed Harry Nichols was the city editor then.

About a dozen other eager hopefuls had applied for the job of copyboy on that blustery, cold day of March 1941. Harry Nichols had asked each why he wanted the job. When he asked Frank, Frank simply turned around, raised his coat jacket and exposed a big hole in the seat of his pants. Nichols, impressed with such simple honesty, took a chance on him.

When Frank was hired, George Dixon, later a humor columnist in Washington, was rewrite man at the *News*. Unable to stand the sight of so much exposed territory erupting from the threadbare suit, he bought Frank an overcoat.

A year later, Holeman arrived in Washington as a cub reporter and was sent up to Capitol Hill by *News* bureau chief, John O'Donnell, who didn't know what else to do with him. "Just hang around a few days and get the feel of things," O'Donnell instructed him.

This was June 1, 1942. Holeman remembers it as if it were yesterday. He hurried back to the office at the end of the day and tried to report on all the amazing things he'd seen and learned. No one would listen, least of all the bureau chief. Next day he learned more amazing things. Again nobody listened. On the third day Holeman's timing seemed to be right. O'Donnell was leaning back resting. More for comic relief than anything, he asked Holeman if there was anything doing on the Hill.

"Well, I think there was something that might make a piece for the paper," said Holeman hesitantly. "We declared war on Rumania, Bulgaria, and Hungary." O'Donnell contained his emotions so as not to frighten the raw beginner out of ruining an earthshaking story, and told him to go ahead and write a piece on it.

Holeman wrote it. O'Donnell read it, deadpan, still afraid to panic the youngster, and handed it to the teletype operator to send.

As George Dixon later told it "Half an hour went by. Then came a phone call from New York.

"It was editor Tenold Sunde. 'This is no kind of story for clowning around with phony by-lines!' he snarled at O'Donnell. 'Who really wrote this war declaration piece, you or Dixon?' To convince Sunde that his ex-copyboy, Holeman, could possibly have written a printable story, we practically had to take blood oaths."

One year the Club had a problem electing a member of the foreign press president of the Club.

There was nothing against this in the Club constitution but if they voted him in, they could no longer serve liquor in the Club. The D.C. code stated that no organization owned or headed by a foreign subject could hold a liquor license, essential to Club income. John Heffernan, known to one and all as "Pat", was a British subject and not about to change his allegiance.

Pat's boosters converged on Capitol Hill. So well did they succeed as lobbyists that they got a special bill passed exempting private clubs from the ruling. And for good measure they also got an amendment permitting Sunday drinking of liquor for the first time in the District of Columbia in this century.

Heffernan's term in office was a great comfort to Press Club members who had feared that all the power of the press had gone down the drain.

The typical Club president is the head of a news bureau, writing for newspapers or trade papers. In the Club, as in most organizations, there is an escalator system. A member gets named to a committee, becomes chairman, gains notice for good works, and is elected to the Board of Governors.

Then comes the big treat—running for vice-president, and if he wins he almost automatically becomes president a year later.

This system has the merit of educating those heading for the top but it confines the selections to the ruling clique.

Once in a decade or so an escalator breaks down when some raiding clique shoots its way in, bringing ideas without the experience to carry them out.

This happened in 1971 with the ascension of Warren

Rogers of the *Los Angeles Times*, a friend of the Kennedys, Helen Thomas, United Press correspondent of the White House, and Peter Lisagor of the *Chicago Daily News*, who was also one of the nation's top panelists on TV.

It raised the tone of the Board. But these luminaries did not have time to attend meetings. So nothing was gained.

Bill Lawrence of the *New York Times* was president when Fidel Castro came as a luncheon speaker in 1959. Lawrence did well in the number of illustrious guests he introduced at news-making luncheons.

At the end of his term, the club gave him a little party and Bill, over the drinks, grew a little expansive. "The highlight of my year," he said, "was to have the three big *K*'s. I introduced them all—Kennedy, Khrushchev, and Castro." Someone said, "You don't spell Castro with a *K*." Bill looked at the quibbler with scorn. "You spell it your way and I'll spell it mine."

Bill and Kennedy had a very close relationship. In fact Jack Kennedy used the Press Club forum to announce that he would seek the presidential nomination, as did Carter later. Bill Lawrence practically walked off the podium with Kennedy and right on to the campaign trail.

A few years later, in January 1961, President Kennedy became a member of the Club, sponsored by Lawrence. As a former newspaperman, he paid the $90 nonactive initiation fee by personal check.

He attended the ascension of the new National Press Club president, John Cosgrove, *Broadcasting* magazine bureau chief, just eight days after his own inauguration. As I recall, this was the first time a U.S. President participated in a Press Club inaugural since Herbert Hoover, about 1930.

However, Kennedy had to leave before the actual swearing-in by Chief Justice Earl Warren. As he was leaving JFK looked at Cosgrove and said, "Be sure to keep your hands on the Bible." There had been a flap in the press over whether Kennedy had truly had his hand on the Bible when Warren had given him the oath a few days before.

What a night it had been! Kennedy's appearance had fouled up the schedule. Secret Service men had been busy checking behind every curtain. Phones were hooked up. Pierre Salinger, the White House press secretary, had worked out a prearranged signal. Secret Service would give Cosgrove a long ring that would sound in the club's East Lounge when Kennedy left the White House.

Salinger was waiting with Cosgrove in the lounge, ready to rush down to the lobby's Fourteenth Street entrance to greet the President. The signal must not have been given after the President left the White House. Poor Kennedy was in the lobby all alone, pacing and cooling his heels in front of the elevators. When his greeters came, he met them irritably, "Where have you been?"

Fortunately, just then some people realized who he was and rushed over to shake the young President's hand. His mood escalated rapidly. So expansive did he become, that he even praised the club members for making him pay for his Press Club membership card—No. 2973, calling it the decent thing to do.

Bill Lawrence was president in an era when you didn't worry about offending ethnic groups. Members still talk about the night he spoke at a farewell party for Ernie Barcella of UPI, leaving the news profession to become a General Motors flack.

Ernie had brought with him all the people who were dear to him—his family, friends, and parish priest. Bill Lawrence, speaking in the East Lounge, looked down and said, "This is a typical Italian celebration. The priest is always there for the three most important times in their lives—the baptism, then when they're married, and finally when they're electrocuted."

The history of the Club's dealings with presidents—those of the United States and its own—has many highs and lows.

One of its lows was its custom, in the old days, of extracting money from eager inaugural parade watchers who would pay almost any sum to get a good view of a new President riding down Pennsylvania Avenue and Fifteenth Street en route to the White House. When the Club had an excellent view from its rented quarters above a tavern at Fifteenth and F streets, the going price was one thousand dollars a window.

As Brian Kelly, *Washington Star* reporter, tells it, "The only inaugural that was missed was Woodrow Wilson's, in 1913, when, after a typical Press Club disagreement over who was getting the money, the windows were painted black."

At that event, I would have been better off had I missed it too. My seat was on an improvised stand inside a building. Jumping down, I tore my pants on a nail, to the snickers of the

54

audience. My mother had to buy me a new pair before she could take me home.

When Don Larrabee was sworn in as National Press Club president in 1973, the Inaugural Committee chose Don's old friend Elliot Richardson to do the job. Richardson has held many top government jobs in various departments—Justice and HEW, for example. At that time he was Secretary of Defense. Richardson always seemed to be at the center of every administration problem with abuse flying around his head.

It seemed reasonable, therefore, when Richardson asked Larrabee to put his left hand on a stack of Massachusetts newspapers, for which Don was the correspondent, and swear never to print anything unkind about him.

A second much-beleagured man, about whom Larrabee also wrote tons of copy, helped officiate—Senator Edmund Muskie. The presidential chances of both men seem faint. Larrabee has been accused by some bar habitues of giving them the kiss of death while he had them there together.

They point out that Larrabee seems to have had a strange effect on world leaders as well. It is a matter of Club record that Larrabee's list of luncheon speakers in 1973 included a dozen foreign heads of state. None are still in power. They included Britain's Prime Minister Edward Heath; Israel's Golda Meir; Australia's Gough Whitlam; Japan's Kakuei Tanaka; South Vietnam's President Nguyen Thieu; and Germany's Willy Brandt, among others.

Larrabee's term had the distinction of drawing the largest stand-up crowd to any National Press Club event. More than nine hundred jammed into the ballroom for a Congressional Night party where columnist Art Buchwald did a memorable slide presentation and commentary on Watergate, using old silent-film comedy characters like Laurel and Hardy and Charlie Chaplin to make each needling point and discuss the Watergate cast of characters.

Robert Farrell became Club president in 1977. He was bureau chief of McGraw-Hill world news and formerly Paris bureau chief.

Declaring that under Farrell humility is out, the old Imperial Presidency is in, the Inaugural Committee traced a parallel with Nixon. Though Farrell could not learn how to be imperial by moving into the White House, "He is as much the aristocrat as fifteen years of high living in France on a company expense account can be expected to make of a humbly-born New York City Irishman."

At Farrell's inauguration party, "populist" members insisted that the new president follow in President Carter's footsteps, with at least a show of humility—"a walk down the twelve flights of stairs from the club's ballroom to the street." Though his deputy bureau chief, Herbert Cheshire, offered to have an honor guard of thirty-seven staffers along the stairs, Farrell did not think the walk imperial enough.

A special issue of the McGraw-Hill publication *Business Week*, issued for the investiture, explained in a fantastic chart the history of the Club from 1908 to 1978, and from 1926 all Club landmarks tied in with Farrell's own life.

- 1926—Coolidge lays Press Building cornerstone—R. E. Farrell born.
- 1932—Press Building in receivership—Farrell enters school.
- 1933—Prohibition repealed—Farrell drinks his first glass of wine.
- 1946—Member protests poor service by dangling waiter from thirteenth floor window—Farrell hides out in college.
- 1949—Farrell graduates from college—Russians detonate first atom bomb.
- 1956—Farrell joins McGraw-Hill—Hungarians revolt.
- 1968—The Willard Hotel closes—Farrell returns to Washington—D. C. riots devastate downtown.
- 1973—Farrell elected to NPC board and buys round of drinks.
- 1975—Farrell discovers gin and tonic.
- 1977—Farrell falls from high board post into presidency.

Among Farrell's campaign promises was one to "begin an immediate inventory of Club assets."

Farrell said the Club is richer than it knows. A search of an abandoned top floor barroom yielded dividends. Among the finds, which Farrell says will be converted to cash: the perfectly preserved remains of a member, fully attired in authentic 1930s dress, complete with vest and spats, who apparently was over-looked when the old bar closed in April 1936.

When Frank Aukofer of the *Milwaukee Journal* became the seventy-first president of the Club in February 1978, he had to take a lot of ribbing about his cigar-smoking. The headline of the special issue that the *Milwaukee Journal* printed for the occasion ran: "What Press Club Needs: Aukofer and 8-Cent Cigar." The story, written by John Kole, chief of his bureau, said:

> *It may ring alarm bells at the Environmental Protection Agency because Aukofer is partial to the Muriel Coronella which he often buys at five for 37 cents. It could not really be described as a good 8-cent cigar, but it's cheap.*
>
> *A few years ago, Aukofer encountered Henry S. Reuss, the aristocratic Milwaukee congressman, at a Capitol Hill reception. Reuss, the heir of a Milwaukee banking family, bummed a cigar.*
>
> *He lit up and took one puff before withering Aukofer with a look of haughty disdain. "One good thing about Aukofer," Reuss declared, "nobody's ever going to roll him for his smokes."*

In keeping with Club tradition, "When Aukofer was running for president last year, the greatest campaigning was not for him but to boost Arthur Wiese of the *Houston Post* into the pivotal post of vice-president, from which his rise to the current presidency was almost inevitable.

"Bottom Line Wiese" his campaign handlers called him for the fact that as treasurer of the Club, he had wiped out its deficit and even brought in a little profit. Also if anyone cared to know, he had won nine journalism awards along the way.

Wiese himself doesn't refer to them. His mind is filled with other things. As Board member Vivian Vahlberg interprets him, "Inside Art, yearning to be set free, is someone much like Fred Astaire, Gary Cooper, and Humphrey Bogart rolled into one.

"He's actually an incurable romantic at heart, who would rather be at the helm of the *African Queen* than of the NPC."

Well, it takes all kinds to fill the presidency.

5/Churchill Smoked Here

In more than seventy years of the Club's existence, thousands of famous guests, including the last fourteen consecutive presidents of the United States, have come through NPC doors and visited— Teddy Roosevelt, William Howard Taft, Woodrow Wilson, Warren G. Harding, Calvin Coolidge, Herbert Hoover, Franklin D. Roosevelt, Harry Truman, Dwight D. Eisenhower, John F. Kennedy, Lyndon B. Johnson, Richard M. Nixon, Gerald R. Ford and Jimmy Carter. Presidential press styles change.

Harding came to the Club to mingle with reporters. He was a lonely man.

Coolidge was not keen on publicity. For a while he was not to be quoted but made statements to be attributed to a "White House spokesman"—himself.

Hoover, in his high starched collar, was a bit stuffy. Once, when a Hearst paper reported that his son had gotten a job with an aircraft company, he indignantly stated that his son was a good engineer trying to make it on his own and that any inference to the contrary was "a dastardly attack on the President."

Roosevelt was a masterful manipulator of people, including the press. He came to the Club and reveled in bantering with the reporters. He was a man's man and liked an off-color story.

So did Truman. Felix Cotten recalls the tale President Truman told on Congressional Night at the Club, when no women attended.

It seems Truman was always telling stories about a Judge Lewis of Memphis, who was famed as the "talking judge" of Tennessee.

The way the story goes, a young woman was testifying in court after accusing a certain man of raping her in her sleep, and the man was on trial charged with this bizarre thing.

She was attired in her best—dark satin dress, broad-brimmed hat trimmed in flowers, and white gloves to her elbows.

After a while Judge Lewis interrupted the witness because he found it a little hard to believe a woman could be raped in her sleep. So he said, "Young woman, yo' mean to tell this heah coat that this man raped yo' in yoah sleep?"

She said, "Yes, judge."

Judge Lewis said, "Young woman, how far did this man penetrate your person before you woke up?"

She reached up to the end of one of her white gloves and said, "To here."

Whereupon old Judge Lewis said, "Young woman, I am putting yo' on judicial notice. Don't yo' go to sleep in this heah coatroom because I don't think there's a man round here who could wake yo' up."

Ike almost became the only President not to join the National Press Club. The reason was, according to Frank Holeman, who was correspondent with the *New York Daily News* at the time, that candidate Eisenhower had learned, through a poll conducted by a news magazine, that most reporters were Democrats.

Looking back, Holeman says this should have come as no surprise. "It is well known," he says, "that most news correspondents are Democrats who call themselves Independents, just as most publishers are Republicans who call themselves Independents—it evens out."

But it did come as a painful surprise to Ike that the people who were covering his campaign were for Adlai Stevenson. "When he was elected, he saw no particular reason to join a club made up largely of his critics," Holeman says, adding that the Club was not terribly upset by his decision until they really needed him in 1958.

That was when the Club was getting ready to celebrate its fiftieth anniversary and needed a President of the United States to give the celebration a touch of class.

Never short of ideas, a Board member suggested the Club invite Ike to the big gala, where he would be presented with a *free* honorary membership card. It worked.

There are about five thousand members of the National Press Club currently—the most diverse group you'd ever want to meet—from the presidents of the United States, to ne'er-do-wells who can barely scratch up the two hundred dollars or more dues every year.

Among the members, fortuitously, is Warren Lane, vice-president of the Security National Bank on the first floor of the National Press Building. Members turn to him for loans to start new newsletters, new public relations businesses, and new news bureaus. Among the more unusual loan applications was for a boat to steady the nerves of a self-employed newsman. He got the loan and paid same.

The year 1928 is historic for the Club in that it chose to blackball an applicant for membership—a rare event. As member Don Curry tells it, "The Club, while the most political in the country save the United States Senate, did not elect people to membership on the basis of the ideological backgrounds. If they met the standards for membership, that was it.

"What happened in this notable exception is that a member made a trip to Italy and did an interview with one of the political leaders of the time.

"Since the dignitary had had a newspaper background, he was eager to be proposed for membership. His application was submitted. However, his name had to be posted in the Club for two weeks. If as few as ten of the brethren signed a petition, he was blackballed.

"Such a petition was signed in this, the only case of membership blackballing I can recall. Then President J. Fred Essary, chief of the *Baltimore Sun* bureau, had the unpleasant duty of writing his regrets. "The dignitary's name? Benito Mussolini."

The list of famous visitors who have come to the Club is mind-boggling: Sarah Bernhardt, Orville Wright, Charles A. Lindbergh, William Jennings Bryan, Will Rogers—who, by virtue of his syndicated newspaper column, was an active member— Andrew Carnegie, H. G. Wells, Victor Herbert, Champ Clark, and Kaiser Wilhelm's pre–World War I ambassador, the Count von Bernsdorf.

Charlie Chaplin was lucky to visit the Club at the precise time papers were being drawn up to finance the present National Press Building and he signed those papers as a witness.

And the list goes on: Samuel Gompers, Andrew Mellon, Nicholas Longworth.

Admiral Robert E. Peary, explorer of the North Pole, came to the Club to tell all about it.

The old F Street quarters didn't do so badly, either, as a place for entertaining big names. On the night of May 18, 1908, the big opening night of the Club, more than a hundred members of Congress came, as well as a half-dozen members of Teddy Roosevelt's cabinet, to mix and mingle with reporters and get a look at the guest of honor, Buffalo Bill Cody.

The Club luncheons, which began officially in 1932, have made history every year since. Truman's Secretary of State, Dean Acheson, announced the Truman Far Eastern policy from here.

In 1956 Winston Churchill set a new tone to international relations by calling for peaceful coexistence between the United States and the Soviet Union.

In 1958 Secretary of State John Foster Dulles announced plans for the first East-West summit conference.

In 1959 the largest event ever staged by the Club took place—a mammoth press conference for Nikita Khrushchev to state his views. Female reporters were permitted that day as guests, and my co-author, Fran Leighton, was the guest of member Mike Trupp of the *Times-Herald*. Khrushchev spotted her long red hair and asked who she was.

In 1969 LBJ made his emotional "farewell address" at the Press Club.

In 1974 it was a governor—Jimmy Carter of Georgia— who announced his candidacy for the presidency. Few took it seriously. Four years later, they found themselves listening to him again at a Club luncheon when, as President, he unveiled his plan for overhauling the Civil Service system.

First Ladies have come as guests rather than speakers, with two notable exceptions. Eleanor Roosevelt spoke in 1938 and Rosalynn Carter, exactly forty years later.

Some memorable photographs have been made at the Press Club. For example, the most famous picture of Harry S Truman was taken there. It shows him with movie star Lauren Bacall perched on top of a piano as he plays.

The inside story on this picture is that he was most annoyed when some overenthusiastic PR man boosted Lauren up to improve a photograph he wanted to take. Truman was only a Vice-President at the time and nobody bothered to ask his permission.

He was playing the piano to entertain servicemen to whom the Club opened its doors in World War II.

After his presidency, Truman would come to Washington to visit old friends. Once the Club had a party and promised a mystery guest would be onstage. At the right moment the Club members were called to attention and through the curtains came the strains of the "Missouri Waltz" on the piano. Everyone laughed and the word went around the room that old Harry was back in town. Then the curtains parted and there sat Vice-President Dick Nixon playing Harry's tune.

It was a good joke and it gave the Club the idea of inviting Truman and Nixon to play a duet. But Truman turned the invitation down flat, saying he refused to be a phony by becoming friendly with Nixon.

Nixon probably never knew why the stunt had not worked, even though he had accepted. Eventually he went to Truman's own turf at Independence, Missouri, bearing a gift—the very piano that Truman played at the White House. By now Truman had mellowed. He graciously accepted the piano for the Truman library. It's hard to say no to a President who knocks on your door.

When Robert A. Taft took his Senate seat in 1939, he was spotted at once as a presidential hopeful and spoke at a Club luncheon. First, a look-alike member was introduced as Taft, said a few words, and yielded to another bulky and bespectacled look-alike, who finally brought on the real Taft.

The introducing of famous guests is an art in itself. Press Club presidents have a long tradition of not fawning on celebrities but, if anything, gently putting them down.

When Frank Holeman as prez in 1956 introduced the governor of New York, Averell Harriman, he summarized Harriman's career, taking it from the top. Here was an average American boy who gets out of college, goes on the board of Union Pacific Railroad, and becomes in turn secretary of commerce, Roosevelt's ambassador to Moscow, and finally governor of New York.

Then Holeman paused and commented, "Very few people with his beginning would wind up where he is today. It was a long hard struggle downhill."

Bob Butler, senior editor of *Traffic World*, was for years NPC entertainment chairman. Every time he thought he had enough of wrestling with schedules of the stars and trying to talk them into participating in Press Club stunts, the Club wouldn't let him go. He was just too damned good at roping in the greats.

For example, when Vernon Louviere of New Orleans was to be sworn in as president of the Club in 1971, and a hot New

Orleans Mardi Gras inaugural was in order, Bob managed to snag Louis "Satchmo" Armstrong as the star attraction. Satchmo was not in good health but Butler talked with his wife and made arrangements for the great musician to have a place to rest if he needed it.

Louis Armstrong came and saw and conquered the National Press Club. Refusing to rest, he responded to the wild enthusiasm and played his heart out. The Club recorded his appearance. A long-playing record is still on sale there. It was Satchmo's last major performance. He died a couple of months later.

Bob remembers with nostalgia sitting with Louis and his wife, Lucille, at dinner before the NPC Inaugural Ball. "He told me how he happened to propose to his wife, a waitress until she shared Satchmo's glamorous life in show business."

The way Bob Butler remembers it Satchmo said, "I just love hamburgers and the best place to get them was this little cafe where Lucille worked. Every day I got to going in for some of Lucille and her hamburgers. She was a great kidder. One day she saw me coming. She took the menu and crossed off the hamburger.

"I walked in and she said to me, 'Louis, I just scratched what you like." So I looked at her and said, 'Well, you just go wash yo' hands and bring me a hamburger!'"

Satchmo realized if he wanted those great burgers, he was going to have to take Lucille too, in a package deal.

Bob recalls how Satchmo refused money. "Being the great guy he was, he only charged us for plane fare for two from New York. And we gave them a hotel suite in the Sheraton Carlton.

"Speaking of hotel suites, we also got one for David Frost, who was our emcee for the Inaugural Ball. The day before the ball I got a call from Frost's secretary in New York City. She said Frost was bringing his friend Diahann Carroll.

"I asked if he would need another room. She said she really didn't know. So we decided what the hell, one suite is enough for two. It was. But they split shortly thereafter. I hope it was nothing the Press Club said."

The Club rarely honors one of its own at its famous newsmaker luncheons. But in November 1977, it invited Eric Sevareid to speak on his retirement. Members' hearts swelled with pride and there were many misty eyes as he explained the importance of the Press Club so much better than anyone had ever done before:

"I have sat out here in this room over many, many years and listened to presidents and kings and generals and admirals and dictators and candidates. It never occurred to me that I would be up here as the centerpiece. It took me quite a while to get up here—but I made it.

"This room really is the sanctum sanctorum of American journalists. It's the Westminister Hall, it's Delphi, it's Mecca, the Wailing Wall for everybody in this country having anything to do with the news business; the only hallowed place I know of that's absolutely bursting with irreverence."

Felix Cotten likes to tell about the off-the-record luncheon press conference which he helped set up for Winston Churchill. It was in 1943, when Felix was president of the Club.

"We didn't have enough room for the crowd of reporters that wanted to come so we held a luncheon at the Statler Hotel with the Gridiron, the White House correspondents, and the Washington Overseas Writers club all sharing the guest of honor, the great Winston.

"I remember it was in October or November of '43. Reporters were permitted to ask anything they liked, after the luncheon, with the understanding that what he said was strictly off the record.

"As I recall, only one man—Paul Ward of the *Baltimore Sun*—wrote anything at all about him, breaking the rule. For my part, I sat up there at the head table with Churchill and wrote notes on the back of the small menu card.

"Then I went back to the office and wrote thirteen pages of double-spaced notes for Hutch, my boss, the INS bureau chief—giving him the war situation as I had learned it. Nothing went out on the wire.

"I will never forget that luncheon. First we had a little head table reception for Churchill on the eleventh floor of the Statler.

"Paul Wooton said, 'Mr. Prime Minister, would you like something to drink?' "Churchill said, 'Oh yes, bring me a martini.' He downed three or four at a good clip.

"From there we progressed to the Presidents Room at the Statler and got Churchill, who was in very good spirits by now, to the head table.

"Again Paul Wooton, who was president of the Gridiron

Club, said, 'Mr. Prime Minister, would you care to have a little something with your lunch?'

"Churchill brightened and said, 'Yes, I believe a Scotch and soda.' He sipped Scotch right through the meal.

"By the time the press conference started, Churchill showed his drinks but his pipe-organ voice and sharp mind were not impaired. He started talking at 1:30 and the conference lasted till 4:30. Nobody who was there ever wished it was one minute less. It was the most scintillating press conference I ever attended. He became poetic and his command of the language carried us to heights of emotion.

"I remember an old congressman from Minnesota who said about Churchill that the more he drank, the more brilliant he got. I don't believe Churchill was ever quite that brilliant again."

What happened to Paul Ward, who broke the secrecy pledge? "Well, he got away with it," Felix said, "but to the honor of the press corps, no one else jumped to do the same thing as, I am afraid, they would today."

One of Felix's greatest regrets is that he does not have a copy of Churchill's remarks. When asked what had happened to the transcript, he said, "I made three copies. I gave Hutchinson one, saved one for myself, and let Hutch send the third to the editors in New York, for their guidance on war stories.

"I happened to tell Clare Boothe Luce, then a congresswoman, about Churchill's eloquent remarks and off-the-record war progress report. She wanted to see it. I made her promise to return my copy. She sent it back eventually with a flattering letter.

"Then one day I made the mistake of mentioning the Luce letter to Hutch. He pleaded to see it. I gave it to him and never saw it again. He also asked to see my only copy of the memo. It also slid off the face of the world. I wonder how many historic memos and documents that would help shed light on the past are tucked away forgotten."

Another person who vividly recalls the Churchill visit is Naomi Nover. Her husband, Barnet, a syndicated columnist, was president of the Overseas Writers club of Washington, co-sponsoring the luncheon.

It was Barnet who called the White House, where Churchill was staying, to invite the Prime Minister and make the arrangements. But it was Naomi who phoned to ask what the Prime Minister's favorite food for luncheon was. Roast beef, she was told.

"Wartime food and gas rationing was on," Naomi recalls. "Churchill was the only one who had roast beef that day, an inch thick. The rest of us drooled. We had chicken, also fruit cup, vegetables, salad, ice cream and demitasse.

"I had found that Churchill did not care for the sweet things that the rest of us were having so he had consommé to begin, instead of fruit cup, and cheese and biscuits for dessert.

"I arrived early and noticed that the waiters were acting peculiarly and picking up every single plate and centerpiece on every table and examining them, even looking underneath. Later, when Barnet received a bill for thirty five extra lunches, we understood why. The waiters had been Scotland Yard men in disguise."

According to Mrs. Nover there was only one small emergency during the meal. That was when Churchill had finished and called for a cigar. Barnet Nover didn't smoke and so he went over to Eugene Meyer, publisher of the *Washington Post*, to ask if he had one.

"Wouldn't you know it," Meyer exclaimed. "Every day I carry a Belinda but today all I have is a fifteen-cent cigar."

While Barnet emoted over whether one offered a man like Churchill a fifteen-cent cigar, the maître d', who had witnessed the whole scene, said just a minute, and came rushing back with a box of Churchill's favorites. The New York Statler had been told about the famous visitor the Washington Statler would be having and had shipped down a box.

The Club takes advantage of the parade of politicians, statesmen, movie stars, and what have you, who pass through Washington for one reason or another. Because actress Claudette Colbert was appearing in a play in Washington in 1974, Clyde La Motte, the newly elected president of the Club, thought he was pretty lucky to be getting her as his first luncheon guest. That is, until he met Madame Colbert for the first time.

Not only did she come without a speech, but she seemed frozen with fear. She confessed to Clyde, before he escorted her to the ballroom, that she could only speak if she memorized and rehearsed lines written for her. La Motte was getting green around the gills as he tried jollying her a bit to prepare her for what was expected—a speech.

"But I can't get up in front of an audience and make a speech. The thought of it terrifies me," Claudette wailed, rolling her eyes.

As Clyde tells, now that he can joke about it, "I began to perspire. I finally said somewhat desperately 'I'll tell you what we'll do. Since you have been interviewed many times for fan magazines, I will simply interview you. You will not have to make a speech. How would that be?'

"She said she guessed that might be all right but she was far from enthusiastic. To make her feel better I told her that she would be heard over one hundred fifty radio stations. 'Oh, no,' she gasped, 'no radio.'

"I went over and talked to the radio technician so that our shivering star would think that radio had been canceled but I merely warned him to stay out of sight. She would have no way of knowing during the luncheon whether she was on radio or not because the network pickup was off the public-address microphone. I didn't exactly lie. I simply went back and told Claudette it had been taken care of.

"This was one luncheon I was anxious to get over with. I explained the Club tradition to Claudette—how after everyone else was seated the president of the Club and the guest of honor enter the ballroom alone and proceed to their places at the center of the head table.

"She asked which side of her face would be exposed to the audience. I told her the right side of her face. " 'Oh no!' she gasped, as if I'd struck her. 'That's my bad side. I always insist on being photographed from the left.'

"Now I was really in trouble. I could see there was no way she was going to walk in from the direction that had been good enough for kings and queens and prime ministers. Then I had an inspiration. While the head table, which had already been seated, waited nervously and wondered if the star had broken a leg, I walked her through a circuitous route, down long hallways to the other side of the building, so we entered from the opposite entrance. Needless to say, everyone was watching the door in the other direction. Our arrival was hardly noticed at all.

"As she took her place the applause started, camera bulbs flashed, and Claudette stood happily posing for a moment with her left cheek to the cameras."

La Motte started his introduction as the luncheon plates were being taken away. She had hardly tasted her food. He was conscious that "a gentleman always remembers a lady's birthday but *never* her birth year."

"Claudette Colbert was born August thirteenth..." he began, but before he could say another word Claudette called out loud and clear, "1906." The audience burst into applause, delighted at her candor. Encouraged by the response, Claudette continued to interrupt, correcting his statements about her. The audience enjoyed this hugely. Clyde was still sweating.

Suddenly she said, "You are stepping on my purse." Poor Clyde, when he finally realized what she was saying, discovered that he was indeed standing on her purse which she had placed on the floor. He muttered that he was sorry then suddenly added, "But *you* have been stepping on *my lines*."

Claudette exploded into laughter, which ignited another round of applause from her fans. Now the crowd was having a good time and Claudette reacted like a trouper, responding in great fashion to questions that were now coming up from the audience. No longer nervous, she had the audience in her hands.

Clyde La Motte shakes his head as he recalls, "When it was over she received a standing ovation. I escorted her to her car that was waiting on Fourteenth Street, in front of the Press Building. As crowds of office secretaries, who could not go to the luncheon, watched, she kissed me on the cheek. As she drove off, I immediately went to the Club bar, ordered a tall drink, and took it with me to the president's office. I needed to wind down after this ordeal by fire on my first stint as prez. I was going to relax and bask in the success of that first luncheon.

"The telephone rang. It was an irate member calling from the Club restaurant. 'I ordered a hamburger well done, and it was served to me so rare it was bleeding. What are you going to do about it?'"

Bob Loftus now hangs his tie and jacket at the House Public Works and Transportation Committee, but he calls himself "a reformed reporter" since he was for years at United Press. He also is a reformed emcee, having introduced the guests for so long at Club parties that some felt he should go on salary to the Club.

He was a phrasemaker and some of his phrases stuck. For example, it was he who once introduced Eugene McCarthy as "the president of the McCarthy-Stassen School of Political Science."

The comment ricocheted around the world.

The National Press Club follows the rule that nothing is sacred at the news-making luncheons. Any question can be asked, no matter how embarrassing—as long as it doesn't contain four-letter words.

When Khrushchev was a guest, President Bill Lawrence made him squirm by reminding him of his infamous kitchen debate with Vice-President Nixon in the U.S. model home exhibit in Moscow. Lawrence told him that he was glad to be taking him out of the kitchen and into a ballroom.

That was only the beginning. After Khrushchev's speech, when the Premier was glowing with goodwill and looking for a show of friendship, Lawrence hit him with the question, "What were you doing when Stalin was committing the crimes you chose to denounce only after he died?" Mr. K. was furious. Instead of trying to justify himself, he merely labeled the whole thing "malicious rumors and lies."

The questions did not get much better, and finally he decided he'd had enough, when he was asked to tell just exactly what he'd meant be telling the United States "We will bury you." He explained that he had not meant he would physically bury America. But that was the end of the questioning.

Between 1973 and 1978, Jimmy Carter made three separate appearances at the National Press Club. After he became President he spoke at the Club on March 2, 1978, and recalled how he had announced his candidacy from the same podium in 1975.

What he did not mention, however, was his first dismal appearance at the Club in February 1973, when Don Larrabee was Club president. As Larrabee recalls, "There were less than a hundred advance reservations for *Governor* Carter, instead of the four hundred or five hundred we had hoped for. Embarrassed aides at the National Governors' Conference, who had helped promote the appearance, padded the house with freebie tickets and managed to round up about five hundred live bodies."

Larrabee, with tongue in cheek, likes to take credit—or blame—for introducing Carter to Washington, although he admits, "I had no idea that this governor would end up in the White House. Apparently the audience was oblivious to Jimmy's long-range plans. There were no questions about a possible presidency, although one person asked if Jimmy had his eye on the Talmadge Senate seat. He politely dismissed that one."

When 1978 Club President Frank Aukofer went to the White House with Club officers in March of that year to present Carter with his gold membership card, Larrabee went along to give him a photograph taken in 1973 and a copy of the tape from the luncheon. Carter grinned and said that he had never worked harder on a speech or worried more about the impression he would make.

Larrabee asked if he had decided at that point whether to seek the presidency. Carter tossed the question to Jody Powell, who replied: "Let's see. Was that after Nixon delivered his State of the Union address?"

When Larrabee replied in the affirmative, Powell said: "Yes, we were running." These days, Larrabee has to take a little ribbing about his head table back in 1973. Press Club speakers are given the privilege of having personal friends at the head table. The only headliners present in 1973 who later moved into top positions with the Carter administration were Andrew Young and Peter Bourne, both of whom have been embarrassments to the President.

Talking about his early impressions of the future President, Larrabee says, "Carter's talk in 1973 is fascinating in retrospect. He spoke even then about the need for a balanced budget. He made a strong pitch for zero-based budgeting. He spoke of the need to shake up the bureaucracy. He insisted that the mood of the country was one of basic conservatism. He said he considers himself a fiscal conservative but also a 'benevolent conservative.' He complained that too much power had been shifted to the executive branch of government. He said Washington was too pervasive in peoples' lives. And Carter was doing his best to ingratiate himself with the press."

Larrabee recalls that Carter started off his talk by saying, "I have to admit I'm not a news reporter." Then he had looked around at his newspaper audience and added, "But I have the same tendency to try to judge people."

It's hard to say whether one invitation Larrabee extended to President Nixon might have changed the course of history. What happened is that Nixon had totally stopped holding press conferences. As a stunt, Larrabee sent word to the White House that the beleaguered President would be welcome to put in an appearance at the Press Club luncheon series, where he could say what he had in mind, yet be spared the ordeal of dozens of reporters shouting on their feet for his attention.

As he explained, the Club traditionally requires written questions, which are sifted by the Club president to avoid duplication and to make certain that the most interesting and timely ones are asked within the time limitations. Nixon never took advantage of the offer. A year later Ron Ziegler, his press secretary, surprisingly phoned Larrabee to say that Nixon was now sorry he had not accepted the invitation.

6/A Club by Any Other Name (Gridiron, WNPC, WPC, ANWC, WHCA)

The Washington Press Club started in 1919 as a protest group. Since women were banned by the National Press Club, they formed their own group, defiantly calling themselves the Women's National Press Club.

Its list of presidents, before and after its name change to the Washington Press Club—with the advent of male members—reads like a *Who's Who* of American women writers:

Lily Lykes Shepard, the first president—a firebrand on the *New York Tribune*; Cora Rigby, who succeeded her—a gentle lady writing as Washington correspondent for the *Christian Science Monitor*. As proof of her gentleness she had the longest term in office, never since equaled, eight years.

Sallie Pickett became the first president from a Washington newspaper—the *Evening Star*. The next year the honor went to the *Washington Post* when Ruth Jones made it, and she was succeeded the following year, 1931, by Martha Strayer of the *Washington News*.

Doris Fleeson of the *New York Daily News*, close friend of Eleanor Roosevelt, became president in 1937, and Hope Ridings Miller, top society writer of the *Washington Post*, succeeded her the next year.

Esther Van Wagoner Tufty, called the Duchess, said to be the most powerful female reporter in Washington because she headed her own news bureau, was president of the Club at the time of Pearl Harbor.

Christine Sadler of the *Washington Post* and May Craig, whose hats became known to everyone for her appearances on *Meet the Press*, also served in war years. The famed Bess Furman of the *New York Times* was president the year that peace came, 1945.

Author of books about the occult, Ruth Montgomery—then with *New York Daily News*—was president in 1950. An early radio figure, Hazel Markel of Mutual Broadcasting, was president in 1953, followed by Liz Carpenter, who represented Texas newspapers but would eventually work at the White House as Lady Bird Johnson's press secretary.

The role of honor goes on—Gladys Montgomery, McGraw-Hill, 1957; Helen Thomas, UPI, 1959; Frances Lewine, AP, 1960; Bonnie Angelo, *Newsday* and *Time* magazines, 1961; Patty Cavin, NBC, 1962; Elsie Carper, *Washington Post*, 1963.

Pulitzer-Prize-winning Miriam Ottenberg of the *Washington Star* was president in 1964. A very serious girl, Miriam was succeeded by a madcap Mary Gallagher, of the *Cincinnati Enquirer*, who would do almost anything for a gag.

When Mary Barelli Gallagher, secretary to First Lady Jackie Kennedy, wrote her revealing tell-all memoir, *My Life with Jacqueline Kennedy*, Mary took to identifying herself on the phone with "This is the other Mary Gallagher calling."

Gallagher was succeeded as president by another eminent reporter, Eve Edstrom of the *Washington Post*, who had the further distinction of being married to a president of the National Press Club.

Eve was followed by Gerry Van der Heuvel of the Newhouse papers, who was press secretary at the White House for First Lady Pat Nixon.

Came then, in succession, Margaret Kilgore, UPI; Marjorie Hunter, of the *New York Times*; Louise Hutchinson of the *Chicago Tribune*; Vera Glaser of Knight Newspapers; Mary Lou Beatty, of the *Washington Post*; Wauhillau Lay Hay, Scripps-Howard columnist.

Then in 1974 a strange thing happened—something Lily Lykes Shepard, founder president, could never have foreseen. A male reporter, Ron Sarro, of the *Washington Star* became president and the Club has never been the same.

The special pride of the Club is that the first event of Washington's official social season at the beginning of every year, when Congress has returned from Christmas vacation, is the Washington Press Club Congressional dinner. All the House and

Senate leaders are there and, in fact, the wittiest are picked to make the after-dinner speeches—always short.

In January 1979, Congresswoman Olympia Snowe of Maine brought down the house when she rose at the congressional dinner to comment on one of the potential presidential candidates for 1980. "There are only two things I don't like about Jerry Brown," she said. "His face."

Only new congresspersons and senators were invited to speak, and another favorite that evening was Senator Nancy Landon Kassebaum of Kansas, who apologized to the assemblage for having "broken a family tradition. I got elected," she said.

The American Newspaper Women's Club stands aloof from both clubs and is elegantly social. It permits no male members, has no plans for male members, and maintains a clubhouse in the embassy section of Washington, with room for sleep-in guests.

Into its drawing room come the most famous names to sip cocktails, partake of a buffet dinner, and rub elbows with newspaperwomen and their guests, who may or may not be men. First ladies, famous writers, ambassadors, movie stars.

Here the decorum is practically the same as at the White House. Long dresses are *de rigueur* and a formal receiving line is used to introduce the guest of honor to the several hundred guests who file past.

True, to live up to the name of the Club, there is a small press conference that takes place after the receiving line, but it is a gentle thing. Embarrassing questions are not asked, as are customary at the other two clubs.

Interesting newsmakers walk up the red-carpeted steps of the Club—such as Rose Mary Woods, personal secretary to President Nixon. She was *not* asked about the mysteriously erased segment of the Watergate tape.

At the Club, too, Hugh Carter, cousin of the President and author of *Cousin Beedie and Cousin Hot*, as told to Frances Spatz Leighton, gave a little talk about family feuding and clans after standing in a receiving line. And it was here he revealed that Miz Lillian, the President's mother and his own aunt, had commented about his revelations in the book, when she met him in an Atlanta airport, "You are the scum of the earth for what you said."

In 1978, when the White House was working to improve

its image, Rosalynn Carter sent formal invitations to each member of the American Newspaper Women's Club to a reception at the White House.

As a present for the First Lady, Club president Lillian Levy had ordered a pair of glass bookends, to be made by glass sculptor Herman Perlman, with the name Jimmy and the presidential seal etched on one, and Rosalynn on the other.

It is amazing how one can tell the tenor of an era and the flow of history by the humorous speeches and stunts used to amuse congressional and other guests at the various dinners given by the press clubs.

Let's take January 26, 1972. That was the night of the "Salute to Congress" dinner of the Washington Press Club, the dinner given every year to welcome back the Congress of the United States from their Christmas holiday with their constituents.

The world situation was that President Richard Nixon was getting ready to go to China. Henry Kissinger, who was naturally going along, was not yet married and every week his name was being linked with some girl other than Nancy Maginnes—the aide to Governor Nelson Rockefeller—whom he eventually married. He was linked with Jill St. John, Joyce Haber, Marlo Thomas, Margaret Osmer, to name a few.

It was a tribute to the Club president, Vera Glaser, that she was able to get Henry Kissinger for the "A Night in Peking" dinner.

Kissinger, who, at the time, was White House adviser on national security affairs, had been making almost no public appearances, and was trying to keep a low profile—except for his romantic image.

Vera had risen to the occasion and ordered everything Chinese that she could think of for the gala occasion— "It was complete down to a Chinese dragon and popping firecrackers and fortune cookies."

As Vera recalls it, "I came down from my room, all primped with a new hairdo and Chinese red evening dress, to learn that the White House was trying to reach me on the telephone. It was Jerry Warren, then assistant presidential press secretary, calling from the White House.

"He said Nixon was going to call Kissinger during the dinner to surprise him and that I was to tell absolutely no one, but he wanted to coordinate the time. We settled on nine-fifteen—after the guests finished eating, after the Chinese dragon had cavorted around the room, and before the speeches.

"Meanwhile a crew of telephone men were frantically installing a direct line to the White House behind the head table in the Sheraton ballroom. It added to the mind-boggling tension that usually accompanies a mammoth affair like that.

"To top it off, the committee chairwomen for the dinner wanted to know what the devil the telephone men were doing. The women were irked when I acted innocent. The line fed into the public address system, so that the conversation could be heard throughout the ballroom.

"At the appointed time the phone rang. Before putting Kissinger on the phone, I gaveled for order, using a Chinese gong, and said we needed a little quiet because an important call was coming through to the security adviser from the White House.

"Kissinger looked a little puzzled and when he said, 'Hello, Mr. President,' he realized that everyone could hear it. But he really started to get nervous when Nixon's voice said, 'Henry, I'm going to give you hell.'

"No wonder he was nervous. There had just been a Jack Anderson column in which Anderson said that Kissinger was complaining that the President 'gives me hell.'

"Nixon and Kissinger talked for a few minutes, with Henry turning his back to the audience, thinking it was an official call, and trying to keep his voice low, but hearing it boom through the hall.

"It was one of the funniest things I've ever seen—Kissinger trying to carry on a private conversation in public. Afterward, Kissinger confessed that he had been edgy because he thought the call was confidential."

Senator Frank Church had been chosen to make the after-dinner speech and here are some of the comments that resulted. First he commented on all those going with Nixon—"Henry Kissinger has already been to China twice. Recently, Ron Ziegler went over. Next week, I understand, Ehrlichman and Haldeman are going. Frankly, I'm worried. The last time so many Germans went into a country, World War II broke out!"

Then the ghostly names of the past come back to memory as we see how Church enumerates what the various members of the Nixon gang and entourage were doing to prepare for the trip.

"Henry is studying the Peking phonebook for out-of-the-way Holiday Inns.

"Bebe Rebozo is studying Chinese real estate, figuring out ways to subdivide China.

"Even Spiro Agnew has been eating fortune cookies—ten pounds a day—looking for the one that will tell him he'll be on the ticket again!

"Nonetheless, on balance, I do think this trip is necessary. I admit, we've always had *somebody* mad at us, but this is the first time I can recall when we've had *everybody* mad at us. So I say, if the Chinese are willing to talk, let's talk. We've got to make a friend somewhere!"

The most prestigious club for the elite of newspaperdom is the Gridiron Club, whose sole function is to have one big party a year.

For a new member to get into the Gridiron, an old member must die or leave town permanently. Only fifty-five active newspapermen—and now women—may ever belong at the same time.

It is to this Club that every year, the President of the United States feels compelled to come and make a humorous speech. It is off the record but widely quoted around the Press Club the next morning.

The rest of the entertainment at the Gridiron dinner consists of skits in which about twenty members of the Club "roast" the President, and whoever is in the public eye at that time. Usually the roastee is in the audience and supposed to take the barbs in good grace.

Sometimes they do and sometimes they don't. LBJ was annoyed and commented that listening to the Gridiron's insulting stuff "is about as much fun as throwing cow chips at the village idiots."

One President—Teddy Roosevelt—got into a shouting match with another guest, a Senator Foraker, one year, which wrecked the mood of the evening.

Another guest once walked out in anger. That was Supreme Court Justice Hugo Black, who had been needled in the one area in which he was most sensitive—bigotry. It has been proven that Black had once belonged to the Ku Klux Klan in Alabama and Club members rose and sang to him, "There is a Klavern in the town," substituting the hated word for the word *tavern*.

Gridironer Jerry terHorst, columnist with the *Detroit News*, claims that the committee in charge of writing new lyrics to old standards these days tries to be kind. "We only want to roast people and not burn them to a crisp. Cruelty is the easiest thing. Cleverness is harder."

Sometimes it works the other way, and the famous guest being roasted loves it—especially when well oiled with the liquor that flows like a bubbling brook through the dinner hour.

Gridiron members say that by the way guests handle themselves at the Gridiron dinner, they can almost predict their future. When they heard Senator Robert Taft speak, for example, they decided that he could never become President no matter how hard he tried, because he had "the three D's"—he was too damn Drab, Dull, and Dreary."

They also crossed the then-Congressman John Lindsay off their list of presidential potentials because "he didn't know how to go by the rules." Warned, as all speakers are, that no blue language is used in speeches, because, figuratively, "ladies are always present," Lindsay peppered the air with bathroom references.

J. P. Morgan was another man who enjoyed seeing himself roasted—the Gridiron cast him as the operator of "a bucket shop." He chortled.

Publishers are positively delighted when one of their correspondents make it into the Gridiron Club, even though tickets to the dinner go for fifty dollars apiece or over—not counting the liquor served at side parties.

The prestige value cannot be overemphasized.

Breaking the sex barrier to Club admittance did not come easy.

Famous women reporters, like Helen Thomas of UPI, Eileen Shanahan of the *New York Times*, and a raft of others, formed a group to run a Counter-Gridiron dinner on the same night, to steal away some of the top guests and force the chauvinistic Club to open its doors.

Eileen, who was the *Times* financial expert, even resorted to angry threats about making the Gridiron Club decide whether it was social or professional. If social, she pointed out, the Club could exclude women, but if professional, it could not continue to qualify for tax deductions from the IRS while excluding professional female newspaper writers.

"Take your choice!" she told them. "You can't have it both ways."

The Club chose and Helen Thomas became the first female in history to be initiated into membership.

Not absolutely every newspaperman who is not a member yearns to become one. There is a long list of reporters who have been nominated for membership by sponsoring members, and as members leave or die, the name at the top is the next one called.

Usually when the sponsors notify the next in line that he may soon receive the coveted membership invitation, he practically dances a jig. Ben Bradlee, managing editor of the *Washington Post*, stunned the Club by pulling a takeoff on the if-elected-I-will-not-serve bit.

Why did he do it? He did it, he explained later, because to him the whole Gridiron concept smacked of seduction of the press by government establishment. He said as a guest in the past, he had witnessed the coziness of big-name press with big-name government and business, and wanted none of it for himself.

But for the most part, reporters do feel that the "one night out"—which costs publishers, who foot the bill, something around $150,000 for dinner, travel, and so forth—results in valuable intimate contacts and eventual stories that more than pay for their share of the tab.

You have to be a mighty popular guy to become president of one of Washington's prestigious press clubs. Edgar Allen Poe, however, is in a class by himself, holding in one year—1972— the presidency of two clubs—the very exclusive Gridiron Club and the White House Correspondents Association.

To complete the picture, he was also president of Sigma Delta Chi's Washington chapter.

Poe was born with printer's ink in his veins, the grandson of James R. Gunter, country editor of the *Mountain Eagle* in Jasper, Alabama.

There was never any question of what he would be and he covered the political campaigns of all the deep-south political families—the Longs, the Talmadges, as well as Theodore G. Bilbo, and a raft of others.

He remained popular with all candidates by refusing to editorialize and by insisting on reporting in a strictly objective way.

But in his own life and as a club member he did fight for his personal views. When the Senate and House Standing Committee of Correspondents wanted to bar Soviet Russia's Tass correspondent from admission to the galleries, Poe fought to let Tass be admitted and won. It was not that he was pro-Russian, but as he explained, it was "in keeping with America's free-speech tradition."

During World War II, Ed Poe, who is a collateral descendant of the writer whose famous name he bears, became a war correspondent and was one of those who covered the Japanese surrender on the U.S.S. *Missouri*. His wartime reporting won him a commendation from Navy Secretary James Forrestal.

What do the guests hear when the banquet room is plunged into darkness and the president of the Gridiron Club rises to make the traditional "Speech in the Dark"? When it was Edgar Allen Poe's turn to speak in the year of his presidency, 1972, the nation, as usual, was in an uproar—political conventions were upcoming, school busing was still an issue, as was inflation. He had something to say on each subject, and concluded:

"There is a lot going on in Washington.

"Confusion has become better organized.

"A petition has been filed with the FCC to merge ITT with the GOP.

"Martha Mitchell is no longer in the Cabinet....A tall Texas Democrat is trying desperately to keep the country from going broke, and the price of groceries down, while Secretary of Agriculture Earl Butz is bellowing like a wounded steer to keep the price of steak up.

"President Nixon is concerned because the Hotel Pierre in New York charged John Connally five dollars for two eggs, while poultrymen are getting only thirty cents a dozen. Only a Texan could afford to pay five dollars for eggs and then get hard-boiled about it.

"Now let us relax in the friendly flow of the Gridiron.

"The Gridiron may singe a bit, but it never burns.

"In its eighty-seven years the Gridiron Club has had but two rules. Ladies are always present; reporters are never present. Now that ladies are really present, the rule still applies.

"So relax and forget the problems of our times.

"On behalf of the Gridiron Club I extend to each of you a warm welcome.

"Please be seated."

part two * * * *

RUM ROW
AND
NEWSPAPER
ROW

7/Rum Row and Newspaper Row

Rum Row and Newspaper Row were right around the corner from each other in the early days of the nation's capital. It was convenient. In the days circa the Civil War and after, reporters hung around their front doors, sat on their stoops and waited for a story to come to them. Often it did.

Congressmen who liked to see their names in print wandered down from the Hill and made themselves available, stopped to chat and to answer questions, and even meandered around the corner to one of the bars or private gambling clubs for gentlemen.

For anyone interested in a romp, the girlie area was just across Pennsylvania Avenue. Bold creatures swished around in skirts so short they almost showed their calves. They were called Hooker's Division, after a Civil War general of that name. Gore Vidal says rather it was because they hooked their arms with male passersby.

Various words now taken for granted in the newspaper world came out of the Civil War era of newspapering in the nation's capital. For example, calling reporters newshounds. It wasn't a compliment. It was a term dreamed up by Secretary of War Edwin Stanton, who was furious because the reporters were finding out and reporting on troop movements, to the aid and convenience of the South. He meant that all reporters were dogs.

Stanton was so incensed that he issued an edict that all reporters sign their stories so that such writers could be caught and punished if they helped the enemy.

It had the opposite effect. Reporters were made famous overnight and military men continued leaking information to them on a large scale. So it is the military we have to thank for by-lines. Before this time most newspapermen made up names for themselves, signing a letter to their hometown newspaper "Ulysses" or "Scribbler" or "Your Washington Traveler."

When they said "correspondent" in those days they meant letter writer and the story was signed the way a letter is, at the end.

It was under President Jackson, who grasped the reins of power, that Washington began to be a news center. But until the Civil War, there were no more than fifty reporters in town.

By the 1870s the block of Fourteenth Street between F Street and Pennsylvania Avenue was ablaze with oil lamps into the night as correspondents scrawled their handwritten reports for transmittal clickety-clack over the wires. The broad avenue runs from the Capitol, a bit over a mile to the east. Westward it runs to the Treasury at Fifteenth Street, jogs around a corner to the White House beyond it.

The world of the Washington reporter was along this narrow strip. Across the street from Newspaper Row was the Willard Hotel, where statesmen could be found at the bar. Or they called at the news offices, eager then as now to keep their names before the folks back home.

The early Washington correspondents had trouble covering Capitol Hill. For some time the Senate held that only those reporters who belonged in town because they wrote for a Washington newspaper should be allowed to see the Senate in action.

There was much grumbling of course, but invention was the great leveler. With the advent of the telegraph, editors had gotten the notion that maybe they should keep track of Congress.

Suddenly dozens of reporters came to Washington in the 1840s and there was no keeping them out of the halls of Congress. In fact, congressmen now had a real complaint—the nosey newshounds were dogging them everywhere, and meddling in legislative matters. To get them out from underfoot, Congress gave reporters space in certain galleries. The galleries are still there today.

Legends of the press are many.

The handwriting of editors was surpassed in illegibility only by doctors' prescriptions. That of Horace Greeley of the *New York Tribune*, with his fringy whiskers and advice to "go west young man," was notorious.

The story is told that one crusty old editor was unreadable to everyone but an aged compositor. The staff dipped a roach in ink and had it walk over a sheet of paper. The printer set type with frequent pauses to scratch his head. Finally he came to the editor, apologizing that one word was indecipherable. The editor looked over his spectacles and thundered, "*Unconstitutional*, you dummy! Can't you read?"

Although the old style of writing tended to be flowery and prolix, in time the A-B-C of journalism became Accuracy, Brevity, Clarity. As one editor told a neophite, "If you were reporting the crucifixion, all you would need to say is, 'An agitator named Jesus of Nazareth, who called himself Christ, was crucified today on Mount Calvary. Citizens and Roman soldiers attended.'"

Literary pretensions were derided by the tough old breed of editors. A classic yarn is told about a reporter at the Johnstown flood. Eager to produce a lead paragraph for the ages, he began, "God looks down from a little hill upon a scene of devastation." As the story came over the wire, the editor broke in. "Never mind flood. Interview God. Get picture if possible."

Dirty tricks between competing newspapers are nothing new. Edgar Allen Poe had a tale about one town's newspaper feud. The editor of the leading paper wrote purple prose with frequent use of the exclamatory *Oh*. The rival editor, after twitting him in print, had a henchman steal all type for the letter *O* from the font.

The printer's devil had been taught to substitute *X* when type ran out for any letter. To the readers, this looked like a secret code and the poor editor was run out of town.

Speaking of codes, a short story by O. Henry demonstrated how old-style journalism ran to stereotyped phrases. A war correspondent sent his paper a mysterious cable, a jumble of words such as *witching, foregone*, and *shadow*.

The staff could not make heads or tails of it. They asked an old German employee whether the paper ever had a code. He said, "Ya, but it butted the editor and he said get rid of it."

Realizing that he thought they said "goat" they continued to ruminate till one had an inspiration. Witching hour of midnight. Foregone conclusion. Shadow of doubt. They decided that the battle was fought at midnight with the outcome still in doubt and got a great scoop.

Apprentices on old newspapers had a hard life. The unwary, invited to see type lice that were barely visible—and in fact nonexistent—would bend over to look and have their noses pushed into acrid-smelling printer's ink.

Obscene typographical errors were dreaded on the copy

desk. The caption for a picture of a divorced woman who remarried was SOCIALITE WHO REWED. By faulty spacing it became SOCIALITE WHORE WED.

A city father who signed a lot of papers was headlined MAYOR'S PEN IS BUSIEST IN TOWN. It became MAYOR'S PENIS....

A friend of mine was almost fired when a man who was to take a sanity test was said to face a "sanitary test." Thus it was in the good old days.

The first wire service entered the picture before the Civil War.

The Associated Press has a formidable record, and its Lincoln connection is always mentioned when people ask, "But what have you done that's historic?"

The way the story goes, on the night of April 14, 1865, an AP reporter named Gobright was lingering in his office after having wired his news copy on "President Lincoln's theater party."

A friend rushed in with alarming news about what had happened at Ford's Theater. His first impulse was to rush out to cover the story, but he paused long enough to dash off a bulletin which went to all client points and read:

Washington, Friday, April 14, 1865—The President was shot in a theatre tonight and perhaps mortally wounded."

AP began in a very low-key way with an organizational meeting in the offices of the *New York Sun*, in 1848, a year when Europe was in turmoil, but the United States was relatively serene. Six New York newspaper publishers were there and decided to pool their resources to get more stories with less cost from areas outside New York.

The operator of a carrier-pigeon news service, Daniel Craig, takes the honors for establishing the AP's foreign bureau the following year at Halifax, Nova Scotia. His job was to telegraph the six newspapers all the exciting overseas news that he got from incoming ships on their way to New York.

By the time of the Civil War, AP correspondents were underfoot on the battlefield, during many a bloody contest, and learning much about battle plans. General Sherman was so infuriated by security leaks that he was almost grimly pleased when three reporters were reported missing. The general snorted, "We'll have dispatches from hell before breakfast."

Memorable moments in AP history have paralleled U.S. history....

1876—An AP stringer named Mark Kellogg rode his gray mule into the Valley of Death with Custer, and was part of Custer's last stand. He had been told not to go but went anyway. Only one living creature—a horse—came out of that bloody massacre alive.

1895—The first time news of the America's Cup Yacht race, covered by AP, was carried on Marconi's new invention—the wireless.

1906—A new journalistic term was born to get attention for news of the San Francisco earthquake. Walter Winchell would later use it every day to get attention on radio to indicate hot news. The word was: *Flash*!

1912—An AP telegrapher picked up the first distress signal of a famous ship. The message was: "The *Titanic* is sinking!"

1921—The first AP by-line ever used went to Kirke L. Simpson. It was put above his stories of the burial of the Unknown Soldier at Arlington National Cemetery.

1932—AP correspondent Sam Blackman first flashed the news that the Lindbergh baby had been kidnapped, the news scoop of the year.

The UPI—United Press International—is the only major wire service in the world under private family ownership. It was founded because E. W. Scripps, publisher of the Scripps-McRae Newspapers—which later became Scripps-Howard—came up against the news dominance of the Associated Press.

When his newspapers were refused AP wires, under the restrictive membership rules as they existed then, Scripps said the devil with it. He started his own news service in 1907 for the express purpose of providing news to any publisher who wanted it, whether his paper was competitive or not with the Scripps papers.

"I do not believe in monopolies," said Scripps. "I do not believe it would be good for journalism that there should be one big news trust such as the founders of the Associated Press fully expected to build up." It was called United Press until it merged with INS.

Today UPI has more than 7,000 subscribers throughout the world—7,079, to be exact, more than 2,000 of them outside the United States.

INS—its slogan was "Get It First But First Get It Right."

International News Service was the smallest of the wire services but it was the feistiest. It also paid the least to its reporters. "We were always woefully underpaid," its financial writer Felix Cotten recalls, "but Hutch still expected us to work twice as hard as the other services and now and then we would score a newsbeat.

"Hutch was always emerging screaming from his office. He was either cursing in fury that someone had failed to get a story or had been scooped or had gotten it wrong, or he was hooting with glee that we had beaten the sons of bitches at AP and UP by ten minutes."

Those who worked for Washington Bureau Chief William K. Hutchinson became immune to hearing him scream, "I don't give a shit about what the White House says. This is what *I* say," or, "That shithead has screwed up this goddamn story again. When he gets in here I'm gonna chew his head off." And when the unfortunate reporter came slinking in, Hutch did just that and everyone would sit very stiffly at his desk and pretend not to notice.

One of Hutch's greatest triumphs he owed to his White House correspondent George Durno. Because of Durno, Hutch and INS had a full day's beat—a twenty-four-hour beat—on the execution of the German saboteurs in World War II. Everyone knew that six spies had been captured soon after arriving on the east coast by submarine. There were all kinds of rumors but nobody knew what was going on.

"The truth," INSer Felix Cotten recalls, "was that FDR himself had given George Durno the newsbeat as a going-away present—Durno was going into military service.

"Durno had made a friend of the President by looking after Eleanor on a few occasions when she traveled, and FDR was grateful for that and for the fact that Durno had kept from printing a story on a couple of occasions. FDR owed him one. FDR told him exactly what was going to happen to the six men—which would be executed and which sentenced to prison.

"He said to Durno, 'If anyone asks me I will deny it but this is what is going to happen. And just as protection I am giving you one small error so that I can say the story is not accurate.'

"Well, it was the damndest clean beat I ever knew. It was twenty-four hours before anyone could get it confirmed. Meanwhile for twenty-four hours INS had the story alone and every newspaper who didn't belong to INS and the other wire services was forced to say, 'INS says ...' which was music to Hutch's ears.

The INSers get downright sentimental as the talk moves to Hutch and his incredible temper.

The most foul-mouthed person in the Washington newspaper world was undoubtedly Hutch.

"He bawled the hell out of people," Felix says, reminiscing about Hutch at the National Press Club.

"Hutch cursed everyone and everything and forgot it the next day. He wanted perfection and that was his problem. It infuriated him because he could never get it from anybody else and he kept trying to give it himself.

"I remember when he filed the wire on the Japanese surrender and he was scurrying around the INS newsroom so fast and working so intensively, he was covered with perspiration and hysterical. INS had the flash first—the news the world had been waiting for."

As fate would have it it was Felix Cotten who was sitting at a typewriter writing the surrender story under the signature of another reporter, Frederick "Fritz" Tuttle, who was dictating from the White House.

"Hutch was grabbing it off my typewriter," Felix recalled. " And he was dictating to the wire. There were two flashes dictated by Hutch. One was 'War Ends!' The second flash was 'MacArthur, Jap Boss.'

"Actually, I had been working on the surrender story for three days till the final surrender was announced at the White House. We had the whole step-by-step development in advance and I had been updating it and rewriting during those three days until Fritz Tuttle phoned the final step in from the White House as Truman announced it.

"We had a beat of perhaps a minute, but a minute is a hell of a long time in wire service business. I will never forget the thrill I felt as almost instantly horns started honking on the street below as motorists heard the news and rejoiced."

"It was the one day Hutch was finally satisfied."

The horsey set among the INSers still talk about their "sporting" life.

A little gang, with Felix Cotten as their fearless leader, would go horseback riding every Saturday.

Felix must have had courage because he rode the wildest horse in the stable, a former racehorse named Greystone.

"The fastest traveling I have ever done," Felix still

claims, "was done on the back of Greystone whenever we were following a fence. Greystone interpreted any fence as meaning racetrack."

Others in the group were usually INS girl reporters— Frankie Music, who covered the Pentagon, also Jean Van Vranken and Pat Kriegbaum; general reporters.

All were attractive, but Pat Kriegbaum was a renowned local beauty who once had six marriage proposals in one week.

One day, in starting out, Pat's horse stepped on a snake and panicked, throwing her and breaking her collarbone. Greystone also panicked and sent Felix straight into the air five feet, landing him flat on his back on the ground. He was luckier and got up still walking. Kriegbaum left by ambulance. She recovered and moved to London.

"If your book can help locate Pat Kriegbaum, it will have served a worthy purpose on that score alone," Felix told my co-author.

INS staffers had their share of heavy drinkers, whose praises are sung at their alumni's annual bash. But the two who were most famous for their escapades were Fred Tuttle, whom everybody called Fritz, and Jim Lee, a rewrite man.

If Fritz was buying, he never ordered anything but beer but he was known to go along and drink anything that anyone else was drinking and offering to share.

"Fritz Tuttle was a man of integrity," Lou Brott, a PR man and INS alumnus recalls. "He never drank while he worked and he always gave Hutch full value for his money. I recall when I was working weekends on INS night desk, Fritz would sleep on a desk if he had started on a toot, instead of going home.

"I'd wake him up in the morning, when it was time for him to go to work, and he'd start writing copy, as sober as a judge. He didn't need the hair of the dog; he didn't even need a cup of coffee. He'd be ready to rush out and cover a story. He was a fine writer, too. One of the greatest. And I wonder what he would have become if he hadn't wasted his time and talents drinking."

A different kind of person altogether, Jim was the rewrite man at INS and surely one of the best in the trade. As Hutch would say, he could take any piece of junk and make it sound good. Or to quote Hutch more precisely, "You give that son of a bitch Jim any piece of shit and he gives you back a major story."

But Jim had a dream and so he was not content. He hated rewrite. He wanted to go out and cover stories. Hutch knew that this was very risky because Jim's feet had a way of turning in to any bar. But one particular time, Jim had been on the wagon for weeks and weeks, and maybe even months. He had put on weight. The ghastly pallor was gone from his face.

Hutch was tempted to take a chance. He needed someone to take a trip on an important story to be phoned back. Jim could do it better than anyone if he would, and Hutch called him into his private office to sound him out.

"Don't worry," he assured Hutch. "Drinking is not my problem anymore. I'll be back tomorrow."

"Now you listen here, Jim," Hutch warned him. "If you take one goddamm drink, I'll have your ass. And I'll never trust you again in Christ's world. Do you hear me?"

Jim heard and smiled his reassuring smile, hurrying out before Hutch could change his mind, clutching a sheaf of money.

"Remember, you have to file copy tonight," Hutch screamed after him. "Phone me!"

Jim did not phone. Hutch waited around and gave instructions to the night man to speed the story when it came.

The next day there was still no sign of Jim or his story. A phone call established that he had not checked in at his hotel.

Days later Jim appeared a little paler than usual and sat himself down at his old rewrite desk. For once, Hutch said nothing. There was nothing to say. He just ignored him for a while, but the day editor immediately tossed stories to him as if he had never been away. You just didn't fire a dream of a writer like Jim. You just kept him prisoner in the office.

INS produced some fine writers and important executives, and public relations men. It produced Les Whitten, who went on to share by-lines with Jack Anderson and be his number-two man. Whitten also became a fiction writer, even breaking into Hollywood.

It produced Al Spivak, a fine writer who is now Washington representative of General Dynamics; also Bill Theis, who was one of the great political writers of the country covering Capitol Hill for many years, and who now is chief public relations official of the American Petroleum Institute, heading a large staff.

It produced Felix Cotten, who was a top financial writer

for many years before becoming a senior editor at the Commerce Department, serving a succession of secretaries of commerce, including Juanita Kreps.

It produced Rose McKee, who became a government official, an early women's libber. Eventually Lyndon Johnson picked Rose as one of fifty women to whom he gave high government positions. Her job was in the Small Business Administration.

And my coauthor Frances Spatz Leighton, who'd been a mere dictation girl, went on to become a best-selling book writer whose "as told to" books have been translated into a dozen languages.

I am looking now at the invitation my coauthor, Frannie, received for the most recent INS party. It comes from "a self-appointed committee of two—Al Spivak and Howard Handleman," who worded their invitation this way:

Are you feeling pangs of NOSTALGIA?
Do you suffer from attacks of SENTIMENT?
Do you wake up at odd hours to REMINISCE?
You can overcome those burning yearnings for the past, if you attend the....
TWENTIETH ANNIVERSARY MEMORIAL REUNION
of the alumni of
INTERNATIONAL NEWS SERVICE

8/There Were Giants in Those Days: Editors and Publishers

Many of the legendary figures of journalism were publishers. Under President Jackson, the Postmaster General was Amos Kendall, who founded the *Globe* in Washington as a party paper. A man of influence, a mysterious figure, he was seldom seen. When he came to a gathering, a whisper went around the room, "Kendall is here."

Horace Greeley was an apprentice printer who eventually came to Washington. He wrote political papers in New York and founded the *Tribune* in 1841 as a liberal journal. When his name became a household word, he served a term in Congress and ran for president in 1872, during a split in the Republican party.

He was a curmudgeon. Mark Twain once wandered into his office by mistake and was told to get out.

The name Pulitzer brings chills and shivers of dismay and delight as Washington news media people get the news of who has won a Pulitzer Prize.

Joseph Pulitzer emigrated from Hungary as a Union Army recruit in the Civil War. After he arrived in St. Louis penniless, he published German-language newspapers, and combined two weak papers into the still great *Post-Dispatch*.

When his aide shot and killed a political enemy there was understandably public reaction against his paper. Pulitzer moved to New York and bought the *World* from financier Jay Gould in 1883.

He was elected to Congress in 1885. To the everlasting advancement of journalistic standards, he endowed the School of Journalism at Columbia University and the annual prizes that bear his name. But the "end of the *World*" was a sad day when his heirs sold out that haven of brilliant writers.

The influence of Colonel Robert McCormick was felt in Washington as it was felt in Chicago. Even before he bought the old *Times-Herald* for $4.5 million in 1949, the much feared publisher of the *Chicago Tribune* the "World's Greatest Newspaper," was a thundering rightist. He went forth across the world in a converted World War II Flying Fortress to interview chiefs of state and send voluminous dispatches. He reassured his readers that flight was safe as the four-engine plane could fly on two engines if the others failed—but just in case, when he traveled by air, rescue ships always waited in the Atlantic.

The rival *Chicago Daily News* was owned by another man important to Washington, W. Franklin Knox, former general manager for Hearst, a Republican who became Secretary of the Navy when Roosevelt was seeking national solidarity in preparation for World War II.

There were publishing giants in those days. The most colorful was William Randolph Hearst, important in Washington newspaper history, where he owned the *Evening Times* and the *Morning Herald*. He was born in San Francisco, where his father made a mining fortune and was elected to the United States Senate. The younger Hearst also tried politics and became a two-term congressman. At Harvard he spent much of his time observing Boston newspaper methods.

Gaining control of the *San Francisco Examiner* he developed new ideas; bought the *New York Journal* in 1895; and built a news empire from city to city with dozens of papers, two wire services (International and Universal), and a flock of magazines.

Hearst's success was based on sensational news—"yellow journalism," as it was called. His editorials were strongly nationalistic, a force in the precipitation of the Spanish-American War in 1898. President Teddy Roosevelt, who gained his reputation by his rash cavalry charge in that war, ungratefully blasted Hearst as an "exploiter of sensationalism." But Hearst was a Democrat and Teddy a Republican. Such are the ways of politics.

It is legend how Hearst spent his latter years in his vast estate at San Simeon with movie star Marion Davies, not able to return to New York where his estranged wife might serve legal papers. Often heard in the newspaper world before naughty words were printable is the rhyme widely believed to be the words of sharp-tongued Dorothy Parker with which she amused her friends after a visit to San Simeon. As I recall it as it was passed by word of mouth:

> *Upon my honah, I saw a Madonna,*
> *Set within a niche*
> *Above the door of the favorite whore*
> *Of an eminent son of a bitch.*

There was love, or at least a deep affection between the two. Marion drank a wee dropee too muchee but was not known to stray much. Once on a Hearst yacht, a guest disappeared overboard. It was rumored that he had been making up to Marion, but who knows?

Hearst, William Randolph Senior that is, was a lord, a tyrant, a king maker. It was said one politician was so owned by Hearst that his slogan was "Hearst in peace, Hearst in war, and Hearst in the hearts of his countrymen."

Hearst lay down editorial policy, but one policy did not have to be written down. It was: Be kind to Marion Davies and her family. Marion was a low-talent actress whom Hearst was determined to build into a superstar.

Reporters who wrote unkind things about her acting would be fired outright. Let other papers pan her, in the Hearst papers she was the queen of Hollywood.

At the Press Club the story is told that after Hearst died, Marion married and was honeymooning in the Nevada desert just when some atomic tests were being made. When Marion heard and felt the explosion, she leaped from bed and said, "My God, Willie's back."

The new newspaper king makers play it low-key. No so Hearst. He gloried in his power and did not care what people said.

In the depression, Hearst had to pool some of his newspapers and issue stock. He also had to sell from his vast collection of antiques. He had given Marion a good deal of property. She put it all at his disposal to tide him over. In World War II his empire made money again. The Hearst publishing empire continues under his sons with more profits from the magazines than from the papers.

To win the old man away from Marion in his late years,

the New York management once hatched the "Jessie Plot" to send out a slim blonde beauty, but she declined. This is all she will tell me. Had she gone, I think she would have made it.

When Hearst died, Marion Davies might have had legal control of all the properties. Instead, she worked with the sons and let them take over. All told, she should be remembered as a nice person.

The old egomaniac publishers drove hard bargains, closed down papers and fired many people. But some had a streak of kindness. Hearst looked for talent and paid well for it. As for Colonel McCormick, one of his former Washington bureau chiefs was pointed out to me by a friend. "Poor guy," said he, "I feel sorry for him."

"Why?" said I.

"Because he has retired on a life-long pension of two thousand dollars a month." That was a lot of money then.

Hearst sent out efficiency experts, the "wrecking crew," to pare expenses by firing people. In prosperous times, the local papers would hire extras to throw to the wolves when the pinch came. But Hearst did not believe in cutting salaries, and kept his best people.

Not so with Roy Howard of the Scripps-Howard papers, whose symbol was a lighthouse, to enlighten the world. He won note by reporting the World War I armistice two days early. He was not disgraced for bad reporting. Instead he was applauded for having given the public two celebrations instead of one.

It is said that when Roy visited the paper where he had made his start, an old-timer who encouraged his ascent was waiting to greet the great man. "Is that son of a bitch still around," said Howard. "Fire him. He's too old."

The cruelty of some publishers is notorious.

As for the holy name of Pulitzer, hundreds of people were terminated with two weeks' pay when the *New York World* was scuttled by heirs. Reporters had no minimum wage, no tenure against immediate firing, no sick leave, and few, if any, pensions.

A cub might work for ten dollars a week to gain experience. A wire service might keep a man with a series of piddling raises, fire him before he could draw retirement pay, then hire a cub at half the cost.

The Washington bureau chief of the McGraw-Hill magazines once returned from vacation to get a notice by special delivery, postage due, that he was finished, just before he was due to retire with a pension.

After the formation of the American Newspaper Guild, the tables were turned. From publishers impoverishing reporters, it was the other way round as wage demands from the guild and other unions weakened many a paper until it sold out or merged.

The influence of the old giants—Greeley, Pulitzer, Hearst and the rest—remains as part of the heritage that has shaped American journalism and America itself.

A few editors from the heyday of the wire services, in the thirties and forties, are also well remembered.

Lyle Wilson, UPI Washington chief, was the nonchalant type who loved to throw into the conversation something that would make the others cringe. You just got used to it and didn't pay it much mind. One day he was sitting around the Club talking to Bascom Timmons, who owned a large news service and apropos of nothing, Lyle suddenly said, "You know, Tim, they're not using the word *fuck* much anymore. Styles must be changing."

Timmons just sort of nodded and went on with whatever the conversation had been about before he'd been interrupted.

In the old days editors were judged by their tempers: the hotter, the greater. On that basis William K. Hutchinson, bureau chief of the International News Service, was one of the most famous guys in town.

Then there was Casey Jones!

His name still comes up at the Press Club bar, when older members reminisce about where they were and what they were doing when the ships at Pearl Harbor were bombed. Scott Hart is always called on at such times to tell his famous story of what it was like at the *Washington Post* on Pearl Harbor Day, Sunday, December 7, 1941, when the formidable Casey Jones was trying to put out an extra.

"I was in the city room with Jones, who had the most violent temper on the *Post*," Scott recalls, "and Eddie Follard was trying to make some sense of things at the White House.

"Poor Casey was cursing away because he was trying to make up a paper without facts and it was rough as hell. What we were trying to do was to find out how much damage had been done to the fleet. How many ships down. How many men killed. The extent of the disaster.

"Well, in the middle of all this tension, in comes Robert Tate Allan at a dead gallop.

"This fellow Allan covered churches—no one else wanted to do it. He was a gentle soul, religious. So to see him rushing in like that, you knew he really had something on his mind.

"And he did. 'Hold everything,' he hollered at Casey. 'I've got a real scoop for your extra. The Reverend So-and-So in Georgetown has finally decided to leave Washington and go to another vineyard.'

"Casey Jones sprang from his desk, a mighty growl rising from his throat. His face turned purple and I thought, God Almighty, he's going to have a heart attack!

"But it was a different kind of attack that Casey had in mind. He started for Allan as if he were going to kill him, and poor Allan ran out of the city room for his life, wondering what he had done."

Scott well remembers his early days on the *Post* in the thirties when a sixty-dollar wage was considered a princely sum. That's what Shirley Povich, the young sportswriter was making in 1937, when Bob Considine came to Washington.

Shirley heard that Bob Considine, over at the *Times-Herald*, was making $110 a week, and was amazed.

"Shirley couldn't get over talking about it," Scott recalls. "And he wasn't even jealous. What Shirley wanted to know was: What in the name of God would someone do with so much money? And coming in every week, what *do* you do with it?"

But most of all when he remembers the *Post* of old, Casey Jones and his temper stand out in Scott's mind. "For some reason I was about the only person Casey wouldn't scream at. Maybe he liked my feature stories. Everyone else seemed afraid of the man—Eddie Ryan, for example, was in terror of him, but I had too big a temper of my own. I would get mad and resign every three weeks over something that had been done to my copy or some dumb-ass assignment Casey would give me that was an insult to my intelligence. I would tell him I quit.

"Casey would not say anything and eventually I would forget it. But one time I really meant it and I put it in writing and flung my resignation on his desk.

"Casey read it and then he came around the desk and said, 'Scott, I'm not accepting this. You wrote it in anger.'

"I wanted to say, 'Look who's talking about anger,' but I said instead, 'How do you know it was written in anger? What the hell are you talking about?'

"Casey looked like Sherlock Holmes as he smugly said, 'See here? You hit the typewriter so hard on this last word that it went right through the paper.' Then he balled up my resignation and threw it on the floor."

Cissy Patterson was possibly the most colorful woman in Washington. Surely the most independent. William Randolph Hearst brought her to the *Washington Herald* to help save the paper. He gave her the title of editor and a salary of ten thousand dollars a year. That may have sounded like a lot of money in those days, but it was a drop in the bucket to what he had already lent her. Later she became the owner of the *Herald*.

From the beginning Cissy—a member of the Patterson McCormick newspaper family—became a Barnum and Bailey character at the newspaper. Her first issue carried a drawing of herself, surrounded by tributes to her as a great writer. Her next issues launched into a feud with Alice Roosevelt Longworth, who, it had been reported, was going to be campaign manager for the widow of United States Senator Medill McCormick, who happened to be Cissy Patterson's first cousin.

Cissy's real name was Eleanor Medill Patterson and she used it to write a front-page story which certainly showed her prose style and quickly got her labeled as shrewish which she was in conversation as well as print:

Reports that Mrs. Alice Roosevelt Longworth will manage the Senate campaign of Mrs. Ruth Hanna McCormick are interesting but not true.

Mrs. McCormick takes no advice, political or otherwise, from Mrs. Longworth.

Mrs. Longworth could not possibly manage anyone's campaign, being too lofty to newsmen and too aristocratic for public speaking.

Mrs. Longworth gives no interviews to the press.

Mrs. Longworth cannot utter in public.

Her assistance, therefore, will evolve itself, as usual, into posing for photographs.

Cissy became famous for her entertaining, in her home at Dupont Circle, where the liquor flowed free. She seemed to prefer the company of women to men, and she hired many beautiful young things, who were frequent guests in her home. Frequently she gave them expensive gifts, such as clothing.

Though she was gentle with her favored female employees, she was hell on wheels with the men in the city room.

If she passed a reporter who did not seem busy at his typewriter, she might fire him outright if her mood were bad. She once fired an editor because he had bad breath.

To prove her great writing ability she once had a young reporter named Frank Waldrop do a series on poverty and suffering in the Appalachia area, under her by-line.

Once she embarrassed a young reporter in the Senate press gallery by laying her head on his shoulders. He didn't dare move until she did some fifteen minutes later.

Cissy Patterson's attitude toward little girls has not been ascertained at this writing. Old-timers conjecture that she invited them to her parties as decoys to lure a great variety of men into attending.

How many of these men Cissy ended up inviting for private parties later is not known either, but according to various reporters, Cissy Patterson was promiscuous—and proud of it.

When someone once told her, after a party, that her bra had been found in or under the sofa, she is reported to have retorted gleefully, "Yes, and you'll find my panties in the chandelier."

Since there were many editions—ten editions a day at one time—there were always people working at the *Times-Herald*. Cissy loved to pop in to "look around and check out" after a party.

She would wear dresses with just little straps at the shoulders and she'd walk along among the horny men and lean over and suddenly a breast would come popping out of the skimpy top. What happened next is not recorded.

But some of the men, in private conversations, did feel pressured by her to get a little closer.

Cissy, it was said, would become furious if someone she liked seemed not to be interested in her. There is the classic story told about Cissy and a certain good looking male reporter, who shall remain nameless. The willful female publisher had her eye on him and invited him to parties. He wouldn't attend and would explain that demands of family kept him away.

Finally, Cissy ordered him to come with her on her private parlor car to New York. The fellow, on the horns of dilemma, again hid behind family and said he couldn't leave his wife and children.

Cissy fired him. End of story.

Cissy Patterson was famous for her feuds. One person she could not stand was Drew Pearson, who was her ex-son-in-law. She hated his guts for many reasons, most of which involved outsmarting her.

She refused to publish the radio schedule of WMAL because Drew Pearson's once-a-week broadcast was one of their programs. She didn't care if she was bitchy.

Bill Odlin, when he was a young reporter filling in at the night desk on the *Times-Herald*, lived to regret having treated Cissy Patterson in a high-handed manner. She had phoned in asking about some story that was breaking and he had mistaken her for some supercilious suburban socialite.

He had given her only cursory answers and gone back to his work.

"My life became a hell. I never knew what time it was. I was given alternate days of one A.M. to nine A.M. and then ten A.M. to six P.M." Bill recalls.

"I had a baby in the house and I needed the job so desperately that I took anything she could throw at me—and she did with vigor. I was so confused about time I was almost out of my mind.

"To wind down, instead of going home, I would just go to the Press Club and sit and drink. It was a miracle my marriage survived. As for me—I'm not sure I have."

George Waters, *Times-Herald* assistant city editor, was one of those lucky ones who got away. As Bill Odlin, still haunted by the *Times-Herald*, recalls, "He married a very lovely young lady and took off for Hollywood, to be a writer as it turned out. With his luck, his bride not only had beauty but entrée into Hollywood circles.

"Anyway he was the envy of the *Times-Herald* crowd for a while. He just seemed so lucky.

"Some time went by and Cissy Patterson was gone from the scene—dead by now—and here came a long expensive telegram from lucky George, still playing it grand. He said he would be coming back to Washington with a 'mission' to do a documentary on Cissy Patterson. And he would be getting a suite at the

Mayflower Hotel—which was the height of elegance of course—and he wanted everyone to be available to him.

"He was going to honor us all by taking us in one by one and getting our stories about Cissy.

"Harry Gabbett volunteered to reply to George's high-handed four-page telegram.

"He sent back the telegram in three words: *How's that Again?*

"I don't recall that anything ever came of George's documentary."

Harry Gabbett was the most versatile writer on the *Times-Herald*. Anytime they needed a humorous twist to something, they threw the story to him for rewriting.

Gabbett would just sit there thinking and then he'd root around his desk a while, and suddenly he'd have some angle to bring the story to life.

It was unbelievable the things he had squirreled away for possible future use, like the statistical abstract of 1936. His desk was full of crap, but then so was everyone else's.

One day the city editor announced that an efficiency expert was coming in and reorganizing the office and that anything that did not have SAVE THIS written on it would be thrown out over the weekend.

Harry Gabbett considered this announcement a personal affront and he went into a whirlwind of activity for two days. Not only did he mark everying in his own bulging drawers SAVE THIS but he rushed around bringing in everything he could mark for saving as well. For a week it was impossible to find anything you really needed.

Eventually, the *Washington Post* hired Harry Gabbett away and instead of making use of his puckish humor, they turned him into a police reporter. It was the greatest waste of talent the town had every seen.

To show the kind of humor Harry Gabbett indulged in, one day, for office reading only, he wrote an item about Eugene Talmadge, the arch-bigot and political boss of Georgia. It was a whimsical thing, absolutely untrue, of course, written in police-court style, saying that Talmadge had been arrested for refusing to go to the back of the bus as the bus crossed the Potomac River into Virginia.

The Jim Crow laws were in effect in Virginia but not in the District of Columbia, so passengers from the District would have to switch to the rear as they crossed the bridge.

The first editor Gabbett handed the item to thought it was funny and passed it along for the next desk man to have a laugh. However, an edition deadline was coming up and someone on the newsdesk took only a cursory look and flipped the item into the slot marked for page one, for use as a box.

As Bill Odlin, who was there, remembers it: "The next thing we knew, it was on page one and the heavens fell in. There were copious retractions. But then the policy of the *Times-Herald* was to entertain the public—and this day it certainly did."

9/In the Beginning Was the Star

A battle of the Titans is now in progress, pitting two giants against each other in mortal combat in the nation's capital—the *Washington Post* and the *Washington Star*. Each has an army of troops from a powerful news magazine.

The *Post* owns *Newsweek*. The *Star* was bought by Time, Inc., in 1978.

How will it end? After fears that the *Star* would fold, Washington remains a two-newspaper city with its news sharpened by rivalry.

There was a time the *Star* could afford to be magnanimous. In 1885, after a fire burned out the *Post* and two other papers housed with it, the *Star* lent the use of its presses. It long was Washington's leading newspaper and remained so until the 1960s.

In the first half of the century, Washington had five daily newspapers. Competing with the *Star* was the *Evening Times* and with the *Post* was the *Morning Herald*. These two Hearst papers were sold to the flamboyant Cissy Patterson who combined them into the round-the-clock *Times-Herald*, later bought by the *Post*.

The fifth paper was the *Daily News*, a Scripps-Howard tabloid dealing mostly with local items. It was bought by the *Star*.

As a child, I was not permitted to read the Hearst papers. My parents thought them "trashy."

My first exposure to the *Post* was when I was in baby dresses at the age of less than three. I remember crawling on the floor where the paper was spread. In a piping voice, I could spell out each letter of the *Washington Post*, in Old English type as it is now.

My parents once tried to show off this accomplishment to visitors. I refused to perform and uttered no more than goo-goo noises. Some think the *Post* still does this.

The *Post* did a big thing when it bought the *Times-Herald* which then had the greatest circulation and advertising. The *Star* tried to match this coup by buying the *News*, but results were disappointing, and the *Post* had supremacy.

The *Times-Herald* was bought from the heirs of its cantankerous female publisher. When Cissy Patterson died, she willed her newspaper to seven top executives, in effect giving each the value of a million dollars or so.

One unlucky fellow just missed sharing. Ash DeWitt was managing editor off and on. Hot-tempered, he would quarrel with Cissy, resign, and be brought back. Unluckily, Cissy died when he was on the outs and he lost his million.

Today, Washington's two newspapers, the morning *Post* and the evening *Star* are among the world's most influential—because they are read by the top people of government. Every president, plus Congress, Cabinet, and ranking officials, reads both papers.

The *Post*, glamorized by its part in forcing Nixon out of office, has an edge on the *Star* and even on the *New York Times*. It is the paper with clout, famed for its daring and its colorful managing editor, Benjamin Bradlee. The *Star* holds its own on sprightly features. It's easier to read.

But each is more than a paper; each is the keystone of a news empire tied to radio and television and linked to the top news magazines.

What is the difference, from the viewpoint of the reporter, between working at the *Post* and the *Star*? Some like the prestige of working for the *Post*, simply because it is world-famous and frequently quoted in other newspapers.

Some prefer working for the *Star* for the exact opposite reason. It is interesting to talk to reporters on both papers and hear what they have to say—some expressing the feeling that they are being squeezed by big-business journalism, and others happy that they are permitted to grow and flower at their own speed.

Ron Sarro, until recently on the *Star's* Hill staff, says, "I preferred to work at the *Star* though originally I applied at both papers at the same time.

"In a way the *Star* and the *Post* compare with the National Press Club and the Washington Press Club. The *Post* is like the NPC—bureaucratic, dominated by editors who seem to be always jockeying for the upper hand. It's big-rich, tends to consume its people.

"The *Post* has changed the meaning of the words *creative*

tension to *hysterical tension* and all you have to do is watch how upset their reporters are on a day-to-day basis, to see what I mean.

"The *Star* is a reporter's paper, a writer's paper. Most of the people have been through a lot together, especially in the last eight years trying to save it from disaster.

"What I hope will not happen, and I see some signs of it, is that purchase by a large corporation like Time, Inc., will promote a lot of cut-throat executive jockeying in the newsroom. I think advertisers really ought to take a good, hard look at what it would mean if the *Washington Post* had a monopoly on newspaper advertising in this city and start buying more ads in the *Star* in self-defense." Sarro is now a writer for the House Majority Whip.

Through most of the first half of the twentieth century, the *Post* was in a building fronted with dingy stone with a peaked roof on E Street near Fourteenth, around the corner from the present site of the National Press Building at Fourteenth and F.

The *Post* was flanked by two well-visited bars—the "University of Gerstenberg," which reeked of Limburger and newspaper talk, and Shoomakers, which had such low ceilings it boasted that its cobwebs had brushed the hat of Henry Clay.

The *Star* was in a white stone building three blocks from the *Post* at Eleventh and Pennsylvania Avenue. The *Times* and *Herald* were on H Street near Thirteenth and the *Daily News* on Thirteenth Street near I.

As on the old Newspaper Row of the 1800s, the papers were in close proximity and handy to their favorite watering hole—the National Press Club.

Before radio, people were totally dependent on their papers for news. If something exciting happened, special editions were printed. Boys and men ran out crying, "Extra! Extra! Read all about it!" Folks came running out of their houses to buy, often disappointed by a minor story puffed up to sell papers.

The papers posted news flashes that passersby could read and gave scores of ball games. On election nights, screens were placed in front of the *Post* and *Star* to flash returns to crowds standing on the avenue.

As a youngster, I was allowed to go with another lad. When the crowd cheered, we enthusiastically piped up but found we were rooting for both parties when someone asked whose side we were on.

No one was allowed to stand on anything to block the

view. A cop came to admonish a man he thought was on a box and was surprised to find his feet on the ground—about seven feet below. One year the election outcome was signaled by blinking the new electric street lights which had just replaced gas. The *Daily Evening Star*, as it was then called, applauded such modern progress.

Radio and TV changed all this. This was not competition for the *Post* and *Star*. Rather they bought their own stations, which added to their income, though it brought problems about news monopoly with the FCC.

In the beginning was the *Star*—the *Daily Evening Star*. It has burned with a fierce light ever since 1852, before anyone had even thought of the *Washington Post*.

So many newspapers had flashed through Washington as shooting stars and comets, only to die, that there was nothing to indicate that this one would climb higher in the sky and survive the longest.

Surely that first edition on December 16, 1852, was no blockbuster. A heavily bearded young printer named Captain Joseph Borrows Tate, an officer in the Washington militia, decided that he could make a go of it in a place where about one hundred newspapers had already failed.

True, the captain had only five hundred dollars and an old hand press, but he had a good idea. His would be a penny paper. People couldn't afford to subscribe to newspapers because they couldn't pay for lengthy subscriptions. He would charge just a penny, cash and carry, or delivered to the door. Of the first printing of one thousand about a fourth were dropped at doorsteps.

It's fascinating to see what the news was in the Nation's Capital on that first day, which happened to fall on a Thursday. About the biggest news on the front page, was an item headed "An Arrival at Brown's Hotel," which informs the reader that a man named W. L. McCauley, of Baltimore, had just sent over: "One case of patent cork-sole boots, one case of double-sole boots, one case dress boots."

Elsewhere the first edition reports, "Our courts are sitting but the business with which they are engaged is not of a very interesting character."

Taking up most of the front page was a short story concerning two cranky women, entitled "The First Cross Word." The reader is mercifully spared the name of the author.

But even if this seemed like a strange approach to newspapering, at least it had more breadth than other newspapers of the time, which tended to be nothing more than propaganda for a particular political party. A man's politics were known by the newspaper he subscribed to.

The *Daily Evening Star* known today as the *Washington Star*, was born into a world grown tense over the issue of slavery. The population of the nation's capital was 41,000 of whom 2,000 were slaves. An early *Star* item reported that a "white buffalo cow" had strayed from Mrs. Bryant's home on G Street between Thirteenth and Fifteenth streets." It is unknown whether the unfortunate creature ever strayed back in the right direction. If it did it must have passed a lot of geese, ducks, chickens and pigs, as well as a few goats who overran the dirt streets.

Pennsylvania Avenue, leading from the White House to the Capitol Building, was the jewel of the city and it even prided itself on having gas lamps along the way. Since they were considered a bit frivolous, they were only lighted "on moonless nights."

The *Star* crusaded against many things—the throwing of garbage in the streets, the shooting of ducks in the marshes so near the White House. It could be dangerous to wander around in those days. If the flying garbage didn't catch you, a stray bullet might.

Women who read the *Star* knew they were properly dressed for daytime if they wore either red or black. And they were properly dressed for evening, and even fashionable, if they had cloth or embroidered blossoms trailing over a hoop skirt.

An early newspaper tried to upgrade the behavior of men in the capital city by castigating them for their habit of "ogling beautiful women" on the streets. The newspaper pointed out what a proper lady could do if she did not wish to encourage such behavior. As was pointed out, a lady who was not being escorted by a gentleman "might properly visit a public building if accompanied by a child." Even if she had to borrow one.

One of the things the *Star* is proudest of today is a copy of the first inaugural address of Abe Lincoln, dated March 4, 1861, in which he vowed to preserve the Union.

As soon as Lincoln finished giving the address, which carries corrections in his own handwriting, he gave his copy to the *Star* reporter Crosby Noyes, for printing in the newspaper.

Ironically, it was Lincoln's assassination that brought

about the first news illustration the newspaper had ever used—a drawing of the bullet that had killed Lincoln. The *Evening Star*, as it was now called, reported this story three days after the shooting:

> THE ASSASSINATION
> THE LATEST PARTICULARS
> *The Assassination a Conspiracy!*
>   *Developments have been made within the past twenty-four hours showing conclusively the existence of a deep-laid plot on the part of a gang of conspirators, including members of the order of "Knights of the Golden Circle," to murder President Lincoln and his Cabinet.*

As for Noyes, in 1867 he was one of five men who scraped together the lordly sum of $100,000 to buy the paper. The others were Samuel H. Kauffmann, George W. Adams, Alexander R. Shepherd and Clarence B. Baker. The Noyes and Kauffmann families continued to own and operate the *Star* into the 1970s.

But back in the 1860s there was no way for reporter Crosby Noyes to know that he was founding a dynasty. His greatest problem of the day was covering the impeachment trial of President Andrew Johnson, and the *Star* still has the special press pass Noyes needed for the occasion.

Signed by Sergeant-at-Arms George T. Brown, the card says:

> *Reporters Gallery—U.S. Senate*
> *Impeachment of the President*
> *Admit the Bearer*
> *March 13, 1868.*

On May 16, Crosby Noyes' article correctly predicted the President's later acquittal:

> IMPEACHMENT.
> THE GREAT DAY
> *Scenes at the Capitol, Intense Excitement!*

Noyes' story goes on to say that the vote was thirty-four yeas and nineteen nays on a particular article which "admitted to be a virtual acquittal!"

The *Star* headline on February 16, 1898, heralded the event that would lead to the Spanish-American War:

THE MAINE BLOWN UP
> *Awful Disaster to United States Battleship in Harbor in Havana.*
> *Number of Killed or Missing, 253.*

In 1908 Orville Wright took off from Fort Myer, Virginia, to demonstrate his "aeroplane" and crashed, causing the first American death in a plane disaster. The story in the *Star* of September 18, 1908, shows that the future of aviation—at least the Wright brothers involvement in it—hung in the balance:

WRIGHT WILL LIVE; SELFRIDGE IS DEAD
> *Wilbur Wright Tempted to Abandon Aerial Work by Accident to Brother, but Rallies and Will Go on—Principle All Right, But Faulty Construction to Blame.*

The year 1908 was especially important to the *Star* because that was the year Crosby Noyes died, felled by an attack of influenza while on a trip to California.

Samuel Kauffmann had died two years earlier. Theodore W. Noyes, son of Crosby, who had studied law, took over the management for just a short time but then Frank, his brother, took complete command.

Frank loved the paper, having gotten his first taste of newspapering in the business office of the *Star* at the age of thirteen.

Already he had influenced the policy of the paper. As a youngster, he had talked his elders into changing the standard four-page newspaper to an eight-pager and had come up with the idea of a sort of supplement added to the newspaper on Saturdays—a very radical idea.

So astute was young Noyes that he had been made business manager of the newspaper but had quit in 1900 to further his career and had become editor and publisher of the *Chicago Record-Herald*.

When Frank Noyes was brought back in 1909 to head the family enterprise, it was to assume the title of company president.

The innovations he had instituted had certainly borne fruit. The supplement had become a twenty-four-page magazine which now appeared on Sunday—the first issue of a Sunday paper had made history on March 20, 1905. It had been a tremendous fifty-six pages, plus the twenty-four page supplement—a total of eighty pages.

The *Star* had also begun featuring political cartoons on the front page by a young artist named Clifford K. Berryman, whose little bear in the corner of each cartoon became a *Star* trademark.

The bear idea came from a cartoon entitled "Drawing the line in Mississippi" where President Teddy Roosevelt, on a hunting trip, had refused to shoot a cub offered as an easy trophy. Manufacture of the ever-popular teddy bear followed, just as Smoky the Bear caught the public fancy in later years.

Under Frank Noyes, the *Star* not only continued to flourish but set up its own fair-business practice. It announced that it would stand behind any advertisement it published.

This was 1910, before government laws protected consumers, the *Star* invited the reader to tell the truth about painkillers and other "miracle" drugs.

As a result of this attempt to protect the public against fraud, the *Star* eventually led the entire nation in volume of advertising.

In 1948 Frank Noyes resigned as president but died within a few months, before he was able to enjoy his retirement. The presidency then went to Samuel H. Kauffmann, the grandson and namesake of one of the original purchasers.

In the 1960s, the great prestige of the *Washington Star*—which had been run from 1867 by an unbroken line of the original Noyes and Kauffmann families—began to slip as the *Star's* style became stodgy in comparison with the ambitious *Washington Post*.

It was said that the *Star's* ruling families—the Kauffmanns and the Noyes—had a list of family and friends that every reporter on the staff had better recognize, say no ill against and prominently mention in party lists on the women's page.

The *Post* was getting fatter and the *Star* thinner. As *WJR (Washington Journalism Review)* tells it, "Once Washington's dominant newspaper, in 1970 the *Star* lost $886,000, and by 1974 the loss was running to $7.7 million."

In 1974, the family dynasty era was over when the *Star* was bought by Joe L. Allbritton, a Texas banker and businessman.

It is hard to say exactly what Allbritton paid for the *Star* because the newspaper was part of an estimated $50-million-plus deal which included the *Star's* TV and radio stations in Washington as well as stations in Charleston, South Carolina, and Lynchburg, Virginia.

The best estimate seems to be that Allbritton paid somewhere around $12 million to $15 million for the *Star*, give or take a mil or two.

His triumph was such that by 1977 the yearly deficit on the paper was reduced to $1.3 million operating loss for that year.

Reporters felt that the improvement in the paper's exchequer was taken out of their hide.

Perhaps the happiest reporters in town were the *Washington Star* reporters when the newspaper was bought in 1978 by *Time* magazine for some $20 million plus the assumption of an $8-million debt. How did it feel? Ron Sarro, congressional reporter, said it best, "I no longer feel that I work in a lifeboat. Well, I may be in a lifeboat, but now at least it's safely secured to an ocean liner. *Time* is a wealthy, journalistically proven organization. It doesn't like failure and has given every indication it will put money and time and effort to help the *Star* succeed."

To help save the *Star* during its recent Allbritton lean years, Sarro was one of hundreds of reporters who worked a four-day week, taking a twenty percent cut in pay for one year.

The *Star* still does not have the staff at its command that the *Washington Post* does. On Capitol Hill, for example, "Reporters from the *Washington Post* often outnumber me six, or even eight, to one," says Ron Sarro, who for years headed the *Washington Star's* congressional reporters. "The part that really griped me was that most of them were paid $150 more a week to give me the privilege of working my tail off to beat them every opportunity I got."

Times have definitely changed at both newspapers. One famous editor among the Washington press corps greats was Ben McKelway, of the *Star*, who lived to attend the fiftieth anniversary of the National Press Club at the Sheraton Park Hotel.

Ben's favorite story, which he told a few Club members as they stood around having drinks, was the time, many years before, when he was running the newspaper and a scared cub reporter came up to him and said, "Mr. McKelway, how does a fellow go about getting a raise on this paper?"

McKelway, feeling sorry for the lad, took the time to lay it out. "Well son, if you feel you have been doing a good job, you just go to the city editor and you tell him you feel you've been doing good work and deserve a little raise."

Then something made McKelway ask, "What are you getting now?"

"Nothing," said the boy.

McKelway is gone, and so is the pre-Guild world with its minimum pay. No longer does the *Washington Star* take on kids who work for nothing—or just about.

Today at the *Star*, even the humble copyboy/girl makes $192.22 a week. The cub reporter makes $253.83 and the seasoned reporter, after three years, pulls down a salary of $471.12.

The *Star* is now the third highest-paying newspaper in the country. The second highest, according to David Eisen, research and information director of the Newspaper Guild, is the *New York Times* and the top pay in the newspaper world goes to those on the *Washington Post*—$213.25 top minimum for copyboy/girl, $284.65 for a starting minimum for a cub reporter, and $560.50 top minimum reached by a reporter after four years.

As comparison, the wire service reporters earn considerably less than *Post* and *Star* reporters, but more than the average reporter is paid outside Washington and New York.

At Associated Press, a reporter starts at $236.40 and works up to $410.00 in six years. At United Press International, the same reporter would start at $224.04 and work up to $392.07 in five years.

Murray J. Gart is the relatively new top editor of the *Washington Star*, holding the position equivalent to that of Ben Bradlee, though Bradlee calls himself "executive editor" and Gart calls himself "editor."

A new man on the job, brought in after *Time* took over, Gart seems like a worthy newsman on the Washington scene as well as a member of the National Press Club, which he has just joined.

Members welcomed him as one of them—reporter first, administrator second, with a string of past by-lines, first on the *Honolulu Star Bulletin*, then the *Weekly Independent Record* in Cape May County, New Jersey, the *Wichita Beacon*, and the *Wichita Eagle*.

Finally, Gart moved over to *Time* magazine, where he learned to live without by-lines. At *Time* he worked his way up from stringer in Wichita to bureau chief in and out of the states—Toronto, Boston, Chicago, London.

What Press Club members admire most about Gart is the way he distinguished himself by masterminding a plan to get an off-limits story.

As former Club president Frank Aukofer tells it, "Gart put on his dark glasses and posed as a police inspector to slip a *Time* reporter into a private New York reception for Nikita Khrushchev.

"And then," says Aukofer, "Murray was indignant when he learned the *New York Times* had done the same thing using their own ruse."

The *Star* is exceedingly proud to have a man known for his toughness at the helm to counteract the generations under which the *Star* was run as a mom-and-pop, father-and-son, family affair—by the gentle Noyes and Kauffmanns.

They are especially pleased at the *Star* when Murray Gart is compared in toughness to Ben Bradlee of the *Post*. But, says at least one staffer, "Bradlee may be the sweeter of the two."

10/From Pillar to Washington Post

It is said that the *Washington Post* was born a bastard child of politics.

Its founder, in that year of 1877, was a vitriolic Democrat who refused to acknowledge that Rutherford Hayes had won the election against Tilden.

The *Post* would *not* even dignify the election enough to call Hayes "President Hayes," no matter what a specially created electoral commission had decided.

According to *Post* founder Stilson Hutchins, a tall, fine figure of a man, Hayes had stolen the election, and he carefully avoided giving him his due, referring to him only as "the bogus President," "his fraudulency," or "the acting President."

The few times that Hutchins called Hayes "the President," readers chuckled and said Hutchins' pen must have slipped.

The *Post* founder had a colorful background, and the *Post* was not the first paper he had founded. In 1862, he had put out a sheet supporting the secessionists in Dubuque—the *Dubuque Herald*. So strongly did Hutchins feel in his Southern sympathies that he named a son Robert E. Lee Hutchins.

When Grant took Appomattox, Hutchins moved to St. Louis, where he and another man started another paper, the *Times*. To Hutchins' credit, he gave a young foreign-born reporter named Joseph Pulitzer his first English-language writing job.

Hutchins' private life was as colorful as his political battles. After his wife of some twenty years sued him for divorce in 1882 on grounds of adultery—and won—he quickly found a replacement. He married a girl whom he had met through the author of *Little Lord Fauntleroy*, Frances Hodgson Burnett.

For his new bride, Sarita Brady, he built a beautiful palace on Massachusetts Avenue, the heart of Washington's embassies.

But soon tragedy struck. A little over a year after the wedding, Sarita died giving birth to their child.

This time Hutchins waited several years before taking a third bride.

The year the *Washington Post* was born there were only thirty-nine states in the Union. Aside from politics, which the *Post* could be counted on to give only the Democratic viewpoint, news items included these important events:

A "dashing cock fight" in which some New Jersey fighting cocks had won a slashing victory over some New York birds—"to the disgust of the New York sporting men."

Alfred, Lord Tennyson was being besieged by romantic Washington ladies writing him to plead for "locks of his hair."

The White House held a social event for the ladies called a "kettle-drum," at which Mrs. Hayes, "attired in black silk, relieved with white lace at the throat," served tea at five o'clock. The guests left at six. A young lady, who favored the group by playing the piano may have helped clear the "Executive Mansion" an hour earlier than traditional.

Already in that year of 1877 readers were sending angry letters to the editor. One such letter of December 12 demanded to know if there was not an ordinance "requiring streetcar conductors to call out the streets." The person, signing himself "A Subscriber," indignantly told how a nursemaid with an infant and two-year-old child had to wander around lost on the streets of Washington because she hadn't known where to get off.

But there was a happy ending. "The children were restored to their distressed parents by a policeman."

Going through old issues of the *Washington Post* is a feast of history and famous names:

In 1879, the *Post* ran an extra when Governor William Sprague of Rhode Island drove Senator Conkling of New York off his property "at the point of a shotgun because of Conkling's alleged attentions to Sprague's wife, the beautiful and accomplished Kate Chase, daughter of Supreme Court Chief Justice Chase."

Two years later, the *Post* followed up with the story of the governor filing suit for divorce at Providence and commented archly that it was "the kind of incident to make tongues wag."

In my attic I have a little table that had belonged to this same beautiful Kate Chase.

In 1882 the *Post* snorts at a visit to Washington of the "social lion" Oscar Wilde, newly arrived from London. "To have treated the *ass-thete* seriously would have been an enduring indictment against our judgment," comments an editorial.

116

AN HISTORIC RIP OFF: Minutes after Lyndon Baines Johnson graciously signed the National Press Club guest book, someone ripped out the page for its historical value. Though an ad was placed in the Press Club *Record* for return of the page with no questions asked, it never reappeared. Red faced, the Club president, Reuters chief John W. Heffernan, shown here standing to the left of Lady Bird, eventually told LBJ what had happened and the President agreed to sign another page. *(Credit: John Metelsky)*

THE DANCING PRESIDENT: LBJ could be very charming and even frolicsome. He loved to dance and frequently twirled female reporters as well as White House guests around the dance floor. When he danced with Naomi Nover of the Denver *Post*, he teased the other press gals by playfully dancing Naomi over to them and proclaiming, "Naomi is the best dancer of all of you." And he may have been right.

HAIL TO THE CHIEF: President Nixon could be very gracious and relaxed with reporters on social occasions. It was only on a one-to-one basis that he acted uncomfortable and sometimes gruff. Here Ted Knap, Scripps-Howard White House correspondent, toasts the President at a dinner, while Secretary of State Bill Rogers joins in the toast. Incidentally, it was the morning after this White House Correspondents Dinner in April 1973, that Nixon learned that the Justice Department had uncovered the Watergate coverup.

GOOD FRIENDS: Helen Thomas, UPI White House correspondent, and First Lady Pat Nixon had an especially warm and friendly relationship. When Helen Thomas was secretly planning to get married to fellow White House correspondent, AP's Doug Cornell, it was Pat Nixon who scooped the White House press corps by announcing the engagement.

THE PERFECT DINNER COMPANION, according to Edgar Allen Poe, *New Orleans Picayune* Washington correspondent and president of the White House Correspondents Association, is Betty Ford. "She's witty without for a moment losing her feminine charm." Here Betty's wit has Poe and Supreme Court Justice Lewis F. Powell in stitches at a 1975 dinner. *(Credit: Stan Jennings)*

THE CARTER STYLE: Such southern hospitality does Rosalynn Carter exhibit, that it was perfectly natural for Lillian Levy, president of the American Newspaper Women's Club, to take along her visiting eighty-year-old mother and sister to a party the First Lady gave for the Club. Proudly posing with the First Lady and their own family's star at the White House are Mrs. Clara La Valle (left) and Theda Mann (extreme right), both of California. *(Credit: The White House)*

AND THEN THERE WAS JOHN FITZGERALD KENNEDY: He was just a freshman Senator when TV moderator Ruth Hagy invited him to get TV exposure by appearing on her panel show, *College News Conference*, to answer questions of the college crowd. "He jumped at the chance." Ruth recalls, "He needed that exposure. The youthful Jack Kennedy was a great hit with the kids but did I think that he would be President? No." *(Credit: Collection of Ruth Hagy Brod)*

PRESSING THE FLESH: This is what it's really like when a President attends a party—more compacted than a New York subway. A few faces in the crowd around President Jerry Ford are NPC president Robert Alden, in glasses; former NPC president Ken Scheibel, lower right corner; and above Ken's head, correspondent-author Frances Spatz Leighton. *(Credit: John Metelsky)*

THE PRESS OFF GUARD

THE SYNCOPATED TRIO: They dance, they sing—and sometimes even in time with the music. Either way, they bring down the house at private NPC parties. The National Press Club stars are, from left, Bob Butler, senior editor of *Traffic World*, Tiger Farley, National Association of Realtors, and Carl West, investigative reporter for Scripps-Howard. *(Credit: Berny Krug)*

CONGRESSIONAL NIGHT 1971 celebrating the vote that permitted women to become members of the National Press Club for the first time in its sixty-three-year history. From left is Don Curry, with a "Texas fifth," to signify that the influx of women might drive him to desperate drink; Jim Srodes, signifying that life with the ladies will be a piece of cake; Lew King, partially hidden, diplomatically smoking a peace pipe; Sarah McClendon, the happiest woman on the stage with her sign which reminds the crowd of the old rule around the club that women could enter "Accompanied by Male Members Only"; coauthor Fran Leighton, who like Sarah was among the first female writers to be invited to join the Club; and Bob Herzberg making like Teddy Roosevelt—he is promising to speak softly to the ladies, but just in case, he's carrying a big stick.

INVESTIGATIVE REPORTER IN DISGUISE: Ron Sarro! He may have been a hotshot investigative reporter for the *Washington Star* by day, but by night he was Dottore, in little theater.

INVESTIGATIVE REPORTER WITHOUT DISGUISE: Eric Ruff, who sleuths his stories for the Donrey Media Group, has a different way of getting away from it all. You will find him beside a river in quiet contemplation with his beautiful black Labrador retrievers, Moose and Jessie. (*Rebecca Ruff*)

CBS ANNOUNCER IN DISGUISE: Wearing a Turkish fez, Kim Gregory, announcer and producer of CBS, takes a chess lesson from the National Press Club's "Friendly Philosopher," bartender "Grand Master" Johnny Prokoff. Prokoff, who usually keeps three or four chess games going on the bar of the Tap Room while taking orders and mixing drinks on Saturdays, once considered giving up bartending to devote full time to chess. "But I like to eat," he explains. Incidentally, it took special permission from a member of the Board of Governors to take this picture in the bar, which is off limits to cameras. *(Walter Fisk, U.S. News Service)*

HALLOWEEN AT THE PRESS CLUB: "It's better than bobbing for apples," says member John Metelsky, who took advantage of the preinflation price of fifty cents at the "Kongressional Kissing Booth" at the 1973 Halloween party. Pretty Press Club member Patricia Young is the moneymaker with Representative Ken Gray of Illinois waiting his turn. Gray's guest for the evening was the soon-to-be famous Elizabeth Ray, who dressed in a costume matching his. *(Credit: Berny Krug)*

THE MOST POWERFUL WOMAN IN WASHINGTON, that's what they call Katharine Graham, Chairman of the Board of the *Washington Post* and *Newsweek*. They also call her the shiest millionaire, the most powerful woman in the publishing world, and surprisingly, one of the nicest persons you could ever meet. With her, at the National Press Club, are past Club presidents Robert Alden of the *Post* and Bob Farrell of McGraw-Hill. *(Credit: Stan Jennings)*

UPI WIRE CHIEF Grant Dillman works beside his reporters in the hurly-burly newsroom of the wire service's National Press Building quarters.

AP CHIEF Walter Mears works in an elegant private office in the much more staid and somber atmosphere of the wire service that prides itself on dignity and the exclusiveness of its member newspapers. So is AP's address more exclusive—a modern building at Twentieth and K Streets.

TOUGH GUY AT THE WHITE HOUSE: Sam Donaldson of ABC, a native of El Paso, Texas, has the reputation of asking the toughest questions of President Carter and of his Press Secretary Jody Powell. Here he is at the spot from which he frequently broadcasts.

KING OF THE NEWSLETTERS: Llewellyn King is one of the most successful newsletter publishers—*Energy Daily*—which King admits brings in three quarters of a million dollars a year. Here the "King" has a quiet word with Energy Czar James Schlesinger, who admits he starts every day by reading King's newsletter. *(Credit: Stan Jennings)*

KING OF THE GENEALOGISTS—Alexander Haley, right, is a millionaire now, but the Press Club gang is inspired and proud that they knew him when he was a down-and-out writer, under their own roof, and owing the Press Building three thousand dollars back rent. It was Ofield Dukes, left, now a top Washington public relations man, who officed next to Haley and kept him going until his long book-writing ordeal was over and he sprang to fame with *Roots.* Here they are at a reception given to honor Haley at the embassy of the Ivory Gold Coast.

LEGAL EAGLE: Charlotte Moulton of UPI, in front of the Supreme Court, which she has covered since World War II. The hardest decision to cover, she says, was school desegregation in 1954, because Chief Justice Earl Warren elected to read the whole decision aloud. "It was not until Warren had virtually finished reading," Charlotte recalls, "that it could be said with certainty that a racially dual school system was unconstitutional." *(Credit: United Press International)*

NO, THAT'S NOT A HIGHBALL IN JACK ANDERSON'S HAND: That's plain ginger ale Jack Anderson is drinking at the National Press Club with his friend and neighbor from five miles down the pike, Press Club member John Metelsky. Everyone asks John what Anderson is really like. "I've known him for years," John laughs and says, "and I once asked him for a job. He asked for a résumé. That cooled my ardor for the job, but not for the man. He's just a good guy. He's driven me home sometimes. He's tops in his field and as a conversationalist. I may not always agree with him, but I admire and respect him."

LIKE FATHER, LIKE SON: Austin Kiplinger, left, now carries on where his father, W. M. "Kip" Kiplinger, left off, putting out the most famous newsletter ever, the *Kiplinger Newsletter*. Austin keeps the folksy touch in his newsletter which is still considered the bible of investors.

BEST KNOWN WASHINGTON SO-
CIETY COLUMNIST is the very social
Betty Beale, whose Washington connection
is the *Washington Star*. Here, stepping out
in twin evening costumes are Betty and her
husband, industry representative George
K. Graeber. *(Credit: City News Bureau, Inc.)*

PULITZER PRIZE WINNER Miriam Ottenberg is sworn into the presidency of the
Women's National Press Club (now the
Washington Press Club), by Attorney General Robert Kennedy in 1964. The picture
has further historic importance because
this was the very day President Lyndon
Johnson had called Bobby Kennedy to the
White House to tell him that he did not
want him as his running mate for Vice
President. "Because of that," Miriam recalls, "Bobby almost didn't make it to my
swearing in." One can only wonder what
the course of history would have been had
LBJ not, in effect, freed Bobby to run for
the Senate that fall, deferring his White
House aspirations. In the center is Ben
McKelway, then editor of the *Washington
Star*. *(Credit:* Washington Star)

THE ONE AND ONLY BEN BRADLEE:
Most famous editor in the country is probably the *Washington Post*'s Ben Bradlee. It
was he who guided Woodward and Bernstein in the Pulitzer Prize-winning investigation of Watergate. He is also credited
with helping Katharine Graham grow into
her difficult job as publisher of the *Washington Post*, after the tragic death of her
husband, Philip Graham. *(Credit: Kathleen
Summers,* The Washington Post)

FEMALE INVESTIGATIVE REPORTER Vera Glaser of Knight-Ridder managed also to be a Club leader, becoming president of the Washington Press Club in 1971. Here she is having a one-to-one interview with President Lyndon Johnson at the White House.

SEPARATE BUT EQUAL CAREERS: One of the top writing couples in the nation's capital is Marianne Means, Hearst columnist, and *New York Times* Washington correspondent Warren Weaver. Here they are in the garden of their Georgetown home, which is big enough to have his and hers writing dens.

MR. 4TH ESTATE: CBS anchorman Walter Cronkite beams on the night the National Press Club made him its first recipient of its "4th Estate Award" in 1973 for his "distinguished career in journalism." With him are NPC members Don Curry and Linda Vance, chairman of the Club's Board of Governors and correspondent for the Commodity News Service.

FAMED CARTOONIST Herblock, of the *Washington Post*, is honored at the National Press Club in 1977 when he became the first cartoonist to receive the 4th Estate Award Here, he and Doree Lovell share a laugh at a take-off another cartoonist had done on perhaps Herblock's most famous cartoon. Herblock's cartoon had shown candidate Nixon arriving at a rally climbing out of a sewer, and the caption had been "Here he comes now." The take-off, in a much kindlier vein, shows Herblock—whose real name is Herbert Block—arriving at a rally crawling out of an inkwell of black ink and Nixon is there to greet *him* with a welcome sign. Again the caption is, "Here he comes now."

THE CHALLENGER: Pat Oliphant, political cartoonist of the *Washington Star*, is the cartoonist universities say the new generation of artists is trying to emulate. Oliphant's cartoons are so grotesque they're beautiful and as works of art, are collectors' items. The amazing thing is that Oliphant understands us so well—he's a native of Adelaide, Australia.

BACHELOR AT LARGE: Because press men's wives, like all other wives, don't relish their husbands doing escort duty to beautiful and powerful women, such as Ambassador Shirley Temple Black and movie star Claudette Colbert, and because the Club had its own most eligible and social bachelor, Don Curry was pressed into escort duty, to the mutual enjoyment of both Don and Indira Gandhi. Even the female head of the world's largest democracy fell under the spell of the Club's macho bachelor before a Press Club luncheon at which Indira Gandhi was guest speaker, and had to be reminded it was time for more serious things. *(Credit: Stan Jennings)*

In 1884, the air at the Capitol made *Post* news. Under the heading "Atmosphere Most Foul," a long article told how congressmen sitting on the floor of the House side of the Capitol were suffering "a feeling of lassitude and often times severe headache, while cases of vertigo are not uncommon."

Many believe the lassitude is still there. The headaches go to the taxpayers. In 1884 a "Committee on Ventilation and Acoustics" found that the foul air was being drawn from a low part of the grounds suspected of having "malarial influences."

> *The air which is at present forced into the hall is drawn from the west side of the Capitol grounds from near the bed of the old canal, a locality the most unhealthful in Washington.*

In 1887 there was a different complaint. Bells on the horses that drew streetcars made a cheerful jingling but were abolished because they disturbed the sleep of a district commissioner.

More recently a curfew was put on aircraft at Washington National Airport because they woke the wife of an aviation official who lived in Alexandria.

The more things are different, the more they are the same. The top-hatted men with whiskers, gold-headed canes, overdressed women, and overstuffed sofas made out as well as we. But let us move along to our own century.

Teddy Roosevelt began it with boundless verve and a hearty grin, not realizing that before the next year was over, President McKinley would be dead and he would be President.

Thanks to the *Washington Post* of Saturday, September 14, 1901, we know how President McKinley, shot by an assassin, spent his last moments of life and what his last words were.

With Mrs. McKinley at his side during the night, he recited the hymn "Nearer, My God, to Thee." Then, after saying good-bye to those assembled, his last words were, "It is God's way. His will be done."

In 1905 the *Post* was sold to John Roll McLean, the son of a boilermaker who made a fortune building steamboats. The new owner had moved from Cincinnati to Washington in the 1890s to head the gas company, start a suburban rail line, invest in major banks—and entertain lavishly.

A Democrat, McLean backed William Jennings Bryan, who ran against Teddy Roosevelt in 1904, and gave Bryan a dinner with a hundred guests as consolation after his defeat. The Bible-spouting Bryan lived near me in my boyhood in the Meridian Park area of northwest Washington. Strong for temperance, he believed that Jesus changed water not into wine but to the unfermented juice of the grape and he kept a bottle of grape juice ostentatiously on his window sill.

In 1889 a chance meeting between editor Frank Hatton of the *Post* and a music professor John Philip Sousa, resulted in Sousa's writing a stirring march to be used on the occasion of the *Washington Post* giving a prize in an essay contest in the public schools.

Sousa named his tune the "Washington Post March," and the newspaper has proudly used it ever since. It was played on the flagship of Admiral Dewey as he steamed into Manila Bay.

McLean hobnobbed with Republicans too, including his fellow Ohioan Nicholas Longworth, later the House Speaker and husband of Roosevelt's daughter Alice, who wed the dashing Nick in the White House. Sharp-tongued "Princess Alice," as she was called in the *Post*, was not impressed by publisher McLean's amiable comments and publicly spoke of him as "a dreadful man with a big belly."

McLean loved the power and prestige of owning news-papers—he also bought the *Cincinnati Enquirer* and *New York Morning Journal*—but he liked to work in subterranean ways. He did not permit his name to go on the *Post* masthead. Nor did he permit the *Post* to write about him or his fabulous parties. When it came to other people, he kept a file of damaging facts to hold over them if need be.

John McLean would have been amazed to know that his *Washington Post* would, in the 1960s and 1970s, become world-famous for its investigative reporting. "The people," he wrote, "don't want to read unpleasant news, no matter how true."

In 1916, while America was being drawn into the Euro-pean struggle, the old publisher lay dying. Even then his days were stormy. The family feared he would make a deathbed marriage or otherwise dispose of his estate. After angry scenes, he was put under restraint "to prevent him from endangering himself," as his doctor certified. Before he passed away, he still managed one dramatic outburst, throwing a million dollars' worth of bonds at his doctor.

Stormy days did not end with John Roll McLean. He had tried to keep his son, Edward B. McLean, from controlling the *Post* after he died, but in the long run he failed. Edward, who was known as Ned to all his drinking buddies, almost succeeded in wrecking the *Post*, in spite of his father's will.

Ned was a wild youth, living it up with wine, women and fast cars. It was said he managed to spend the more than half-million dollars a year his father's will gave him plus his wife's wealth as well.

He had married Evalyn Walsh, who inherited her father's mining fortune. The couple entertained royally in their sixty-room mansion on Massachusetts Avenue, which is now the Indonesian embassy.

This was only one of their places. There also was Friendship, a seventy-five-acre estate out Wisconsin Avenue beyond what then was the edge of the city, and the 2,600-acre Belmont Farm at Leesburg, Virginia, where they kept racehorses.

According to the elder McLean's will, Ned had only part control of the newspaper. A bank was trustee. Ned set out to break the will and won enough additional power as cotrustee and editor-in-chief to siphon off money as needed.

Ned sought power like his father but unlike his father gloried in publicity. The McLeans helped Harding campaign for president, using their private railroad car. The Hardings stayed at McLean's mansion after the 1920 election and Ned was chairman of the Inaugural Committee, a coveted honor.

Ned thought he would have things pretty much his way in Washington, and for the most part he did. Once he stubbed his toe when he sought the appointment of a district commissioner who was expected to let him name the chief of police. After Ned failed to get his way, the man's name never appeared in the *Post*.

Ned's wife, Evalyn, not only thrived on publicity, she insisted on it. Today the mammoth "bad luck" Hope diamond is displayed at the Smithsonian, where it is one of Washington's chief tourist attractions. Evalyn wore it dangling around her neck and it was always mentioned in the society columns of the *Post* after every party.

She hit the papers in a more sinister way when she was conned into giving $100,000 to the rascally Gaston Means, who said he could ransom Lindbergh's kidnapped baby.

A friend of mine lived in a house once occupied by Means and thought the money might be hidden there. He never found it, as far as I know.

Being friendly with Harding and his gang eventually

got Ned involved in helping to cover up the Teapot Dome scandal—the Watergate of its time.

Harding's Secretary of the Interior, Albert Fall, gave rights to oil companies in the nation's naval petroleum reserves. From Fall's sudden affluence it was suspected he had been bribed.

With the Senate bloodhounds baying on the trail, Fall asked Ned McLean to say he had lent $100,000. Ned backed him up. But to avoid questioning, Ned went to Florida "for his health" and kept in touch with Washington by leased wire.

Senate sleuths decoded his messages. Ned came out of the affair looking foolish rather than sinister.

Ned was more than a little touched with madness and grew more and more erratic. Even under Harding, he was said to have urinated in public, once in a White House fireplace and once down the leg of the Belgian ambassador, a story Ned denied.

Every old-time newspaperman in the Washington area has heard stories of Ned's partying. One that I remember concerned an orgy he held in an apartment with a bevy of girls as his guests. When the house manager came to complain, I was told, he was tied to a chair and the ladies made free with him in sundry ways.

In 1930 Evalyn could stand Ned's dalliances no longer and sued him for separate maintenance.

By now Ned was in such sad shape that he was in danger of losing the paper. He decided to sell before he would be forced into bankruptcy.

There were offers from Eugene Meyer, and William Randolph Hearst, and David Lawrence for several million dollars, but Evalyn was determined that their sons should inherit the *Post* and went to court to get a delaying action.

The McLeans kept Washington society buzzing. In 1932, Ned was ousted from the *Post* and a year or so later committed to Sheppard Pratt, a mental institution at Towson, Maryland.

The *Washington Post* did fold and was auctioned off in 1933. Evalyn McLean, the Hope diamond flashing on her bosom, watched haughtily from a *Post* window as the bidding took place on the steps. Averell Harriman was one of a group of three who bid a half-million dollars for the paper. Hearst bid through his attorneys. Even Bascom Timmons, the successful owner of a news service, bid a quarter of a million dollars. But the winning bid belonged to an attorney named George E. Hamilton, Jr. When the dust cleared the owner of the *Post* turned out to be Eugene Meyer. Vengeance was his. He had gotten his Washington paper for a mere $825,000.

Ned died in 1941, still in the asylum.

It is an eerie thought that years later, yet another *Washington Post* publisher, Philip Graham, would be institutionalized and would be considered of unsound mind when he died of his own hand.

When Eugene Meyer took over the *Post*, it was little more than an empty shell, rated low for quality and influence. Deficits topped $1 million a year.

Meyer set out to learn the business. He was an apt student and soon learned the tricks of making money—new writing talent and comic strips.

Cissy Patterson, at the *Times-Herald*, also knew the value of comics. She put up an intense struggle to get Dick Tracy and Winnie Winkle, claiming that their contracts to the *Post* were voided by the sale of the paper.

It took a ruling of the Supreme Court to prove they still belonged to the *Post*.

Cissy was furious and expressed it in her own inimitable way. She sent Meyer a prettily wrapped gift package. He opened it and grimaced. In it was a hunk of raw beef—a pound of flesh for Shylock. Actually, though born of Jewish parents, Meyer had become a Lutheran and married a Protestant New York beauty, Agnes Ernst.

Cissy and Meyer hated each other with a passion. When Meyer wanted to buy the *Herald* from Hearst, Cissy lent Hearst $1 million to keep Meyer from getting it.

When F. D. Roosevelt took office in 1933, the New Deal spread its wings and federal employment doubled. Washington boomed and everyone had money to spend—for newspapers and for the things advertised in newspapers.

Agnes Meyer followed the lead of Eleanor Roosevelt in traveling around the country and investigating conditions—sometimes even making news. But as they say, a prophet is without honor in his own town. Sometimes it would be a letdown to come back to Washington.

It was especially so once when she arrived at Union Station and couldn't find a cab. Annoyed, she called the city room and asked the assistant managing editor, who answered, to come and get her.

Deke, as he was called, was in the middle of getting out the bulldog edition and informed her bluntly that she should not expect him, adding words to the effect that he was not a flunky.

Mrs. Meyer told her husband about this as soon as she saw him—having gotten herself home—and publisher Meyer, feeling this should go through channels, called Casey Jones, Deke's superior.

Casey declared that he stood by Deke but not his language and would censure him for it. But the man had been within his rights and he was not a flunky.

For months Agnes Meyer stayed away from the *Post*.

When Christmas rolled around, her heart softened a bit. She gave Casey a bathrobe, which must have cost a lot of money, but gave nothing to Deke. It was interpreted as a peace offering of sorts.

Even in boomtown, Eugene Meyer had a hard time building the *Post* into a profitable venture. Meyer worked hard to turn the tide, prowling the creaky old *Post* buidling to see what everyone was doing and to figure out how it could be done better. Staffers could hardly sneak a drink on the job without getting caught.

Eugene Meyer was almost puritanical. He would not print romantic scandals about people in high places. When Jerry Kluttz, one of his columnists, told him about Roosevelt's involvement with Lucy Mercer Rutherfurd, he indignantly dismissed it as filth.

But Meyer did not hesitate to point a finger at government incompetence, which brought about a brush with Jesse Jones, Secretary of Commerce, that vastly amused the Washington press.

A *Post* editorial had ascribed the wartime rubber shortage to Jones's mishandling. The ambitious Jones, it was charged, had tried to be czar of more government operations than he could manage, and couldn't do justice to any of them.

Furious, Jones grabbed Meyer, whom he spotted in the Willard Hotel, and shook him until his glasses fell off.

Meyer had just about gotten himself in position to punch the tall Texan when friends grabbed his arm—a good thing for Jones, since Meyer had taken boxing lessons from heavyweight champion "Gentleman" Jim Corbett.

The story did not make the *Post* but was gleefully seized by the *Star*.

Truman was a great supporter of Meyer, as Meyer had

supported Truman, and appointed him as the first president of the World Bank, a job he left after a few months.

Earlier, after a career as a financier, he served on the Federal Reserve Board and was the first chairman of the Reconstruction Finance Corporation among other high posts.

As Truman's years ran out, Meyer broke from his usually neutral stand and declared for Eisenhower, saying, "The very air of the nation's capital is poisoned with scandal and corruption."

When Kennedy and Johnson came into office, the *Post* was closer to the throne than ever before. By now, Philip Graham, Meyer's son-in-law, had inherited Eugene Meyer's mantle. Meyer had died in 1959 at the age of eighty-three.

Katharine Graham, current Chairman of the Board of the *Washington Post*, is basically so shy a person that it is hard to imagine that she is chief executive of one of the world's largest news media empires.

She didn't set out to have it that way, and would have been content to live in the shadow of her dashing husband, Phil Graham, former publisher, the rest of her life.

Some say the irony is that Philip Graham wanted power so much that it drove him to madness, and that she wanted it so little that she hid from sight, yet was forced to become one of the most powerful women of the world.

In Washington newspaper world, Katharine is given much sympathy for the abusive way she was treated by her husband in his last tumultuous years.

A further irony is that when Katharine Meyer first fell in love with the handsome, charismatic Philip Graham, he made it clear that he wanted nothing to do with her wealth. He wanted to make it on his own.

But Eugene Meyer took a liking to Phil and literally forced him into the management of the paper. Meyer knew talent when he saw it and Phil was truly talented.

It may well be that Lyndon Baines Johnson owed his presidency to Phil Graham. Phil claimed it was true and the story is told that at the 1960 Democratic Convention Phil had the brainstorm of telling Kennedy he must pick LBJ for vice-president.

At that point Johnson had said he would take the presidency or nothing. "The vice-presidency," he had sneered, "is a good place for a young man who needs training in politics."

When Phil had convinced Kennedy that Johnson would be a good man because he could carry the South, there was still the problem of getting Johnson to accept—Kennedy was sure LBJ would turn it down.

Phil was adamant and insisted that if Kennedy turned on enough charm and spoke soothing words, Johnson would break down and say yes.

As it turned out Phil was right, but his take-charge attitude in a campaign that really wasn't his own, or even his business, may have been a symptom of mental illness. Graham was diagnosed a manic-depressive. During the 1960 convention at Los Angeles, fortunately for LBJ, he was in the manic swing of the cycle.

Later came a downswing, followed by more ups and downs, until even Kennedy, busy as he was, became alarmed and started calling mutual friends to find out what they thought and what could be done to help Phil.

Graham was subject to great fits of temper in some of his mood changes. He would even call the President to lash out at him for something JFK had done that publisher Graham disapproved.

Once, on such an occasion, Kennedy tried to sidetrack him, and Graham became furious. "Do you know who you are talking to?" he demanded of the President. At that moment his mental condition was such that in his mind a publisher far outranked a mere President.

JFK, understanding and sympathizing, did not hang up but gently chided him, saying, "Well, I'm sure whom I'm talking to is not the real Phil Graham, who is my friend."

Katharine, too, had to exercise forbearance when he lashed out at her, even in public. But the unkindest blow was when her husband moved out early in 1963 and went to live with a pretty young secretary.

Phil took his sweetie to Paris and other posh places and frequently announced he was going to divorce Kay and marry his new love. But eventually the relationship fell apart and the girl left town.

No one realized that two great men were fast approaching tragic deaths—Phil Graham and Jack Kennedy. Graham had gotten so belligerent, distressed, and hyperactive that on and off he was committed to Chestnut Lodge, a private psychiatric institution in Maryland.

To show the sort of thing he did, at a publisher's

conference in Phoenix, Arizona, Graham started to make a speech but became so abusive of certain other publishers that he had to be restrained and flown back to Washington.

On August 3, a Saturday, the world looked just a little more cheerful to Katharine, his wife. Phil seemed to be himself again.

He had been institutionalized again on June 20, but his doctor had felt he was so much better that he could go with her to their farm in Virginia for a weekend. It was going to be fun. Katharine drove. The servants all welcomed Phil home to Glen Welby.

They hadn't even finished making all their plans for the weekend. Katharine went up to her room to freshen up, leaving Phil downstairs. Suddenly a shot rang out. Graham had killed himself. He had been only forty-eight, a friend of presidents and Cabinet officers, possessor of lavish estates, cars, horses, servants. Not to mention a loving and forgiving wife.

It didn't make sense. And three months later Jack Kennedy met death at the end of another bullet—and that didn't make sense either.

Into the breach came Ben Bradlee.

Even before friend Jack Kennedy was elected President in 1960, Bradlee secured his position with the *Washington Post* owners for all time. He was with *Newsweek* when he had his brilliant brainstorm.

He engineered the sale of *Newsweek* to the *Washington Post*, his old alma mater. After that coup he could name his job. He chose to be Washington bureau chief of *Newsweek*, helping to build the magazine into a stiff competitor to *Time*.

After Graham's breakdown and suicide, Katharine grew more and more dependent on Bradlee, whom at first she admits she didn't even like.

Necessity made her take another look and she now found him a strong brain and shoulder to lean on. In 1965 she named him deputy managing editor and managing editor a few months later.

Ben took over from Ed Friendly, the former managing editor, who was shuffled into a foreign assignment, in what some Friendly fans considered a very *unfriendly* manner.

True, Ed had been permitted to choose his assignment but he had been hurried on his way.

Today the most talked about editor in Washington does

not like to talk about himself. Ben Bradlee, now executive editor of the *Washington Post* is given much of the credit for making it one of the greatest newspapers, perhaps the greatest, in the country. He likes to quote his predecessor, Russ Wiggins, on the subject: "Editors should be off the stage in the audience."

Even though he tries to maintain a low profile, everything he does is observed. For example, the reporters would claim they knew how he felt about a person by where he took him to lunch. If he liked the person, he took him to the posh Madison Hotel across the street. If he didn't give a damn what the guest thought, he took him to the lunchroom bar, Durty Annie's next door.

Everything he says or does is duly passed along in the trade, cherished and saved to tell to editors back in the hinterlands. There is the famous story told of the way he answered some complaint against the paper that came from Pat Moynihan, then working at the White House. Bradlee sent over a note saying, "You are picking fly shit from the pepper with boxing gloves."

His language is often quoted and judged by some to be among the most profane in Washington, and also the most elegant, when he so chooses.

The Watergate reporters Carl Bernstein and Bob Woodward, in their book *All the President's Men*, attest to this and report how he told Woodward early in the investigation. "Our cocks are on the chopping block now and I just want to know a little more about this."

Bradlee was even tougher on Reed Irvine, a columnist for *Washington Weekly* and chairman of the Washington-based AIM—(Accuracy in Media), who sent several letters to the *Post* protesting that the paper was failing to cover certain early reports of genocide in Cambodia.

Bradlee shot back a letter calling Irvine "a miserable, carping, retromingent vigilante."

"I had no idea what he meant," Irvine told Fran Leighton "until I checked and found he was accusing me of urinating backwards. I framed the letter and hung it on the wall."

Bradlee is a dropout from the field of fiction writing and actually took a course in fiction under James T. Farrell, the author of *Studs Lonigan*.

Unfortunately, he didn't hang in long enough to find out if he had the stuff of which novelists are made and grabbed a job as copyboy at the *New York Times* for thirty dollars a week in 1945. He ended up working in the paper's library rather than hustling copy,. So intrigued did he become with newspaper writing that he used his savings and money borrowed from his family to buy into a newspaper in New Hampshire.

His first job at the *Washington Post* was as police reporter at eighty dollars a week. "But if you want to know what I'm earning now, I'm not telling," he says.

Bradlee had a fatal flaw in those days—he couldn't take notes fast enough. Ben Gilbert, his boss, advised him to study shorthand, so he went to a secretarial school and learned speedwriting.

The speedwriting came in handy. He once risked his own neck to climb out on the top floor window of the Willard Hotel, across the street from the National Press Building, to record the complete conversation between a man threatening to jump and the policeman who was trying to save him. That earned him his first by-line.

Reporters point to Bradlee's career as proof that you sometimes have to quit your newspaper in order to get ahead on that same paper. Bradlee was fed up with police reporting. He had written such powerful stories that once a police chief had spit in his face. Yet he could get no further. He managed to get a job as press attaché for the American embassy in Paris. It was there he met Art Buchwald, still his closest friend.

What is Ben Bradlee really like? He's hard to describe because, according to those who see him most often, he is seldom twice the same. Sometimes he looks a bit seedy, like an old-time police reporter. Once he had on such a loud suit that someone mistook him for a gambler.

Romantic-minded females see a resemblance to tough James Cagney at his prime. Women in the *Post* newsroom have been known to sigh at the sight of his biceps flexing as he works in rolled-up shirt sleeves in his glassed-in office. He has earned those biceps the hard way—chopping wood and doing other labor at his West Virginia retreat.

He works at physical fitness with a desperation born of having had a bout with polio when he was a youngster. He and another classmate were struck with the dread disease. The other boy died.

Since it is known that he was Jack Kennedy's next-door

neighbor in Georgetown, when Kennedy was senator, many want to know if he talks much about his old friend and neighbor. As a matter of fact he is careful not to appear to be bragging about his close friendship and seldom refers to JFK, even though he did write a very interesting and elucidating book about him, entitled *Conversations with Kennedy.*

One insight to Bradlee is that though he cares little what is written about him, he was hurt when an article in *Esquire* said that he had forced people on the *Post* to buy his book.

"It's just a silly point—not true," he told Fran Leighton. "The *Post* buys wholesale, books that are authored by our reporters, and the authors autograph the books. They can be bought at the wholesale price by anyone on the staff who wants them. My book was treated like any other."

It is hard for those who know Benjamin C. Bradlee as a tough-talking editor to reconcile him with the fellow who studied and enjoyed Greek and poetry at Harvard. He handles quotes from the classics just as well as he handles scatology.

And that middle initial C., incidentally, packs some quaint history. As mentioned earlier, it stands for Crowninshield, a family name which dates back to 1864, when Ben's great-grandfather married a member of the Boston Crowninshields. One Crowininshield served in President Madison's Cabinet. The best family story concerns Ben Bradlee's wealthy great-great-great-grandfather, Josiah Bradlee, whose untimely death at the age of eighty-two is chronicled in the *Proceedings of the Massachusetts Historical Society.*

Because of his wealth, Josiah could afford to have servants to warm the seat of the outdoor privy at the family home. As the *Historical Society* tells it:

"A servant sent to warm the seat of the privy behind 142 Tremont Street, in preparation for his master's visit, carelessly left the warming pan within the building, which was so airtight that Josiah Bradlee succumbed to the charcoal fumes and died there."

Of course Bradlee has enemies among newspeople who have severed their connection with the *Post*—but it would be a miracle if he didn't. Some say he is like a Roman potentate pitting two gladiators in the arena to fight until one is mortally wounded.

They seem to feel that Ben Bradlee gets his jollies from seeing fierce competition among members of the staff. Even the

Watergate pair, Bob Woodward and Carl Bernstein, have indicated that they too were nudged toward competition but managed to become a cohesive team in spite of it.

To give the devil his due, Washington newspeople generally agree that without Ben Bradlee, there would have been no Watergate exposé on the dimension which caused a president to resign from office, for the first time in history. "It took an editor with balls of iron to stand up against the pressure that was being exerted on the *Post* by Nixon's White House to call off the investigative dogs," one journalist said. "The White House was trying to intimidate Bradlee and his boss, publisher Katharine Graham, by hinting that their TV licenses could be revoked."

Bradlee also deserves credit for okaying the exposé of the Pentagon Papers, which, for a time, were stashed in his house. But though Bradlee has the power of life or death over stories, he does not mix into editorial policy and he lets the editors thrash it out themselves.

His type of control is simply to wander around the newsroom several times a day, seeing what's going on, letting writers and editors talk things through with him.

Balancing the bitter things said about Bradlee, is the comment that he is a regular "Gentle Ben" in showing concern for reporters who become ill or have personal troubles. Also, Bradlee supporters claim that the competitive attitude in the newsroom forces every writer to do his very best and fight for space on the newspaper. Though *Post* reporters may gripe about the tension they work under and the stories they write that get cut to ribbons or thrown to the winds, they are the most envied newswriters in Washington and their pay scale is the highest.

As of this writing, as Bradlee told Fran Leighton, "Our average reporters make $475 a week under the current old contract, but under the new contract they will be making $525 and more."

Of course the top reporters and columnists get considerably more.

Though Bradlee may use locker-room language and drive reporters to excessive work, he prides himself on the fact that he doesn't scream. "I don't lose my temper. People can tell when I'm angry, but I don't explode. I take out my energy on physical exercise over the weekend in the woods."

A different sort of person is Bradlee's new publisher, Donald Graham, son of Katharine. Donald is quiet and low-key. He worked his way up in the paper in various departments, including sports. For a time he was a Washington cop to learn about the town. Donald did not pause to sample Bradlee's job but recently jumped to publisher.

What took him so long—he's all of thirty-three? As his mother says, "Donald felt ready for the job long ago, but I didn't."

11/The Battle of the Sexes

The battle of the sexes has ranged over Washington pressdom. As the angry woman said in a take-off on Churchill's impassioned speech, "We shall fight them on the streets of Washington; we shall fight them in the newsrooms, and we shall storm them in their Club."

To reconstruct the Washington scene before women's lib, it is necessary to see what *was* going on in newspaper offices.

Casey Jones, managing editor at the *Washington Post*, was hell on wheels when it came to romance in the city room. He would rather have an editor walk naked through the city room than have him embark on even the most harmless flirtation.

When a city editor dared marry a *Post* reporter, Jones never recovered from it and would start cursing whenever anyone reminded him of that day of infamy. That was the situation when a young and beautiful graduate of the Columbia School of Journalism with a Master's degree came to see the famous Casey Jones. She told him her background. She asked for a job.

Casey listened coldly, paid not the slightest attention to her proud recital of her training in journalism and said, "We don't want any romance around here."

He hadn't even bothered to find out her name—Virginia Imlay.

Miss Imlay leaped up, furious, and stomped out of his office. She went directly to the office of her father, Charles Imlay, a noted Washington lawyer, legal scholar, and linguist.

Imlay needed a cane to get around because he had been afflicted with polio. But when she told him her version of her mistreatment at the hands of the male chauvinist pig, he became so incensed, he offered to go to the *Post* and beat the devil out of Casey with his stick.

Somehow the confrontation never came about and Virginia sidestepped the whole problem of chauvinism by going to work for Ruby Black, who had a news bureau for Wisconsin newspapers.

She later became Washington correspondent for *Barrons*, writing financial news, and eventually worked for the *Wall Street Journal.*

Virginia's career as well as what she thought of Casey Jones was well known to the Press Club members because she married INS correspondent Felix Cotten—thus confirming Casey's fears that she was indeed the kind of troublemaking female who could disrupt a city room.

If you believe the movies, sleek newswomen are forever risking their virtue to coax secrets out of men. It has been true to some extent.

Employing beauties to charm statesmen is an old ploy with mixed results. An O'Henry story told how a lady lobbyist wangled a postmaster appointment, only to find it was for the wrong town.

The persistence of news lassies goes back to the very first occupant of the White House. When John Adams swam in the Potomac, he didn't have a chance when a female reporter sat on his clothes till he granted an interview.

For my own part, I have always found the flashier types effective. I once hired a high-octane news gal named Celeste to prowl Capitol Hill for aviation news.

She swished about in a leopard coat, a dangerous animal as she herself said. When old Josiah Bailey, Senate Commerce chairman, took his daily nap, she was the only one he would receive as he lay on his couch uttering Bible quotes and information.

Her sister Rose was horseback riding with General George Marshall, Army Chief of Staff, on the Sunday morning of Pearl Harbor.

Celeste was chased around a desk by Congressman Andrew Jackson May, House Military chairman, who later went to jail. Hunting bigger game, she met and married the elderly chiarman of Pan American Airways, blossomed into mink and diamonds, and became a wealthy widow.

In my time, the more luscious girl reporters were the protégées of editors and publishers who did not want to be lonely on visits to Washington. Those hired by Cissy Patterson, flamboyant publisher of the *Washington Times-Herald*, were considered U.S. Choice.

A friend of mine, George Stone, an Ohio manufacturer, missed getting a high federal post due to one of these ambitious young protégées. George was slated to be named assistant Secretary of Commerce for Air. In Washington about the job offer, he shared a hotel suite with an oil magnate.

The Texan brought in a lady writer. George retired to his room. Next morning his friend's door was closed. The woman's purse and gloves were on a table outside. She came out and engaged in what George thought was just a polite conversation. Who was he and where was he from, she asked innocently.

Her premature story spoiled his appointment because as is well known, presidents hate to be scooped. A bit later, George was killed in a flight he would not have made had he gotten the job.

One of the worst male chauvinists in Washington newspaperdom was Scotty Reston, *New York Times* bureau chief. He once wanted the talented *Washington Star* reporter Mary McGrory on his staff but when he told her she would also have to learn to operate the switchboard mornings, she quickly lost interest in Reston and his "kind" offer.

She went on to win a Pulitzer Prize in 1975 for her incisive and what the judges called her "trenchant commentary."

Bess Furman, who did write for him was confined to doing stories considered "women's topics"—the First Lady, education, and health.

When Bess retired, Scotty hired another talented female writer, Marjorie Hunter, for the same assignment. Only in his final days as bureau chief, before he switched to writing his column, did this obdurate sexist permit more than one woman among his reporters.

Felix Cotten remembers when the battle of the sexes centered on placing a ladies' rest room in the Senate press gallery:

"This was a hotly contested issue," Felix recalls. "The male reporters in charge of the standing committee argued that it was not necessary; women were fully capable of marching down the hall to the public powder room.

"Some said that women reporters were already too aggressive and this would only encourage them—if they had their rest room in the press gallery—to hang around after they got their work done.

"As I recall, when the vote came up among those who

voted against the female 'invasion' was Hutch, the INS bureau chief, my boss."

When the furious ERA women marched on the Capitol of the United States, Sunday, July 9, 1978, led by Bella Abzug, Gloria Steinem, and Congresswoman Margaret Heckler of Massachusetts, to demand more time to get the Equal Rights Amendment passed, a little knot of National Press Club members reminisced about earlier groups of angry women—suffragettes and prohibitionists.

After expressing amusement that the 1978 marchers were wearing white dresses for purity and carrying banners proclaiming "Men of Quality Are Not Threatened by Women of Equality," Felix Cotten, the senior member among them, was the only one who could speak of personally being assigned to cover activist women of the past, and his story was applauded by every chauvinist.

The story goes back to the early thirties when Cotten was a cub reporter for the *Washington Post* sent out to interview a group of "angry, aggressive women who had come to Washington to demand that the Army and Navy be used to enforce prohibition."

Felix recalled, "Carrie Chapman Catt was in charge of the big rally in one of the large hotels. Pressure was being brought to bear to have a resolution passed that cocktails not be served at parties. But I noticed that Miss Catt failed to bring the resolution up for a vote.

"So afterward I went over to her and said, 'Miss Catt, your women wanted a resolution that cocktails not be served at parties, why didn't you put it up for a vote?'

"Miss Catt looked at me with the tolerance a teacher has with a thickheaded child and said, 'Well, we can't upset our Washington hostesses.'"

The men fell to discussing how the story would have been handled today and how Madame Catt would have been ripped to shreds for this show of hypocrisy. "What had Felix done?" they demanded to know.

"Well," he drawled in the Mississippi manner that has never left him, "now I would, of course, write the story telling what she said and pointing out the hypocrisy of her stand. But in those days men—even male reporters—were kind to the ladies. So I just never put that in, or anything else that might be unchivalrous."

Until the female reporters learned the vernacular of men, they hadn't a chance of being treated as equals. I doubt, for example that this could happen with today's sophisticated women. An editor had sent a girl reporter to do a story on some school and she wrote, "During the lunch hour, the girls go over to the boys' gym and play with the boys' tools."

This gaffe was caught at the desk, but the original became the only school story in history to be special reading at the Men's Bar at the National Press Club.

Considered far more choice was the item written by a girl who was assigned to do some story on gardening. She toured the town diligently and wrote, "Secretary of State Cordell Hull has the biggest aspidistra in Washington."

Jesse Jones, chairman of the Reconstruction Finance Corporation, was famous for the stories with which he ended his press conferences. No women attended. His offerings were crude and were called "Texas tales" by the reporters.

One day to everyone's surprise Betsy Yeager of the *Wichita Beacon* was sent to cover the RFC press conference. At the end of the conference, the men shuffled around a little tentatively expecting a story, yet very much aware of *la dame* Yeager.

Betsy spoke up innocently and said in her sweetest voice, "Mr. Jones, I understand that you tell some very interesting stories at the conclusion of your press conferences. Won't you tell us one?"

Jones looked at her and his mouth fell open but nothing came out. For once he was stumped. As the reporters explained to Betsy with relish as they walked out, "You ought to know, Betsy, the man doesn't know any clean stories."

Ruth Hagy was part of the battle of the sexes in the TV media. As she tells the story, "In 1956, ABC-TV asked me to attend both national political conventions in Chicago and L.A., and assigned me to work the floor with the male reporters. No woman TV reporter had ever before worked on the floor so I was not permitted on camera.

"I set up the interviews and then a man took over. Finally, Speaker Sam Rayburn complained to the news director on the phone and said, 'Let the little lady go on with her interview. She is quite able to ask the right questions and is prettier too.'

"And that is how the big breakthrough came. No other

network had ever had a woman's face on the floor of a political convention. Pauline Frederick was in the booth and did commentary for NBC for both radio and TV. That was it.

"By 1960 at the next convention, every network had many women reporters working the floor and they have done so ever since."

For the flavor of what it was like to be a woman reporter in Washington before women's lib, a great raconteur is Winzola McLendon, known to her friends as Winnie, for many years a women's page writer at the *Washington Post.*

"If a woman was the subject of a story, the *Post* sent a woman to cover it. Some of the best stories were written on the women's page," Winnie recalls.

"When Francis Gary Powers, the U-2 pilot was shot down over Russia, the *Post* learned that his wife had come to Washington to go to the Russian embassy and plead for him. The *Post* called me at home and told me to rush downtown to cover this story. A new reporter, Judith Martin, was to stand outside the embassy until Mrs. Powers arrived.

"She had instructions not to speak to Mrs. Powers but just follow wherever she went and phone the paper to tell where she was and I would go there. Eventually I found myself in the Statler Hotel on the ninth floor. Judy pointed out the room she was in.

"But what you won't believe is that Judith, being new but not shy, had ordered room service sent to the hall of the hotel and her food had arrived. I knocked on the door and Mrs. Powers's attorney comes out. I'm saying, 'I want to talk to her,' and he is saying 'Absolutely no. There will be no exclusive interviews.'

"This gave me an idea and I changed my tactic and said, 'I agree, she absolutely *should* hold a press conference.' The lawyer went back in to discuss it and came back saying Mrs. Powers thought that was a good idea.

"I looked at my watch and realized that if they had the press conference too soon I would outsmart myself and be scooped by the *Star.* So I said to him, 'On this press conference you need time to do it properly and it takes time to get it on the wire so I advise you to have it at four o'clock.'

"Back he went to discuss that and while I'm waiting for an answer, all at once here comes the house detective. He has been informed about the hall room service which has been interpreted as meaning that someone is soliciting.

"So I'm telling him that I'm not soliciting and hoping that the lawyer won't hear this inside. The detective is making sounds like he is throwing me out.

"Suddenly, Judy, who is wandering around eating her sweet roll, comes back around the corner, and I am trying to motion her to get out of sight so she won't be thrown out too.

"Unfortunately, just then a door opened. As I waved at Judy, a man stepped out of his door and thought I was waving at him. The detective turns in time to see the man waving back, a very friendly wave. Now the house dick is really angry because he has caught two of us and he's about to drag me out.

"When all else fails, try anger. I said, 'Look, I'm with the *Washington Post* and if you lay a hand on me, my paper will sue Hilton for everything he has. You call Bill Rolle, your publicity man, and he'll tell you who I am.'

"The detective did call him and Rolle came and rescued us. Ever since, he has never failed to ask me whenever we meet if I've done any soliciting lately."

Judith Martin has come a long way from the time she was slinking in the Statler corridor trying to stay out of sight. Today she does a much read, nicely humorous column syndicated by United Features and appearing in the *Washington Post*, entitled "Miss Manners"—illustrated with Victorian sketches of refined young ladies and with comments on the mores of then and now, speaking of herself in third person.

In one column, Miss Manners talked about the new practice at the Carter White House of giving receptions for money   renting the place to organizations at five to fifteen dollars a head like a hotel ballroom, but with the added attraction that "the package always includes a welcome from either the President or the First Lady." Judith reports that several associations have already availed themselves of the opportunity and tongue-in-cheek discusses the nicety of it.

"Miss Manners does not mean to suggest that a president who won four years of White House residency, fair and square, does not have the right to invite whomever he wishes, at so much a head..." but she felt such a guest had certain privileges for which he was paying. He should no longer have to observe protocol in having to stay until after the President has left the party. And "He would certainly feel free to mention politely any deficiencies in the establishment."

Miss Manners came to the attention of the Press Club bar gang when she answered the question: "What is your opinion of women who nurse their babies in public?"

The acidulous answer: "Miss Manners is against the public nursing of babies or anyone else."

When Winzola McLendon, who recently wrote a book about Martha Mitchell, *Martha*, was with the *Washington Post's* women's section, she was delighted to receive an invitation to a party at the Russian embassy in honor of Prime Minister Khrushchev.

She was pleased to learn that a similar invitation had not been given to any of the political reporters or State Department staff who were covering the State visit of the Russian leader during the Eisenhower administration.

"I figured," Winnie told Fran Leighton, "that I was asked because I had now and then written about their military attaché in my Sunday column. But the world desk at the *Post* was furious and wanted me to give up my invitation.

"They practically said I had to, though I protested I would not. I told them, 'You can't transfer it anyway.'

"They said, 'Call the embassy and tell them you can't make it and can someone from the world desk go in your place.'

"I made the call but the embassy wouldn't transfer it and the *Post* had to let me go.

"As I walked past all the reporters on the sidewalk, I will never forget their dirty looks. I was early. The receiving line hadn't been formed. There were Nikita and Ambassador Gromyko talking together informally.

"Gromyko introduced me and said I was a journalist. Khrushchev said, through his interpreter of course, 'Oh no, a journalist could not be so attractive.' So we were laughing about this when all at once, whoever was supposed to let the receiving line start gave a signal and everything began to happen at once.

"I stepped back and wound up standing one step back between Khrushchev and his wife on the TV cameras. In fact, that night my husband had a call from his sister asking what in the world Winzola was doing in the receiving line with Khrushchev.

"But I didn't know or care. I was having a wonderful time and hearing everything that was said. Vice-President Nixon arrived and I was in the middle of that. I was moving right along with the honored guests to dinner when I realized the Russian security guard had stopped me with an elbow in my ribs. He looked straight ahead but he knew very well what he was doing.

"I spotted my military attaché friend, a general. He spoke in Russian and the security man didn't try to push me back again.

"Afterwards I went happily to my office prepared to write the 'tip of the iceberg' story but the world desk writers took all my important stuff and I ended up being permitted to write only a party story.

"Today, of course, no man would dare take a story away from a reporter just because she happened to be a woman. Thank goodness that couldn't happen today—or could it?"

Winnie received another invitation to the Russian embassy when Van Cliburn won the Russian piano competition. He gave a concert at Constitution Hall and the embassy gave a party for him afterwards.

"We thought it would just be a reception with a few drinks and a chance to take a few pictures so I was assigned a photographer and I was supposed to drink fast and get back to do my story.

"We were doing a big spread for the Sunday *Washington Post* and I had to have the copy in at three A.M. Marie Sauer, a great gal and great women's page editor was staying late to get my story edited and blocked in.

"All at once the photographer was gone. I was ready to leave the party when they opened the ballroom door and there was a big midnight supper, complete with place cards.

"Again, as with Khrushchev, I was the only reporter. Seated on the inside of the U-shaped table, I had a great view of Cliburn. The guests who included Mrs. Alben Barkley, widow of the vice-president, Mrs. Merriweather Post, the breakfast food heiress, and a lot of congressmen and senators.

"Caviar was served, and there was a vodka toast with each course. When I didn't come back the paper called and tried to find out what happened to me. The embassy would only say 'Private party,' and hung up.

"Time passed. The *Post* was alarmed and sent a copyboy to knock on the door of the embassy and ask if I was there. They slammed the door in his face. I was unaware and untroubled. Finally, we got through eating and drinking and Van Cliburn gave another concert. It was two A.M. when I got out.

"I rushed to the office and there sat a worried Marie Sauer. As soon as she saw me, fright turned to irritation. She almost shouted, 'Where have you been? Why didn't you call me?'

"'I couldn't,' I said innocently, hoping to soothe her. 'I was on the inside of the U.'

"Marie gave me a disgusted look, threw the pages at me and stalked out. She had dummied in the pictures and length of story and size of heading. I had the job of writing to fit the exact space for everything—my story, the head, the cut lines under the pictures. "If it had not been for the vodka, it would have scared the wits out of me but I made it by the deadline."

No matter what anyone may say, it is still not easy to be a female writer in fields previously closed to women. Marilyn Millstone writes in a previously all-male scientific field, turning out a biweekly newsletter, *Water Information News Service*. Some days in her office at the National Press Building, she all but despairs of getting the information that a male reporter would get in a hurry.

"I have been sitting here for two hours and not one of the six people has returned my calls. Because I have a soft, young voice, any number of secretaries have called me 'dear.'

"The complexity of the story I am working on is overwhelming me. I am trying to resist the urge to be simplistic. Still, since not an 'expert' in Washington seems to have a better grasp of the problem than I do, I am forced to figure it out for myself.

"It is not a good day for me. To residents of my hometown of Beaver Falls, Pennsylvania, I am somewhat of a folk hero, having gone to the nation's capital to pursue the glamorous life of a journalist. Having people be curt and rude to you over the phone or in person because you are a member of the press and a female is not glamorous.

"What glamour, if any, surfaces from all this is hard to see, but I suppose it comes from seeing one's by-line—the—hopefully—accurate spelling of one's name which appears above a story that is, one prays, accurate, unbiased. And which bears at least a passing resemblance to what you set out to write in the first place."

So why is she there waiting at the phone, beating her brains out and eventually getting the story? "I guess because of all the rudeness, curtness, and derision, there are moments when the story-within-the-story is revealed," Millstone says, "and the challenge. The pleasure of finding that secret is worth struggling with the torrent of vague press releases and tedious testimony that floods this town.

"Most important is that I have rarely been bored. The challenge remains to get the story in spite of everyone and everything—the battle of the sexes included."

Esther Van Wagoner Tufty is one of the most colorful members of the National Press Club and one of the first females to be admitted.

When she was sworn in, she recalled how furious she had been for many years because though she was owner of the Tufty News Service, which went to many newspapers, and hired male reporters, she had to stand by while her male employees took visiting editors to the Club for lunch.

"It was positively insulting," she said. "The worst thing that any male Club member ever said was what Bill Lawrence of the *New York Times* commented when someone asked him what he thought of having women admitted so they could use the Club restaurant: 'I don't mind sleeping with a newspaperwoman but I'll be damned if want to have lunch with her at my Club.'"

Esther is, I believe, the dean of the women journalists with offices in the Press Building. But she is seldom called by that name—everyone calls her "the Duchess."

Women were not admitted to the Club till 1971. Earlier there was a ladies' dining room near the entrance foyer. Then the East Lounge, on the other side of the ballroom, was used for this purpose. But ladies were not allowed in the Club proper till after 6 P.M.. They could watch Club luncheons with celebrity speakers from the balcony.

The Men's Bar, now called the Tap Room, remained a male citadel till 1971 and the cardroom in effect still is. If a lady entered the bar the conversation was likely to turn raucous till she fled, contrary to the rule of the Club: "On ladies' night, members will please refrain from using words ending in *ick, ock, it, unt, uck* and *ucker*."

There is a true story of how Molly Thayer, a particularly dignified female writer, barged into the Men's Bar, bent on ordering a drink as a challenge. The men looked at her in horror. One of them exclaimed, "Molly, you can't come in here. We don't even permit ladies."

There is a report that one time a woman ventured into the NPC cardroom only to make a hasty retreat when attacked by a man using his cane.

To the outside world the name of Mable Cornett might not ring bells, but among the legends of the National Press Club she is a star. When she retired from her awesome job as guardian and supervisor of the front desk, all the past presidents from miles around dropped everything to honor her at a big bash and remember their many adventures with her.

Every past president has taken Mabel's "abuse"—before, during and after being prez. Rank made no difference to her. She treated everyone alike. She was as adamant as any chauvinistic male about keeping women out of the hallowed all-male premises in the old days.

Members well remember Monday, August 17, 1970, when a young and exceptionally pretty girl reporter for the *Washington Daily News* thought the male foolishness had gone on long enough and attempted to bull her way through the Club lobby into the Men's Bar.

The story sounds best coming from Ann McFeatters herself. She quickly received the Mabel treatment. "A female voice followed me and stopped me with its iciness. 'Miss, you're not allowed in there.' Darting from her perch behind the cash register, Mabel fixed me with beady eyes and drew me out into the lobby.

"'Why not?' I asked, thinking my tone of phony innocence sounded pretty effective.

"'Women are never allowed in there. We discriminate,' she said.

"'Do you mean to tell me that as a reporter, I cannot go into the bar of the National Press Club and have a drink?' I asked.

"'With my bare face as a woman hanging out, I'm telling you,' she said. I think it was her no-nonsense voice and the feeling she had a dagger strapped to her cash register that stopped any further thought of a frontal assault on the bar."

It is only fitting that a female be permitted to tell her story as an eyewitness to the traumatic day in 1971 when the last great bastion of male exclusivity came tumbling down.

She was Vivian Vahlberg, a twenty-two-year-old firebrand who had just gone to work at the Washington bureau of the *Daily Oklahoman*. It was one of the first stories she covered for that paper.

She had come to Washington some months before as an intern and graduate of Northwestern University, and had distinguished herself in her job as intern by being the first person to use the word *shit* on an Amarillo, Texas, station—KGNC News. The station manager, who happened to be driving his car at the time, heard the news report and almost had a wreck.

"I watched the proceedings at the National Press Club from the balcony," Vivian recalls, "the only place women could sit during the historic debate on whether to admit women as members of the National Press Club—and whether, if admitted, they should also have access to the members' bar, poolroom and cardroom.

"The speeches were spirited. There were men who argued that the Club should be kept as 'the one place in Washington where men still wear the pants.' They said, with much emotion, that letting women in 'would destroy the tasty character of the sixty-three-year-old institution and its tradition of male journalism.'

"For a newcomer, such sentiments seemed surprising coming from a press which at the time was being roundly criticized as being too liberal by then-Vice-President Spiro Agnew. The funniest part of the debate was when one member, claiming that everyone knew 'the female of the species is more talkative than the male,' threw up his hands in horror, objecting on the grounds that letting women in would mean that 'we would be subjected to female chatter from morning to night!'

"At this point, the floor of the NPC ballroom, crowded with male members, had become so noisy that the chairman had to gavel them to order, over and over.

" 'Gentlemen, gentlemen,' he cried. 'The chair hopes this meeting can be carried out in a gentlemanly and orderly fashion. Gentlemen!' Many times during that debate he had to gavel down the members to keep them quiet. So much for *female* chatter!"

The vote was taken just as it is on Capitol Hill. Members poured into the aisles to be counted while someone kept the tally. The vote was 227 aye and 56 nay. There were wild shouts of hurrah.

Not from everyone. One man at that moment left the Club with a vow never to return—and he didn't. His case was considered special and all sympathy went to his resolve because he was also the man whose wife once came storming into the Club and into the Men's Bar—now the Tap Room—to march him out by the ear. We hope he has found another refuge.

A second vote did permit females into the bar and game rooms but women seemed to be content to leave cards and pool alone and concentrate on drinking.

When at last the walls were breached, some two dozen of the press, of assorted ages and sizes, were inducted into full card-carrying membership while the orchestra played, "Thank Heaven for Little Girls."

Fran Leighton was in the first batch, with a gardenia on her bosom and her long hair cascading. Sarah McClendon shed tears of happiness as she, who had made the greatest clamor about men barring women, was sworn in.

A photographer, who had missed Sarah's tears and had heard of them on his way out, came rushing back, but Sarah was all through crying. Indignantly, he demanded, "Sarah, cry some more!"

And she did.

Other new female members took it more philosophically—Helen Thomas of UPI; Jessie Stearns, Stearns News Service; Esther Van Wagoner Tufty, Tufty News Service; and Katharine Graham of the *Post*.

When Sarah almost immediately began to use her talents as an investigative reporter to delve into Club affairs, from the kitchen to the Board room, the results were explosive. She uncovered an auditor's report that pointed out the lack of security of liquor supplies and other violations of rules, and waved it in the Board members' faces.

However, except for Sarah, women's arrival on the scene went smoothly enough. The new female members survived even the most blatant passes from drunks in the Club. Every dire prediction has proved unfounded. Not only have they survived but they have reacted with class.

Linda Vance, the first woman chairman of the Board and one of the prettier reporters of the Washington Knight-Ridder Service was in the Club talking with a few of her friends when some drunken member kept interrupting with a laying on of hands.

The more sober members considered walking over to help Linda but soon decided it wasn't necessary, as they heard her tell the drunk, "Sam, I'm busy right now. If you want to maul me, why don't you come back later."

"Okay," he said cheerfully, not even insulted that she'd picked a name out of the air, and shambled off.

More and more women joined and appeared at lunchtime, an aid to the ever sagging revenues of the Club. Two were elected to the prestigious eleven-member Board of Governors. Life went on without incident until a special election over the sudden resignation of Club president Clyde La Motte. He quit in a dispute with his Board. Vice-president Kenneth Scheibel stepped up, leaving a vacancy in the number-two spot.

Enter Sarah McClendon on a white horse, galloping into the campaign. Knowing her propensity for work, I offered to help her get elected. To reach the scattered voting membership, I outlined a mail canvass and let her campaigners use my handily located office as a command post.

On the night the votes were counted, she phoned me to squeak joyously, "I won! I won!" My help was kept secret as after past misadventures, I shun any involvement whatsoever in any sort of club politics.

After Sarah won the vice-presidency, the fur began to fly. She approached her job with the zeal of a crusader and charged forth to police the Club, uncover any shenanigans, and find out why the Club wasn't making money.

Instead of backing her reforms, the Board members felt she was attacking their ability and integrity. It all boiled up in a special meeting of the full membership that Sarah had called to vote on removing Clyde LaMotte from the post of president of the National Press Building Corporation which he had kept after resigning as Club prez. He was ousted but the debate was so acrimonious that one old member moved to have Sarah expelled. That failed but the damage was done and it dampened her enthusiasm.

At one point, Sarah jumped up and said, "If LaMotte is so innocent why doesn't he prove it?" Don Byrne, a Board member, retorted, "Sarah, that isn't the way we do things in this country."

Clyde LaMotte will be remembered for arousing Sarah's ire, but he will also be remembered for starting the coveted 4th Estate Award, which has been won by such media stars as Walter Cronkite of CBS, John Knight of Knight-Ridder Service, Richard Strout of the *Christian Science Monitor*, Vermont Royster of the *Wall Street Journal*, James Reston of the *New York Times*, and Herb Block of the *Washington Post*.

Somewhere along the line the Club's Board of Governors censured Sarah for hostile behavior. It was a unanimous vote except for Sarah's. She did not appear in the Club for several years. Most of her criticisms turned out to be right but her explosions of Irish temper turned opinion against her and the Club continues to plod along unreformed.

In the bar, Sarah McClendon's name comes up with surprising regularity. The most often recounted story involves Sara and the AA. As Felix Cotten and others recall it, Sarah one dreadful day decided that all the habitués of the Press Club bars should be incorporated *en masse* into Alcoholics Anonymous.

"The members found out about it when an AA official called back," Cotten recalls, "and said, 'Who in the hell is that woman over there who wants to enroll the Club?'

"He explained that AA only accepts people who have shown an *individual* desire to swear off drinking. I believe it was President Ken Scheibel who got that call. 'I know, I know,' he said and quickly assured the man that he needn't worry about having his AA membership roll abruptly doubled or tripled."

So that was the story of women's entry into the National Press Club. But in all honesty, it must be admitted that the Women's National Press Club had already beaten them in opening its doors to the opposite sex by several days, and would even score an historic first by electing a male president—the kind of equality the National Press Club shows no signs of being ready for.

Louise Hutchinson of the *Chicago Tribune* was President of the women's club in the fateful year, leading the fight against female exclusivity. But the biggest fight was still to come—whether to change the name of the club. Many members felt it would be good for men's souls to become members of the *Women's* National Press Club, and poetic justice, as well. The majority opted to be gracious. After long and spirited debate over what to call the club so that male reporters' feelings would not be hurt by the feminine title, the name suggested by Fran Lewine of the Associated Press, was finally voted in—The Washington Press Club. It was hoped this would make it different enough from the NPC to avoid confusion.

But there still is confusion. The National Press Club occupies the thirteenth floor and the Washington Press Club has space on the fifth floor of the National Press Building and must exchange mail frequently, as well as redirect phone calls.

A slight air of condescension still exists on both sides but both clubs agree that the battle of the sexes has abated—at least on their turf.

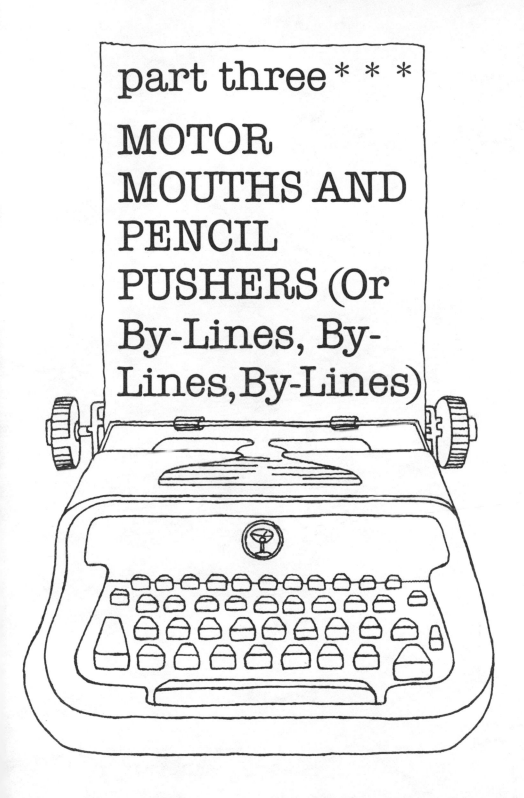

part three***

MOTOR
MOUTHS AND
PENCIL
PUSHERS (Or
By-Lines, By-
Lines, By-Lines)

12/Investigative Reporters

Bob Woodward and Carl Bernstein of the *Washington Post* are now the most famous investigative reporters. Their Watergate saga not only made them household words but brought movie millions. But they didn't invent this sort of journalism. Early in this century it was called muckraking. Nor does such reporting necessarily mean *macho* maleness.

One of the first female investigative reporters in Washington must have been May Dixon Thacker. She studied the diary of Gaston B. Means and wrote *The Strange Death of President Harding*, published in 1930.

May Thacker pursued Gaston Means right into the Atlanta Penitentiary where she sweet-talked the chaplain into introducing her to the man serving a three-year term for his part in the Teapot Dome misuse of public lands.

Somehow during that secret meeting, May convinced him that he should talk. When he emerged from prison on July 19, 1928, he was ready to spill all to her.

The story that May Thacker was able to piece together is a shocker still worth reading and points up the fact that the death of President Kennedy is not the only twentieth-century presidential death mystery still open-ended. According to Means, Florence Harding, the president's wife, killed Harding, not only because of the Teapot Dome scandal brewing and ready to pop, but because of her own fierce jealousy of Nan Britton, a beautiful blonde. According to May Thacker, Harding sent Nan money from the White House, as well as a fur coat for herself and one for the little girl who was supposedly his illegitimate daughter.

Such stories as Thacker dug up are enough to titillate any reader. Mrs. Harding trying to keep the existence of the child from becoming known to the public. Mrs. Harding ordering Means, a former investigator with the Bureau of Investigations of the Department of Justice, to keep Nan under surveillance. Mrs.

Harding ordering Means to intercept Nan on a train approaching Washington and arrest her on any pretence.

According to Thacker's account of what Means had learned, Florence Harding had slipped the president poison. Mrs. Harding had recapped it later in a private conversation with Means, saying she had been alone with the president, had sent the nurse out of the room, and had done what she felt she had to do.

If it is true, the poison must have been administered in several parts. First there had been "ptomaine" poisoning at Anchorage, Alaska, which the president alone suffered, even though he had eaten just what everyone else did. Then he had been taken back to the States where he got as far as a San Francisco hotel where he died, while Mrs. Harding was alone in the room with him. He was not taken to a hospital because it would alarm the public, but only to the Palace Hotel.

According to May Thacker, Florence Harding told Means she had been alone with the president "only about ten minutes." The quote from Mrs. Harding to Means allegedly continues. "It was time for his medicine. I gave it to him. He drank it." The president then suddenly opened his eyes wide and looked straight into her face. Mrs. Harding is quoted as having told Means, "I think he knew," and describing how he had turned his head away and after a few minutes she had called for help.

She had asked Means in this very private conversation how to avoid an autopsy. Mrs. Harding had told Means, May Thacker's book says, that she had no regrets, that had Harding lived twenty-five hours longer "he might have been impeached," but this way he had "died in honor."

Mrs. Harding maintained that even in Alaska, the president had been writing a letter to Nan Britton. He had pretended it was to someone else but she had intercepted it.

Mrs. Harding had also refused to permit a death mask to be made—a tradition in earlier days. The implication was that some of the poison—or whatever killed him—might remain on the mask lips.

Not all investigative reporters deal in political scandals or CIA cover-ups. Marian Burros will go down in history as the Paul Revere of modern times, riding through the countryside sounding the alarm about the food we eat—the harmful, the downright poisonous, or the merely *nonfood* food.

Marian, the food editor of the *Washington Post* and Emmy Award–winning consumer affairs reporter for NBC-TV, made waves on three important investigative stories.

She was the first to discover the banning of the dangerous red dye No. 2; the first to write about powdered wood pulp being added to one company's bread; first to reveal the presence of asbestos in talcum powder.

Even Ear, that rascally purveyor of gossip in the *Washington Star* finally heard of the crusading Marian Burros and wrote an item that had Washington—if not Marian—rocking with laughter:

> NUTRITIONAL FLASH. . . *Marian Burros, NBC's Foe of Junk Food, has been offered five figures by a baking industry lobbyist to pose with a Hostess Twinkie. Strictly platonic, Ear's sure, but is impressed anyway.*

Unstoppable Burros recently frontally attacked the food industry by writing a book, *Pure & Simple*, to help consumers prepare "nearly pure, additive-free meals."

More than that, her cookbook also teaches housewives how to save money by making their own convenience foods and storing them in the fridge, freezer, or on the kitchen shelf.

The *Washington Star* had a Pulitzer Prize–winning investigative writer long before the appellation was popular. That was Miriam Ottenberg.

She won the big one for a series of articles exposing used-car frauds, and went on to further glory. In 1963 she broke the Joe Valachi story.

She was the first reporter to write that the Mafia was doing business in the United States as the Cosa Nostra, and that an insider, Joe Valachi, was talking.

In 1962 Miriam made a splash with her first book, *The Federal Investigators*, which featured not only J. Edgar Hoover but all the other chiefs of agencies that protect the public.

Miriam once almost got stuck on the women's page, back in the forties. One day the managing editor, B. M. McKelway, called her in and sat, leaning back in his big swivel chair, puffing his pipe, as he surveyed her.

"What are you doing now?" he asked.

"I'm covering the police beat," she said.

McKelway nearly fell backward out of his chair.

"Do you like that?" he asked, incredulously.

"Very much," Ottenberg said, wondering what he wanted of her.

"Fine," he said, "you can go now."

Years later he told her that that day he had called her in to make her women's club editor. "I would have died in that assignment," she laughs, remembering.

Walter Riley is an investigative reporter who hates the name. "I follow the story wherever it leads," says the writer of the syndicated column "Dateline Washington." "The name investigative reporter infuriates me. Every reporter investigates the facts before he writes them if he is going to stay in business," Riley fumes. "It's just that some reporters spend a lot more time investigating, and I guess I'm one of them."

The life of Riley is a good example of how tough it is to be that kind of reporter and how brickbats can fly in both directions. During a series of his on a congressman, the congressman in turn investigated Riley and found a "criminal record," a fact that did not slow Riley down in the least.

Walter Riley is the pen name of Clyde Riley Wallace. His writing career began at the age of fourteen when he wrote fiction for *Dime Western* at $7.50 per story. "That was a hell of a lot of money in 1939," Walter says. "I didn't change my name to avoid the law. I used that pseudonym because I was afraid that publishers would be able to check out Clyde Riley Wallace and find he was only fourteen and not buy his stories."

Now his syndicated column earns him a tad more than his fiction for *Dime Western* and is distributed by Trans-World News Service.

The piece of reporting that resulted in the expo of his own legal problems of the past has become known as the Frasergate. It began with a column appearing in over a hundred papers headlined: "Congressman Fraser Refuses to Explain $47,500 Mystery Salary." To show how gently such things sometimes start out, this is the lead on Riley's first column:

> The financial records of the Clerk of the U.S. House of
> Representatives show that Rep. Donald M. Fraser
> (DFL–Minn.), chairman of the prestigious Subcommittee on

*International Organizations, has been involved in some rather
strange financial arrangements. The taxpayers are paying the
freight, and the only questions that remain are: "Who is being
paid, for what, and for whose political benefit?"*

Riley goes on to tell that a particular $47,500 salary "turns up as a
'payroll change' on Fraser's required monthly 'House Payroll
Certification Report.'"

Each column investigated the congressman's finances a
little further under such headlines as "Congressman Fraser Pays
Off Favored Witnesses with Contracts," the second story; "Crony-
ism Surfaces in House Probe Unit," for the third column, and
"Frasergate in the Making?" for the fourth.

The congressman did a little investigating on his side
and, as Riley tells it, "attacked my credibility by telling all who
would listen that Riley, known as Wallace, had a criminal record
from his youth and therefore his writing could not be reliable."

Also Riley charged that Fraser, who was seeking reelection, had placed "a news blackout against me on Capitol Hill as far
as his powerful subcommittee could reach."

Riley comments, "It was the news blackout that infuriated me. Attacking my credibility, exposing my criminal record, all
of that is fair game—truth must out. But the congressman knew
little of history—a news blackout to a reporter is like waving a red
flag at a bull.

"Incidentally, the criminal record had nothing to do
with guns or violence. It concerned a promissory note I hadn't paid
off. I was put in the pokey—a debtors' prison. The year was 1949.
You couldn't get away with that anymore—debtors' prisons are
out."

In spite of any blackout, Riley continued to investigate
the congressman's finances. It was a red-letter day when he was
able to write his fifth column headlined: "Congressman Fraser
Confesses Illegalities in Payroll: Will Make Restitution." This day
the story ran in three hundred papers and was also quoted by AP
and UPI. The lead, as it appeared June 14, 1978, read:

*Rep. Donald Fraser (DFL–Minn.) attorney and law school
graduate cum laude said he only just now found out that it is
illegal to pay his House office employees a year's salary in
advance. This was, of course, after the "Dateline Washington"
column brought it to his attention. Fraser said the "problem is*

*being corrected" and added: "the practice will be discontinued
in the future." He reassured that there was nothing to really
worry about, and full restitution would be made.*

Investigative reporters are always on the search for truth, says
Riley. "Anybody can go out and chase a fire, covering something
that's already happened. The trick is, when there is no news, to dig
and make news by finding out where it is hidden. Corruption in
politics, government, business. Exposing deceptive practices that
hurt the public. This is real reporting as far as I'm concerned."

Because a reporter is investigating something doesn't
mean that his publisher will print it. Some of Riley's columns end
up on the cutting room floor of timid newspapers, he says. What
troubles him is "the current attitude toward Communist activities
in this country. Anybody who writes about communism has trouble
getting editors to publish it as a result of the McCarthy stigma.
They say, 'Don't bring me any of that McCarthyism.'

"They are afraid to look foolish. Everyone on a newspaper desk shies away from the word *communism*. The *Washington
Post* and other papers have style books that indicate that better
words are *left wing, ultra liberal,* and *extreme leftist.*"

What is it like to be an investigative reporter? The only
trouble with it, says Walter Riley, is that everyone gets a little
nervous when you come around. Along this line Riley recalls what
happened after his stories had exposed Fraser's office finances. "As
a result of the stories," says Riley, "one of the candidates for Fraser's
seat, Washington Senators former owner Robert Short, had his
press aide call me. He congratulated me on the Fraser series and
asked for assistance in any other dirt I might have on Fraser.

"I said, 'Number one, I'm apolitical. Number two, I have
a strike against your boss too.'

"I paused and the press aide got very nervous. 'What's
the matter? What's wrong? What have you got on my boss?' I could
almost see him shaking in his boots. I laughed and said, 'He stole
the Washington Senators baseball team and hijacked them to
Texas. And, as if that isn't bad enough, he stole their name, and
now they're known as the Texas Rangers.'"

Incidentally, there were seven columns on Fraser and, to
complete the set, the final two headlines were: "Frasergate Continues," which told how "General Accounting Office officials have
confirmed they are exploring the idea of a 'full audit' of Fraser's

handling of the public funds," and, "Fraser's Raid on U.S. Treasury Stopped by Rep. Derwinski"—Derwinski being the powerful Representative Edward J. Derwinski, Republican of Illinois.

The thirteenth of September 1978 turned out to be unlucky for Congressman Fraser and the *Washington Post*. Fraser went to bed the night before thinking that he had won his Minnesota Democratic primary campaign. The morning *Post* of the thirteenth claimed him as the winner. But a little later Fraser had a rude awakening and the *Washington Post* wound up with egg on its face.

Businessman Robert Short, and not Fraser, had won the primary for the Senate seat formerly held by the late Hubert Humphrey.

Walter Riley's telephones began ringing in his National Press Building office and before the day was over more than thirty calls had come from reporters, editors, and publishers in Minnesota congratulating Riley for the part his columns had played in Fraser's defeat.

"The call I enjoyed most," Riley said, "was from Eric Nathanson, press assistant to Fraser. He told me, 'If there's anything we learned throughout all this, it's don't pick a fight with a reporter.'"

How true. Prior to the payroll exposure, polls showed Fraser ahead with a 72 percent voter preference.

Investigative reporter Walter Riley frankly admits that he now protects himself by burning all his papers after he has written his story.

"Police state tactics reminiscent of the Nazi era are now being employed against the press, and against churches," Walter says.

"Court decisions leave jail as the alternative for those clergymen or reporters who would defy court orders to reveal the names of persons who had confided information, under former guarantees of confidentiality to their newspaper or church.

"Though the May, 31, 1978, Supreme Court ruling stated that police have a right to conduct no-notice search warrant raids on news offices, as they did at the *Stanford Daily*, lawyers say this ruling would apply to churches as well.

"At any rate, I now feel that shield laws are necessary to protect newspapers in order to guarantee free flow of information to the press.

"The Supreme Court ruling in the *Stanford Daily* case has caused me to destroy or remove evidence of any kind or nature that would give access to or identify my sources.

"I have resorted to an intricate code identification for my unimpeachable and normally reliable sources. God help us! The Supreme Court has rewritten the First Amendment."

Is there enough protection for reporters in the law as it now stands or should there be new legislation?

Jack Nelson, who has become an expert on the subject through his own abuse at the hands of FBI and southern local law enforcement figures, does not want any new laws, unless it is simply a shield law that echoes the First Amendment.

Nelson holds that if the government is demanding that a reporter reveal his sources, "the reporter already has a First Amendment right not to reveal sources."

The best liked of Washington's investigative reporters among his colleagues, strangely enough, is this reporter from the *Los Angeles Times*, a place once known for its conservatism.

Yet Jack Nelson has broken icons. Instead of being booted from his newspaper, he has been boosted up into the position of chief of its Washington bureau.

There was no more hallowed icon than FBI Director J. Edgar Hoover and it took a feisty guy like Nelson to investigate the investigator and write a story showing him as incompetent and evil.

Hoover waged a vendetta against Jack Nelson, calling him a drunk and charging that he had gone around town spreading the word that Hoover was a homosexual.

John Lawrence, who was then bureau chief of the *L.A. Times*, stood firm and did not fire Jack, and Jack stood firm and kept on investigating Hoover, finding out, among other things, that the FBI had paid some $36,000 to set up two Ku-Klux Klanners so that the FBI could look good closing in and arresting them for planting a bomb in a Jewish home.

Around the Press Club it is said that anyone can take on J. Edgar Hoover now that he is dead, but Nelson gets their vote because he took him on when Hoover was alive.

Nelson has always lived dangerously. When he was just a beginning investigative reporter for the *Atlanta Constitution* he blew the lid on so-called respectable citizens in Georgia who were cooperating with gangsters involved in various forms of vice.

His series ended up with several dozen people under indictment, and young Nelson ended up with a very severe warning to get out of town and never come back.

Nelson survived to fight again and end up at the top of the heap of Washington's investigative reporters.

You can't tell me that reporters don't develop a sixth sense. This is hard to believe but it's true. In 1943, fully two years before the atomic bomb was tested in the New Mexico desert at Alamogordo, Arthur Hachten, night editor at INS—possibly with the help of his boss Hutch's radar mind—decided INS should find out what was doing in the field of atomic energy.

He assigned Frankie Music, who was a fresh young reporter at the Pentagon, to dig around and see if anyone was still working on that quaint notion of developing an atomic bomb.

Frankie dug and dug. And dug. She studied everything she could find, all of which was in the public domain. And when she had put all the pieces together after about three weeks of research, she came into the office and wrote her story.

The public had never even heard anything about an atomic bomb but with the bits and pieces she had, it seemed that there could be a very powerful explosive made of atoms and involving a chain reaction.

Hachten read her story and was much impressed. He felt it just needed a new lead that would give it a little zip and so he wrote something like this: "The United States is pushing forward with all haste to develop an atomic bomb in order to bring the war with Japan to a rapid conclusion."

All sensitive stories concerning the war were given for clearance to Byron Price, former chief of the Washington bureau of AP and head of the voluntary Office of Censorship.

The instant the story hit that office, alarm bells rang all over town. Price was sure some damn fool in government had leaked information and Frankie was interrogated and tailed by the FBI for three weeks.

The story was, of course, killed instantly, and poor Frankie was lucky she didn't land in jail. But in August 1945, when the atomic bomb dropped on Hiroshima, Frankie Music was some kind of heroine to the little group who knew what her kind of investigative reporting could piece together.

Sometimes credit is given for great investigative report- ing when in truth the scoop is actually a plum that falls into the reporter's mouth. That's the way the shocking news was uncovered that Governor George Wallace of Alabama planned to divorce his wife, Cornelia.

An anonymous caller directed station WSFA-TV to go to a certain Montgomery grocery store and look under some vegies. Under the greens was a copy of a divorce petition, which had not even been filed yet.

The whole trick of being an investigative reporter, some say, is making people confess things you only surmise. Jack Anderson and his staff have the technique down perfect. Anderson admits that he calls someone he is planning to expose and gives him "a chance to explain your side."

The other man, thinking Anderson has everything, starts blurting out his justification, and suddenly Anderson is learning much more than he originally knew of the story.

Sometimes Anderson and his men will invite a man to their office or other meeting place and do a squeeze play. Anderson will play the good guy, saying, "Let's not be tough. Let the man explain," while his staffer acts aggressive and mean.

The man ends up appealing to Anderson for understanding and spills out everything.

The difference between Anderson and his old boss Drew Pearson is that Pearson would go ahead and print a story before it had been completely checked out and confirmed by other people. His reasoning was that he didn't want to risk losing an exclusive.

Even with all his checking, Anderson sometimes has to make a retraction. Once an amusing situation developed in which the victim of an error pleaded with Anderson not to apologize.

What happened is that someone tipped off Jack that Donald Rumsfeld was having his OEO director's office extravagantly redecorated—naturally at the taxpayers' expense.

Anderson was even given the architect's designs for it. So he went with the story. It turned out that Rumsfeld had canceled the redecoration for exactly that reason—the high cost to the taxpayer.

Anderson immediately offered to print a retraction, but the director of the Office of Economic Opportunity told him to just forget it because a second printing would simply stir it all up again—and some people would still believe it.

Eric Ruff, Washington correspondent for the Donrey

Media Group, once went up to Jack Anderson, after Anderson had appeared on a National Press Club seminar for young reporters, to ask a question. "With your type of work," he began, "you question bureaucrats and their decisions. Should every reporter develop that cynicism?"

Anderson said, "Now wait a minute. Cynicism is unhealthy. Skepticism is healthy. It does not immediately condemn. It gives a man a chance to explain himself."

"That was an excellent bit of advice," Ruff recalls. "My respect for the man shot up. I don't have respect for pure muckrakers but I do respect investigative reporters.

"You've always got to be skeptical as a reporter, but when you turn cynic, your whole perspective in reporting the story sours. You can no longer see the light at the end of the tunnel—everything is negative."

Jack Anderson is acknowledged to be the top investigative reporter of Washington—and possibly of all time. So it's interesting to see who works for him and whom he rates as tops on his staff.

According to Jack Anderson, Les Whitten is the best investigative reporter one could be—fearless, hardworking, and exercising good judgment. Not that staffers Joe Spear or Britt Hume are lacking in any way.

It is hard to say who will inherit Anderson's column, should Jack ever wish to retire. Each has a background quite different from the others. Les Whitten has the most varied of the three, and in a way, Jack is more emotionally bound to him because Les came to him just days after Drew Pearson died in 1969.

Les simply wanted to work for Jack in order to do stories in greater depth. He had worked as a police reporter for the *Washington Post*, had worked for Radio Free Europe, and had risen to be assistant bureau chief at INS, before it folded. He had even worked awhile for United Press.

But when Les came to see Jack Anderson, Jack at first discouraged him, claiming that Les needed too much money with all that experience, and was getting a little old to be starting out again.

What Whitten didn't know was that Anderson himself had been paid only a measly $14,000 a year by Drew Pearson.

But the men took a liking to each other and Les was hired at the age of thirty-nine.

Newspaper people are always curious to know more about the Anderson-Pearson story and what Jack paid to inherit the column.

The truth of the matter, according to Jack, is that he did not pay anything for it—but the story is a little more complicated than that. What happened is that Anderson got fed up with working for Pearson and never seeing his own by-line, so he quit the "Washington Merry-Go-Round" cold in 1954, without even a new job to count on.

This took courage because he had a wife and a growing family. Luckily he was able to get a job as Washington correspondent for *Parade* magazine, the Sunday supplement.

Eventually Pearson tried to get Jack back, because he needed his kind of dogged dependable investigative reporting. Jack pondered what to do but Pearson said the magic words that would bring him back to the fold—he promised that Anderson would inherit the column.

Joint by-lines of Pearson and Anderson became commonplace and Jack had the ego satisfaction he had yearned for.

When Pearson died Jack could have taken over and let it go at that, since there was no contractual obligation to Drew's widow, Luvie. But Jack, with his own moral code, decided to send her a check every month.

He still does—amount unknown. Possibly the world will never know just what is on that check. At this writing it is a closely held secret.

Joe Spear, who moved over into top back-up position when Whitten took a leave of absence to write fiction, came to Anderson by way of the public school system—he had been a discontented high school science teacher in Maryland.

Deciding to switch to journalism, Joe went back to college, moving to Washington to enroll at Georgetown University. It was clever of him to pick Jack Anderson as guest speaker on campus and that was how they first got together.

Anderson happened to mention to someone else in Joe Spear's hearing that he was looking for someone to write for *Parade*. Joe quickly asked for the job and later became part of Anderson's whole operation.

The story of Britt Hume is that he was discontent with his job at the *Baltimore Sun* because it was not one that permitted him to do really hard-hitting investigative reporting. He had even gone on his own to write a book revealing the results of his investigations of what United Mine Workers union officials were doing with the miners' union dues.

With Jack's operation, Hume is in his natural element, having complete freedom to tell it like it is. Since Anderson has no advertisers to placate, he doesn't worry about what he reveals as long as it is true.

Bruce Keidan of the *Philadelphia Inquirer* is an investigative reporter who spends almost full time traveling. He goes wherever a story takes him. Though *Knight-Ridder* Bureau has expert reporters they could send out to get the information he needs in Washington, Keidan spends considerable time on Capitol Hill making his own contacts and gathering what he needs.

Bruce Keidan freely admits that this life of travel finally broke up his marriage and yet it's in his blood and he cannot stop. "My marriage survived twelve years. I have a child whom I have custody of for about a third of the year. Though he's only five, I take him traveling with me on some of my assignments."

At the Press Club Keidan reminisced with Frances Leighton about his favorite travel experience. "The Managing Editor called me in during the strike of the Baseball Players Association in the spring of 1972.

"I had just returned from spring training in Florida, as a matter of fact, and I had written myself out. He called me in and said, 'We're running your exclusive story on the strike in the Sunday papers.'

"I said, 'What story? I've written everything I know about the strike.'

"He said, 'Well, you better find out something that's new because we're already advertising your story.'

"So I packed and was on the plane in one hour to Chicago, where the baseball owners were. I got nothing. The week was moving along and the deadline was Friday for Sunday news. I was getting desperate. I had overheard that there was one player representative who hadn't voted for the strike in the secret ballot.

"That was Wes Parker of the Los Angeles Dodgers. So I called him in Santa Monica and said, 'I know you're the guy I have to see. Will you talk to me?'

"He said, 'If you want to come out, we'll sit down and discuss it.'

"I was on the next plane out of O'Hare bound for Los

Angeles, and I met with Wes the next morning.

"He is a very sensitive man, really bared his soul and told why his conscience had not allowed him to vote for the strike.

"I was elated. I had my story. I was the only reporter who knew he had abstained and why he did it. In triumph I called my sports editor in Philadelphia and said, 'I've got the exclusive.'

"He asked where I was. I said I was in Los Angeles and told him what I had.

"Later that day, when it was all over and I was still high with the excitement of my news break, I got the playback of how the managing editor had reacted, 'What? He's in Los Angeles? He couldn't have gotten the story by phone?'"

Bruce Keidan, incidentally, was nominated for a Pulitzer Prize on a Washington story, the same year Woodward and Bernstein won the Pulitzer for their coverage of the Watergate scandals. His series concerned the holy war between the Sunni Muslims and the Black Muslims, after the slaughter of a Sunni family in their Sixteenth Street home in Washington.

Keidan is also known for his in-depth stories about people in the news, such as his profiles on Wayne Hays and Howard Jarvis.

According to John C. Behrens in the *Typewriter Guerillas* less than one percent of America's newspeople can, in the truest sense, be labeled "investigative reporters." The total employed full time on such work might number in the hundreds for the entire country.

The reason they are so few is that few news organizations can afford them. A true investigative reporter might work months on a single line of inquiry with local expenses and perhaps large sums for long-distance calls and travel if the story is of more than local scope. And it might all come to naught.

On a report about drugs in Europe, *Newsday* employed as many as a dozen people for a year at a cost of $300,000. This won a Pulitzer Prize but it was at too high a cost. The investigative team was disbanded.

There are more lone investigators than teams. Although these men and women may not be loners by choice, the pursuit of guilty secrets must proceed cautiously. Typically, these muckrakers do not discuss anything they are doing with their news colleagues or with their own families.

Part of the job may involve long, tedious scrutiny of

financial records. In most cases, inside contacts are the key. A writer must find sources, win their confidence, and keep current with them through the years. It can be a day-and-night affair. Mysterious phone calls; secret meetings with people who could lose their jobs, or even their lives, if seen. And a writer must protect them at all costs, even at the risk of going to jail for refusing to name them.

The most famous informant was "Deep Throat" of Watergate, whose identity was known only to Woodward and Bernstein; not even to the top executives of the *Post*.

Threats and harassments await the digger who comes too close to hidden truth. It is no job for those of nervous temperament or with spouses who expect normal home lives.

Nor do most investigative reporters draw much more pay than other reporters. Yet those who have dedicated their lives to muckraking would have it no other way. Some are out for results; for action after they have blasted out wrong-doing. Some think their job ends with telling the story, let come what may. And we have a better country because of them.

Reams have been written about Bob Woodward and Carl Bernstein and how they hung in tough until they had ferreted out the whole of the Watergate story and the men involved, right up to the President.

But what other press people ask about most is what were these two characters really like before they were "Woodward and Bernstein."

The answer is that they were very *human* humans, with more than their share of foibles.

Bernstein had a habit of borrowing both money and cigarettes and liking to be seen in only the best and most expensive Washington restaurants.

One of the words used to describe him in those early days is *arrogant*. Strangely enough—or maybe not so strange— becoming a millionaire from book and movie rights helped gentle him down and made him a much more pleasant person.

Bob Woodward was a much more stable, or plodding, type of person. He had less flair and flash than Carl and less experience in reporting.

But he had demonstrated to his editors that if they sent him out to get a story someone else had failed to get, he hung on like a bulldog and didn't come back till he had it.

Bernstein, on the other hand demonstrated a real dislike for editors telling him what to do. From the beginning, he made sounds like an investigative reporter, wanting to bird-dog his own leads.

They were unlike in almost every way—even in looks, Woodward being considered a rather handsome devil, on the order of Robert Redford, who did indeed portray him. In their political leanings, Woodward was also more conservative.

But as they say in the newspaper business, whatever turns a reader on. .... And this combination in style and content did just that—turned the reader on.

Today, Bernstein lives in New York while Woodward remains in Washington, near his child and estranged wife.

Under their financial agreement on the paperback rights alone of *All the President's Men*, each of them receives $45,000 a year for five years—and that's only part of their financial picture.

Bernstein, a college dropout, who also had trouble buckling down to work long enough to finish high school, liked his old pose as a bit of a slob. But deep down he did care and he was driven by ambition. In fact, at the *Washington Star*, where he got his first taste of journalism as a copyboy for three years, he was known for his drive to learn as much as he could as fast as he could.

Getting a chance to become a reporter for the Elizabeth, New Jersey, *Journal*, Bernstein graduated from copyboy status and distinguished himself by winning the 1966 New Jersey Press Association's prize for a story he wrote.

Now he was ready for bigger things and he applied at the *Washington Post*. He wrote a series for the *Post* on slum real estate which was well received, but Carl was not happy when he was assigned to cover Virginia politics.

He felt it was a dead end, because who in Washington cares about Virginia politics?

Not too many did. That was certainly true. But because he was "expendable" he was available when the paper needed someone to help run down a puzzling break-in and robbery at the Watergate. He was brought in from the cold.

Serendipity worked in his case, to give Bernstein fame and fortune, just as it did for Bob Woodward. There are some in Washington social circles who say that serendipity worked in giving Bernstein a reward he hadn't looked for but it also worked in taking one away.

Bernstein and Woodward both met a beautiful and socially prominent girl of a fine Texas family, Frances Barnard, at the same time, and Bernstein flipped for her.

Francie, as she was called, went bicycling with Bernstein several times. But when it came to marriage, she flip-flopped and married his partner, Woodward, in a marriage that eventually came apart at the seams.

Bernstein nursed a singed ego and got married two years later, in 1976, to Nora Ephron, who wrote for *Esquire*. Bernstein too, found that marriage was not easy, especially to a fellow writer, even though he'd been down the marriage path before in a turbulent marriage to a *Post* reporter. At this writing all is well and the happy couple have a new child.

At the *Washington Star*, Ron Sarro was a major investigative reporter. It was he who first discovered that Agnew was in serious tax trouble. In fact, he was one of the reporters that Agnew subpoenaed to try to learn their source of information and silence them. Ron has a little smile of satisfaction as he recalls, "We were due in court the same day that Agnew resigned as Vice President and pleaded no contest to one tax charge. We were in court, of course, but the subpoena became moot."

During the "Koreagate" days Sarro was the only reporter from the *Star* covering the Korean investigation. He was the first to name the four congressmen who would be investigated by their colleagues for allegedly accepting money for favors.

One thing is missing today—a sense of pattern that corruption takes. Investigative reporters keep exposing corruption in specific cases but give no general idea of how the system works.

Lincoln Steffens, the pioneer muckraker, did this in his day. From his series on the "shame of the cities," he found that each was much like the others.

Once, in a lecture at Greenwich, Connecticut, he said he would prove that the local government was as corrupt as any other. Without a word about Greenwich, he talked of San Francisco, Pittsburgh, Minneapolis: How were votes bought? How did the political boss protect vice and crime? How did cities let their contracts?

As Steffens talked, Walter Lippmann, later a famed columnist, drew squares on a blackboard charting how graft was organized. At the end, Steffens asked, "Have I not shown that Greenwich is as corrupt as the places I have named?"

When the audience looked blank, he added, "Isn't this a

picture of the government of Greenwich?" Then there was laughter and applause as the truth sank in.

It would be a service if someone made a series of blueprints on how a weak or crooked congressman is financed and controlled; how an unscrupulous industry works to advance its interest in Congress; and items more sinister.

The public needs to know these things to combat them.

One doesn't have to be an old political pro to cover Capitol Hill. Christopher Bonner, called Chris by his friends, is barely thirty, yet he has been covering the Hill since December 1976, when he went there to size up the situation the newly elected Carter would face.

Chris, who works out of the Knight-Ridder offices in the National Press Building, is a regional correspondent and specializes in the Alabama and Georgia delegations in the House and Senate. He's the new breed of investigative reporter, who follows a story wherever it leads.

"I don't hang out much at the press galleries. Most of my leads come from walking around sniffing them out and then I come back to write in the National Press Building."

If the story he gets is hot enough it is one of those selected to go into the combine of Knight-Ridder, *Chicago Tribune* and *New York Daily News*.

One investigative job Chris Bonner is credited with helped open the whole question of Senator Herman Talmadge's finances. "I traced a land deal that he had inside information about. He knew there would be an interchange on an interstate highway in Georgia for several years before it was made public."

What does it feel like when you are dealing with a senator who knows you are writing nasty, though true, stories about him? "Let me say that I like Talmadge personally and I think that he is a very effective senator. But as a professional reporter I have grave questions about his conduct. I try not to let the two interfere."

Bonner says that Talmadge is equally professional about his attitude. "He takes no special notice of what I have written about him and still answers questions. Throughout all my stories, he was available for comment and his staff remained cooperative. I appreciated that.

"But in other cases, when I did an investigative story, I have been avoided."

168

Bonner gives as a sample the case of Representative Douglas Barnard of Georgia. "I wrote that Barnard accepted money from a tobacco company to appear at a luncheon at the tobacco company's plant. It wasn't illegal but it was embarrassing to him. The amount was close to a thousand dollars. The response of his staff was to cut me off from all information and hunt for whomever it was who leaked it to me."

On the Talmadge case, Chris credits Edward Pound of the *Washington Star* for breaking the major part of the story, and spending full time working on Talmadge.

Chris Bonner was political editor of the *Macon Telegraph* covering the Georgia General Assembly when Carter was governor and during the time he was campaigning.

One story Chris did on Carter got Carter a little annoyed. "It was nothing I could help. It was just that my story was being used to hurt Carter by an antagonistic publisher.

"What happened was that I covered Carter in early 1976 at Fort Lauderdale, before the Florida primary, when what he said came out sounding as if he was for gun control. He cut a very fine line on that in his remarks.

"But to me it was just another campaign story and I didn't follow it up. The campaign speeches tend to blend together and you forget which is important or which is not important. What you are looking for is what is new.

"So a couple weeks after that story appeared, I was in New Hampshire. It was a few days prior to the New Hampshire primary, and there on the front page of the *Manchester Union Leader* was my story, which William Loeb had picked up from the *Macon Telegraph*.

"It was obvious that the story was prominently displayed on the front page to force Carter to answer questions before conservative voters about the issue of gun control. So he was stuck with answering questions on gun control and he didn't like it.

"Loeb was against gun control and against Carter.

"I met Carter at a dinner that night and I said, 'How have you been doing, governor?'

"He had an icy look about him as he coldly replied, 'I've been doing all right, but I see *you've* been busy.'"

Not all Washington stories originate in Washington, D.C. Jack White of the *Providence Journal-Bulletin* scooped the whole

Capital press corps with the story that Nixon had paid less than one thousand dollars income tax two years running.

Then IRS found he owed over $425,000. White got the clue when flying around the country to write about cuts in Navy strength.

To get involved in writing true spy stories you have to slink around, as columnist Ralph de Toledano found.

"Back in the early fifties," he told Fran Leighton, "I picked up a rumor that Igor Gouzenko, the Soviet file clerk in Ottawa who defected and broke up a spy ring, would be ready to talk to a reporter if he trusted him. I was with *Newsweek* then. I asked my editor, 'How would you like an interview with Igor Gouzenko?'

"'My God,' he said, 'Are you kidding? Go. But what will it cost us?'

"'A three-cent stamp,' I told him.

"The three-cent stamp was for a letter to Gouzenko, care of the Royal Canadian Mounted Police. About a week later I received instructions.

"I was to check in at the Royal York Hotel in Toronto on a specified day and wait. The deal was that I would be contacted there. A car would meet me at the hotel, I would get in, be blindfolded, and driven to an unknown destination where Gouzenko would meet me.

"I flew up to Toronto, checked in at the hotel, and waited. Finally my phone rang and a Russian-accented voice said, 'Is this Ralph de Toledano?' 'Yes.' 'This is Meester Brown. May I come up?'

"A few minutes later there was a knock on my door and Gouzenko walked in. 'When you write your article,' he said, 'please make our meeting very mysterious. I do not want the Russians to know that I come to your room.'

"I got the interview—it was a world beat—and returned to New York. *Newsweek* gave it a full page!

"Several days later, a friend of mine in the United States Intelligence community called me. 'Do you think you could see Gouzenko again?' he asked.

"No problem. He gave me a list of about fifty questions on codes, enciphering and deciphering, all so technical I couldn't understand most of them.

"'What's the point of this?' I asked. 'The FBI or the CIA

must have asked him these questions.' To my surprise, my friend said, 'No, they haven't.'

"'One thing about Gouzenko,' I told my friend. 'He's scared to death that the KGB will discover what his assumed identity is. Even his kids don't know who he really is. And he keeps moving from place to place every time he spots what he thinks are suspicious characters prowling about.'

"'Maybe you shouldn't tell him,' my friend said. 'But the KGB knows who he is and where he lives.'

"I returned to Canada and read off the questions on the list. His answers were also too technical for me to understand, but I wrote them down verbatim and delivered them to my friend.

"'Wow,' he said. 'This really opens up a lot of things for us.'

"Not long thereafter, Gouzenko's best-selling Book-of-the-Month novel, *The Fall of the Titan*, was published. Some son of a bitch stole my copy."

Sy Hersh of the *New York Times* won the Pulitzer Prize for his stories on the My Lai massacre. And that's only one of his many awards.

But it will do to show how an investigative reporter operates. It started with a call from a lawyer he knew. The lawyer said he had heard a rumor that a soldier was being held at Fort Gordon, Georgia, for killing seventy-five civilians in Vietnam, and there was going to be a court-martial.

But it seemed there was no story. Fort Gordon said nothing was happening there, certainly not a court-martial. Hersh felt his antenna twitch just a little bit and he made dozens of calls in the next few days until he had uncovered the fact that there was indeed a soldier being held for killing civilians but the number was wrong. It was more like 109.

The more he dug, the more shocking the story became. Finally, after several months, he had it all together. The only trouble was no newspaper wanted to use it. At least not to buy it.

At this point in his career, Sy was working on a book and had resigned from the Associated Press. It had been an expensive investigation for him.

Finally, he got a small syndicate—Dispatch News Service—to take on the distribution of his stories on Lieutenant William Calley. So exicted did the public get in reading the gruesome stories and arguing about whether Calley was justified in doing the deed he was charged with, that newspapers suddenly were fighting to print the series for one thousand dollars or more.

Sy Hersh is possibly the most looked-up-to investigative reporter in Washington for his true grit and willingness to take a chance on his own intuition.

The My Lai material ended up as a book and Sy Hersh ended up with a safe berth on the *New York Times* Washington bureau. But he didn't set out to play it safe. It's just that such talent and hard work and independence are valuable commodities in the newspaper world.

Clark Mollenhoff is in a class by himself—a man who has come full circle from working for Nixon's White House to becoming one of Jack Anderson's top investigative reporters.

One of the brainiest writers in Washington, a Nieman Fellow, a lawyer, and author of books too numerous to mention, it's ironic that Clark suddenly thought he should do his bit for God and country by helping Richard Nixon spot incipient scandals in his administration. This was in 1969, when Nixon was the new broom, sweeping into office after many years of Democratic stranglehold.

Amusingly, Mollenhoff didn't last long. He soon realized that he was never going to be able to report any wrongdoings directly to the President, because he would never be able to get past Nixon's German mafia, Haldeman and Ehrlichman.

Government's loss was journalism's gain though it was evident Mollenhoff was a better fighter on an investigative story than he was fighting "the Berlin Wall," as the duo was known around the White House.

A great bear of a man, Mollenhoff is considered the dean of Washington investigative reporters. At the Press Club bar they still talk about Clark's fearlessness, even back in the Eisenhower administration, when he had a role in the departure of Ike's aide, Sherman Adams, for accepting gifts from a favor-seeking manufacturer.

Some of Clark's greatest triumphs included reforms in federal laws governing grains, commodities, and stockyards. Mollenhoff is also the holder of a Pulitzer Prize—for investigative stories that triggered the government's probe of corruption in Jimmy Hoffa's Teamsters union.

Freedom of the press, an American principle all too rare in the world, is too much taken for granted. I sometimes think the proper phrase would be "Freedom of the Press—If Any." Through the ages a man could have his ears cropped or his head chopped for unwanted utterances. The pioneers who settled the New World left some of the old restraints behind.

Fledgling newspapers in Britain's American colonies did not seem to have problems in saying what they wanted till 1734 when a printer named John Peter Zenger was tried for libeling William Cosby, a corrupt and unpopular governor of New York.

After Cosby had stacked the case by naming a new judge, an eighty-year-old Philadelphia lawyer, Andrew Hamilton, came to defend Zenger.

The wise old man argued for the first time that there was no libel if truth could be proved. The jury upheld him and the burghers of Manhattan celebrated by holding a great dinner at which freedom of the press was the honored guest.

Freedom of the press was again breached by the Alien and Sedition Act of 1798, passed in fear of France under Napoleon just as free thinking was dimmed for a time through fear of communism in the 1950s.

Fiercely partisan and in some cases bribed, the newspapers friendly to the French not only boosted their cause but tried to discredit opponents.

Benjamin Franklin Bache, a young grandson of the great Ben, was one of the worst offenders. He had even libeled George Washington by publishing a letter known to be a British forgery during the Revolution, making the President seem a traitor and a coward.

Later indicted under the Sedition Act, he died of yellow fever before he came to trial.

Another scurrilous writer, James Thompson Callendar who worked with Jefferson to slander the opposite party, went to jail under the Sedition Act; was pardoned by Jefferson; and then turned against him. He later drowned by falling from a ferry boat when drunk.

In all, six men went to jail before the Act was permitted to expire in 1801.

The remarkable thing was that the targets of all this slander nevertheless held steadfastly to the principle of press freedom. George Washington, in a Cabinet meeting, blew off a little steam against the press corp, just like President Carter did years later. History records Washington "got into one of those passions when he cannot command himself, saying he would rather be on his farm than be made emperor of the world, yet they were charging him with wanting to be king."

Through all manner of mudslinging, the early leaders of the new Republic defended the press as an institution no matter how much its early editors abused them.

There was no real challenge to press freedom for more than a hundred years except that Andrew Jackson, on behalf of slave owners, tried to get abolitionist newspapers barred from the mails. Congress did not back him up.

In the wars, of course—Civil War, World War I, and World War II—military information was censored but newspapers were left as free as they cared to be in criticizing the government and the generals.

The 1950s saw the nation gripped in wild hysteria whipped up by Senator Joseph McCarthy in his "witch hunt" for Communists in government. Eventually Hollywood became a target, and a parade of stars filed before his witness stand.

Writers were blacklisted in Hollywood and elsewhere on the basis of unproven suspicions that they were friendly with or even once had talked to a Communist—guilt by association. The end result was that McCarthyism made fear of communism look so silly that the reds in our midst have been able to run unchecked ever since. It was television that brought the nation to its senses by picturing this madman.

If the American principle of freedom of the press is to keep working, one main essential to the flow of news is that confidential sources be protected so they will not be silenced.

A reporter whose informants are exposed cannot be trusted. I had this drilled into me as a cub. Never having embarrassed a news source, I am told things that would take my informants' heads right off if caught.

Paul Wooton, my mentor in the business, inadvertently wrote something not supposed to be known. A high official leaned on him to tell who spilled it. Finally, this mild-seeming little man lashed back: "I know you can make my life unpleasant. At worst, you might drive me to suicide. But you will not make me betray a trust."

Though few of us want to be heroes, we must keep the faith. Once I nearly was on the hot spot. It was in 1949, when the

Air Force and Navy were fighting for their share of the defense budget and trying to discredit each other's weapons.

The Navy was trying to plant scurrilous stories about the big slow B-36 bomber, hinting that the contract was influenced by visits of Air Force Secretary Stuart Symington to the ranch of Jackie Cochran, wife of aircraft magnate Floyd Odlum, at Indio, California.

On the Navy side, an affable fellow named Cedric Worth was hired as a public relations aide, an old friend of mine from my year with the Republican National Committee.

To impress newsmen, he would show a document stamped SECRET, hoping this would make them want to read it, and I did.

Always eager to impress my publisher, who fired people on whim, I wrote him what I had seen in a Navy paper with SECRET stamped in red letters all over it, to show what a newshawk I was. An air-power zealot, my publisher passed the word to the Air Force of what I had seen.

During the House probe of the B-36, the Navy PR man, Cedric Worth, was called by irascible old Armed Services Chairman Carl Vinson to explain what seemed a breach in security. I was to be next before the inquisition.

I had decided what to say. Had I been put on the stand, I would have expressed shock that such a good American as Mr. Vinson would ask me to do such an un-American act as to reveal my sources.

As it turned out poor Cedric bore the whole brunt of the questioning and I was never called. Vinson put down Cedric by identifying him as a writer of mystery stories. The Armed Services chairman left the impression that anything Cedric said about a B-36 plot had to be wild imagination.

In truth, it was not Odlum's wife who socialized with Symington in California—it was Harry A. Bruno, Odlum's public relations man, who entertained General Hoyt S. Vandenberg, Chief of the Air Force, at his Long Island hunting lodge. But Cedric still had a potent point in the fact that industry was entertaining the Air Force.

One of the things I saw in the document marked SECRET was that bombers would not protect us against the Reds for lack of a bombardier's map of Russia.

Not true. Secretly, the lumbering B-36's being criticized

had made such a map, long before the U-2 spy plane—a story never told.

Recurrently through the years, reporters have faced contempt charges for failure to name sources. In criminal cases, this can be called obstruction of justice.

There are shield laws in some states to protect the press. Press people are divided on whether there should be a federal shield law.

In 1973, the U.S. Supreme Court, always ready to do injustice in the name of justice, ruled that newspeople may not withhold confidential information. This would strip them of the protection given to lawyers, doctors, and priests.

At the time, a dozen or so reporters across the country faced trouble, including a Los Angeles man in connection with the multimurder Manson case.

In New Jersey, Peter Bridge of the *Newark Evening News* went to jail through a quirk in the state law. It protected against revealing news sources but in this case a source had been named.

Bridge refused to answer questions about threats and bribery that might have endangered his informant. The judge insisted. After the Supreme Court decision, Bridge was jailed until the grand jury he had defied was released.

Peter's newspaper meanwhile had discontinued publishing.

No one helped him pay his legal bills. He came out of the experience jobless and broke but proud that he had "paid his dues" to his profession. There stands a man!

Comes now the same Supreme Court and says police may search files in a newspaper office. So alarming is this new undermining of the very foundation of freedom of the press that the National Press Club held a conference on this subject, which was attended by such notables as Katharine Graham, publisher of the *Washington Post*; A. M. Rosenthal, executive editor of the *New York Times*; Howard K. Smith of ABC News; and Jack Nelson of the *Los Angeles Times*.

This "First Amendment Rally" had co-sponsorship of every important press group—NPC, Washington Press Club, National Press Foundation, Women in Communications. Society of Professional Journalists, Newspaper Guild, and White House Correspondents Association.

The key-note was struck by Rosenthal, who rose and said, "We'll come out okay as long as we resolve to fight!"

All proceeds from admission to the rally went to the Reporters Committee for Freedom of the Press.

Whether Congress should enact a shield law to protect reporters in every state is a matter hotly contested in the Press Club. Some continue to claim it is unnecessary because they are already protected by the Constitution. But under a Chief Justice hostile to the press, how much of a shield is that?

Pressure to reveal sources is not the only squeeze that reporters feel. There are subtler kinds of coercion to report with a bias toward some special interest.

During the interservice feuding of the late 1940s I was trying to report impartially on the Air Force obsession with big bombers while the Navy was hell bent on building supercarriers.

To my thundering old publisher, Frank A. Tichenor, there was only one side. "The Air Force is right," he told me, "even when it is wrong."

To make me see the error of my ways, he invited me to New York for a private lunch with Air Force General James H. Doolittle.

I had looked forward to meeting one of America's living legends. Jimmie Doolittle stories abounded, such as how he broke an ankle jumping from a balcony when surprised in a lady's bedroom in South America.

As he had explained it, he fell while trying to prove that he could walk on the railing.

But it was a serious warrior I met that day. The great Jimmie—round-faced, earnest and outspoken—lectured me on the absurdity of the Navy, even though he himself had launched his historic sneak attack on Tokyo in World War II from *the deck of a Navy carrier.*

Had I followed Jimmie's Air Force line, and agreed with him that the Navy view was "pure and unadulterated horse shit," I might have become a Reserve general. But I could not refrain from sniping at Air Force Secretary Stuart Symington for his ineffectualness and failure to fight against cuts in Air Force strength. Instead of calling me in to enlist my aid, Symington tried to influence my publisher by the lure of a slice of Air Force suppliers' advertising.

Again to New York. This time for an aviation luncheon

at which my publisher, Tichenor, arrived with both Doolittle and Symington. Their topic was my reporting. Symington had come armed with several pages of "objectionable items" culled from my stories.

Tichenor was a proud man who stood behind his people. But he was hurting for cash. After his attacks on the Navy, his magazine *Aero Digest* was getting no ads from naval aircraft suppliers such as Grumman and Martin. Now they were looking for Air Force linked contracts to fill the void.

Symington broadly hinted, Tichenor later told me, that "if these companies expect to do business with the Air Force, they ought to advertise with our *friends*, shouldn't they?" And Tichenor, of course, was a friend.

Though not told what to write, I became a bit more circumspect and went to see an Air Force general in public relations toward friendly contacts. But my name was mud there.

The general did not want to listen and had his secretary call from outside so he could leave abruptly.

There was a good deal of uneasiness among press people in those days about censorship. In an effort to get fair rules, I got myself named chairman of a committee on press freedom and ethics for the Aviation Writers Association. My ten-point code was approved by the membership and printed in *Editor and Publisher.*

My tenth point was that impairing press freedom should be denounced whenever observed. It is still being *observed* and problems remain.

According to *Aviation Week*, November 14, 1977, the Carter administration was in trouble with Congress for having managed all phases of national defense by "covert attempts to manipulate the media to slant the news, punitive investigations into alleged news leaks, and discrediting critics of the SALT II proposals being discussed in secret with the Soviet Union."

An impediment to reporting is overprotection of information. I met with it as a fledgling reporter. I had seen a little Navy plane that I described as having a "cigar-shaped body."

In order to find out that the Navy had bought three of these planes, I had to go all the way to the Secretary of the Navy—his subordinates were overprotective and would not talk.

More recently, the length of the Minuteman missile was "classified" although Eisenhower had proudly posed beside it for news pictures. Anyone could call the White House and learn that

Ike stood five feet ten inches, a good two-yard measure with shoes on.

In recent years, the Freedom of Information Act has made it possible for reporters to dig out much that was previously hidden. One need only file written questions, citing the law, and federal agencies must give priority to answers.

Also, "sunshine" rules, throwing open sessions of Congressional committees and federal boards previously closed, make reporting easier.

Happily, the press scored at least once recently when the Supreme Court refused to review a defamation case in December 1977. A *New York Times* story had quoted a source that called three scientists "paid liars" after they belittled the effect of insecticides on birds.

These scientists had been awarded $61,000 damages but the Second U.S. Circuit Court of Appeals overturned it. Chief Judge Irving K. Kaufman ruled: "The public interest in being fully informed about controversies that rage around sensitive issues demands that the press be accorded the freedom to report such charges without liability for defamation."

Another impediment to truth is the dismal fate of "whistle blowers." Anyone in government and industry who tells unpleasant facts from his job, in an effort to get reforms, is likely to find his career cut short.

As that crusty old genius Admiral Hyman Rickover said, "If you must sin, sin against God; not against the bureaucracy. God may forgive you but the bureaucrats never will."

A prime case is that of A. Ernest Fitzgerald, a top Pentagon procurement official, fired in 1969 for blowing the whistle by revealing the $2 billion cost overrun on the Lockheed C-5, the huge trouble-plagued Air Force cargo plane.

He sued the Civil Service Commission to win reinstatement but was put on minor work. Even so, he labored on and fought the spending of $800 million for Project Max, an Air Force logistics system that Congress had ordered stopped. This made him no dearer to the hearts of the Pentagon brass.

When running for President, Carter pledged that there would be no more firings for truth tellers. But Fitzgerald, after incurring $400,000 in legal fees, still is suing for full reinstatement and $3.5 million damages.

Another whistle blower I once knew was in the Washington office of a major aircraft company, and was an able young man. In a congressional hearing he told that Secretary of the Air Force Harold Talbott had been giving business to his own consulting firm. This forced Talbott out of office.

My friend got no medals—he simply disappeared from Washington. As Eisenhower warned, the military-industrial complex has unholy power.

As for the influence that may cause reporters to slant their stories, one old survey seems close to the mark.

In 1934, Leo Rosten, author of the H*Y*M*A*N K*A*P*L*A*N tales and other humorous books, went to Washington to interview some 150 newsmen as part of his work toward a doctorate. Updated twenty-five years later, Rosten's findings held up well—and as far as I can see they still do. Cynics had told Rosten the Press Club gang would never talk fully and frankly but they did.

One finding was that reporters are not under instructions to slant their news but that they read their own papers, they find what their editors want from how their stories are run or played down, and knowing which side their bread is buttered on, learn to write accordingly.

One does not write anything the least offensive to advertisers. I found this out in my first days as a cub. Nor can ill be said against any racial or ethnic group or any religion or against women's libbers or organized gays. Such groups, ready to attack with the venom of angry bees, are becoming untouchable.

So perhaps it is for lack of other allowable targets that reporters take shots at our elected officials more than ever before.

As this is written, the Supreme Court has made the astounding decision that in a libel suit a court not only may search reporters' records but may demand that they tell "what was in their minds" when they wrote the alleged libel.

If they succeed, Pandora the box-opener hasn't seen anything yet. Opening a reporter's mind might reveal some of the damndest things!

writer" —there is a
hat.

f party treatment.
of reporters and
Party for him.
d guests, Novak
n the hall from
ffice boy back

change his
now boring
g."

rts buff.
rs got a
andout

White
big-

a

...lines in the
...sion. As such the
... their private lives.
... Tom Wicker, Rowland
... immediately passed around the
... ropriate laughter or sympathetic

...cidentally, are nicknamed the Odd
... say Evans "belongs to the horsey
...chool of journalism and Novak is a
...gernail school of reporting."

...people, who love giving labels and nick-
...k the Prince of Darkness, for his swarthiness
...disposition.

...they say, he and Rolly can laugh all the way to the
...they write one of the most successful columns.

...he team of Evans and Novak is very important in
...n. Their critics say they try to cover too much territory—
...y are jacks of all trades and masters of none.

Novak has been put down, behind his back, as a "pom-
...s know-it-all" who demands special treatment on stories and
ppears to be self-centered.

This would mean he is very self-centered indeed, because almost any reporter must be self-centered and pushy to get
the story he is after. It does take a bit of cheek to set oneself up as a
columnist, guiding the thinking of thousands, and even millions, of
people.

One thing held against Rowland Evans is that he practically never invites newspaper people to his home. His wife, Kay
Evans, is very social and takes care that reporters are not even
present to write about their parties.

Rowland Evans is described as a straight shooter who
married a rich wife and got into society. Though some claim it's a
pity Evans couldn't have been poor and made it the hard way—

oly would have been a bette

in their voices when they say

vak commands a different kind o

ad his forty-eighth birthday, a group

s threw a Prince of Darkness Birthday

were the mode. As one of his colleagues tol

so tight that when he stopped in on a party dow

own office and they ran out of liquor, he sent an o

to his office to bring back *one drink* for himself.

Bob Novak, for his part, does not seek to
image. Commenting on the party, he said, "No matter
an evening turns out to be, you can still learn somethin

Like many nonathletes, Novak is a dedicated sp
He is a Redskin season ticket holder. Not long ago report
good laugh when Novak flunked out trying to recruit a st
high school football star for the University of Maryland.

He tried to dazzle the lad by taking him to a
House press briefing and to lunch at the Sans Souci, where
bucks columnists like Art Buchwald can be found.

It didn't work. The press gang decided Novak wa
better pencil pusher than he was a motor mouth.

David Broder, whose column appears in the *Washingto
Post,* is a columnist many journalist students wish to emulate.

He is one of the most respected all-round columnists in
Washington—as a man and as a writer. "His column is the
journalistic bible," some say, though Broder himself is a bit more
modest.

Columnists come in for a great deal of discussion
around the National Press Club. Whenever someone comments on
how great Scotty Reston is and how powerful, someone else is sure
to comment, "Well yes, but did you know he started out as a caddy
for Sulzberger [publisher of the *New York Times*]. You've got to
know how to gain fame by association."

Pulitzer Prize–winning Mary McGrory is praised by
some and put down by others for "never writing a story with which
she is not personally and emotionally involved." As one critic put it,
"She was the first reporter to give the lie to the notion that to be a
successful reporter you have to be objective."

Those who covered the McGovern-Nixon presidential
campaign of 1972 well remember how passionately she spoke for
George McGovern and how she suffered when he didn't seem to be
making it.

In spite of many signs that Nixon had it sewed up, Mary McGrory still had faith, and even went out on a limb a few weeks before election to write from Detroit, "Here in Michigan, they have failed to get the word about the Nixon landslide. They're talking victory—not big, not easy—but victory for George McGovern."

Her calculations had been based on the results of polls of voters of Polish descent at Hamtramck. Thereafter, Mary had to take a lot of ribbing from the rest of the gang following McGovern. Good-naturedly, she didn't exactly admit she could be wrong but she did vow that if McGovern lost she would leave town.

To be a writer is probably the hardest work on God's green earth. Ditch diggers at least get exercise. Writers just develop ulcers and cirrhosis of the liver. Knowing too much about doctors and the medical process, through covering hospitals and malpractice court cases, they put their faith in the bottle.

At the top of the writing heap, earning hundreds of thousands of dollars a year if they click, are the columnists. Since each paper pays only a small amount to carry a column, a columnist is more apt to starve than any other breed of newsman, except the stringer, who is paid by the inch.

So the problem is to get as many newspapers to run your column as you can. But if you manage to snag very many, earnings are amazing.

Let's take a look at just one columnist and his earning capacity, based on one column a week. That is Walter Riley, who writes "Dateline Washington," whom we met earlier.

He has something over 400 newspaper clients. Those under 25,000 circulation pay $3.00 a column; from 25,000 to 75,000 circulation, $6.00 a column; 75,000 to 250,000 circulation, $10.00 a column; and over 250,000 circulation, $25.00 a column.

It takes no genius to multiply 400 by $3.00 and get $1,200 as his minimum per week and to multiply that by fifty-two weeks to show a yearly income of $62,400. However, some of his papers pay more than the minimum and some weeks, when the news is fast breaking, he puts out more than one column, doubling his earnings.

The case of Walter Riley shows that with even one column a week a writer can do very well.

The most valuable thing a would-be columnist can have is an original idea—or a takeoff on an old idea. The writing profession is littered with skeletons of ideas and columns that crash-landed.

Columnists, since they give opinions and strike a pose, have to take the greatest amount of abuse—much of it out of their earshot. And a surprisingly large amount of it comes from their own profession—at whatever bar reporters meet.

Everybody, it seems, has at some time tried to take a verbal poke at Joseph Alsop.

The bill of particulars against Joe Alsop have the sound of the squashing of sour grapes.

He's acquired an English accent— "the damned fool sounds like an eccentric Englishman. He's a British snob out of Connecticut."

"He's given his ancestral portraits to the National Portrait Gallery."

"That SOB Joe Alsop would rather go to a dig on Crete than come to a Press Club party for the Pope."

Alas, it's true. It's all true. Alsop spent enough time in England to pick up the proper clipped speech of a member of the House of Lords.

He did give the family portraits to the National Portrait Gallery because they are important and historic. He is some sort of cousin to President Teddy Roosevelt. And he did indeed go on a dig in Greece, being a collector of ancient Greek and Chinese art.

Such an expert is he on ancient art that he lectures at the National Art Gallery. His education is strictly Ivy League—Groton and Harvard.

When he took a job as a budding journalist on the *New York Herald Tribune* someone once had to look for something in his desk. Rummaging around, the staffer came across four or five salary checks. Evidently young Joseph hadn't thought thirty dollar checks were worth cashing.

Those who know Alsop best say it was at precisely that moment that his colleagues started to look askance at Alsop, which they continue to do to this day.

For some reason Joseph Alsop rubbed the Washington Press Corp the wrong way. He was "smug," reporters said, and he "swaggered."

And what was even more unforgivable, he seemed to make a success of everything he did. Because he was overweight, his envious colleagues had an excuse for calling him "All-Slop."

And again he did the unforgivable—he lost all his fat and made money writing a feature for the *Saturday Evening Post* on how he had done it.

I remember Joe Alsop from before World War II. He was often in the Club then, always well-dressed. I remember him as pleasant to talk to.

A friend of mine, a bureau chief for a major paper in Vietnam, had a less admiring view. He was told once to get a room for the great man at a time when rooms were so scarce that reporters were sleeping on pool tables and in bathtubs for lack of housing.

My friend was so incensed at the order and so resentful that he avoided Alsop altogether by going out to the battlefront to see what was doing there.

One classic Alsop story involves the 1960 Democratic primary in West Virginia. In a resolutely Protestant state, it pitted John F. Kennedy, a Catholic, against Hubert H. Humphrey, a Protestant, and was regarded as a test of the paramount religious issue.

Kennedy had charmed Alsop into his camp—as he had a number of newsmen—and the columnist went off to interview rural West Virginians in the poor back hollows.

Alsop knocked at one ramshackle cabin and asked the barefoot woman who answered for whom she planned to vote. When she responded "Humphrey," Alsop drew himself up to his full height and proclaimed with disdain: "Madam, you are a bigot."

Kennedy and he struck up a friendship and in fact, the whole Kennedy family seemed to have adopted him. When Kennedy went to Austria in June 1961, for his summit conference with Khrushchev, and then visited in London, the press almost spit nails.

As they stood outside the home of Prince and Princess Radziwill, behind Buckingham Palace, while the President was entertained at a big party by his in-laws, Joe Alsop sashayed right in as a guest—the only member of the press to be invited.

Another pundit, Arthur Krock, one of Washington's most powerful columnists for many years, did not suffer from overmodesty. Although he had no legal training, he took great delight in analyzing the decisions of the Supreme Court and privately considered himself a sort of adjunct justice.

President Lyndon Johnson had reason to fear Krock, because the *New York Times* man was lambasting him in his column every other day.

Being skilled in the art of persuasion, LBJ invited Krock over to the White House and, in effect, swept him off his feet.

The story that is told around the White House press regulars is that Lyndon was so successful that he even got Krock to accept a ten-gallon hat as a gift.

But after he accepted it, the columnist suddenly realized he would have to walk through the lobby in which the White House correspondents sat around waiting for newsbreaks.

Slightly shamefaced, Krock left the hat behind, telling the President he would send a messenger to get it.

"So when is a gift a bribe?" the reporters asked. There is no hard agreement.

Another newspaper columnist Scotty Reston of the *New York Times* also piques the curiosity of the Tap Room gang. Why would someone named Jim Reston be called Scotty?

James B. Reston acquired the nickname "Scotty" by being born in Clydedale, Scotland, in 1909. His parents moved to the United States a year later, but he returned to Scotland for seven years of private schooling.

He was publicity man for the Cincinnati Reds in 1934, then graduated to reporting for the Associated Press in New York. Fortunately for Scotty, AP assigned him to London in 1937, and after two years of foreign seasoning shifted him to the *New York Times* bureau there. His move to the *Times* Washington Bureau came in 1941.

As Washington bureau chief, Reston assembled a star-studded cast of reporters—Allen Drury, who went on to win a Pulitzer Prize for his insider's political novel, *Advise and Consent*, Tom Wicker, Russell Baker, Anthony Lewis, and Max Frankel, among them.

As a reporter, Reston was unexcelled. As a bureau chief he ruled with a firm hand, and finally, as a columnist, he is known as one of the most influential newsmen in Washington.

What makes a columnist memorable? Much of the trick is that they have truly mastered the technique of the colorful lead.

A lead simply does what it says—it attempts to lead the reader into the premise of a story. A perfect example of an intriguing lead is the opening paragraph of a *New York Times* column by Tom Wicker, entitled, "The 'Standby' Presidency":

"President Carter was asked at his news conference this week about charges that he was 'exhibiting weakness and impotency' in his foreign policy. Keeping his cool almost to the point of rigor mortis..."

The reader is hooked!

In Washington newspaper circles, they say that Jack Germond is the most totally political person around. It is said that he can go into any New York or Washington bar where politicians meet and the bartender will say, "Hi Jack, how you been?"

Germond, all agree, relishes his work as if it were a hobby and seems to have radar vision into the future. He identified Jimmy Carter as a serious presidential candidate before anyone else, for example, and he traveled with Jimmy when he was the only reporter with him.

Jules Witcover, Germond's writing partner in the column they call "Germond and Witcover," is quite the opposite from Jack Germond in appearance and personality.

More reserved, Witcover is tall, thin, and dark to Germond's short, rotund, and balding figure. Germond is the more extroverted.

As a writing team, they make it easy for themselves, usually alternating writing days. If one is on a trip, however, the other just keeps writing until his partner gets back or takes over from whatever dateline he finds himself in.

Their column appears in the *Washington Star* and elsewhere around the country.

When you get together political pundits like Jack Germond, Bob Novak, and David Broder, you are apt to come away laughing at the whole political scene. At one such Press Club gathering, Novak tried to explain the Republican party, which periodically seems to be going out of business and then ends up gaining more seats in Congress. "The Republican party is like a fungus growth," he said. "It may not seem alive but you can't kill it."

Speaking of persons who are elected to public office, David Broder commented, "You can compare it with sausages. The product is always more savory than the process by which they are made." As for the position of Ted Kennedy, perennial presidential candidate, Broder described his condition as "the loneliness of the long distance liberal."

Jack Germond told this story when colleagues asked him how to predict the outcome of an election:

There was a confirmed horseplayer who used inspiration to determine what horse to bet on. If he saw a license plate he would be inspired to bet on that number, and if he saw an address he would feel compelled to bet on that number. One day he was besieged by number 5s. A license plate had 5s. He glanced at the clock and it said 5:55. His car odometer said, 5,555. He had to drop something off at 555 Fifth Avenue. The taxi fare was $5.55.

He could stand it no longer, "Take me to Aqueduct," he said. He arrived in time for the fifth race. He raced to the fifty-dollar window and said, "Quick, give me five tickets on number 5." The race started. Number 5 came in fifth.

Jack Germond is credited with developing the Germond Rule for reporters that holds that a luncheon bill is evenly divided so they won't look like a bunch of club people saying, "You had the egg rolls and I had the spinach."

Though the Germond Rule is rigorously adhered to, reporters who go light on booze in the lunch hour have been forced to order the most expensive food on the menu—Tournedos Rossini and Cherries Jubilee—in self-defense against their hard-drinking buddies.

Almost anybody with a clever mind and fresh idea can earn a living with a column datelined Washington. You start with one newspaper client and you build from there, if you can't find a syndicate to handle you. The main point is to get started.

The perfect illustration of a clever man and a clever idea getting together is Phil Steitz, who came up with a column for the financial pages— "In the Pits."

He started with just one newspaper, the *Wichita Eagle*, but hopes to have fifty newspapers using the column by the time this book is published.

The column is an adventure in playing the commodity market. Steitz started with a mythical bankroll of $9,925, on November 28, 1977.

By spring of 1978, Steitz's fortunes had gone up and down and he was still hanging on. The day's heading for his "In the Pits" column on Monday, March 6, said, "Losing Streak Finally Ends." One editor's comment at the top of the column sounded a jubilant note: "The *[San Francisco] Chronicle's* commodites hand-icapper has come to the end of a four-week losing streak. He is worth $10,141—up $851 from last Monday."

Phil Steitz's own lead tells it this way:

"Washington—I began last Monday with $3,397 in mythical trading capital in reserve. There were three transactions at the opening bell Monday that I said would take place...."

The column goes on to tell how Steitz liquidated some beef and hog spreads, losing $255, but made up for it in corn and sugar.

By the end of July, Steitz had suffered upsets and triumphs in futures of beans, corn, and soybeans and had almost doubled his original mythical bankroll, making him worth some $20,000—on paper.

His happy lead on July 31 read:

"Washington—Listening to my sweet tooth paid last week. After four long bearish years, bulls are big in sugar.

"I bought 112,000 pounds of October 78 #11 sugar at 6.29 July 17. Little happened at first, and I was in the red through Thursday...."

Steitz goes on to say how the next day his paper profit was $594 on this single contract, how he had not fared well in the grain pits, losing $108 on soybean oil futures he had bought in December.

What happens if Steitz makes some bad investments and gets wiped out? Will that end the column?

"It will never end," he says. "I didn't know beans about commodities when I started and I've learned as my readers learn. I'm getting smarter every day. But say I do go 'broke.' Then I believe I will be rescued by the fortunate death of a mythological relative who leaves me a small inheritance. The show must go on."

Editorial page cartoonists are the equivalent of editorial writers molding opinion with drawings that speak louder than words.

Two syndicated Washington cartoonists—Oliphant of the *Star* and Herblock of the *Post*—have fans who follow them with the rabid devotion of sports fans. Both are collected and Herblock has put out several anthologies of his work.

Herblock, whose real name is Herbert Block, is older and a native of Washington, D.C. His style is more traditional. The humor is in the things the characters do.

Oliphant's humor is in the ridiculous dumb-ass way he makes everyone and everything look. Such as Jerry Ford as a Neanderthal man.

Oliphant is the wild new breed of cartoonist, whose grotesque drawings are unbelievably ugly and funny. He's a six-footer, mustachioed, with dark, crinkly hair, a native of Adelaide, Australia. His Carter is a dumb kid character whose face is all teeth and squinty eyes.

Grotesque animals drawn with very thick lines frequently tell his complaints. One scene flashes to mind of a huge rat in a cage zonked out from cigarettes with butts all around while another rat, in obvious good health, lounges outside, with one elbow on the bars of the cage asking the dumb question, "Apart from that, how do you like them?"

To illustrate Carter's situation with Congress, Oliphant shows the little figure of a dumb-kid Carter sitting alone at a little table in the Congress Restaurant, looking at a menu. In the doorway from the kitchen, completely filling it, stands a Stone Age–faced cook whose apron reads, "Chef O'Neill."

The waiter is telling the tousle-haired Carter kid, "I'm sorry sir, but the chef says if you want anything other than hamburger, you know what you can do."

Herblock cartoons tend to look more like comic strip characters of the Blondie-Dagwood school but are generally more complicated. To give his comment on the issue of smoking and how confusing the industry and government reports have become, Herblock shows a couple in a smoke-filled restaurant.

The couples behind them have polluted the air. However, the husband is comparing two newspaper articles. One headline says, "Study Financed by Tobacco Industry Finds Cigarettes Hazardous to Health." The other flip-flop headline says, "Cancer Official on 'Tolerable' Cigarettes—Carter On 'Even More Safe' Smoking.

The confused husband is saying to his wife, "I think all this smoke has affected my eyes."

Pat Oliphant is said to be the biggest thing in journalism to come out of the seventies. It is said that his earnings are well over $100,000 a year.

He appears in some four hundred newspapers—the largest circulation for any cartoonist. To look at Oliphant you would not think he was an angry man. He smokes a pipe

190

thoughtfully, wears conservative dark suits with conservative striped ties and does not even holler when he knows he has just invented a great idea—"If it works, I laugh inwardly," he told my coauthor.

But as for feeling inward anger, he does—at least enough to draw with a pen that is like a sword. Nor does he dare attempt to get friendly with any of his subjects.

"You can't consort with the enemy," he told her. Just once, Oliphant admits, he met someone and started to like him. That was Senator Barry Goldwater, and he was immediately sorry. He determined not to let it happen again. "It's easy to lose your objectivity," he says. "The only way to do it is to stay away."

He doesn't even belong to the National Press Club—or want to belong. Too many Establishment types come in. When he comes to the Club, as someone else's guest, he stays at the stand-up bar in the Tap Room rather than relaxing in the more elegant bar and lounge.

Unmarried at this writing, Oliphant has a dangerous hobby—when he has time for it. Aerobatics, otherwise known as stunt flying.

Fortunately, Oliphant and his greatest competitor, Herblock of the *Washington Post*, are friendly rivals.

Oliphant is the first to sing the praises of his colleague, saying, "You have to honor Herblock for what he did in the McCarthy years and how he fought Nixon."

For his brave cartooning, Herblock won three Pulitzer Prizes.

Horrified at the atom bomb, Herblock invented a character in 1947 known as Mr. Atom to be the symbol of nuclear warfare. Mr. Atom was a gruesome character and he grew even more so as atomic bombs became scarier.

When Mr. Atom became a MIRV—multiple warhead missile—he suddenly sprouted snakes curling from his head like a ghastly Medusa.

Herblock has never been a fan of Nixon's and had always pictured him with a sinister five o'clock shadow and beady eyes that registered suspicion or disapproval.

"Herblock was such a Nixon hater," a Press Club member commented, "that the only thing he ever gave Nixon was a shave." This kindly act occurred when Nixon won the election.

Oliphant believes that humorous editorial cartoons

eventually will be used on TV. They can be animated by a computer and would give variety to a newscast.

Some time ago he and a group of cartoonists worked out some possible animated editorial cartoons which would take thirty seconds but could find no network willing to take a chance.

Still, it's a fresh idea for the future.

It is strange that someone born in Australia should be so vitriolic about American politics, but such is the case. He has come to love—and hate with passion—American politics.

But even more than he hates what goes on at the public trough, he hates what cartoonists call "creeping timidity," which is the growing desire of some editors to play it safe.

Oliphant answers to no man about his cartoons. He thinks them up, makes a little trial sketch in about two and a half minutes and then spends two and a half hours making the final draft.

Originally hired for the *Star* by famed editor Jim Bellows, who is now with the *Los Angeles Examiner*, Oliphant's new boss is editor Murray Gart. Gart lets him have his head—does not try to censor him.

Oliphant seems to know by instinct and long training just how far he can go in good taste and avoid the furies being unleashed or stepping over into the field of libel.

Though he is in his early forties, considerably younger than Herblock, Oliphant has been drawing cartoons since his high school days. In fact he quit school to become a copyboy on the *Adelaide Advertiser.*

His talents quickly took him into the art department of the newspaper, where he tried his hand at editorial cartooning.

His big break came in 1964 when the *Denver Post* gave him his first American cartooning job. Soon he was commuting to Washington also to do cartoons for the *Washington Post.* Eventually, Bellows of the *Washington Star* stole him away and he built a style that has been widely syndicated.

What advice does he have for beginning cartoonists? How does he approach cartooning political leaders? "You have to start with the premise that there's not a good one in the bunch," he says. "But you've got to show their behavior in a humorous way. Ridicule helps keep politicians in line."

It's always been a fact of newspapering that cartoonists lampoon politicians. Comes now a cartoonist, Jeff MacNelly, who has taken on the whole journalistic field, doing a syndicated comic strip that appears in the *Washington Post*. Under the name of "Shoe," the strip shows the daily adventures of two disreputable birds—the kind that fly—who have set up a newspaper office on the limb of a tree, complete with typewriters, press releases and overflowing wastebaskets.

Some of the news they cover is somewhat less than earthshaking, such as the "Dedication of a new stomach pump for the Snakebreath County Rescue Squad."

Readers get emotionally involved with their newspapers and sometimes send threatening letters to cartoonists and columnists, who bear the brunt because they openly take sides. But there are all kinds of hazards in the writing game.

Vera Glaser and Malvina Stephenson learned how harrowing it could be to write an investigative column. "Among other things," Vera recalls, "Malvina and I were threatened by then-Attorney General John Mitchell, who told us if we quoted him he'd see that we never got inside the White House or Justice Department again. That was because we tracked down Martha Mitchell's first husband and learned she had a twenty-five thousand dollar lawsuit pending against him."

After Malvina left the column, Vera continued alone and managed to get many exclusive stories, such as the problems of being the White House token female—Midge Costanza.

"I had the first story on Tongsun Park's skullduggery on rice deals in March 1975," Vera Glaser proudly recalls. "The *Washington Post* exposé began the following October.

"I racked up another scoop when the Carter White House sent some of their young eager beavers around to the agency heads, trying to get them to create Schedule C jobs where none existed before, so that they could be filled with Jimmy's political pals. They stopped it fast after my story came out."

Though Helen Thomas of UPI became world famous when Martha Mitchell started calling her in the middle of the night to give her scoops on the Watergate scandals—for example, when Martha called to say she was being held captive and had been forcibly injected in the rump with sedatives—it was Vera Glaser and Malvina Stephenson who first made Martha famous.

As Malvina tells it, "Martha was comparatively anonymous until our first column in October 1969, which proved her a talking doll. She would call us very early in the morning.

"Her last call to us, which resulted in a joint by-line story, concerned a suit she had filed to try to collect twenty thousand dollars from her former husband, Clyde Jennings, Jr."

"She claimed that he still owed her money for child support of their son, Jay Jennings, who was then aged twenty-two and a graduate of Virginia Military Institute, on active duty at Fort Hood, Texas."

Malvina did not rely simply on Martha's woozy calls but tracked down and checked out the former husband, who was a colonel in the army reserve. "He told me," Malvina said, "that he had tried to work out something with Martha but that Martha would tell him to talk to her husband, John Mitchell, the Attorney General. Then when he would call Mitchell, the Attorney General would say, 'That's between you and Martha.' So we knew that there were many problems in the Attorney General's home life."

Vera Glaser and Malvina Stephenson, whose column for Knight Newspapers was called "Washington Offbeat," were each used to being a star in her own right, yet they forgot their egos long enough to put out a column so unified that it seemed to have been written by one voice.

It finally stopped, not because of temperamental differences but because each had so many other projects to concentrate on.

How did the unique arrangement get started?

As Malvina tells it, "In the summer of 1968, Vera Glaser called me and suggested the possibility of a joint new syndicated column from Washington. The idea of working with her on such an experiment appealed to me. Although several pairs of male reporters had successfully teamed up from Washington, she pointed out that a double by-line for two women would be a novel challenge.

"We made several trial runs to determine that we could work well together before signing with Knight Newspapers nearly a year later.

"Some of our friends made dire predictions about the 'shackling together' of two strong-willed, independent women. I think they gave us but a short time to last. We fooled them.

"If anything, we were spurred on to see how much each of us could contribute to the common product. Being willing to go more than half the way is the only way to assure a happy marital team and a happy writing team.

"Our working relationship was harmonious mainly because we first agreed on the approach and content in advance. We relished the prospect of a good story and spared no effort in going after it. Our dissimilar political backgrounds—Democrat for me, Republican for her—provided a wide range of diverse contacts. When we got our heads together and our resources assessed, there was almost no assignment that could stump us."

According to Malvina, "There are only two liabilities in a writing partnership, which might stop some people—it takes more time to coordinate the activities of two people, and there is the hard fact that you have to divide column income in half. In the early days of the column, before there are many clients, this may mean very small earnings."

Before starting a joint column, Malvina Stephenson recommends that a couple try working together to see if their styles mesh—not only in writing but in mode of operation.

Malvina and Vera Glaser first tried out their teamwork on election night of 1968 at the Waldorf-Astoria in New York City.

They were determined to get into the inner sanctum of the Nixon headquarters.

"While other correspondents were penned up in the large ballroom, being pacified with booze and briefings," Malvina laughingly recalls, "we latched onto Lieutenant Governor Bob Finch of California and rode in on his coattails. How heady to forge past the barricades of police and security guards, escorted as 'ladies' in the company of VIP Finch.

"In the exclusive precincts of the thirty-fifth floor, we had a field day, taking mental and scribbled notes on such top Nixonites as John Mitchell, the future attorney general, and Murray Chotiner, Nixon's old hatchet man, who had been kept under cover in this campaign.

"We were able to linger on the excuse—to this day I don't know if it was real—that Vera had a headache and was ordering some pills.

"Before being kicked out, we obtained a batch of exclusive interviews which were worth the price of the entire excursion.

"But even as we retired from that battlefield we managed another triumph. Since we were both sober, we were able to concentrate on a bunch of what seemed like routine releases on another floor of the hotel, only to discover that one was a secret memo prepared by campaign director Bob Ellsworth, coaching his aides on the handling of election returns.

"Using it as our source, we were able to write an

hilarious report comparing the confidential analysis with what the campaign spokesmen were feeding out to the public as the returns came in."

Malvina and Vera's basic approach to the column was that they would always find the offbeat angle and treat the subject with irreverence or humor wherever possible.

They also avoided following other reporters. "When so many writers were covering the Kennedys at the time of the so-called Chappaquiddick case," Malvina says, "we focused on the Kopechne family and angles, including attending the funeral of Mary Jo Kopechne, who had been drowned in a car driven by Senator Edward Kennedy.

"I'm not sure the Kopechne family appreciated it and later we were the syndicated columnists referred to in Mrs. Kopechne's magazine article in *McCalls.*

"She said we took advantage of her sister, who was under sedation. Her sister always seemed to me to be in complete possession of her senses, as well as of the family secrets. I don't know about her sedation, but the facts she gave use were never denied.

"From her, we learned of the Kopechne effort to get a hefty financial settlement, probably from Kennedy's insurance company. Later, we discovered that the Kopechnes were building a comfortable retreat in the mountains north of Wilkes-Barre, Pennsylvania, their home territory. It was an eerie trip into sparsely populated area by car to check it out.

"This ultimately led to the revelation that Kennedy personally had settled more than ninety thousand dollars of his own money on the Kopechnes as a result of their daughter's fatal accident in his car."

Marianne Means is one of the prettier faces around journalistic circles, who has had an impact on the Washington scene. She sprang to fame in the sixties for having a special inside track at the White House because of a special friendship with President Kennedy and then President Johnson.

Both presidents enjoyed her good looks and kidded around with her. Sometimes there were rumors that the friendships went still deeper and that Kennedy had boosted her career by taking her under his wing.

But all of this Marianne denies. Since my coauthor, Fran Leighton, has known Marianne from the early sixties, when each was married and lived in northern Virginia, Frannie was able to get Marianne's version of the story as an exclusive for this book.

"There has been a lot of misinformation about how I originally came to Washington," Marianne told her. "You knew me in those days, so perhaps you already know the real story. But Paul [Means] and I came here because he had been admitted to George Washington University Law School—where I also graduated twenty years later.

"We had met Kennedy when he addressed a University of Nebraska student convocation which Paul and I had helped to organize. His secretary was Evelyn Lincoln, from Nebraska, and his assistant was Ted Sorensen, also from Nebraska. They were the only people we knew when we came here.

"But Kennedy did not get me my first job at the *Northern Virginia Sun*; I applied and got that on my own. After two years, I became the first woman in the Hearst Washington bureau—again with *no* Kennedy help—was assigned to the 1960 presidential campaign, and after that to the White House.

"It is taken for granted nowadays that women reporters are as competent as men to cover the White House. But I was the first woman assigned to cover a president's activities on a full-time basis—Helen Thomas covered the First Lady then—and I therefore was the object of some controversy.

"I covered the White House for five years, then began the column on national affairs for King Features Syndicate."

As for LBJ, Marianne says, "My former husband, Emmet Riordan, was a Johnson administration official, and we spent many social evenings in small groups with the president and Mrs. Johnson.

"This was, of course, a technical conflict of interest, since I was still covering the White House during much of the period—although I later began the column and was able to write about other subjects than the presidency.

"But I felt that the opportunity to observe a president at such close range comes once in a lifetime and should not be missed.

"The understanding of the pressures on a president and the internal administration conflicts, which never surface publicly, that I gained from that experience have made me, I believe, a wiser observer of the Washington power scene than I could have been otherwise."

Marianne interviewed three past presidents to write a

book on the influence of First Ladies on their husbands— Eisenhower, Truman, and Kennedy. Marianne chuckles as she recalls that "Truman was outrageous—he told me he'd spank me if I didn't write nice things about 'the Madam,' as he called Bess."

Marianne found that Jack Kennedy, of all the presidents she'd known, seemed most adjusted to his office. "Six months after his inauguration, I asked President Kennedy if he had changed in the White House. 'I've forgotten what it was like not to be President,' he replied."

Marianne Means' most traumatic memory and greatest reportorial fiasco concerned Kennedy. "I was in the White House press corps that accompanied him on the fatal trip to Dallas," she told Frannie. "Our press bus was left behind when the President's car sped ahead after the shots were heard.

"We proceeded to our scheduled destination, not knowing what else to do.

"The President and his entourage were not there, so we all rushed to the telephones. By accident, I was the first to connect with my Washington office.

"The wire operator there said, 'How's Kennedy?' He had just read Smitty's [Merriman Smith of UPI] wire story and that's how I learned Kennedy was shot.

"'Where is he?' I yelled, and when he told me Kennedy was in Parklawn Hospital, I dropped the phone and screamed at the others, 'Let's go, he's in a hospital.'

"We all ran out to the busses and with much cursing and shouting got the driver to take us to the hospital. We were supposed to be covering the president but we had less idea what had happened to him than those in Washington reading the wire services."

There are two famous society columnists in Washington and both their columns appear in the *Washington Star*. The *Washington Post* evidently does not feel the need for such a column.

But originally Betty Beale did write for the *Post*. It was during World War II, when Hope Ridings Miller, the new society editor for the *Post*, contacted Betty and invited her to write a column because she knew everyone in Washington society, and Hope needed someone with at least a knowledge of the names and the feuds.

At that point Betty Beale was a society girl whose greatest writing contribution had been press releases to help her Junior League projects.

Ymelda Dixon's previous writing experience was even more laughable. "I'd never written anything except a check," she admits. "I followed Dorothy McCardle around to see how she did things and when someone said, ' You have fifteen minutes to deadline,' I said, 'Deadline for what?'"

Both women are proof that training for newspaper work is not a prerequisite to success. Betty Beale, a product of Holton Arms School and Smith College, majored in history. Her own history is distinguished and begins in this country when the first Beale arrived in Virginia and settled in Williamsburg in 1640.

Ymelda Dixon was the daughter of Senator Dennis Chavez of New Mexico and her knowledge of Spanish has been of great help in the diplomatic world she covers. She was a special friend of the most social of all the ambassadors stationed in Washington—Ardeshir Zahedi of Iran, who left that post following the Iranian revolution.

Betty Beale's specialty is the White House and she has frequently been a guest there, though it was rumored that as a Christian Scientist she was not on the same wavelength as Jack Kennedy.

Helping to give that impression is the fact that she was the one who broke the story, during Kennedy's Camelot days, that Ethel Kennedy, the wife of the Attorney General and the President's sister-in-law, had dared push a fully clothed presidential adviser, Arthur Schlesinger, into the pool at her home as a whim.

The story made front pages around the world. At the *Star*, however, it appeared on the fifth page of the B section.

Proving again, as all reporters know and frequently complain, that a prophet is without honor in his own land.

Two D.C. gossips have the city divided between them. One is a man, the other a woman, calling herself, "the Ear."

The man, Rudy Maxa, owns Sunday. His juicy bits fill two pages or more of the *Washington Post Magazine*, the paper's own Sunday supplement.

One column segment is called "Suspicions?" And answers questions like this one of July 9, 1978: "Did the late FBI director, J. Edgar Hoover, really try to impress a date by having agents arrange for an artificial full moon one night?"

The answer, incidentally, was yes and the gal was a movie star.

In another segment called "Joker," Maxa told what happened when Atlantic City was opened to gambling and newspapers sent reporters to gamble with company money.

Result: "A reporter for the *Wall Street Journal* lost the entire one thousand dollars her newspaper gave her to gamble."

So did a male reporter for the *Detroit Free Press*, and male and female reporters for various other newspapers lost smaller amounts given them. Only one reporter won—a *Trenton Times* scribe was given $200 and returned with $410.

But the biggest secret disclosed by Maxa in the "exposé" was this: Jimmy the Greek does not gamble and hasn't since 1961. According to Maxa, Jimmy thinks thirty dollars is the right amount of money to gamble in a weekend because that's what you would be paying for other entertainment.

Rudy Maxa leads a maximum busy life, even confessing that he has done some moonlighting, turning out articles for the popular tabloid the *Enquirer*.

"The Ear," written by a British import, Diana McLellan, is Rudy Maxa's greatest competition, and some say she outshines him. Hard to say. Rudy gives more complete stories. " The Ear" is hit and run—a sentence or two.

As one Press Clubber said, "They couldn't call it 'the Rear' so they called it 'the Ear.'"

Ear speaks a language of its own; things are trendy or else awfully tacky. And there is no judge but the Ear. French of sorts is spoken: " 'Comme il faut ... Linda Ronstadt,' says clever little *People* maggie, roller-skated to her dinner date with Jerry Brown at LA's El Adobe restaurant. It's getting rough to keep up, darlings....Monday, Barbara Howar and Ham Jordan didn't even try. They just clodhopped into the Palm together, on their feet—along with three total strangers—giving everyone quite a turn. Let's try to do our part, darlings."

Ear is affectionate, sends woks to newlyweds and ends wedding announcements with the comment that she is sending a wok.

Much of the column deals with the new "super trendy" media types, the "pols" and the TV stars. For example, a July 1978 column starts out by describing a media party thrown by Dick Goodwin and Doris Kearns for Bob Healey, executive editor of the *Boston Globe*. Ear reports: "Peter Falk wore a clean shirt. Joan Kennedy boogied. Ed Brooke didn't show. All anybody talked about was the Red Sox. Ear actually had a hot date with a meatloaf."

When Carter finally got mad at UN Ambassador Andrew Young for saying during the Russian trial and imprisonment of dissidents that the United States too had "hundreds if not thousands" of political prisoners, many Ear followers looked back at what Ear had said the month before:

"OVERHEARD: '... Carter has named as UN ambassador Andrew Young, probably the least qualified diplomat since Caligula named his horse consul. But at least Caligula named the whole horse.'—Pat Buchanan."

Diana McLellan is rumored to be making something over $50,000 on her column, a nice raise from the original $25,000. The way the story goes, Diana got the raise when more timid souls would have been bounced out or at least been hiding out of sight of editors.

What happened is that Ear printed a terrific boo-boo on a little item concerning Amy, the President's daughter. The column had said that after Amy lost a relay race at her school, she had kicked up such a fuss that a Secret Service agent had gotten her a trophy anyway.

There was hell to pay. Everyone at the White House was calling the *Washington Star* to complain, including the President himself.

As a result the *Star*'s ombudsman, George Beveridge, printed a soothing column, which was a semiretraction of the item, as a small human interest bit dreamed up by Ear.

Instead of being contrite over the slap on the wrist, Diana marched into the editor's office to demand a raise because of all the attention and publicity her gossip column was getting for the *Star*.

It is certainly true that Ear is being credited in great part for having pulled the rocky financial position of the *Star* to safety.

She has become must reading in Washington, which loves seeing its stuffy officialdom laid low and treated with complete irreverence.

To her credit, it must be said that Diana McLellan treats her own life and husbands with the same irreverence as she would treat others'. Of her second husband, she says, "He was an historian just back from the North Pole or somewhere."

Hopefully she will find out someday, because they are still married.

Nor does Diana mind anyone knowing that her jobs, before the column, were perfectly dreadful, low-brow things like switchboard operator at a third-rate hotel in Washington, the Cairo

Hotel, now defunct; sales clerk; animal-pet artist; and finally, clerk at the business counter at the *Star*.

Diana managed to back into her gossip column by writing newspaper ad copy and TV commercials. It was Kay Elliott, editor of the women's page section now known as "Portfolio," that gave her her first chance to break into newswriting by covering high society parties.

Instead of being impressed, Diana found the Washington social life of cocktail parties and embassy benefits highly amusing—so amusing that she talked another writer, Louise Lague, into joining her in doing a fun column anonymously.

From the first, Ear was noticed—but negatively. Louise admits that the insults and sneering she had to take upset her so much that she eventually dropped out of the writing team.

Diana, however, thrives on abuse and even sends thank-you notes to those who say the meanest things. She calls her job "popping the mighty with a toothpick."

Now here's the hottest columnist in the country, Jack Anderson. He's full of surprises. Just as you think he has calmed down and started to run dry, up comes a blockbuster, such as his columns in September 1978 alleging that fugitive businessman Robert Vesco, working through Georgia acquaintances of top presidential assistant Hamilton Jordan, was trying to get his legal problems "fixed."

Were the phone calls really about Vesco and not just friendly visits?

How much money passed hands and to whom?

What did President Carter know, and when did he know it?

Were the documents, which were "reconstructed," really the same as the originals?

Truly it was a cliff-hanger series as only Jack Anderson knows how to make them. The search for Jack Anderson takes you to what his friends and staff call the "Charles Addams house" on Sixteenth Street—a huge, dark-red mysterious-looking mansion, with turret and wings converted to an office building which he shares with a firm of lawyers.

Go in the huge arched entranceway, past security, and up the stairs, and there you will find the top investigative writer of the country—Jack Anderson himself.

But what a difference between the inside and the outside of his house. Inside it is warm, friendly, cheerful; Anderson is a very serene person. It is hard to believe so many deadlines are riding on his shoulders—his column, his daily TV stint on ABC and radio, an article for *Parade* magazine, a newsletter he now puts out, and, yes, even speeches for which he gets from one thousand to five thousand dollars a go. He calls them "lectures."

And *go* is what he does. Sometimes one of his sons drives up to take him to the airport. He has a brood of nine. Sometimes he is too busy to talk to anyone, but other times, day after day, he will hold staff meetings every morning where ideas are thrown around and sometimes land on his receptive ears.

The speeches are his eating money, about $100,000 a year—add or subtract a lettuce leaf or two. He plows the rest of his writing income into his office and his investigative column, an expensive operation involving paying the salaries and travel expenses of his huge staff of fourteen, a close-knit office family. Investigating government is not cheap.

Also, as a good Mormon, he tithes.

Jack doesn't like to talk about money but his column by the early 1970s was reputed to be clearing something in the neighborhood of $120,000 above expenses.

His staff is amazed at how he can survive the onslaught of work, phone calls, ideas, emergencies.

Yet, as Sam Fogg, who works for him now, says, "Anderson is a very relaxed person. He runs a relaxed working operation. He has an open door. The staff is free to just walk in. I find Jack a very honest person with great integrity."

Then Fogg grins sheepishly and adds, "Obviously we will never become drinking buddies. He's a Mormon and doesn't drink. But professionally I respect and like him."

In behavior, Jack Anderson is an oversized cherubic smiling figure, walking around his office on a chilly morning under his own halo, wearing an Oriental robe and comfy slippers.

He neither drinks, smokes, nor swears, but those around him more than make up for it, and he seems not to hear when his staff mutter such expletives as, "Oh shit," "Damn it," and "Tell that joker to go fuck himself."

The "angel's" favorite expression of disgust is "Oh brother!"

As for the drinking, staff members keep a little supply

of vodka on hand, a drink that does not leave a telltale breath. But that's only a courtesy. Anderson would not say anything even if he could sniff a telltale whiff of strong drink on his dedicated aides who have stayed late to work on one of the columns, TV bits, or other projects.

Cigarette smoke also swirls around the offices, and a little pipe smoke from Joe Spear, Anderson's second in command on many writing projects—all of which does not seem to register on the "angel."

Jack Anderson is undoubtedly the most read political columnist in the nation—over fifty million readers.

This is a triumph because when Drew Pearson died in 1969 and Anderson inherited the column, more than thirty newspapers canceled. But little by little, Andreson proved that he was a more exciting and more accurate writer than Pearson, and today he has about 125 more newspaper clients than Pearson ever had. He has, in fact, more than 750 newspaper outlets!

There is the story that when Drew Pearson unexpectedly died in 1969, he left no written instructions about the future of his muckraking empire. However, according to Anderson, he did have an oral agreement since 1954 to be the successor.

Some papers run his column on the Op Ed page, but others lump him in with the funnies. Jack doesn't care. The funny page assures he's reaching the young set.

Youngsters by the dozen apply to be interns at Anderson's office. He chooses the brightest and the best and always has three or four on the job.

True, they don't earn much more than they would as dictation or copyboys or girls on wire services or top newspapers, but this is the best training they could get for becoming investigative reporters. And they can almost choose the paper they want to work on after a few years with Jack.

So valuable is this experience, that some jokingly commented to my coauthor that they would be willing to pay for Jack's training. But Jack is not interested in that. His only concern is to have the best column that is humanly possible.

What is his goal? What is he trying to do in his column, which has shaken all of government from the White House to the CIA to the GSA to the dome of Capitol Hill?

A more careful reporter than Pearson, though he still admits mistakes, Anderson has assembled a staff that digs into an amazing variety of misdeeds from official bribery, corporate greed, and organized crime to dangerous consumer products and the woes of migrant farm workers.

Since Jack Anderson is always pointing the finger of scorn at those who take freebees, he must himself attempt to stay Simon pure. Usually he achieves this perfect propriety but every once in a while he is called to task to explain something that looks, from the outside, as if there might be some small conflict of interest.

Once the questions concerned some Oriental art pieces, especially a valuable Korean screen in his Bethesda living room.

Jack confessed that the screen had been given to him by a Korean government official, after he had made the mistake of admiring it in the man's home. Jack had wanted to return the screen and had checked protocol at the State Department.

He had been warned that returning the screen would be an insult to his host, who had operated in the Oriental code of courtesy by giving the guest whatever the guest praises.

With this lesson in protocol learned the hard way, Anderson tried to take away the onus by sending a valuable gift to his host.

Now that the column is his own, he is indeed a more cautious man. One of his favorite points of attack is junketing and free rides by congressmen and officials.

I had a personal experience with Anderson when he was working for Drew Pearson in the fifties. At that time I worked for a group of nonscheduled airlines that Pearson's staff favored with occasional items.

When Anderson went on vacation, I had to furnish free coast-to-coast transportation to Jack, his wife, three children, and a baby-sitter.

He was less grateful for the ride than annoyed, because he could not be picked up on the return trip from some point in Utah.

At one time, he was on the Board of Directors of Riddle Airlines, a cargo carrier whose successful management had been ousted by a group of raiders who pushed their way in. Their idea of how to curry favor with the powers that be was to fly a planeload of political supporters free from Washington to Las Vegas to put a little pep in the reelection campaign of Howard Cannon, chairman of the Senate Aviation Subcommittee.

Included was the notorious influence peddler Bobby

Baker, Senate aide who later went to prison. Cannon survived this kind of help and got elected in spite of it.

I had the passenger list of those who were flaunting the election laws by not paying for campaign travel. At the time, Ken Scheibel, later president of the National Press Club, was writing for a Las Vegas paper that was fighting Cannon's reelection. Ken was doing an exposé series on Senator Howard Cannon and my material added fuel, which he was happy to have. It came to naught, because the owner of the paper suddenly decided to back Cannon after all, so the attacks stopped.

Anderson felt a little heat when it was revealed that he was on the board of the airline, not quite in keeping with the journalistic objectivity expected of a member of the Senate Press Gallery.

He felt a little more heat when John Dean, Nixon's counsel and Watergate whistle blower, said Anderson and Pearson got $100,000 in 1958 to write favorably about Cuban Dictator Batista. Jack replied that his own writings were on the record and he wrote no such columns.

What do you get if you hire Anderson to speak to your club or association? Malfeasance in public office is a favorite subject and he gives a lively speech.

Though Jack Anderson doesn't cuss, he likes to open a "lecture" by quoting an Alben Barkley story that soon has the audience convinced that Anderson's a regular guy.

Anderson tells how old Alben, the super politician, was delivering one of his usual speeches at an Indian reservation in Kentucky, his home state. Alben was convinced that this must be the most loyal group of supporters he had ever had because whatever he said the crowd shouted "Hoya!"

Barkley promised that if reelected to the Senate, he would see to it that the reservation had a new hospital.

The crowd shouted "Hoya!"

Barkley promised a new school.

Again the crowd shouted "Hoya!"

Alben Barkley promised free hot school lunches for the reservation school children.

"Hoya!" the crowd cheered.

Barkley left the crowd feeling mighty uplifted and headed through a pasture, where horses were grazing, toward his automobile that was parked a little distance away.

As he walked, his Indian host suddenly steered him to

the left, saying, "Oh, you almost step in hoya!"

After the laughter dies down, Anderson becomes serious as he makes his big point: "In Washington, this is the year of the hoya and I want to tell you just what kind of hoya."

In his column every day, Anderson digs down through a lot of hoya.

Among those who toppled from power or public favor because of Anderson exposés have been former senators Tom Dodd (D-Conn.) and George Murphy (R-Calif.), ITT's Dita Beard, and Postmaster General Ted Klassen.

Anderson has collected many feathers for his cap in recent years. Not all the kudos for Watergate reporting go to Woodward and Bernstein. Anderson was the first to implicate Attorney General John Mitchell and H. R. Haldeman, Nixon's top aide in the ongoing scandals.

He was first to reveal that Nixon had "participated in the Watergate coverup," although he reported that Nixon "had no advance knowledge of the Watergate break in."

Anderson himself was called on to testify when Watergate investigators learned he had been hidden in an adjoining room during discussions over the hush money and that an official attending the meeting had gone to him at intervals to give him progress reports.

And there were other things, such as the revelation that the CIA had attempted to have Cuba's Fidel Castro assassinated—not once but in six assassination attempts. And that the FBI and other law enforcement agencies were spying and keeping files on "law-abiding Americans."

Now, in large measure thanks to Anderson, any person can demand to see files kept on himself by the federal government.

Anderson's greatest reward is that he sees the changes in government that he has inspired. But in 1972 he finally did receive public acknowledgement—a Pulitzer Prize for his investigative reporting that proved that both Nixon and his Secretary of State, Henry Kissinger, had lied to Congress about the U.S. tilt toward Pakistan in the India-Pakistan conflict.

For as long as Jack can remember, he has been interested in newspapers and the written word. When he was twelve, growing up in Utah, he edited a Boy Scout page for the *Deseret News*. The same year he got an even more important writing job at seven dollars a week on the *Murray Eagle*.

Jack still proudly recalls that one of his first stories at age twelve was to explain the town's yearly tax report, and he laughs as he says, "It is probably the only tax story ever written that could be understood by any twelve-year old."

Jack was a firebrand in high school. Not only was he president of the whole student body, but he was earning his own money writing stories for the newspaper at fifteen cents a column inch.

In college, too, for one brief year he combined reporting for the *Salt Lake City Tribune* while attending the University of Utah in the 1940–41 school year.

After leaving to become a Mormon missionary, he never returned to college but instead joined the Merchant Marine, which he again managed to combine with reporting.

He talked the editors at *Deseret News* into giving him credentials as a foreign correspondent in China. His assignment was to find home town—or at least Utah—soldiers and write puff stories about them.

But Jack was, from the very beginning, an investigative reporter. Somehow he managed to hitch a plane ride to the top-secret headquarters of the OSS—Office of Strategic Services, which later became the CIA.

The OSS command was more than a little distressed to find they had been infiltrated by a reporter and to distract and utilize him they quickly dispatched him to get in touch with Chinese Nationalist guerrillas in the area to find out what was going on.

Excitedly, Jack filed the story revealing that a Chinese civil war was raging and that the Chinese Nationalists and Communists were attacking each other instead of the Japanese. But at that time, it was such a far-out idea that the story did not get printed. The editors considered it too implausible.

As World War II was ending in 1945, the draft board discovered Jack, and he found himself inducted into the Army at Chungking. It was the best thing that could have happened to him, because he was assigned to work on service newspapers such as the *Stars and Stripes* as well as the Armed Forces Radio, which he did until 1947.

It was during a bull session with a bunch of reporters in Chungking that another reporter commented that Anderson sounded like the kind of kid who should go to work for muckraker

Drew Pearson. It sounded good to Jack and he headed for Washington as soon as he was discharged.

When he met Pearson, he bore down on the fact that he had been a world traveler and a "war correspondent," which was the kind of person Drew Pearson was looking for—a vastly experienced war correspondent.

Jack let the misunderstanding stand but he chuckles as he recalls, "I'm sure I filed less copy than any foreign correspondent in history."

It is interesting that both Pearson and Anderson practiced minority religions—Anderson a Mormon and Pearson a Quaker.

The difference was that Jack never broke the dictates of his religion, even, as he recalls, when all the reporters in the press room in Chungking were guzzling what they called "air raid juice."

But Drew, though he could talk a good Quaker game and even throw in the "thees" and "thous," enjoyed a stiff drink and the good life as it is lived by Washington society.

Anderson was not interested in Drew's private life. What concerned him was that they were a good writing team and instead of using Pearson only as a short-term teacher, he found himself settling into the job for the long haul.

Part of Jack's heart still remains with his youthful experience in China. His interest in Oriental art is part of this nostalgia. In his home are interesting Oriental touches, just as in his office. A favorite acquisition is a Japanese dinner service for everyday use.

Visitors to his Bethesda home were impressed to see a ceiling of panels imported from Tapei, Taiwan, in beautiful turquoise and gold. At this writing, however, Jack was preparing to move out of the big house to a smaller one, still in Bethesda.

Visitors to Jack Anderson's office building, converted from a three-storied Victorian style house, want to know all about the house and inspect its lovely woodwork, interior shutters, and stair railings. They are told the house was originally built for Vice-President Thomas R. Marshall, the five-cent cigar man. Then after a series of senators, congressmen, and lesser lights, it was taken over by a colorful character who made it into a fancy bordello.

Anderson made only the changes necessary, preserving all the things of beauty of moments past. In Jack's private office there are no modern marvels of decorating. He sits at a large standard straight desk—fairly neat on top, considering it is loaded with items for current columns, ABC programs, radio spots, and letters from the public and from "sources."

There is no conference table but only a small, round luncheon table where he eats with his staff so they can talk while eating and make every minute count—in what is a remarkably relaxed way.

There is an unbelievable serenity around Jack Anderson's office—like the eye of a hurricane. The serenity extends even to the monochromatic look of the office, with its soft off-white carpeting, its white walls and white interior shutters, its table-clothed table set in a circular alcove, where the private cook brings lunch whenever Anderson is ready.

Even the paintings are low-key—soft Oriental scrolls that have been expensively framed, two Chinese and one Korean. On another wall is a subdued Indonesian painting and a few Oriental objects of art stand around.

But the Anderson sense of humor bursts forth in just one delicious touch, in the form of a beautifully framed sketch above the fireplace. The intricately executed drawing shows four monkeys in a row. Three are facing forward in the traditional See no evil, Speak no evil, Hear no evil poses.

But the fourth is leaning over sideways with a grossly conspiratorial look on his face, talking into the phone. The caption says, "Hello, Jack Anderson?"

A word about that fireplace. It is one of many beautiful fireplaces in the house, none of which can be used—on orders of the fire chief. It is the only complaint that any of the numerous staff have—they yearn to light those fireplaces.

As consolation, in good weather they do use the balconies for little cookouts. It's that kind of wonderful house-office.

The word is that Jack almost never loses his temper. Opal, his private secretary, says so, and she is a very frank person, saucy and afraid of nobody—including Jack Anderson.

A former reporter herself, Opal Ginn says, "Once Jack got very quiet and I realized he must be angry. He just doesn't explode."

A tough cookie with a heart of gold—readers will remember her by-line in *Parade* magazine, before Jack hired her away—Opal is like a breath of fresh air around the office, treating her boss and everything else with a touch of irreverence.

Once Anderson phoned Opal to complain that he was snowbound and couldn't keep a speaking engagement in Kansas because of a freak storm. He sounded most annoyed.

Opal shot back with, "Look, Jack, I'll take responsibility for almost anything around here except a snowstorm in May in Kansas."

According to Opal, Jack is the most doting of all grandfathers and is simply a pushover for his three grandchildren, who are the offspring of his eldest daughter, Cheri. But he doesn't have the time or inclination to do things like shop for toys for them.

Any spare time he might have is spent in swimming or in the practice of a martial art, which, considering the emotion his columns arouse, could come in handy at any time—karate.

In the Nixon administration, for example, Anderson was harassed almost constantly and felt there were plots against his life. As Watergate watchers learned, G. Gordon Liddy once thought he had been ordered by Magruder to kill Anderson but was soon advised that such was not intended.

It's amazing that Anderson can be so serene, considering all this turmoil and even perhaps danger to his life. Though Anderson did sue, in the case of the Watergate harassment and physical threat, he dropped the case because to do so would have meant that he would have to reveal his sources—something he never does if it breaks a confidence or endangers other people.

One would think that Anderson would be constantly worried about any bugging of his telephones and would at least use a voice scrambler, but such is not the case. The office seems quite unconcerned about whether they are bugged or not.

Still, to take a reading on his telephone situation, Anderson occasionally makes a call to the FBI to see if his source acts nervous. The theory is that if the source acts evasive or nervous, the source must be afraid that his words are being recorded when he talks to Jack Anderson.

It is true that sources who want to give Anderson secret information sometimes act very paranoid. They will suggest various code words to be used on the phone. And they will suggest meetings with Anderson or his top men—Joe Spear, or Britt Hume—take place at strange places, such as a used car lot or a beanery.

Whatever the source wants, the Anderson staff goes along. Anything to get a truly great story.

Woodward and Bernstein had only "Deep Throat" whom they met in weird places. Anderson has dozens of "Deep Throats."

Why do people spill their secrets to Jack Anderson?

According to Jack, each has a different reason, but they fall into several different categories. Some people simply like intrigue and if they know something they take the chance of getting it to him even if it could mean the loss of their jobs. They love the gamble.

Then there are the angry people who are out to get their bosses or someone else in the public or business world whom they hate.

And finally, there are the conscientiously concerned people who are interested in the overall pattern of American life. They are interested in the public weal and feel the public has a right to know of any transgression on the part of their elected officials.

No matter what the source of the tip, Anderson and his staff spend a great amount of time and trouble carefully checking out the stories so that they are not just trapped into carrying out somebody's vendetta.

Les Whitten, who was Anderson's top staffer until he took time off to write very profitable novels, claims that Anderson always impressed every new reporter with the warning that nothing would be published on the basis of just a tip, unless it was confirmed by two other sources.

Sometimes a good story would get away because word would get back to the subject under investigation and he might rush to break the story himself, using a more kindly reporter. Exclusivity is the life blood.

What makes Anderson so busy is that not only must he work on current stories but he must always keep building his contacts and insider friendships, even when he is not doing a story that involves them.

Fortunately Anderson doesn't expect the people around him to work as hard as he does. As someone on his staff so aptly put it, "He's a workaholic but he doesn't flog other people."

Around Washington, they call Carl Rowan the black Jack Anderson. Rowan is every bit as vocal and almost as famous, paralleling Anderson's career in many ways. Rowan gives hard-hitting lectures,

212

like Anderson, and is very much in demand around the country. Like Anderson, Rowan appears frequently on TV, but his major forum is CBS's *Agronsky and Company*. Rowan is a syndicated columnist, as is Anderson, though Rowan appears only three times a week.

Like Anderson, Rowan cannot do it all by himself, and he has a smaller staff than Anderson's, only five.

Like Anderson, too, Carl comes of humble background. His father had a twenty-five-cents-an-hour job in a small-town Tennessee lumber mill. Carl himself entered the work force the hard way—pick-and-shovel work and carrying coal. Yet so intent was he on lifting himself into a literate world, that he not only became the first member of his family to graduate from high school, but was valedictorian.

Working his way through college, at Tennessee A & I, military service intervened. He became one of the first blacks to receive a commission in the Navy. One of his Navy friends went on to become a U.S. senator—Howard Baker.

After World War II, Rowan went on to get a Master's degree in journalism at the University of Minnesota.

Somehow he managed to get a job on the *Minneapolis Tribune*, and what he learned about racial tensions both in the North and South, resulted in his first book, *South of Freedom*. Partially as a result of the book dealing with segregation, Rowan was named one of America's Ten Outstanding Young Men of the Year.

The year was 1953 and Rowan laughs when he recalls that another ambitious young man who was named that year was Billy Sol Estes.

Rowan's life took a twist that Jack Anderson's never did. Whereas Anderson was always at odds with the administration, Rowan became part of government when he caught the eye of President Jack Kennedy and was offered a slot in the State Department.

Lyndon Johnson went Kennedy one better. He made Rowan ambassador to Finland. When Edward R. Murrow died, LBJ named Rowan to succeed him as head of USIA.

Though Rowan has had experience on both sides of the story—writing it and being a government spokesman, he becomes furious if anyone thinks he is not his own man. Those who know him, know he is every bit as independent as his white counterpart.

14/Washington News Bureaus

The news bureau chiefs are the barons of the press corps. They dominate the prestigious Gridiron Club. Most presidents of the National Press Club have come from their number.

The most influential bureaus are those of the news magazines, *Time* and *Newsweek* and big-city papers such as the *New York Times, Wall Street Journal, Chicago Daily News* and *Chicago Tribune, Los Angeles Times, Baltimore Sun* and other large-circulation journals. Some have national impact through their syndicated news services.

News comes out of Washington from hundreds of offices, large and small. The wire services, TV networks, major newspapers, and newsmagazines each employ dozens of people here. Offices of smaller papers are manned by a half dozen or less. And many a one-person office represents a single publication or a flock of them.

Most reporters consider it a step up—in fact, the ulti-mate tribute—to be sent to Washington, D.C., to head the paper's bureau there. Now and then, it is also a way of getting a tough competitor, or someone who has felt the ire of the newspaper's hierarchy, out of town. In that case, it's a way of shoving out of sight yet up the ladder.

Walk along the corridors of the National Press Building and read the names on the doors. Papers from cities, big and little. News bureaus, foreign and domestic. Specialized newsletters.

Taking it from the top, you might think the wire services—the Associated Press and United Press International—have the most clout, since they reach so many millions in circulation. But for the most part they skim the surface, the obvious events of the day.

Too many of the papers they serve look no farther. The great majority of writers do not deal with the world at large but address some special audience—what's happening in Washington that affects a given city. Boston or Louisville or Denver or wherever. Those regional reporters keep in close touch with the congressmen and other offices concerned with the area.

Even reporters from more obscure states sometimes get an edge over other reporters when a big story breaks that involves someone from their home areas.

"My Oklahoma background gave me an edge on some of the Koreagate stories," says Malvina Stephenson, currently heading her own bureau, which supplies a column to the *Tulsa World*.

"Former House Speaker Carl Albert was from Oklahoma, and I had covered him closely enough to know not only that he had top witness Suzi Thompson on his staff from the time he became Speaker, but that he was close to the Korean Ambassador Kim Dong Jo, the target of House investigators.

"In fact, I attended a small luncheon which the beautiful Madam Kim gave for Mrs. Carl Albert shortly after Carl became Speaker and which would become important years later in the congressional hearings.

"When the scandal began to unfold, I had background on both Suzi and the Kims. Two congressional wives testified, incidentally, that when they had visited Korea, this same Mrs. Kim had left hundred-dollar bills in envelopes for them. They had been insulted and returned the money.

"And when Albert was called back to Washington to give depositions to the House Ethics Committee investigators, I was a jump ahead in national stories. I even had a picture of the luncheon with several of us in it—Mrs. Kim, me, Mrs. Albert and a former U.S. ambassador's wife.

Another reporter with regional approach is Eric Ruff of the Washington bureau of the Donrey Media Group, representing newspapers and radio and TV stations in the West and Midwest.

To be exact, the chain is comprised of thirty-seven dailies, two TV and four radio stations. The states represented are Oklahoma, Texas, Arkansas, Nevada, and California. One of the papers he represents, the *Las Vegas Review-Journal*, is the largest in the state and the *Southwest Times Record* is the third biggest paper in Arkansas.

Ruff particularly enjoys covering Capitol Hill and finds there is much to amuse a reporter who pays close attention to what's going on on the Floor.

He particularly got a kick out of observing the frustration of Senator Paul Laxalt when the conservative Nevadan was helping lead the forces opposing the "giving away" of the Panama Canal.

Laxalt was getting ready to make a big speech on the subject and his aide came on the Senate Floor and handed him the text.

"I could see that his aide was briefing him and Laxalt hadn't read it," Ruff recalls. "Laxalt was recognized and started reading and the speech was technical as hell.

"Laxalt's aide was not the most concise and clear writer and Jake Garn of Utah, sitting next to him, was not helping things by saying out loud, 'Paul, are you sure you wrote this thing?'

"Laxalt stumbled on and Garn said, 'Paul, it sure doesn't sound like you.' Laxalt persevered as long as he could.

"Finally, he just said, 'Oh, the hell with it, Mr. Chairman, I submit this for the record.'"

The quality of writing that comes out of Washington bureaus is almost uniformly excellent and reflects the pride of the reporters who are the "chosen ones."

And speaking of "chosen ones" reminds me of the story of Tom Wicker.

The Washington press set watched with interest Tom Wicker's somewhat stormy trip through the *New York Times* hierarchy a few years ago.

Wicker and Scotty Reston were friends, and when Reston retired as bureau chief in Washington, he was able to pass the post on to Wicker, his protégé, disappointing several other contenders.

Friendship sometimes can hurt as much as it helps. *Times* officials in New York had resented Reston's power for years and, after Wicker had run the bureau for a while, they persuaded Arthur "Punch" Sulzberger, the publisher, that Wicker should be replaced with James Greenfield, a *Time* magazine alumnus working as a *Times* foreign editor, who had the support of A. M. Rosenthal, now the *Times* executive editor.

Word reached Washington of this attempt to purge Wicker. Reston, much annoyed, took Tom to New York for a private confab with Sulzberger.

The publisher was talked into reversing his decision and reinstating Wicker. Now Rosenthal was mightily angered. Wicker served long enough to prove his ability, then became a full-time columnist and associate editor.

The *New York Times* was smarter this time and picked Max Frankel who was acceptable to both Reston and the New York hierarchy, for Washington bureau chief.

There is much good writing coming our of newsmagazines. Fortunately *Time* magazine does permit its Hugh Sidey, who has also become famous through TV appearances, to have a by-line. His views now appear in a column called "The Presidency."

As a lesson to journalism students, this was his lead for his column on the life of former President Richard Nixon at San Clemente: "The empty helicopter pad is a forlorn reminder of power brutally rescinded. The scraggly haired surfers shoulder their boards in the morning sun and scuff down the nearby paths to their emerald waves, unmindful of Richard Nixon, who stirs beyond the fence in the skeletal complex that used to be the Western White House."

A Washington bureau man who rose from the ranks to become the top Civil War writer of his time was Pulitzer Prize-winning Bruce Catton, who still wanted it known that he considered himself "a reporter, not an historian."

Catton was Washington correspondent for NEA—Newspaper Enterprise Association—before becoming a book writer.

It wasn't easy for him to make the break. His first two books, *Mr. Lincoln's Army* and *Glory Road*, hardly made a ripple but his third book, *A Stillness at Appomattox*, hit the jackpot and won him the prize.

Like any good newspaperman, when he heard the news that he had won the Pulitzer in 1954, he said, "Boy, if ever there was a night to drink a bottle of bourbon, this is it."

Women get a break in many Washington bureaus. Karen Elliot House covers energy for the *Wall Street Journal*.

Maggie Hunter covers hard news for the *New York Times*, as well as the distaff side of the White House. Betty Ford singled Maggie out, one Christmas season White House party, to grab her and kiss her in greeting, because they were long-time friends who hadn't seen each other for some time. In fact, both had shared similar surgery and had phoned each other at the hospital.

But the other reporters didn't know all this. All they knew was that Maggie rated very high with the First Lady and they were, frankly, jealous.

Jim McCartney of the Washington bureau of Knight-Ridder Newspapers covers the White House and national security. His life and career is one of the most exciting in the Washington press gang, because he follows a story wherever it leads.

Once it led to a great news scoop.

It was soon after Richard Nixon had taken office—April 1969, to be exact—and the nation was geared to a new president who had stormed into office as a definite hawk.

Still, Jim's antenna told him something was afoot and maybe Nixon wasn't the hawk the nation thought he was. Firing McCartney's imagination was a Sunday story by Phil Potter of the *Baltimore Sun*, which he happened to read.

Potter wasn't really saying anything, just sort of thinking aloud and hinting that maybe Nixon was prepared to withdraw troops.

Jim, who knew Potter well, was sure he didn't make such statements, even thinking aloud, without some firm basis. But how to pin it down?

By good luck McCartney happened to have a luncheon set up with a special assistant to Mel Laird, the brand-new Secretary of Defense. It had been set up to discuss an entirely different subject for a story but Jim innocently threw in a question about whether it wasn't true the administration was ready to take out troops from Vietnam.

"To my surprise," Jim recalls, "He said an immediate and unqualified yes.

"I went on with the interview on the subject scheduled, supressing my excitement, since I didn't want him to know it was a big story. Every now and then I'd slip back into the matter of the troops and advance that a little further. And then I'd go back to the subject he was prepared to discuss.

"I can't even remember the subject I was there to discuss, it was so inconsequential in comparison to this new development in national policy. I got out of there as quick as I could, grabbed a cab to the National Press Building and told my editor, Buzz Merritt, who is now editor of the *Wichita Eagle*, what I was onto.

"Buzz sprang to life, 'Jesus, let's get it out.'

"As it turned out, we had a clean exclusive and the wires were going wild. Nobody knew where to check out the story. Nobody was talking. I had been foxy enough not to even mention that my source was an aide to Laird, or even that it had come from the Pentagon. I merely called him a 'top administration official.'

"As a matter of fact, I am still protecting my source. To this day no one knows who gave me the scoop.

"The next person who scraped together enough to pick up on the story was Scotty Reston, who got it into his column in the *New York Times* a full day after my story had appeared. The *New York Times* didn't know how to nail it down for attribution either.

"Meanwhile our Knight papers—this was before the merger with Ridder—were having a field day. *Miami Herald* and *Detroit Free Press* led the paper with my story as the major headline on the front page. As an amusing sidelight, we had just acquired the *Philadelphia Enquirer* and they were so startled by my story, which they did not see confirmed on the wires, that they were afraid to use it—to their deep regret. They had had a cold exclusive and flubbed.

"Even funnier was the reaction of the *Washington Post*, which was unable to confirm the story and consequently wrote an editorial which I still keep for laughs.

"The editorial criticized irresponsible reporting by a number of people who were suggesting the unthinkable: that Nixon was ready to withdraw troops from Vietnam. They mentioned me by name—James McCartney of Knight Newspapers—and Scotty Reston of the *New York Times*.

"Though the *New York Times* bureau chief Max Frankel—now editor of the *Times* editorial page—did a follow-up story on Sunday, about five days after my story had appeared, the *Washington Post* carried nothing until Nixon's decision to withdraw troops was formally announced six weeks later."

One bureau man stands out above the rest.

Reporters look at Jerry terHorst of the *Detroit News* with a certain extra look of respect. TerHorst startled the nation, and astounded the press corp, by refusing to work for President Gerald Ford after Ford announced that he was pardoning Nixon.

Why did he do it and what kind of a man gives up such a job as press secretary to a president, one of the most powerful jobs in the whole country, and one of the best paid?

"I resigned because I couldn't agree with the pardon,"

Jerry told my coauthor, "I told the President I would do him a disservice to try to defend something that I felt was so wrong. I was told the night before. I did handle it—the announcement of the pardon—I just didn't come back the next day. There is no law that says the President must consult with his press secretary, but I couldn't live with it."

TerHorst has always been known as a tough newspaperman and a very outspoken one. Jerry Ford had known him as such and respected him for it. Their friendship had gone back to Grand Rapids days, even before Ford ran for Congress.

"Ford was a budding young lawyer out of the Navy and I was a cub reporter out of the Marine Corps in 1946, getting started at the *Grand Rapids Press*. I covered his first campaign in 1948 and eventually I wrote a book about him, *Gerald R. Ford and the Future of the Presidency*, published in 1974 by Third Press."

Jerry terHorst was White House correspondent and bureau chief of the *Detroit News* when Nixon resigned and Ford became President.

"I liked the way Ford had given me a great challenge to revamp the White House press office when he offered me the job. After the Nixon-Ziegler years, I felt and every White House reporter felt the office should be reshaped into a professional news operation rather than a propaganda office.

"So I took the job and got rid of enemy lists and all that nonsense. Ziegler had been operating a propaganda mill—things that should be done by the National Republican Committee. Haldeman and Haig had been telling him who to hire to help preserve the Nixon presidency."

TerHorst remembers with an ironic grin how the National Press Club had invited him as one of their own to come and make a speech about what it was like to be press secretary to a president.

"I remember I said, 'Give me a little time to get my feet on the ground. I've only been here a couple of weeks. I'll come over then and have something worth saying.' Thirty days later, I was out of the White House and back on the beat. So then it became a welcome back party, and they gave me a real surprise gift—a three-legged milking stool, such as I had used in my early days in Michigan.

"They had found it in a Maryland flea market."

TerHorst cherishes the stool, not only for the fact that it

is an antique which brings back memories, but for the words inscribed on a brass plate on the seat: "Jerry terHorst, a Reporter's Reporter, NPC 1974."

The first story terHorst cracked after his White House stint was the exposé that during the last ten months of Nixon's presidency, the President, in fact, if not in name, was Alexander Haig.

The *New York Times* picked it up and ran it on the front page, crediting *Detroit News* and Jerry terHorst. At this point Haig was Ford's chief of staff.

Nowadays terHorst maintains his *Detroit News* position but does a political column as well, which is distributed by Universal Press Syndicate.

Newsmen get to liking the appearance of their own by-lines in the newspaper in the same way a newscaster grows fond of hearing his own voice on the air.

There's nothing wrong with it. That's why people go into the news media—to stand apart and be recognized for what one writes and says.

So how does one cope with suddenly becoming an anonymous writer for such a newsmagazine as *Time*? This subject—the need for identity—is frequently threshed out at the National Press Club, where the question is asked: Are the high wages at *Time* and *Newsweek* worth the loss of one's by-line?

Club members love to get old *Time*sman Scott Hart started on the subject of the *Time* segment of his colorful and many-faceted career. And they they almost roll off their chairs as he gives it to them in complete detail.

"My old buddy, John Denson, late of the *New York World*, and in my opinion, the best damn news-desk man of past decades, brought me to the Washington bureau of *Time* as a so-called staff correspondent," Scott begins.

"He and others there told me the difference between newspaper reporting and *Time*'s way of operation. *Time* wanted *detail* along with the story. This meant: Were the subject's trousers pressed? Did he need a haircut? Did his mouth sag? Did he have a trombone nose? Did he fidget? Did he ever belch?

"One staffer remarked: 'They want everything, even to the color of his underwear.' Okay, no kick from me. I knew that *Time* had grown great on such marvelous colorations. Moreover, Denson, whose real greatness lay in his ability to place men where they were best suited, assigned me to go along with the 'heavy boys,' the diplomatic and political writers, and leave them to their thing while I picked the color.

"My stuff went to New York tacked to the heavy story, and it went across big. Indeed, the first thing I did, the light, bright side of the then just-finished Jefferson Memorial, brought a phone call to me from a New York office writer saying he understood I would stay in the Washington bureau and how pleased he was.

"Then, gradually—and really for want of manpower in the bureau—I was sent alone on all manner of assignments. Then, too, I saw disaster ahead. But let's lay a foundation right here.

"Felix Belair had been taken from the *New York Times* to run the zoo of *Time, Life,* and *Fortune* in Washington. He knew Washington newsmen, and selected the cream—mostly men too old for the war, an average age, I would say, of forty.

"They all had been prominent by-liners on the best publications. They, including me, soon learned they had fallen into obscurity. Actually, they became researchers; for example, if *Time* wanted, and anticipated a story to make two paragraphs, the editors wanted, say two thousand or three thousand words.

"And the hell of it was that New York, or somebody I never knew, wanted it written by us as though it were aimed at *Harper's* or the *Atlantic*. There was no need for this, no reason in it. All the actual writers in New York wanted was something like a memorandum—the facts and the colorings.

"Most unnerving was the pressure. Each Wednesday we held a story conference. Each of us was admonished to bring in a minimum of five story ideas. These went to New York by teletype.

"Late on Thursday, the teletypes related to us which of our ideas they wanted—along with literally dozens of ideas they had hatched up. There were only thirteen men and women in the bureau then, compared with twenty-one today, and many of them were on brief assignment to the war fronts or elsewhere, sometimes leaving only a half dozen of us in Washington. The deadline was Saturday night!

"Wartime censorship clamps were really on. And don't forget they would want maybe three thousand words to 'process down'—as Luce used or misused the word *rewrite*. They wanted military and political secrets that the authorities would scarcely whisper in cloisters.

"I saw one harassed guy head for the Pentagon one

Friday morning with twenty-three 'queries,' as they called assignments, in his pockets.

"It is a fact that if the copy growing out of the twenty-three queries had been put into a newspaper, it would have made an entire newspaper—and one of the very best."

As Scott Hart tells it, the possibility of getting on the cover of *Time* magazine made top government officials open up like a sieve. "*Time* had almost mystical prestige," he says.

According to Hart, staffers were not allowed to see press agents or public relations men—only the top officials.

"We demanded and got to see the top people. But here was the hell of it: We once estimated that less than five percent of what we sent to New York ever saw print. This played hell with our contacts.

"After a while, someone would say to me on the phone, 'Do you *really* want a story, or are you just fishing?' He meant but wouldn't say, 'and wasting my time?' I'd feel sorry for the poor joker. Hell, I was having my troubles too.

"A common joke in the shop was, 'Say look, here is a comma I wrote.'

"The writers in New York, I know, felt badly about this, but were helpless under the system. Once I got a query to go out into the Virginia countryside and find a colorful sort of farmer who was much troubled about the general tax situation. A *Life* photographer and I drove there around twilight.

"Like all farmers, this one I finally found in the moonlight, let go a string of damnations upon taxation, hard work, low returns, politicians, his aching corns, beetles, bugs, and birds that dropped things on his head. I believe it was the best story I ever wrote.

"Not one damn line ever appeared in the magazine—though it was exactly what they told me to get. Several weeks later, a writer, whose name eludes me now, mailed me the story from the New York office, stating he considered it so charming that he had asked permission for me to own it and market it.

"Another time, they were doing a cover story on Ernie Pyle. I got hold of Pyle's best friend—and later biographer—and spent an entire afternoon with him. He gave me, with scarcely a murmur, stuff I knew he wanted for himself.

"What appeared from the twenty-three sheets of copy sent up? Two goddamn sentences, and those rewritten. I had sent stuff unknown about Pyle. The material they used was pretty much common knowledge.

"I could go on and on with such illustrations but my blood pressure soars. Under such pressure and frustration some of the men grew ill; some drank. Maybe that's why they're now letting an occasional by-line appear.

"God, what a price we paid! We worked from around ten thirty A.M. to midnight and later, six and often seven days a week. I believe that for a while I bordered on madness. On my day off I'd wander into Rock Creek Park alone and recite poetry to myself to shake myself into reality.

"Then around Christmastime of 1944, some dude was sent down from New York and Belair disappeared. One by one the staff was fired.

"I leaped toward the National Geographic Society and got a job, only to be talked out of it by the new gent from New York. I should have had my head examined.

"The following July a notation came on the teletype from New York saying, 'Kudos to Scott Hart' for some damn story or another I had dug out. That very afternoon I was summoned into the boss's office and told I was fired. I was, he said, the worst reporter he had ever known. And I was told to be out of the office by five P.M. that day."

There is always a hush as Scott finishes his story of how he got fired from *Time*. And then he looks around at his colleagues and says with a fierce grin, "Well, you asked me how the hell it felt to work for *Time*. If it's gotten better I haven't heard it."

The best stories in Washington's news bureaus never make the newspaper. Take the day Barry Sullivan, a dictation boy on the Dow Jones (*Wall Street Journal*) News Service, broke the sugar market.

Barry, with earphones on, was on the typewriter taking dictation. As he tells it to select friends, "It was a terrible day; the desk man had a hangover; the teletype man had been bawled out and was mad at the world.

"Reporters at the Capitol were hollering for service. Things were jumping at the White House, too, as bad news continued to come from Hitler's Germany.

"And just then the time came to take the daily imports from Cuba of tonnage of sugar for the day. Usually, it ran to something like forty thousand tons.

"But in the turmoil, I struck an extra zero and the message went through the desk and out on the wire to all commodity exchanges and brokers that four hundred thousand tons of sugar had been imported that day.

"The market dived for the cellar—and so did I. I almost got fired. If I'd known then what I know now, I would have bought short first before taking the message and sending it along.

"Then, after selling, I could have retired at twenty-one, financially secure for life."

Covering the Hill can sometimes result in bizarre situations, but reporters are always amazed at how dignified the legislators can remain under all circumstances. A *Los Angeles Times* reporter once had a lesson in dignity in a most extraordinary experience.

As he told the story, he went to a particular California congressman's office after the House had adjourned, as he had done before—and since.

The door was open and he walked in and looked around for someone to announce him but no one seemed to be there. So he went over and opened the door to the adjoining room, the congressman's private office.

"It was rather dark but clearly in view was a woman spread-eagle on a desk, and the congressman was giving it to her. I gingerly backed out and closed the door, hoping nobody had seen me. I should have gotten the hell out but I was standing in the outer office in a stunned condition when the congressman came hurrying out.

"He was still stuffing his shirt in his trousers and zipping up and he said, with all dignity, 'I'm sorry I kept you waiting but I was doing a favor for a widow woman from my district.'"

Every bureau has its unprinted journalistic anecdote. A reliable newsman, Morris D. Ervin of the *Cincinnati Times-Star*, told me this many years ago as a true happening. The English Duke of Chester was rumored to be coming to the States to see a lady of lurid reputation—actually it was an Irish noble of similar name.

As Tex, as we called him, told the story, "An American reporter kept calling the British embassy for word as to the arrival of the nobleman.

"Each time he drew a blank. And each time he became more determined to get his story. Finally, he got to the Ambassador, who also denied knowledge.

"'Couldn't he be here without your knowing it?' the reporter pursued.

"'That is scarcely possible,' said the Ambassador. 'Young man, do you know who the Duke of Chester is?'

"'Well, he's some sort of a lord.'

"'True,' said the Ambassador drily, 'but in addition to his other titles, he is King of England.'"

Some reporters climb the reportorial ladder of success by switching from bureau to bureau and some succeed by achieving tenure.

When Don Larrabee came to Washington from Maine in 1946, he didn't realize he was beginning a thirty-two-year career with the same organization—the Griffin News Bureau. He didn't dream that eventually the news bureau would add his name to become the Griffin-Larrabee Bureau, representing at one point, twenty-six newspapers from Maine to Alaska.

Says Larrabee, "The Griffin News Bureau was, I believe, the oldest organization in Washington serving independent daily newspapers.

"At first, every story was exciting, including my year as president of the National Press Club in the thick of the Watergate scandal." But in 1978 Larrabee surprised friends by selling his bureau to two staff members, Betty Mills and Gary Thomas, after agreeing to accept a new challenge—that of opening a Washington office, of which Larrabee is director, for Governor Joseph E. Brennan of Maine.

Why did he do it? everyone asked. He had been a part of the Hill scene for so long—wouldn't he miss the old House and Senate press galleries?

Well yes, Larrabee agreed, but after the first thirty years he had felt himself growing a little stale.

"I must admit," Don says, "that I found little inspiration, after thirty years, in writing some of the same stories over and over again, with only a slight change in the cast of characters.

"There are highs and lows in the news business, as in any other. I experienced one high chasing Senator Edmund Muskie as he chased the presidency. It was a letdown when that collapsed. I have been told by a number of newsmen that they are bored with post-Watergate Washington—when in their lifetime can they ever again write a story to compare with the unmaking of a president?"

Not everyone, however, starts to feel jaded. Listen to

Cyrene Dear, a spritely, high-fashioned senior citizen of 82, who for 33 years has been reporter, editorial writer and newspaper chain vice president and still writes a column "Washington Siren" at the Dear News Bureau. You will be amazed at what she has packed into her colorful career—and she is still chasing stories around the world:

She was tear-gassed during a Panamanian revolt in 1964.

She was accused of starting a flu epidemic in Algeria.

She attended a press conference in the palace of King Hussein of Jordan the day he expelled leading members of his cabinet. On the road between Jerusalem and Amman, the handsome Arab police guide sang Arab love songs to her as she sat in the front seat of the car between him and the driver.

In Robat, Morocco, she was locked in her hotel room. When she finally got out, the study mission had long left for the party, so she got a taxi and said grandly, "Take me to the palace." Unfortunately, she found she was almost penniless. She gave the driver the only money she had, not knowing how she would get back, and ran into the palace.

The party was over. King Hassan had given his speech but she cornered him and said, "When you came to Williamsburg, Virginia, as a young prince with your father's entourage, my husband and I had to give up our room to the King of Morocco.

"It was Thanksgiving Day and as we were leaving the dining room, the royal entourage entered. My husband accidentally bumped into the King, your father, almost knocking him down. But the King graciously apologized first.

"King Hassan seemed amused at the reminder and said, 'I have never forgotten that Williamsburg incident.'"

It was in Rabat that the study mission was entertained by members of the King's cabinet. "We sat on beautiful cushions on the floor at our table for eight. There was plenty of silver, but we followed our host's example and broke pieces of bread and dipped them into the main dish—mostly lamb."

President Habib ben Ali Bourguiba of Tunisia she found living "in a palace that makes the White House look like a summer cottage." And his attitude was very regal too.

"But," Cyrene says, "his son, with the same name, who was his foreign service secretary when I was there, was very democratic. He personally served us excellent drinks in beautiful glasses on silver trays. He also interpreted his father's French for us in a very relaxed way."

A female success story, the name Cyrene Dear is known to many readers because for years she headed the company known as Dear Publication and Radio, Inc.

When her husband, publisher Albert Dear, died in 1959, she determined to keep the organization going just as if he were there. The very day after the tragedy she presided at a news meeting.

"In fact," Cyrene Dear recalls, "both the day after my husband died and the day after a son died, I presided at meetings. Work is the best antidote to tragedy and newspaper work is the best of all.

"I just keep busy. After fifty-two years, I am still married to the newspaper business."

There are about three hundred foreign correspondents in Washington. The largest group are the BE-Jays, meaning the British Empire Journalists. However, there are fairly good-sized groups from Latin countries as well. Portugese-speaking Brazil has five separate newspaper bureaus in the Press Building.

Each group has it own problems, its own puzzlements. The Mexican reporters find the twelve to one luncheon hour in D.C. uncivilized. They are used to a three o'clock lunchtime.

The French find almost everything uncivilized and, it is said around the Press Club, they speak only to each other.

The housekeeper thanks heaven for the soap opera and the Washington press thanks heaven for the foreign press bureaus, who make life bearable on the dull days.

British reporters seem to have the greatest air of irreverence and become downright fanciful when writing about Washington. One Britisher writing for a London paper kept the National Press Club gang amused as well as the readers of his paper with such "inside" stories as a scoop that Jimmy Carter was going to grow a beard like Abraham Lincoln had to improve his image, and that Jimmy Carter's lunch every day comes from a delicatessen, and that beggars in derby hats were panhandling in front of the White House—with seventeen such-hatted characters being hauled off in a paddy wagon.

But according to member James Srodes, what's amusing to the Press Club is a headache to other foreign reporters, who get queries from their editors asking for similar stories.

Foreign correspondents, not having to bear the consequences of presidential acts, view the American presidents with much more humor and sit around laughing at the blunders and inconsistencies they have witnessed. American reporters may join them and laugh a little too, but it's mostly with tears in their eyes—thinking about their taxes.

Bogdan Kipling, the one-man Washington bureau for the *Toronto Star*, amuses the press gang with his recital of what American presidents are all about and "How Presidents Solve the Energy Crisis," his favorite spiel. "Energy produced some of the funniest situations ever witnessed by the eye of man," he said recently, "particularly in Nixon and Ford days. When the energy crisis erupted Treasury Secretary George Schultz announced he could reduce gas use by introducing a five-cents-a-gallon surtax.

"We all thought this was the funniest thing we ever heard. It wouldn't wash. It would make no difference. We were right. Then came energy czar Bill Simon with "Project Independence"—the theory that motion is all. Create a lot of motion, flap around, and people will take it seriously. Of course, they didn't.

"Later he was rewarded by Nixon by becoming Secretary of the Treasury, having made an absolute botch out of the energy crisis. This is the public relations way to solve the problem of incompetence—reward with a secretaryship."

As his appreciative audience laughed, Bogdan continued, "As the country rapidly plunged into near depression, Jerry Ford's prescription was 'tighten your belts'—don't consume too much, don't spend too much."

At this point Bogdan shook his head and exclaimed, "Christ, if the country is to avoid a real depression they have to spend like crazy, just as many experts were saying. What I'm saying is that on the economic policy side, the president watchers are having a time, laughing. I'm underwhelmed. It's a comedy. There is a lot less than meets the eye. Jerry Ford, thinking he could turn the trick with a WIN button. It's pathetic or it's funny."

How does Bogdan view the Carter administration?

"Carter's is a seesaw administration," Bogdan said, "blowing hot and cold. We don't see that this administration sees any better than the previous three administrations what the problems are and how to cope with them."

Bogdan's main point is that Carter started out "too cocksure of himself." He reminisces about his own experience. "When Carter came on the scene, he announced the end of the pork barrel from Watergate days. I happened to be at the White House when the cut in dam projects was announced. I said, 'Jody, would the President veto if Congress reinstates the water bill with the dams. Would you go so far as to veto?'

"He fudged, but we all know subsequently the President had to back down. Carter had underestimated the power of Congress and been too cocksure of himself."

Sometimes the wire services get scooped by the foreign press. Bogdan Kipling remembers his first news triumph.

"It concerned the Watergate story. I had been given a pretty good tip on the Supreme Court decision of Jaworski versus Nixon on the matter of the tapes, I believe that was 1974.

"I filed a story saying, 'It will be eight to zero that Nixon will have to give up the tapes,' and I concluded it was the end of Nixon. I was reporting for fourteen dailies in Canada.

"Of those fourteen papers, only one dared run the story. They didn't believe it.

"Well, AP didn't have it. UPI didn't have it, so they were afraid to touch it. But the story was right. Twelve hours later the wire services confirmed it and I had given one paper a great newsbeat."

What does Bogdan think of the American Press?

"Funny people, these American reporters," he muses. "Very generous in spite of what you hear of this town—really quite soft in terms of generosity. Reporters give dupes of stories to a foreign correspondent even before their own story hits the newspaper, knowing full well we are not competitive. And sometimes they give you leads. Sometimes we have covered for one another."

As for how reporting compares in the two capitals, Kipling says, "It is much more exciting to be a reporter in Washington, since reporters are much more aggressive in Washington than in Ottawa.

"You would never ask such embarrassing questions of Prime Minister Trudeau as were thrown at President Nixon, or Ford or Carter.

"At first I found myself out of my depth and shocked at the guts of the reporters as the monumental Watergate story was breaking. I quickly realized if I wanted to play in this league, I would have to be more ruthless."

The foreign press is known for its great sense of humor and actually are more interested in such things as Polish jokes and Russian jokes than even Americans are.

But the best Polish jokes came right out of Warsaw and were sent back by Michael Getler, the *Washington Post* foreign correspondent. Getler's best Polish story is about the man who gets so furious at waiting in line for meat that he announces he is going to leave the line that hasn't moved in three hours and go murder the Prime Minister.

As Mike Getler tells it, " A few hours later he returns to the line, looking dejected, and reports, 'No luck. There was a line.'"

When a Pole became the new Pope, Polish jokes ran up and down the Tap Room bar. One of the best asked the question: "What was the Pope's first action on moving into the Vatican?"

The answer, according to Al Beitel: "He ordered new wallpaper for the Sistine Chapel."

Even the *Evening Star*, in its "Ear" column, came up with a Polish joke. When readers complained, "Ear" quoted what Pope John Paul II himself has said on the subject of Polish jokes: "I think they are certainly permissible, if in good taste. We certainly have Polish jokes in Poland! We also make jokes about the Russians." And just to be sure, my coauthor checked with John Szostak, a White House correspondent who spent several days with Cardinal Karol Wojtyla before he was elevated to the Papacy, and confirmed that he had indeed said that.

John Skelly runs a one-man bureau and originally came from Cuba. In fact, he went to school with Castro's first wife, who was originally Skelly's childhood sweetheart. Press Club members frequently go to John for understanding of Castro and the Cuban revolution.

Skelly does his best to explain Castro and Cuba but there is a bitter edge to his conversation, because his Castro connection for years kept him from getting good reporting jobs— unfortunately he worked for two months for Castro in the early days of the revolution. When Castro spoke at the Press Club in April 1959, he offered Skelly a job again and tried to get him to come back to Cuba.

Today he is Washington correspondent and bureau chief of *El Nuevo Dia* of San Juan, Puerto Rico, which makes him an American rather than foreign correspondent.

But Skelly is always involved in diplomatic reporting, frequently writing in Spanish.

The fact that another diplomatic reporter had a name that was pronounced just like John's led to all kinds of complications.

But it's better when John Skelly tells it:

"John Scali was the AP diplomatic reporter when I was the UPI diplomatic reporter and we would meet at the State Department noonday briefings. We were always getting confused at the State Department press room. But one day when I was on the UPI cables—which is the same as the AP's foreign desk—I got a call from the Polish Ambassador's secretary inviting me to the Polish embassy.

"I showed up for lunch at the embassy and was escorted in grandly into the Ambassador's library. They had immediately fixed me drinks and I was leisurely perusing the Ambassador's library shelves when the Ambassador strolled in.

"I turned around just as he spotted me and his face changed colors as his expression clearly said, 'Who the hell is this guy?' In a flash I realized he had wanted not me but the 'Sicilian Mafia,' as I always called Scali to his face, just as he called me the 'Cuban Mafia.'

"Just then who is ushered into the library but the Sicilian himself, John Scali, at which time I bowed and thanked the Ambassador for his hospitality.

"The Polish Ambassador appreciated the humor and laughed and asked me to stay, but I decided that two 'Scalis' is more than anyone can take at one time.

"I got my revenge on the Ambassador by having told, to date, forty-six hundred Polish jokes."

The largest of the French news agencies in the United States is France-Presse, which has eight or ten correspondents in its Washington office.

Nelly Stone is the more typical foreign correspondent, working all alone to cover for her wire agency, Intermonde-Presse of Paris, which services about a dozen French newspapers. She also represents an individual newspaper, *Nord Eclair*, of Lille, France.

As Nelly describes it, being a foreign correspondent is not the easiest thing.

"It is a rather lonesome job because we foreigners live in a little world of our own and are not really included in many American functions except the State Department if you belong to their Correspondents Association, and sometimes the White House, which, in my case, has been pretty good about inviting me to some functions.

"Most foreign correspondents seem to live pretty much

a closed circuit and to socialize with other correspondents from the same country or with people from their respective embassies.

"I know it is true of the French, but I think it is also true of most nationalities. On a broader scale, the Europeans seem to know and see each other more and stick together, as do the Asiatics and the Latinos, and Spanish-speaking groups. Of course, they have some American friends, but not an awful lot and they mostly entertain among themselves."

As for how a foreign correspondent decides which story to cover, that isn't easy either. Nelly says, "Something which is big in Washington is not necessarily of any interest for the readers in France or in Hong Kong or in Buenos Aires.

"You have to learn how to decide what is or what is not and sometimes try very hard to convince the editors about the potential of a story."

Still there are the thrilling moments and the foreign correspondent gets to be a regular at the embassy of his native country. He or she also gets to interview all the stars of his country, whom he might never get to meet over there.

Nelly Stone, for example, has interviewed a whole parade of big names from France. "I have even interviewed sports figures occasionally, such as the French skiing champion, Jean-Claude Killy. In Washington I have interviewed a French jockey, the French singing star Charles Aznavour, and sexy actor Yves Montand."

But Nelly's favorite anecdote relates to the TV star-scientist, Captain Jacques Cousteau. "To me, it was my prize interview—one hour with Cousteau, who turned out to be just as fascinating in private as on TV and in his books. He was here testifying on the Hill for a hearing on ocean pollution and in spite of a very tight schedule, agreed most graciously to talk to me at great length.

"One slight and humorous detail about this interview. After talking very strongly at the hearing against pollution and for antipollution measures, Cousteau, as soon as he was finished, produced the biggest, fattest cigar I ever saw in my life and proceeded to light it, generating great clouds of smoke.

"I mentioned it to him later and he laughed about it, saying that it was more to the deterioration of his health than to the environment."

Many foreign correspondents would be at loose ends if

it were not for the Foreign Press Center in the National Press Building.

Though most foreign reporters are completely free to travel and do what they want, unlike our correspondents, going to Soviet bloc countries, the center does serve as a sort of an Intourist service in that it organizes trips for them as well as get-togethers on an informal basis. However, when countries, such as the USSR, place restraints on our reporters, the State Department places what it calls "reciprocal restraints" on their reporters.

Any question they have about American life or how to get a story, can be answered in the plush Foreign Press Center offices by various American aides from ICA (International Communication Agency, formerly USIA), with linguistic talents, such as Bill Gordon.

Not only can they listen in on the State Department press briefings wired into the center's quarters, but the White House press briefings are also broadcast there.

Sometimes foreign reporters are heard to mutter in disbelief after all the help they receive in Washington as compared to what little service is provided foreign press in other world centers.

As one French reporter was heard to mutter "*Mon Dieu,* the Americans are about to drown us all in press releases."

Foreign correspondents make up an important segment of the Press Club and spend perhaps even more time in the bar than their American cousins, who have homes to go to and many more relatives and are not as footloose.

Not all writers for foreign or ethnic readers are happy with their treatment in Washington. One of them—John Szostak— who, as a one-man bureau, writes for three million ethnic readers in the United States and two million abroad, has been particularly annoyed by the treatment he feels he has received by the White House and by his American colleagues.

As a matter of fact, Szostak sued the *Baltimore Sun* for $750 for printing a story making fun of the questions asked at White House press briefings.

The article, by Carl Leubsdorf, had said that some reporters, John Szostak among them, had turned the briefings into "near circuses" by asking "obscure questions about ethnic subjects."

The story had appeared under the headline "Political

Posing Turns White House Press Briefings into 'Absurd Plays.'"
Szostak lost his case when the judge dismissed it, saying that
though Leubsdorf's story had been "unpleasant" it was not
"defamatory."

Though Szostak's action might make him sound rather
grim, nothing could be further from the truth. John is known for
his great sense of humor.

When Marshal Tito of Yugoslavia was visiting the White
House, John Szostak tried to inject a little levity by kidding one of
the official party about a decoration he was wearing, thinking he
understood American-style jokes.

As Szostak tells the story, "In all good humor and
smiling, I asked the fellow, 'If I go to Yugoslavia, do you think I can
buy one of those with a few cereal boxtops?'

"Not understanding my joke he replied, 'No, no. Marshal Tito gave this to me.'

"Still smiling I said, 'How about that, maybe when I see
the old boy, I will ask him for a few.'

"The man walked away saying in Russian, 'You un-
cultured idiot.'

"I replied in Russian, 'How nice to know someone who
can speak Russian.' You should have seen his expression.

"People would be amazed, when they read the very
serious story that appears in the newspaper, how many irreverent
comments were going on in the sidelines while the press is keeping
itself from getting bored."

Along that line Szostak recalls how the press amused
itself outside the door of the Roosevelt Room, while they were
waiting for the appearance of the President, himself.

Prior to Carter's arrival, presidential aide Midge Costanza was giving a briefing to the representatives of the National
Council of Churches.

"Since Midge was sounding reverential," John recalls,
"one of the White House press said, 'Let's all kneel. Reverend
Midge will give her blessing. Does anyone know how to give a Latin
blessing?'

"Sure enough a reporter stepped forward and gave it to
perfection in Latin. Then to balance the Catholic touch with the
Baptist, the press starting humming in a low voice, 'Amazing
Grace,' the President's favorite hymn.

"At this point, the guests were craning their necks to see what was going on and seemed more interested in our antics than Costanza's briefing. But suddenly President Carter appeared and all nonsense stopped.

"The press may have its fun but it does respect the presidency."

By great good fortune, John Szostak unexpectedly became truly famous among his peers late in 1978 when Cardinal Karol Wojtyla of Poland suddenly was elevated to become Pope John Paul II. Szostak had been corresponding with him for years and had spent several days with him when Cardinal Wojtyla came to the States to attend the Philadelphia Eucharistic Congress in 1976.

Suddenly all his friends were asking John, "What is the Pope really like?" From him they learned that the new Pope was a sports enthusiast, skied, canoed, and played a hot game of Ping-Pong. From him they learned too, that John Paul II had once suffered the exhaustion and mental indignity of being a slave laborer of the Nazis, and that he had been a singer and actor in an amateur theatrical troupe as cover for his work in the underground.

Yet, in spite of personal adversity, Karol Wojtyla came through as a happy and remarkably witty person, when Sozstak finally met him after the long correspondence. "The first thing he said to me was, 'So this is the legendary John Szostak.'"

Szostak had a bit of an exclusive for my coauthor. "I can tell you something for your book that I have not told anyone," he told Frannie. "The Pope is simply mad about blueberries. He called for them every day. About other food, he was not concerned. I would go out to get him a snack and it would be simply toast without butter and black coffee. The fresh blueberries were the special thing he loved for breakfast."

15/Wire Services

What makes a person want to write for a wire service rather than for an individual newspaper?

Sam Fogg at sixty is a good man to ask. "I've worked for two of the three major wire services. I worked for UPI until just recently and for the INS, which folded in the late fifties. I stuck with wire services because I like the competition. Most newspapermen are competitive, but wire service reporters are the most competitive of all.

"A wire service reporter has by far the most exciting life. His deadline is every minute. He has to run for the phone and be looking for his lead while the dictation boy or girl is writing the heading."

Newspapers buy wire services because it's less expensive than trying to staff every government agency in Washington with their own reporters or have reporters stationed in every city and every country.

Ah, how life has changed for the wire service reporters. Reporters seldom get the DT's anymore—at least on the job. Instead, they are concerned with VDT's—a fancy name for a fancy gadget that has taken all the joy out of old time newspapering—video display terminals.

You are the reporter. You have a keyboard. You roll no paper in. You just type your story, which then appears in front of you on a TV-like screen.

You read it and make corrections. Your hand never touches a sheet of clean, crisp paper. Push the button and get a new page.

When you are done writing the story, it goes into a big computer. You don't throw the story on the editor's desk in triumph. When the editor wants to see it, he pushes a button and calls it up. He makes corrections on the screen. He pushes another button and it disappears.

All the stories go to the Big Computer in the Sky—showering down again, like snowflakes all over the world, upon newspapers, radio and TV stations, newsmagazines, and whoever else has paid for the service. Editors and others with no poetry in their souls call this "redistribution."

Your story may go to a newspaper in New York, where that editor, who knows its name and number, may summon it, edit it further, and decide on which page of the newspaper he wants it to appear.

Because wire stories go to so many newspapers with individual policies, the wire service reporter must write as unbiased a story as possible—"straight reporting," it is called.

According to Fogg, "The best wire service reporter I ever saw in action was Doug Cornell of AP," who married UPI White House correspondent Helen Thomas, after he retired. "He was definitely the most skilled of anyone I've ever come across at getting and writing a story, and most important, *knowing what was important*. The lead.

"As if that weren't enough, he was one of the nicer people to work with."

Fogg's happiest memory of Cornell was the time they were covering the investigation of "the Hollywood Ten" by the House Un-American Activities Committee. Or, as Sam says, "the time we used to ride the broomstick together."

Fogg and Cornell, along with George Reedy of United Press, who would later work for Lyndon Johnson at the White House, combined forces and "had a gentleman's agreement" that they would "black sheet" their stories to protect one another—meaning exchange carbon copies.

As Sam recalls, "Since we represented the three wire services, this practice kept us from getting call-backs from our editors in the middle of the night, wanting to know why another wire service had said such and such.

"It also prevented members of the Un-American Activities Committee from taking advantage of a wire service to keep phony stories alive. We would pool resources to find out the truth.

"On one occasion Doug came back and wrote his overnight about the Communist threatened takeover, or whatever, and gave his black sheet to George, who rewrote the lead and goosed the story and gave me his black sheet.

"I was in the process of goosing it to make it still more lively when Doug came over and saw something that really shook him up.

"He said, 'Jesus Christ, where did you get that?' and he

rushed back to rewrite his own story and goose it some more. At that time J. Parnell Thomas was the chairman. He later went to jail for kickbacks."

One of Sam Fogg's favorite drinking stories concerns the time he was with INS and George Reedy was with UPI and they both went up to the Hill to see Congressman Harold Velde of the House Un-American Activities Committee to get an overnight story.

They had chosen well because, as Sam recalls, "Congressman Velde came from Peoria, home of the Hiram Walker liquor distillery and he always had a good icebox full and ready.

"It was getting dusk and we were sitting in the congressman's office in the gloaming, getting a little drunk with him on Hiram Walker.

"We didn't realize how much we'd been imbibing until Velde said, 'You know, fellows, I'm too stupid to be a congressman.' And George and I weren't in much better shape. It took quite a while before one of us spoke up and said, 'You're not the dumbest one, congressman. There are others who are stupider than you.'

"At the time, I thought we were being very kindly, and after a long pause, Velde said, 'Name some.'

"And after a long pause we finally named four. But it took time and trouble."

Expense account stories are, next to sex, the favorite stories of newsmen. Sam Fogg, a veteran of many years in the wire services, shamelessly tells his favorite, which concerns the time back in the early fifties, when he was covering the White House on weekends and had the dullish job of covering Dwight Eisenhower's weekly appearance in church. As consolation, Fogg found the way to make an extra twenty-five cents. He padded his expense account.

As Sam tells it, "I would sit in the back of the church where the secret service men were and fling my little quarter into the collection box when it passed me. Reverend Elston had an affluent congregation and there would be the rustle of dollar bills and even $5 bills until my little coin would go clang against the side of the plate.

"People would look at me and I would look back and pretend the secret service man did it. Well, one day Hutch [INS Bureau chief] called me in and said with an ominous frown, 'Sam, I notice you're putting in a church contribution of fifty cents.' I wondered if he had found me out. But no, he had a different complaint: 'Putting a man's church contribution on an exprense account—that sounds sacreligious.'

"I had no answer. I just looked at him and kept on looking. He finally said, uneasily, 'Well maybe you are right. But for Christ's sake, put it in as breakfast or taxi or some damned thing.'"

But that isn't the end of Sam's story. A girl reporter showed up one Sunday covering Ike's religious experience for UP, and she took the opportunity to get Sam's advice on whether it would be all right for her to put her church contribution on her expense account. Sam had just come through his ordeal with Hutch and was still smarting from it.

"Of course," he said.

"What do I put down?" she asked.

"How much did you put in?" he asked.

She said, "One dollar."

Sam said, "Call it 'rental of pew.'"

She did, not knowing he was pulling her leg, and bureau chief Julius Frandsen raised hell, but eventually allowed it.

Later Sam Fogg was telling the AP man, Marvin Arrowsmith, what he had to call his church contribution and found that Marvin, who also was in the Eisenhower Sunday press retinue, was having a different kind of problem. He had put his contribution on his expense account and the AP New York office disallowed it.

Arrowsmith insisted that the money in the collection plate was indeed a proper expense item.

As Sam Fogg tells it, "Marv became indignant and decided to fight. He told AP, 'Look, I shouldn't even be in this Protestant church, let alone subsidizing it.'" He won!

To show the contrast in expense account stories that time brings about, this is the latest one bandied about the Club Tap Room, and it comes from Howard K. Smith. Smith told of a recent reporter's expense account item, after he attended some foreign economists' meeting, which listed a hundred dollars a day for food.

The editors demanded to know how a journalist could spend a hundred dollars a day for food.

According to Smith, back came the reply, "By skipping lunch."

Many great writers and reporters start as copyboys or dictation girls.

Helen Thomas, UPI White House correspondent, has scored so many firsts that a book could be written about her—and it was—by herself. She was:

- First woman to close a presidential press conference.
- She became the first female officer of the National Press Club—treasurer in 1972—after it opened its doors to women members following many years of male exclusivity.
- She became the first woman officer of the White House Correspondents Association after it had been in existence more than fifty years. She followed that by becoming its first woman president—1975–76.
- She became the first woman member of the Gridiron Club in its ninety-year history.

That is pretty heady stuff, but Helen Thomas has remained a nice human being, approachable and even fun to be around. She does not take herself too seriously, even though the 1976 *World Almanac* listed her as one of the twenty-five most influential women in America today, in company with *Washington Post* publisher Katharine Graham; Coretta King, widow of Martin Luther King, Jr.; former First Lady, Lady Bird Johnson; and Texas Congresswoman Barbara Jordan.

Helen is, in fact, the kind of gal that fellows like to kid and play practical jokes on. There was the time during the 1976 campaign that Helen Thomas spent a lot of time with the political reporters hanging around Plains, in their coverage of candidate Jimmy Carter.

There was little to do in Plains except watch a softball game or listen to the arguments between the two spurs of the Baptist Church, so the correspondents were always working out their own entertainment.

Helen Thomas was deathly afraid of the small planes that candidate Carter used to ride in before he was provided with an Air Force jet. So it became the obsession of Sam Donaldson, the ABC White House correspondent, to lure Helen into a small aircraft.

He enlisted the aid of Tom Peterson, who ran the Plains grass field airport and was formerly Carter's pilot—and still the Carter family pilot—to invite Helen on a newsmaking flight.

The plot was that Pete was going to take them up for a supposedly never-before-seen view of the town and then would pretend he had to make a forced landing on a grass strip used by crop dusters.

They had almost convinced Helen that she must make this flight so as not to be scooped, but at the last minute, she smelled a rat and backed down.

Reporters, male and female, develop a sixth sense about people and their motives.

Helen is a good example of how far one can rise from the humble position of copygirl. She was not proud. That was the closest she could get to a reporting job when she applied for work after graduating from Wayne State University.

It was at the *Washington Daily News*.

It was definitely a step up to get a job at United Press in 1943 but her assignment was something no one else wanted—writing radio news for the UPI wire.

At that time radio was snooted by the regular reporters as an inconsequential adjunct of newspapers, of no importance and with no future.

Radio newsmen were not even permitted to become members of the National Press Club. Helen stuck to the job for twelve years, even though she had to be at work at 5:30 A.M. to get the radio news out in time for breakfast listeners.

She was eventually rewarded by being put on several beats around the federal government agencies, including Justice Department, FBI, and HEW.

Helen Thomas's big break came in 1960 when she was assigned to cover President-elect John F. Kennedy. Mrs. Kennedy was a very colorful society woman of the Georgetown area and a beautiful young mother, so it was felt she deserved special attention.

Helen gave her plenty of attention and Jacqueline Kennedy did not appreciate it. So good was Helen at ferreting out exclusives about Jackie and Caroline and John-John, that Mrs. Kennedy gave special orders to her private secretary, Mary Gallagher, not to tell Helen Thomas "a damn thing."

In Kennedy's administration, Helen became the first woman in history to close a president's press conference with the "Thank you, Mr. President," and she continued to open and close the conferences of succeeding presidents.

An early fighter for women's lib, she has always been an outspoken person. When Martha Mitchell started calling her in the middle of the night to leak Watergate information, Helen Thomas did not pass it off with a laugh. She not only wrote the stories but said that she believed Martha.

More and more Helen became part of the news as well as writer of the news, and honors have been heaped on her. She has received three honorary doctorates—from Wayne State University, Eastern Michigan University, and the International School of Arts. She also received the Matrix Award from the Women in Communications.

In 1975, she was named Woman of the Year in Communications by the *Ladies' Home Journal.* She has also been a president of the Women's National Press Club, now the Washington Press Club.

UPI chief, Grant Dillman, one of the best-loved newspapermen in Washington and elected to the Journalism Hall of Fame in 1977, had a little idiosyncrasy.

He was legendary for firing reporters when in his cups. After a three-martini lunch at the Press Club he would fire whoever touched off his ire, which wasn't hard to do.

His saving grace was that the firing resulted in nothing more serious than the sacked person being rehired by breakfast.

Some miss the good old days. Things are duller around UPI now. "I've given up martinis and I'm on white wine," Grant says with an apologetic little smile.

He doesn't look glamorous but everything about the present life of Grant Dillman, UPI Washington bureau chief, spells glamour. He bosses 120 correspondents and other personnel in UPI's Washington offices on the third floor of the National Press Building and was the model for Gunther Damon in Robert Serling's best-selling novel, *The President's Plane Is Missing.*

Those are the biggies, but you could go on and on about his other connections, like the fact that he is a member of the Gridiron Club, a member in good popularity standing of the National Press Club, and chairman of the National Freedom of Information Committee of the Society of Professional Journalists.

But all those things sound like dry statistics compared to what it is like to live and work around this genius of a man.

He is as unlike his AP counterpart, Walter Mears, as it is possible to be. Older for one thing—all of sixty—though a vital sixty.

Instead of the cloistered office, Dillman sits right in the middle of the hectic wire service newsroom, working like a maniac. If you didn't know who he was, you might mistake him for an aging copyboy—and he has been mistaken for just that. He runs around in rolled-up shirt sleeves, looking not nearly so elegant as his top correspondents, and everyone from the dictation girl up calls him by his first name. When the switchboard is busy, he grabs the phone himself and he has even been known to take some dictation.

Only if he's really sick or disgusted does Grant take to his private office. "I get my ass out in the newsroom where I'm needed. I can't hear a thing in my office or keep on top of the news." Grant keeps on top of the news and on top of every person phoning in the news, checking the stories over the shoulder of the dictation person, if it is hot enough.

He cares about everything and some say he cares too much. And there are those who say it is too bad that Grant Dillman does not have the middle initial O, so that he could officially sign his wire messages "GOD."

There are any number of great stories about the famous Dillman temper but perhaps the best is what happened at the Democratic National Convention in Chicago, in 1956, when Dillman was writing an important story and his predecessor, Julius "Jay" Frandsen, was pushing him by standing and reading over Dillman's shoulder as he wrote.

Dillman suddenly jumped up and simply left, leaving Frandsen to finish the job and do it *his* way.

But true to form, Grant Dillman's tempers never last too long and within the hour he was back to carry on as if nothing had happened.

Dillman's career is one more bit of evidence of the oft-made comment that Washington, D.C., has been taken over by midwesterners. He was born and got his first journalistic experience in Ohio, going to work as copyboy at the *Columbus Evening Dispatch* at the age of nineteen.

He got his education later at night school, taking courses that would help him understand politics.

A first marriage when Grant was twenty-four ended in divorce in three years. "I feel more at home in a newsroom—I guess I'll never be completely housebroken." Fortunately, his second wife, Audrey, works in media, too—NBC TV.

If you go to the AP newsroom, located in a modern office building on downtown K Street, you find an entirely different atmosphere

244

from that at UPI—hushed silence, great dignity, men in ties. Neatness!

Walter Mears, chief of the AP Washington bureau, works in a quiet, carpeted, almost padded, private office, which is protected further by a buffer zone of an outer office.

The man himself does not smile on meeting, seems to have a frozen face and the coldest pale blue-green eyes in the Washington press corps.

It's hard to relate this cold exterior with the man campaign reporters grew to know and treat with affection.

They claim that when he loosens up, he can be as loud as the next, once even joining a group of reporters yelling for escargots in some godforsaken restaurant in Kansas.

Some insist that escargots did finally appear on the table and that someone made a direct hit with one into Mears' ear.

"Not true," says Mears. "There wouldn't have been an escargot within a hundred miles of the place." In Mears' version of the story it was Dick Stout of *Newsweek* who got up on a chair and yelled, "Escargot for the house," but he was whistling in the wind.

Friends of Mears, of whom there are many, say that Mears has the right to have a cold, fixed look. He has sustained perhaps the greatest tragedy a man can endure and still not fall apart. His first wife and children were burned to death in a fire in 1962.

Work became his salvation, and even today Mears is known for his grinding work schedule that keeps him at the office many nights till ten o'clock. An early night gets him home at 7:30. Even remarriage did not slow his work pace.

At this writing, Walter, who is still a relatively young man of forty-three, is building a new house on three acres of land, doing most of the work with his own hands. "I play golf when I'm not digging ditches," he says deadpan.

The house is in the fashionable McLean, Virginia, area where the Kennedys and LBJ's daughter, Lynda Bird Robb and her husband, Chuck, lieutenant-governor of Virginia, live.

While most men would be content to just run a bureau, especially one like the AP, the largest in the world, which must minister to the needs of 1,700 newspapers and other publications and 3,200 TV and radio stations, that is not enough work for Mears. He still writes a three-times-a-week column called "Washington Today."

At the National Press Club bar, where Mears seldom comes anymore— "It's just too far away from the office"—his colleagues, who don't mind a long walk or a short cab ride, talk of Mears' splendid luck in having been in the right location at the right time. In the Kennedy days it was as valuable to be from Massachusetts as it later would become to be a Georgia newspaperman in Carter's administration.

He was born in Lynn, Massachusetts, graduated Phi Beta Kappa from Middlebury College, Vermont. Mears cut his political teeth reporting statehouse news for AP in Boston after college. He was a natural choice to be brought to the Washington bureau of AP in 1961 to cover Congress and national politics since he knew the Kennedy clan so well, and every facet of Jack Kennedy's political history.

But it was writing talent and hard work that earned him the title of chief political writer from 1969 to 1972.

Ever restless, Walter tried switching to individual newspaper reporting, becoming assistant chief and then bureau chief of the *Detroit News*.

In just a year, however, he went back to his first love, wire service writing and more particularly, the Associated Press. Now his whole career seemed to come together and he hit the jackpot. In 1977 he received the Pulitzer Prize for his coverage of the Carter-Ford campaign of 1976, and in the same year became chief of the AP bureau in Washington.

To cap his triumphs, in January 1978, he also became vice-president of the whole AP system.

His old political cronies don't begrudge Mears his new-found glory and they nod their heads and say that Mears' life is proof that good guys don't always finish last. They recall how Walter had an unerring knack for picking the best leads.

As they would struggle with their own jumble of notes and speeches, many was the time they would scream at him to tell them what the lead was. With Christian charity, he would yell back, telling them what he had decided to use. A noble act!

"Let's hoist one for Mears," they chorus in tribute.

Though AP, UPI, and Reuters are the giants in the wire service business, occasionally a man can earn a good living by setting up his own specialized wire service for eager clients. Such a man is James Srodes, who has it made. He pays no rent but has a nice office in the suite of one of his major clients, the *London Daily*

Telegram. He has little overhead above taking a client for lunch and, best of all, he doesn't even have to pay for the printing of a newsletter or a battery of teletype machines. His clients pay their own Telex bills.

What Srodes does is file stories on what's doing in Washington and New York's Wall Street that affects businessmen all over the world—business deals, mergers, interest rates, trade, nuclear power, agriculture exports, imports, new government regulations.

For this Jim Srodes makes good money, grossing in six figures.

But Srodes is not an ordinary man. Though not an economics major, he has a natural bent for figures and business. He started out as a treasury correspondent for UPI from 1967 to 1969, then worked for the *Business Week* bureau and finally for *Forbes* magazine, becoming Washington bureau chief.

His decision to go into business by himself came about when *Forbes* had other plans. "We want you to come to New York and be an associate editor," Srodes recalls they told him. "I didn't want to go because I liked Washington and my wife was just starting law school. But this was the kind of in-house promotion that was mandatory. So I chose to go out on a limb and start my own news business.

"It took off like a rocket. The foreign newspapers really needed an analysis of the American financial news. They had been dependent on their general news correspondents and general news services so there was a market nobody had tried to tap.

"True, the *Lawrence Newsletter* gives similar news but it gets there too late. They need it on the same day. It had to be a wire service."

Srodes sends out three thousand to four thousand words a day to several dailies and a dozen magazines. He even has time now and then to write an additional financial article for other publications using the nom de plume Louis James, which led to an unusual incident.

"I had written a story under the Louis James by-line that was picked up and quoted by the regular press. One of my clients overseas phoned frantically saying, 'Find Louis James and file a matching story.'

"I said, 'I know him very well. I'll do it.'"

Though Srodes learns of many good deals he himself

stays out of investing. "It would be unethical. When I was at *Forbes* if we owned shares of a stock, we weren't permitted to file a story on that stock. It's a good principle."

Only occasionally does Srodes have trouble with clients. Once RCA billed him two thousand dollars for a Telex bill that a client didn't pay. The client claimed he had never heard of Srodes and had never ordered the stories.

"It was a clear breach of contract and I was able to prove to RCA that the stories had been ordered and the service contracted for."

Wire services, like news bureaus, have their own inside stories. The classic, though, is the one that was told by the late George Durno, White House correspondent for INS, and dates back to the days when Eleanor Roosevelt was traveling about as the eyes and ears of her invalid husband.

Given the gentility of the press in those days, the story never hit the newspapers.

According to Durno, the First Lady was on some fact-gathering trip and had a stopover on a South Sea island, where the Chief honored her with a feast and a native dance. Everything was going well except that an old native fellow, who was obviously a friend of the Chief's, had attached himself to Mrs. Roosevelt and taken it upon himself to keep the First Lady informed about what was going on.

This kibitzer, Durno said, was obviously not pleased with a particular dancer. As the dancer leaped about, the friend of the Chief's made disapproving sounds and when the performance was over and the drumbeats had faded away, he turned to Eleanor and said in a firm, loud voice, "Him dancer no fuckin' good."

The Americans waited with suppressed glee to see Eleanor's reaction, but all they got was a sort of frozen look as Mrs. Roosevelt said a long, "O-o-oh?" in a tentative way, as if trying to make up her mind if he was right. Everyone agreed Eleanor's performance was better than the dancer's.

248

16/Newsletters

Old reporters never die— they just start publishing newsletters and make more money than ever.

There are newsletters for good buddies with a citizen's band aerial on their cars. There are newsletters for helicopter owners or manufacturers.

There are newsletters on subjects you haven't dreamed of and most of their founders are eating high on the hog. It is said that the good buddy newsletter man made $50,000 his first year.

I started several newsletters myself. Some of them did fairly well but I do not like to be confined to the routine of production and deadline. When I wrote an electric power newsletter, I recall I sold a subscription to the great Wendell Willkie.

Newsletters are not cheap. Llewellyn King's *Energy Daily* newsletter costs subscribers $450 a year and King doesn't mind letting it be known that it's now a three-quarters-of-a-million-dollar-a-year enterprise.

That more than pays for his staff of five plus stringers in London, Brussels, and Paris.

King has been up and he's been down. Up is better. So is being self-employed. "In fact," says King, "newsletters are the only road still open for a writer or reporter to be self-employed. Newsletters are the last refuge of the true eccentric."

He tried publishing a magazine once, called *Women Now,* which was ahead of its time in women's lib. It was born and died in 1965. Perhaps today he could make a go of that same magazine but King is happy with newsletters, even though, he confesses, they are less glamorous and, as a result, hostesses still don't realize his importance on the newspaper scene.

No matter, he has one of the fanciest offices in the National Press Building, in which he sometimes throws his own cocktail parties. And he can comfort himself with the memory of energy czar James Schlesinger admitting to King that his *Energy Daily* was "must reading" for him every morning.

Almost all the European and Near East countries subscribe, making King, in just a short time, a rich man.

King, who is originally from Rhodesia and still has a slight British accent, was lucky to get out of newspapering, even though Ben Bradlee, his boss at the *Washington Post,* scoffed, "You're actually leaving the *Post* for nuts and bolts of journalism?"

King was leaving to get his training first on *Nucleonics Week,* a newsletter on nuclear energy, before making the big plunge in 1973.

By sheer good luck—from his standpoint—"The Arabs chose that time to cut off our oil and everyone needed new energy ideas in a hurry. Subscriptions for *Energy Daily* poured in."

Newsletter people are loathe to give circulation figures because of the comparison with big-city dailies, but on the other hand $8.80 an issue beats fifteen cents for a newsstand newspaper.

The point is the newsletter deals with a specialized field, fascinating to those who are intimately interested. In comparison, the daily newspaper has to stretch itself in many directions to appeal to a wide audience—it tries to be everything to everyone.

Such wide coverage is very expensive. In comparison a newsletter is very simple and inexpensive to put out.

Most newsletter people write the copy themselves then farm it out to a professional printing and mailing service such as Frank's Duplicating Service in the National Press Building. The service clean-copies the material, proofreads it, asks questions when it doesn't read well, prints it, addresses it, and mails it out— all for a fixed fee.

The cost runs about twenty-five cents an issue for printing and handling, based on a thousand-copy run for a newsletter than runs no more than ten pages.

What does one need as a nest egg to get started? The best estimate is that it takes about $10,000 to set up an office and keep the newsletter going until there are enough clients for the profits to begin.

Some do it for less. Kenneth Callaway, who now has an empire of twenty health and education newsletters, started with $750 a dozen years ago. He and a partner, who both had regular outside jobs at first, did the dirty work themselves, "sitting in the back of the Press Club Tap Room half the night licking labels."

As for the writing of the newsletters, he humorously confesses today, "We paid reporters with all the beer they could drink."

Now, however, Callaway pays reporters with good, hard

cash and his newsletters are published under the name Capitol Publications.

A pioneer in this form of journalism was W. M. Kiplinger—he hated his name of Willard and never used it—who began the *Kiplinger Newsletter* in 1923. Kip is gone now but his son Austin carries on the publication of the longest continuously published newsletter. Dealing with business trends, it is still considered the bible of investors who need to see ahead to make business decisions.

Though Austin has added his own touches to his father's newsletter, he still continues the policy of being frankly folksy, starting it, "Dear Client," and ending it, "Yours very truly."

He must be doing something right because revenues from subscriptions total over $12 million.

Newsletters are on the ascendancy.

The surprising truth of the matter is that now more reporters are earning a living in Washington writing newsletters—over 1,000 reporters and editors—than write for the two local papers—the *Washington Post*, which employs close to 500 and the *Washington Star*, which hires over 300.

It is true that newsletter writers who work for someone else generally earn considerably less than *Washington Post* and *Star* reporters, at least when they are beginners, but on the other hand, some earn more.

One Press Club member tells the story of how he had to leave a good copy-editing job on a Chicago newspaper and move to Washington for family reasons. He hadn't a clue on how to get a new job. His age was fifty-five.

At the *Washington Star* an editor told him, "You're too effing old." At the *Washington Post* they gave no hope—indicating as well that he might be overqualified, a typical cop-out.

Then, wasting no more time applying at newspapers or bureaus, he applied and immediately got a good job on a labor newsletter for $30 more than he would have gotten at the *Post*.

"The final irony," he comments, "was that after I was all nicely set up, I was called to the *Post* to do copy-editing for as many hours as I could spare.

"I was earning double salaries. My wife thought I was crazy but I confess I got nostalgic for the newspaper atmosphere. Once you've worked on newspapers, you're never completely free of them—it's like a drug."

The individual who goes into newsletter publishing usually picks a favorite subject and sticks with it. Leonard Andrews, founder of Andrews Publications, for example, sticks to the subject of legal troubles.

Starting with a newsletter of interest to all the people and firms involved when Penn Central went bankrupt, he now has several dozen newsletters of special interest to litigants and lawyers watching other huge, involved bankruptcy cases.

Andrews even based a newsletter on the chaos of the swine flu vaccine fiasco. It is of special interest to all the lawyers, government and private, and the individuals involved in lawsuits following the deaths of 23 persons and the paralysis of 494 persons allegedly due to the vaccine.

One man who found his special subject and is delighted with it is Jack Botzum.

Back in the late sixties, Jack Botzum shared an NPC office with other writers as a free-lance business and science writer. Today, as head of Nautilus Press, which he joined in 1970, his quarters are considerably larger—and so are his horizons.

When he came to Nautilus, *Ocean Science News* was the only publication in the house. He helped start *Coastal Zone Management,* and later hired reporter Suzanne Contos, who had the idea for a new newsletter, *Marine Mammal News.*

Later Nautilus Press started still another newsletter, *Marine Fish Management,* with Suzanne and Jack as joint editors.

In 1977, Jack founded his latest newsletter, *Weather and Climate Report.* He anticipated passage of a new U.S. climate program and a world conference in 1979, which, he says, "will probably be the start of a concerted worldwide effort to understand our dependence on a greater knowledge of weather and climate in order to survive." Rose Jacobius is joint editor of the weather letter with Jack.

Jack Botzum has come a long way from the beginning reporter who was hired by the *Akron Beacon Journal,* in Ohio, to go to work at sixty dollars a week.

"I was hired at a little before noon one day in 1953," Botzum recalls with a smile, "and shortly after told to go out to get some lunch. When I returned, I was told that I was out of a job because a veteran from the war who had previously worked at the paper had just called, and wanted his old job back. End of phase one of my reporting career."

On his next job, he lasted longer and became an expert on the tire industry.

Explaining why he started his marine life newsletters, Jack says, "*Marine Mammal News* has been recognized as the only source at this time for complete and unbiased news on the question of the survival of marine mammals and their relationship to man.

"*Marine Fish Management* gives the reader the only available monthly coverage of the field of fisheries within the new U.S. two hundred-mile zone, plus world fish management news."

What makes his work so satisfying to Jack is that boating and sea life are also the most important things in his own life, and he spends all the time he can aboard a thirty-six-foot sailing craft.

It's a happy ending to a story of a kid who cut his reportorial teeth on a two-hour job as obit writer for the *Akron Beacon Journal.*

One of the most respected and successful men in the newsletter field is Gershon Fishbein, called Gersh by his friends.

Having risen to assistant city editor at the *Washington Post,* at the age of forty, he decided if he was every going to get into the real money or make a reputation for himself, it had to be now.

The year was 1961, and he planned to go into business as soon as economically feasible. Step one had been to get a specialty and he was writing for *Medical Tribune,* a newspaper for doctors.

The moment of decision came sooner than he planned. "I was covering hearings before the House Labor and HEW Appropriations Subcommittee headed by the late Representative Johnny Fogarty [D–R.I.].

"He was an old friend and I had been covering him for years. He sent me a note at the press table asking me to stop by his office after the hearing.

"To my surprise he opened the subject, asking if I could see my way clear to start a publication of some kind in the field of environmental health.

"He said that as chairman of the committee in which health environmental programs were centered, he had discovered that there was no publication which expressed the view that all factors in man's environment were interrelated.

"He offered to help in any way he could and left the rest to me."

In a way, Fogarty was doing Gersh no favor in pushing him into this particular field. "This was at a time," Gersh recalls, "when nobody knew what the words *environment* or *pollution control* meant. In the summer of 1961, they were wild-blue-yonder concepts.

"I spent my vacation on a pilot issue of the newsletter, however, and Fogarty sent some letters for me recommending the newsletters—a big boost.

"The pilot newsletter I showed him featured the same thing I'm still featuring—the concept that all factors that affect man's health are interrelated and should be treated as such."

At the beginning, Gershon Fishbein's *Environmental Health Letter,* published twice a month, cost fifty dollars a year. Now the subscription price has gone to one hundred dollars.

It is aimed at professionals who have some interest in the health field, government agencies at all levels, universities and industry, and medical doctors.

Gersh's finest hour found him operating as an investigative reporter, and the result was an exclusive newsbeat on the findings of the Surgeon General's Advisory Committee on Radiation, a report so hush-hush and filled with damaging evidence that newspapers were picking it up and quoting *Environmental Health Letter.*

As a result, Gersh found himself "being tailed for two days by the FBI, trying to find out where I had gotten my information. All they found out was where I bought my kosher hot dogs."

Exactly ten years after Gersh started his first newsletter, he was in such good financial shape that he was able to start a second as a spinoff—*Occupational Health and Safety Letter.*

Instead of his clients taking one or the other, about seventy percent of his subscribers get both newsletters.

Incidentally, Gersh's newer publication has also scored newsbeats. For example, he was the first to publish a series of stories "on the asbestos exposure situation at the Pittsburgh Corning Plant in Tyler, Texas."

He had gotten his information from many sources, just as any good investigative reporter does. What makes Gersh happiest, however, is not the newsbeat but the fact that he has influenced industry and government to do something constructive.

Homer Joseph Dodge, the wit of the Press Club, delighted in startling people by announcing that the first newsletter was started by a "Fugger from way back"—actually about 1400.

There would be stunned silence until he went on to casually attribute the first business news service to Johann Fugger, who founded the House of Fugger, which became "bankers to kings" before Columbus had even thought of discovering America.

Actually, Homer Dodge was credited with starting the first Washington newsletter in 1913. He called it the *Bankers' Information Service*. It started as a vehicle to supply banks with news relating to the establishment of the Federal Reserve System, as a twice-a-week or so mailout.

It quickly developed into a daily sent by leased wire to New York, where it was printed. Its coverage eventually included all government activities affecting banks and industry.

Among the most successful and influential newsletter men is George Spencer, who recently sold his *U.S. Oil Week* for a half-million dollars and another newsletter, *Coal Outlook,* for something less.

George, who at one time published six newsletters and has recently added a new one for businessmen, *Diversification Week*, admits that "My revenues for 1977 were $1.1 million."

Spencer does not hesitate to get involved. Evidence that came from his coverage of a convention of the Society of Independent Gasoline Marketers is credited with helping bring about the conviction of several cut-rate oil companies for price fixing.

Spencer did not withhold his evidence but gave the Justice Department the tape he had recorded at the convention.

He also gave his readers facts about oil companies' income tax figures and royalty payments to Arabian princes that do not show up in annual reports to stockholders. Some give him part of the credit for Congress's action on the percentage depletion allowance.

In other cases, however, newsletter publishers are more fearful of losing the support of industries they write about, and because of this fear they tell more about what the government is doing to those industries than what the industries are doing.

Because of the different slants of the various newsletters, some industries subscribe to one newsletter as opposed to another. Of course many newspapers, through their editorial page, also show their bias, but, in general, newsletters are supposed to be less biased than newspapers.

Not that anyone uses the word *biased*. Rather, it is said that the newsletter is interpretive. The Kiplinger letters are traditionally interpretive and filled with predictions, but more recent newsletters are steering away from opinion-giving in the Kiplinger sense.

Putting out a newsletter is not problem-free. If the mails are slow, you are in danger of losing clients to someone with a better distribution system. Then too, it is sometimes hard to find good writers who understand the specialized field. And since the newsletter may be put out by one or two persons, the boss may find himself working straight through the night if his reporter has spent too many hours in the Press Club bar.

But worst of all for newsletters is the growth of the photocopying industry. Companies have been caught duplicating hundreds of copies of a newsletter to pass around to their executives rather than subscribing to a hundred or so copies.

Congress has finally stepped in and has made the photocopying of newsletters illegal and punishable by stiff fines and imprisonment.

The newsletter field is starting to open up to women.

The publication that Marilyn Millstone writes and edits —*Water Information News Service*—is one of six newsletters published by Resources News Service, which is owned by three men:

David L. Howell, who, dressed Western style, is one of the more colorful inhabitants of the National Press Building, is editor in chief. Johnny Allem is business manager and Tom Seay is editor of three of the newsletters—all in the alcohol addiction and mental health fields.

Marilyn Millstone is probably the youngest editor in the National Press Building. At age twenty-four, she still shudders as she remembers how hard it was to get her first job a few years ago because of the competition of interns. She thinks newsletter writing is a perfect place to start in order to develop into an investigative writer.

The editor who gave Marilyn Millstone the most confidence was Tom Seay, who edits *Washington Drug Review*, *Mental Health Scope*, and *Alcoholism and Alcohol Education*.

What makes a reporter a *good* reporter, Tom maintains, is "a healthy curiosity and a sense of righteous indignation."

"I believe he is right," Marilyn says. "Journalism is a game of skill, and the only way to really learn it is to get out and try your hand, and your luck. The time will eventually come, as it came to me, when copy miraculously starts flowing out of the typewriter rather than being wrenched out a word at a time.

"What finally happened, though, was that I tried to fit

my small hand into a very large glove. I was offered a job as editor of a newsletter—a one-man job in a one-man office, at a good salary—ten thousand dollars, up twenty-five hundred from my first job.

"In my gut I knew I wasn't qualified to go from editorial assistant to editor. Yet I did not see how I could refuse to take a quantum leap up the ladder.

"In stretching that far, I strained everything I had to its limits—my ingenuity, my self-confidence, my sanity.

"No matter how many years I put between me and those first months, I will never be able to say the experience was good for me. I desperately needed an editor over me, a string of sources, and another body in the office—anyone to stem the loneliness.

"For me, at that time, the job was all wrong.

"After two months of intense psychic struggling—'Nobody respects a quitter,' versus 'Everyone makes a mistake'—I explained my problem to the publisher and told him to find a replacement for me.

"Instead, he sold the newsletter to a small firm that published five other newsletters and employed three other journalists. While I got no assistance in writing my newsletter, I did get companionship and advice. And the advantage of watching seasoned, talented journalists at work.

"Now I'm making over eleven thousand dollars and feel at ease with the job.

"I knew I had arrived when I went to a conference of the American Society of Civil Engineers, and attended a session on the President's new water policy, hoping to find some definitive discussion about the policy's impact.

"To my great surprise, the speaker held up my newsletter and read my latest story on the water policy to the audience as the definitive information on the subject."

Some newsletter people are among the most respected writers of the nation. Clyde La Motte, a past president of the National Press Club, was one of the nation's veteran energy reporters. He published two weekly newsletters until recently, pulling out at a handsome profit. He began as an energy writer in the Washington bureau of McGraw-Hill and was later Washington editor of *Oil and Gas Journal*. He also wrote an energy column for the *Houston Post*.

Gersh Fishbein agrees with other newsletter writers that after working on a newspaper you forever yearn for the newspaper atmosphere. Though he confesses to earning "three times as much as I would be earning on the *Post* if I had stayed, I'd go back to newspapers tomorrow if it weren't for the money. The newsletter writer lives in an obscure world, writing his own stories in his solitary office, never hearing the excitement of a busy city room."

Of course, some newsletter office setups are much busier than others, because a larger staff is needed to put out multiple newsletters. McGraw-Hill, for example, puts out nineteen newsletters and has an elegant complex of offices in the National Press Building under the direction of its chief, George Lutjen, director of McGraw-Hill Newsletter Publishing Center.

What are the nineteen newsletters about? Almost every subject from energy to fertilizer. One is a *Personal Finance Letter.* The fertilizer newsletter, which brings George in for a lot of ribbing around the Press Club, goes out under the title *Green Markets* and its price is no joke—$270 a year's subscription.

George Lutjen doesn't like to reveal too much of company secrets but he admits the newsletter operation is making something under $10 million.

Current events spawn new newsletters. When the dollar dipped sharply in the world market in 1978 and inflation became a scare word, Daniel R. Kane, a lawyer, economist, and retired government bureaucrat, started the newsletter *Inflation Watch.*

Even the general confusion of Washington bureaucracy has spawned a new newsletter, *Mumblepeg—The Voice of the Bureaucrat,* written and published by the National Press Club's pet humorist, Jim Boren. His slogan, made famous in many speeches across the land, is, "When in doubt, mumble."

Howard Penn Hudson produces the ultimate newsletter. It is called the *Newsletter on Newsletters* and tells all the news of what is going on in the newsletter world. That includes the buying and selling of newsletters; the announcement, for example, of a conference in Chicago, open to all newsletter publishers, on "How To Manage Newsletters for Growth and Profit"; and even job openings in the field.

Hudson, whose *Newsletter on Newsletters* was called "the bible of the industry" in a *Time* article, takes issue with the claim by some newsletter people that Washington newsletters are "merely warmed-up government releases."

"I stand with the newsletter editor who holds that we 'translate releases.' The only thing that could put us out of business," Hudson maintains, "would be if the government began to write in English, but this will never happen in our lifetime."

258

17/PR-PIO: The Image Makers

Image making is nothing new. John D. Rockefeller, once despised as a robber baron, was resold as a benevolent old billionaire who handed out shiny dimes.

President Eisenhower had Robert Montgomery, the movie actor, package him like soap, prettying him up and showing him how to appear less stuffy and stiff on television.

More recently, Secretary Joseph Califano of Health, Education and Welfare, got a screwball reputation. His job was in danger. Quickly his image makers reversed the trend, making him look like a hard-working money-saving official.

I recall when Senator J. Bennett Johnson of Louisiana feared that in the eyes of the voters he seemed too close to the oil industry. So he held hearings on the problems of old people to identify himself with a more heart-warming subject.

Every senator and congressman has a press secretary or someone under another title assigned to PR—public relations. Among the government offices, large staffs of so-called public affairs people feed at the public trough. Some are competent. Too many are political hacks.

The largest such propaganda mill is in the Department of Defense, with 1,340 people costing $24 million a year. This can be partly justified for recruiting. Next comes the Department of Agriculture, with about the same budget and half as many employees. This is largely justified by the good it does in spreading information on good farming methods. In third place is the Department of Transportation, an almost useless agency, with 300 public affairs people costing $9 million a year.

Who does the best job? According to a poll of press people taken yearly by a company called Washington Researchers, the top two agencies in 1978 were the Civil Aeronautics Board and the National Aeronautics and Space Administration. Close behind them are the Senate, the House of Representatives, and the Department of Interior.

259

The ratings were on the basis of openness, helpfulness, and professionalism. Congress does well, it is thought, because it is less bureaucratic and responds more directly to the people. Also its staff can be hired on merit rather than drawn from Civil Service rolls.

At the bottom of the list were the White House, the Department of Energy, the Supreme Court, and the lowest, the government of the District of Columbia.

The Court, according the the press people who cover them, gives out legal gobbledygook. The Energy people, reporters said, "want to know who you are and why you want information. They think they're God Almighty." White House staffers are sometimes pompous, slow to reply, and late notifying the press of available information.

That's the overall story—at least for government public relations. Now what's in it for the individual who chooses PR as a career?

In public relations the sky is the limit for those in the private sector. PR people who get lucky might make $10,000 to $20,000 from one client alone. And much more, if it's the only client they handle.

Salaries in government public relations vary widely. On Capitol Hill each congressman and senator decides what he is going to pay for public relations help or whether to let a staff person handle any press agentry that needs doing. But the salary for congressional press agents can range from $14,000 to $30,000 or more.

The best PR job in government—and the one guaranteed to make anyone famous for the rest of his life—is that of press secretary to the President.

Not everyone can be a Jody Powell, with an open door to the President and a salary of $56,000. But there are other good PIO (Public Information Office) jobs at the White House as well. One woman who is doing very well on the White House PR staff, with a salary of $40,000, is Claudia Townsend, who is only twenty-five.

Claudia is Jody's alter ego and is authorized to answer reporters' questions when Jody is off duty.

Nor does everyone have to be conservative to work in White House information, as used to be the case. Claudia got her training with Nader's Raiders, guaranteed to have a liberalizing influence, and also served stints with the *Atlanta Constitution*'s Washington office and the Cox Newspaper's national bureau.

What is it like to be a public relations man in the private sector?

"It's getting harder all the time," says Lou Brott of Lou Brott Associates, who has been in public relations for twenty years and has offices in the National Press Building.

"A good man can make one hundred thousand dollars easy, but he has to work his tail off.

"Newspapers have become too sophisticated. Now you have to get a straight feature. You can't create a funny, human interest story anymore. They won't listen or buy it."

One time Lou staged a big traffic safety parade and to get the message across he featured coffins and bandaged victims to show what could result from carelessness.

Then as he stood on the back of a truck giving the signal for the grisly motorcade to begin, Lou Brott slipped and fell to the street, breaking his back.

As he tells it, "The procession went in one direction and I went in another in an ambulance. The story hit the papers and the wire service, and Frank Blair, who was then on the NBC *Today Show*, broke up laughing hysterically on his news program when he tried to read the story on the air."

As soon as Brott was out of the hospital, he proved his own axiom that a good public relations man never wastes anything: He had the front and back of his body cast painted with blurbs for his next clients.

Brott admits he has done some weird things to make news or a "story-telling picture." Once, he let some kind of dune buggy with enormous balloon tires run over him to prove that the tires wouldn't hurt the armory floor.

It didn't hurt the floor. But Brott could never wear that suit again.

The hardest people to handle in working out publicity stunts, says Brott, are "nationally known politicos, each of whose ego is a mile high."

He recalls how he once had to placate two political superstars, the crusty, cantankerous Senator Joe McCarthy and FDR's youngest-son-turned-congressman, Franklin D. Roosevelt, Jr.

Brott had dreamed up a television show called the *Young*

Gentlemen, featuring the page boys in Congress and the Supreme Court. Every week they interviewed two 'personalities' with opposing views on the issues of the day.

As Brott tells it, "Came the morning of the program—on CBS WTOP-TV Channel 9—the phone rang. McCarthy was on the horn. 'If I can't be last to sum up on the show, I won't be there.'" Of course Brott had to say, "Sure thing, senator, I'll see to it you will be last."

"Fifteen minutes went by when lo and behold another phone call. This time from FDR, Jr. Same request. 'Either I sum up points last or I won't show.'"

Again Brott said soothingly, "Sure thing, Frank, I'll see to it that you'll be on last."

Brott was really in a predicament. Whatever he did he was bound to make one powerful enemy. The day of the show both men showed up on time but insisted on being in different rooms because they disliked each other so intensively. It was just as well, otherwise they would have found out that both had been assured they had the coveted position.

What to do? What to do? PR people are trained to think best under fire. Up against the wall, Brott's mind clicked and he ordered each of the pages on the show to keep the questions popping no matter what the clock said. Then he told the moderator, Congressman Pat Hillings, that it would look better if the pages were not stifled but were permitted to keep going as long as possible. What happened is that the program ran out of time, the announcer signed off and both political stars went home winners.

Public relations people in Washington consider it a special triumph to involve the President or First Lady in one of their stunts. That gives any project thousands of dollars' worth of free advertising and elevates it to a real swinging newsmaker.

When public relations expert Gerald Rafshoon got the White House involved in a birthday tribute to Bob Hope and the USO, before Rafshoon himself went to work for the White House, it turned the USO stunt into a great news extravaganza.

Jerry had known Jimmy Carter before the White House. This always helps a public relations man. PR people develop a sixth sense about picking winners and they always have an eye out to see who's coming up in the world.

Lou Brott, when he went out on his own to open a public relations office, was glad he had been nice to Jacqueline Kennedy on her way up.

For three or four years prior to her marriage to Senator Kennedy, Jackie Bouvier, as she was then known, would bring herself and her trusty camera down to all the DC armory shows—auto show, boat show, flower show, sports, travel, vacation shows, and all the rest.

Lou Brott, who was handling publicity for the shows, would help Jackie set up interviews for the "Inquiring Photographer" columns she was doing for the *Times-Herald*.

Once Jackie had been on hand and full of awe because First Lady Mamie Eisenhower was going to cut the ribbon at the flower show, and she had been just as nervous another year when the Vice-President's wife, Pat Nixon, did the flower show honors.

"I would take her under my wing," Lou Brott recalls, "and we'd kill time with a cup of coffee, kidding about the affairs of the world. She was very pretty and fun to joke around with, but I never dreamed there would be a time when she herself would be the First Lady, cutting the ribbon at the flower show.

"But it came to pass and there I was and there she was, only this time, instead of being *casually* dressed—to put the most charitable description on some of those gosh-awful outfits she wore—she looked like a dream.

"She was beautifully dressed in fashionable tan, with a lovely pillbox hat smartly in place, and she looked radiant."

But after Brott and the flower show officials had met the First Lady at the door and escorted her to the center of the breathtaking flower-bedecked armory, Jackie saw the crowds and started to get nervous.

Jackie turned to her old PR friend and said, in her breathless voice, "Lou, I'm frightened to death. Shall I cut the ribbon first? What should I say?"

Brott smiled at the First Lady saying, "Honey, you look great! You know you've been here before. Nothing's changed. Just tell everyone how glad you are to be here again, where you had many pleasant times in the past."

She did exactly as he suggested and everything went off without a hitch.

Brott was happy until the Sunday paper appeared and then he recoiled. Betty Beale, the *Washington Star* society gossip columnist, took it upon herself to scold that "brash" flower show publicity man for having the audacity to call the First Lady "Honey."

Probably the most precise and perfect press operation in government is the State Department. Unlike the sloppy briefing at the White House, which is scheduled for 11:00 A.M. but may not begin until 2:00 P.M., the State Department starts sharply at 12:00 noon, ready or not.

Hodding Carter III is the man in charge—no relation to President Carter—and his first dignified words are, "Good afternoon, ladies and gentlemen."

He gives his news and then the elite of the press corps, who cover diplomatic news, ask their questions.

Unlike the often insulting give-and-take of the White House, Carter takes every question seriously, treats all with respect, and writes down questions for which he has no immediate answers. The reporters rest easy knowing that sometime in the next few hours someone will hand them a written answer to the question.

But reporters sometimes bemoan the fact that they don't have a colorful Kissinger to quote anymore. Having Henry Kissinger in the story almost guaranteed it would land on the front page. The effect is not the same if a spokesman says that Cyrus Vance plans something. Kissinger was definitely his own best public relations man and he knew how to please the reporting crowd.

Vance is the complete antithesis of Kissinger and prefers to let Hodding Carter do his glad-handing with the press. In the long-gone fun Kissinger days, the press briefing room used to be called "the zoo," but now it's just a dignified gathering.

One of the things local PR people do is try to get articles about their clients into the top Washington magazines, such as the *Washingtonian.* A strong competitor to national magazines such as *People,* the *Washingtonian* not so long ago was bought for $3.6 million dollars by a newspaper and magazine chain headed by Philip Merrill.

A more sardonically edited publication is *WJR-Washington Journalism Review,* a sort of bible to the Washington newspaper world. As an example of their kind of perceptive article, a November 1978 issue described "The Ten Most Underreported Stories of 1977."

The *Washington Monthly* features an amusing "Memo of the Month," which exposes bureaucratic excesses. This publication lists and reviews most books about Washington and is aimed at more intellectual readers.

Nowadays an important part of private PR work is

helping clients cope with government hearings. Several Washington public relations firms offer clients highly specialized training for appearances.

Considered a leader among such firms, the prestigious Hill and Knowlton has a room fitted out along the lines of an austere congressional hearing room, where the client can be rehearsed in the actual sequence of presentation used in congressional and government regulatory agency hearings. After a grilling in that room, the client is much more relaxed and in command when facing the real-life inquisitors, before the live mikes of the hearing.

Another firm—Carl Byoir and Associates—provides samples of every kind of news media interview. Its "MediaCom" service is capable of recreating the tension and trappings of TV talk show panels or hostile press conferences or even the barrage of questions being fired at a client as he supposedly leaves a hearing room. As Press Club member George Whaley, of Carl Byoir's Washington office reports, "One client company in Minnesota gave the MediaCom treatment to its entire upper-echelon management."

A new development in government public relations is the appointment of talented black women to high positions—such women as Ruth Watson, formerly with the Administrative Planning Council of Loyola.

Ruth accepts the fact that her color is helping her now and enjoys every minute of her career. "Probably one of my happiest moments in government service came in 1970, when I learned that I had been selected to be special assistant to the director of the Welfare Reform Planning Staff in the Department of Health, Education and Welfare.

"My responsibility as a member of the executive staff was to do everything in my power to apprise the public of the importance of the welfare reform bill, known as HR-I, in order to insure its passage. It took less than a week on the new job to find myself totally immersed in public relations work. But what was I to expect, being the token black lady, but to be out front and highly visible.

"My first assignment was to go to the Hill each day and sit in the diplomatic gallery on the Senate side to listen to floor discussion. If the Speaker gave any indication that the welfare reform bill was going to be brought out on the floor that day, I was to call my boss immediately. He was to stop everything and rush to the Senate, where the two of us would sit patiently."

Ruth Watson in her PR job learned about what really goes into trying to get a bill passed—HR-I, which was so named because it had been the first one introduced in the new House session.

"My next tactic in trying to help it get passed," she recalls, "was to go to the Library of Congress and dig through *Congressional Records*, the *New York Times*, and the *Washington Post* looking for statements about senators and congressmen who indicated that they were in support of any kind of poverty legislation.

"The search focused on those lawmakers who were against the welfare reform bill, and I was supposed to find any piece of evidence that would show that they once had supported legislation to promote the war on poverty.

"It wasn't easy. I searched back five years and proceeded to go up to the present time. I would Xerox the evidence and underline significant passages before presenting the information to the director. My boss, John Montgomery, director of the Welfare Reform Planning Staff—we nicknamed it TWERP—would use the information as ammunition to encourage those legislators who were against welfare reform legislation to change their minds. This, to me, was a good example of first-class arm twisting.

"As time went on I was asked to arrange conferences and speaking engagements on welfare reform for Montgomery and his designees. I wrote major speeches for him and kept adding fresh material as the occasion arose.

"I found that it is always better to keep the basic speech and add to it. This doesn't put the boss through too many changes.

"Writing speeches is one of the things I particularly enjoy in public affairs work. I was even asked to supply material and write speeches on welfare reform for the secretary of HEW, Elliot Richardson.

"Occasionally I would be assigned to take over some of the speaking engagements for John Montgomery and I found that I enjoyed delivering speeches as well as writing them. But I was rocked back on my heels when I discovered that the black women in the South, who would be particularly helped by the passage of the bill, were antagonistic.

"What happened is that I went to Birmingham to set up a welfare reform workshop, to work for passage of the bill, only to find that the word *welfare* is an obscene word to black women in the South.

"Since I was black too, they could open up to me and I learned they had become antagonistic because of the many embarrassing and humiliating experiences they had undergone in qualifying for welfare. They would not attend welfare reform workshops I set up in spite of concerted poster advertisements or hearing about it through their minister.

"To entice the women to come I planned a big luncheon at a prominent hotel and then discovered there were no funds for it. Somewhere I had to dig up three dollars and fifty cents for each person who showed up at the luncheon.

"A public-relations type learns to tap other resources. There was an irony, however. The man who donated the money for the luncheon was Senator John Sparkman, who then turned around and voted against the welfare bill.

"I had worked on the bill for two years and then suddenly I was pulled away by the White House, which said it wanted me to switch my attention to another problem, and I became coordinator for black presidential appointees. I learned that I had been taken off the welfare assignment because President Nixon had decided to withdraw his support from HR-I and had not wanted it passed after all.

"The millions of dollars that were spent on national planning to organize the states and get the bill passed was almost all in vain because the welfare reforms for aid to dependent families, which I had been concentrating on and which would make the rules uniform across the country, were defeated.

"At this time everything remains as it was and every state follows its own thinking in its welfare system. However, certain aid to the blind, disabled, and aged did pass and is being administered through the Social Security Administration."

Some government public relations people luck into great jobs, and perhaps the most delightful is that of PIO—"Public Information Officer," as government flacks are called—at the National Park Service of the Interior Department.

Such a lucky one is Priscilla Baker, who travels the width and breadth of the country and takes her job very seriously. When she heard that a White House Secret Service agent had broken off a branch of an in-bloom cherry tree to please little Amy Carter, she made sure that justice was evenhanded. Through channels a little rebuke was sent to the Secret Service with a request that agents not indulge Amy to the extent that park property belonging to all the nation is damaged.

Priscilla, who heads a staff of twenty-three PIOs at the Interior Department's Park Facility, keeps a close eye on the White House grounds. "The White House is a National Park facility and ours is the responsibility for maintaining it. We got a little concerned recently when we learned that President Carter wanted to plant a vegetable garden on the White House lawn. One doesn't dig up property in a national park."

The National Park System includes 295 historic and recreational parks.

As top PIO for the National Park Service, Priscilla must cope with announcements of special events and dedications—which are legion in number—give assistance to the press and movie makers always underfoot in one public area or another, as well as advise the director of the National Park Service, William Whalen, on public relations matters.

The National Park Service has its own code words, calculated not to disturb the serenity of tourists. As Priscilla tells it, "We have many dangerous bears, of course. Every now and then, one gets too frisky and chews up a park visitor, and we must dispose of the animal permanently.

"We refer to this as 'having to remove the bear from the park's ecosystem.'"

But the Park Service is not inhumane and Priscilla laughingly tells of the time a National Park ranger gave mouth-to-mouth resuscitation to a burro.

When film companies arrive from Hollywood to use national monuments as background for action shots, Priscilla must remember many things. "For example, when a film company was doing some shooting at the Lincoln Memorial recently, we had someone there to make sure that the points on the ends of the tripods were encased in cardboard so that they would not damage the marble on the steps of the Memorial.

"In some parks we cannot permit film companies to use motorized vehicles to do filming, lest the motors scare the native wildlife.

"We did make an exception when *Close Encounters of the*

Third Kind was being filmed at Devil's Tower National Monument in the Wyoming-South Dakota area. But when ABC-TV filmed a climbing expedition at Zion National Park and used helicopters, it was a horrible mistake. Somebody goofed. Helicopters aren't permitted there."

How does one get a fun PIO job like Park Service? In Priscilla's case, she sent in a Form 171 application for federal government employment, in response to an announcement she saw about the availability of the job.

"A year and a half later—the government moves slowly—the Park Service called me and requested that I come for an interview. Six months after that, I joined the staff."

She had been chosen out of 139 applicants.

When the movie *Swarm* came out and reporters were worried about killer bees, PR expert Priscilla Baker got the query at Interior Park Service.

Reporters naturally think about Priscilla when they have questions about wild animals. "We're getting all kinds of queries from our editors about the danger from this superbreed of killer bees," they would begin. "When are they arriving in the United States?"

"I'm not into bees," she told the reporters, "I'm into bears and waterfalls. Try Agriculture."

She was right about the Ag and the bees. Bees are considered an agricultural problem. So from Ag, where PIO expert Barry Jenkins is in charge, reporters got the heartening news to relay back to their editors that no one need pack up yet and leave the country.

Reporters were invited to view a fourteen-minute film of reassurance, which cost the U.S. Department of Agriculture $28,000, to refute the terrible message of the Hollywood movie's tale of panic caused by roving swarms of African killer bees.

Why had Ag spent all that money to refute a movie? "We had to give the other side of the story," Jenkins says. "There is danger that people who see that movie might think that any bee is a potential killer. Farmers need bees because they depend on them for pollinating many crops, so we cannot have people going out and burning up bee hives."

Public relations jobs on Capitol Hill are considered choice and prime. If you hitch your wagon to a senatorial star, you may end up traveling the home state or the world in high style.

Or you may end up in the White House press room, speaking for the President. Public relations people help pull an ambitious legislator's career together and help hack him into presidential timber.

As every good PR person knows, it isn't the brainiest man who gets to run for President, but the one with the brightest image.

There are those who say that if the truth were told Hubert Humphrey would never have been Vice-President or gotten a crack at the presidential race if it weren't for a very astute PR man, who got hold of him back in the fifties and milked a mission to Moscow for all it was worth.

The PR man was Julius Cahn, who later worked for Humphrey when he was Vice-President, from 1965 to 1968, when Cahn handled long-range media rather than day-to-day press relations.

But to tell the inside story, before the trip to Russia, HHH was a comparatively little known senator. He had tried in vain to be Adlai Stevenson's running mate in 1956, but had been set aside by the Democratic Convention's choice of Senator Estes Kefauver.

Two years later, in November 1958, when Humphrey started out with Cahn on the European trip, the Minnesota senator was still regarded as a long shot.

But his meeting with Khrushchev propelled HHH into the front ranks of contenders as a public official with international stature. "HHH in '60!" campaign signs read, when Humphrey and Cahn returned from Moscow to National airport.

The interesting footnote to the trip was that HHH had almost completely missed seeing the Soviet premier in the first place, and would have cancelled the trip to Moscow had it not been for Cahn's stubbornness.

Humphrey had been irked by Soviet refusal to grant a visa to a Russian-speaking American cancer specialist whom Cahn had arranged to accompany Humphrey with the cooperation of the National Cancer Institute.

In Helsinki, the night before the flight to Moscow, Humphrey told Cahn to call the trip off unless the Soviets reconsidered the granting of the visa. Cahn, after hours of urging, succeeded in getting HHH's agreement to proceed to Moscow even without the visa. Cahn was convinced that the visa rejection wasn't a snub to Humphrey but a bureaucratic snafu which could be straightened out.

Cahn's guess proved correct—the American doctor joined them in Moscow.

But in the Soviet capital, Humphrey waited for three days without the slightest indication of Kremlin interest in a meeting. There had been no word of HHH's arrival or presence in Moscow in Soviet media. A lowly Intourist guide was assigned by the Soviets to accompany HHH and Cahn on their visits with Soviet doctors as part of Humphrey's international health study.

Finally, word came from the Kremlin that HHH was to visit Khrushchev—on one hour's advance notice. HHH asked if Cahn could be with him at the meeting but was told *"Nyet."*

The rest is history—an eight-and-a-half-hour talkfest by the loquacious premier and the articulate Minnesota senator. But that was only the first part of the story. The biggest battle for publicity still lay ahead.

The hard reality Cahn faced was that though the Minnesota Senator had just met for an unprecedented lengthy talk with Soviet Premier Nikita Khrushchev in the Kremlin, not a word of the meeting was appearing in the Soviet press.

Recognizing that the magic name of Khrushchev could open the doors of Soviet television, Cahn told Soviet authorities that a U.S. senator important enough to see the chairman of the Council of Ministers of the USSR for eight and a half hours was important enough to be seen on Soviet TV.

The request was granted. Humphrey did appear on Moscow TV, conveying greetings and best wishes for *"Mir y druzhba"*—peace and friendship—to the Soviet people. He mentioned his meeting with the Soviet premier briefly but omitted all details in his five-minute TV talk.

Meanwhile, Cahn had alerted U.S. press representatives in Moscow to be watching Soviet TV. The bulletins they sent out were the world's first notice of the historic meeting.

As Humphrey's sole staff aide on the trip, Cahn played his cards right for maximum American coverage. He doled out the contents of the HHH-Khrushchev meeting piece by piece instead of all at once.

As Humphrey and Cahn flew back home, the world learned bit by bit that Khrushchev had let drop a piece of earthshaking news: The Soviets had developed an 8,500-mile

271

intercontinental ballistic missile. And that Khrushchev had bad-mouthed China.

Khrushchev's frankness astonished Kremlinologists in the United States, who studied the interview very carefully.

The Khrushchev interview had a good effect on both Cahn's career and Humphrey's. Before the trip Julie, as his friends call him, had been a little-recognized figure around the Hill, having worked for Senator Alexander Wiley of Wisconsin before joining forces with Humphrey. But after Russia, Cahn became a sort of super star among public relations men on Capitol Hill.

Humphrey, too, was grateful and showed it in a most pleasant way. When a case of rare Soviet caviar arrived as a gift from Khrushchev to Humphrey, part of it ended up as Hubert's gift to the Cahn family table.

It should be mentioned that when Humphrey began his own run for the presidency in the spring of 1968, he chose Cahn to be national deputy chairman of Citizens for Humphrey-Muskie, independent of the Democratic National Committee.

Cahn had thought of everything imaginable to get support from special-interest groups, organizing some forty specialized committees. There were "Mayors for Humphrey-Muskie," "Entertainers for Humphrey-Muskie," "Engineers-Scientists for Humphrey-Muskie"—plus educators, social workers, you name it.

Cahn even booked stars on Humphrey's campaign plane to amuse the press and at rallies to raise money.

He got Frank Sinatra, the king of the fundraisers, and staged a final phone-a-thon in Hollywood with HHH and dozens of stars, such as Burt Lancaster.

Cahn certainly helped boost Humphrey's race to an almost victory. Some believe that had LBJ done his share and boosted Humphrey in the early days of the campaign when he needed it, that plus Cahn's whirlwind of stunts would have tipped the scale to Humphrey.

After Julie Cahn saw victory snatched away when Richard Nixon won by a small margin in November 1968, he felt he'd had it and departed political public relations for a less strenuous private life.

Cahn still shows up in Washington newspaper circles frequently, but now it's as president of *Family Health* magazine.

PR people are the nearest thing we have to Superman, staging happy endings.

Hundreds of private associations and institutions hire public relations people to grind out press releases, which find their way to every news office in the National Press Building—sometimes hand-delivered and thrown in front of every door, sometimes delivered in the mail, and sometimes merely left in a pile for reporters to pick up beside the front desk of the National Press Club.

Some call public relations people "fallen angels" especially those PRs who have switched from journalism to press agenting.

Others call them "flacks." One person who resents both these nicknames is Don Curry, formerly a Hill and Knowlton executive, who worked his way up—or down—to public relations, as your viewpoint may be.

He was a reporter for Gannett Newspapers, a UPI writer, a free-lancer, and an editor for the National Education Association, before going into flackery.

"I think the attitude toward public relations people that holds them a step lower than journalists is wrong," he says, and feels it is unfair that the men and women who write the press releases used by reporters still cannot get equal privileges with reporters in the various press clubs of Washington.

"'Flacks,' as they are contemptuously called," Don says, "can be and are of great service to the working press in Washington, especially when those reporters are on deadline. They provide facts, figures, research material, and much that goes into stories.

"Of course, public relations people do represent a point of view and are paid to represent it. But the entire world is made up of points of view.

"A good reporter should always be willing to listen to all points of view. Reporters, too, have points of view and sometimes are not so innocent.

"I have encountered reporters who present their conclusions and then manipulate the facts to support those conclusions. This type of a-posteriori reasoning is faulty. They do a disservice to their readers. Yet these same reporters often look down at public relations people who are paid to present a viewpoint."

A news background helps one to understand how to handle press people but does not assure success in the art of propaganda. Still, some of the most successful public relations people are from the newspaper world. Sherwood Ross, who is in the $100,000-plus PR category as a representative of various hard news and national quality magazines, once covered urban affairs for the *Chicago Daily News*.

Representing national magazines ranging from the *Atlantic Monthly* and *Harper's* to *Psychology Today,* Ross has broken many sensational stories from his office in the National Press Building.

In 1969 he broke the *Atlantic Monthly* scoop—Attorney General Richard Kleindienst's remark that people who demonstrate in such a way as to interfere with the rights of others should be put in "detention camps."

He also broke, for client *True* magazine, the story of how the CIA tracked down Che Guevara in the jungles of Bolivia and trained Bolivian soldiers to take him in.

And a month before the big dailies carried it, Ross fed to the press the *Penthouse* story on how Chilean diplomat Orlando Letelier was murdered.

He also had the photographs published in the *New York Review of Books* showing a man presenting himself to the Soviet embassy in Mexico City as Lee Harvey Oswald but who bore no resemblance to Oswald, suggesting a conspiracy.

If you walk down the hallway on the tenth floor of the National Press Building you will see a sign on a door: The Smith Group. The Smith Group at this time refers only to Arnold Smith, who has a most unusual client—the Republic of Transkei.

As Arnold tells his incredulous friends at the National Press Club bar, "Yes, Virginia, there is a Transkei." No matter what he says, some still maintain it must be the name of a railroad, like the "Trans-Siberian, or a pipeline like the Trans-Alaska."

But it is a small nation in southern Africa, independent only since late 1976. Now as their public relations adviser, Arnold's job is to correct all the misinformation he finds, even in high places.

Arnold has thrown himself into the job of learning the language of his clients. "The major native language in Transkei is Xhosa," he explains. "Singer Miriam Makeba of the Xhosa tribe introduced its clicking and popping sounds to Americans when she recorded the famous 'Click Song.' It is a hard sound to make unless you were born to it.

"My former father-in-law tried to pronounce the tribe's name and almost lost his upper plate. It really happened.

"When you enter a room full of Transkeians, you hear the voices first, and then in the background a sound like fire-crackers at a distant Chinese New Year's celebration."

Arnold Smith is quite content to base his reputation on this single client. He likes the field of international public relations and would not change it.

After going into public relations for himself, his first client was a car-and truck-leasing association. "They were my first and last domestic client. The fee was small and I had to fill in with odd writing assignments for various organizations needing tempo-rary public relations help—Manmade Fiber Producers Association, the National Alliance of Businessmen, and the White House Conference on the Handicapped's Industry Labor Council, to name a few."

What changed Arnold's life and career was a chance meeting with Ngqoudi L. Masimini, minister-at-large for the Republic of Transkei, who quickly became his friend. "I saw the opportunity to use public relations as a force for positive change," Arnold recalls. "The world had turned its back on this small, struggling nation." Trying to help has given his life new meaning.

Many countries have help with their image. Smith is just a small operator in a big international public relations field. Millions are paid to some of the big PR outfits by major nations seeking to get their viewpoints before the world—and the Amer-ican Congress.

Before the United States was in World War II, the British hired a number of writers, some of whom I knew, in a secret and successful effort to arouse sympathy for the British cause.

Industries go to great lengths at high expense to project images that will help sell their products or downgrade their competitors. The trucking industry long was plagued by cartoons of gorillalike drivers spouting profanities and ready to slug motor-ists after a fender scrape.

Their trade association went to work. A writer I know, William B. Mellor, was among those hired. All he had to do was to research trucking lines and influence reporters to place magazine articles that said something nice about truckers, if only a few words. If he himself wrote the article he could keep any pay he got from a magazine as well as his salary.

The result of the massive effort was to change the public image of truckers to good guys. My coauthor, Fran Leighton, deserves some of the credit for this because she was one of those tapped to write a story with the help of the Trucking Association's research department.

Her story told many touching cases in which truckers had acted heroically as they sped through the countryside by night. Some had stopped to help motorists who had highway accidents. Others had come across burning houses and had rushed in to rescue children and whole families. The title of the piece, which appeared in Sunday supplements across the country, was "Knights of the Highway."

When the U.S. Air Force Academy was built at Colorado Springs, the noted architect Frank Lloyd Wright drew modern designs with a lot of metal and glass, appropriate to flight.

The clay-products people were worried that this might start a trend away from brick and tile if the building became a showplace. Douglas Whitlock, czar of the industry, hired a PR firm to shoot down Wright's plans and make the Air Force use conventional materials.

At a congressional hearing, Wright was shown to have been affiliated with allegedly left-wing groups. It followed that his designs, too, must be suspect. The American Legion snorted in alarm. Any high flights of fancy for the Academy were quickly grounded.

RCA, in the late sixties, was building the image of Robert Sarnoff, Jr., who was succeeding his father, the well-known general, as head of the RCA empire.

A trip was planned, typical of big-business junkets, supposedly to show the press of Washington RCA's new home entertainment equipment.

My coauthor was on this particular junket and remembers, for example, early versions of home video cameras, a radio that could float in a pool—a luxury item that was given each newsperson as a gift.

But most important for the company was a special press conference set up for Robert Junior to meet the reporters, who it was hoped, would see the scion as a great pundit on the future of home entertainment and the future of the world.

No expense was spared by RCA. For entertainment they took the press to Los Angeles, where they stayed in fine hotels, sailed on a palatial yacht, and had a chuck wagon dinner on the Walt Disney lot. This was followed by a couple of nights in Las Vegas with free tickets to the big shows.

Whether enough home sections of newspapers wrote up the RCA innovations to make the trip financially worthwhile is not known, but RCA did get its money's worth in goodwill toward the younger Sarnoff.

However, fashions and freebees have changed since, and newspapers have gotten more stuffy and proper. Some will not let reporters go on any trip for which the newspaper does not pay its share.

This means that a lot of junkets must be passed up, because only the really big events, such as a presidential candidate's campaign or a flight into space or the first test tube baby is worth the newspaper's high expenditure.

18/TV

News reporters are bitter when they hear of the earnings of TV journalists or anchormen. Discussing it one day, investigative reporter Ron Sarro of the *Washington Star* said, "The pay differentials are outrageous, and terribly unfair to the wire services. I've seen AP and UPI reporters paid four hundred dollars a week for busting their guts to cover Congress and put it out on the wire only to have the Walter Cronkites and Barbara Walters of this world read it on TV for half a million or a million dollars a year. It is really outrageous.

"Sometimes these highly paid stars scarcely change the wording. If I were ever on TV I would at least want the dignity of covering my own stories and not have to rely on a hard-working journalist from another media.

"If they paid fifty thousand dollars to a reporter to supply the million-dollar man on TV or the quarter-million-dollar man, it would be a little better, but as it is they would rather pay a TV personality one million dollars for the charade of reading the words of someone who is lucky to get twenty-five thousand dollars."

At the Press Club, when reporters are debating whether TV newspeople have any right to earn so much more than the paper media, someone is always bound to point out that TV newscasters need not be envied because their life at the top is short and the tensions they are under to survive every day are horrendous.

They cite the case of Douglas Edwards, who was at the top of the heap at CBS before Walter Cronkite.

Cronkite himself tells how he learned in 1962 that he had inherited Edward's anchor seat. Edwards suddenly came to Cronkite's office, stuck out his hand, and congratulated him.

No such thing happened when Harry Reasoner was demoted to make Barbara Walters the sole anchorperson.

Barbara Walters is perhaps the most envied and disliked woman in the media—as far as her Washington confreres are concerned. Not for anything she has done, outside of being a little bitchy, but for being paid show biz prices for carrying out an

278

interview in public—a cool million a year. "A pushy woman," they say—even women say it.

Barbara herself, who comes to Washington frequently—and even dated Senator Ed Brooke a bit in the days before his humiliation at the hands of his then-estranged wife and his Senate ethics-conscious peers—is concerned about the media attitude and talks of it often.

As a guest speaker before the Washington Press Club's Editors' Dinner, she spoke almost apologetically of her great success, tried to show her great humility as well as her pride in getting the exclusive interviews she did with such difficult men as Fidel Castro and Richard Nixon.

As proof of their own judgment and excuse of their bias, Washington media people happily point out that on Harry Reasoner's last day at ABC news he did not mention her name in making his fond farewells

As for Barbara—whom her detractors refer to as "Baba Wawa"—she was conveniently off on vacation when Reasoner split; the consensus was that she had planned it that way.

Barbara knows her way around Washington, and has come to the White House to cover big events almost on a regular basis. Female reporters—coauthor Fran Leighton among them—found that she seemed not to know who they were unless she needed them for some background information. Even among reporters there is social climbing and Barbara did not seem to want to be just one of the girls.

Fran tells of introducing herself to Barbara for about the third time, assuming that perhaps Walters could not remember the other times they had covered White House social events together.

"Yes, yes," said Barbara sharply and annoyed, "I know who you are." At that point Fran was sorry she did know, and needless to say there was no further conversation between them.

Dan Rather tells of how ingratiating Barbara can be when she is trying to get an advantageous position. She had crouched down and crawled in ahead of him behind a rope President Nixon would have to pass on his way to church.

Since Rather had been standing there for several hours and had taken the precaution of being early, to make sure he'd get a chance at asking Nixon a question, he was at first annoyed and wanted her to move. But eventually, as she kept kidding him, he could not resist her winning smile and cute comments that she would take up just a little speck of space.

Though Rather had wasted his time and Nixon did not speak to him, at least there was poetic justice in that Nixon did not take notice of Barbara either.

But the anecdote Rather tells in his book, *The Camera Never Blinks*, which some Washington journalists say is worth the price of the book right there, concerns the time he accidentally banged his microphone into her mouth as she was reaching up to kiss him at the Republican Convention in Miami, 1972. " ... Understandably, Barbara did not take to it kindly. I had almost given her a harelip."

Harry Reasoner has, for years, been more or less pitied by his colleagues because it was obvious that he would always be in the shadow of Walter Cronkite as long as he stayed at CBS.

As Reasoner himself said after he left CBS to go to ABC, "I took this job because Walter Cronkite was not showing any inclination to step in front of a speeding truck."

That was typical of the Reasoner openness and brand of humor. Reasoner was jealous of Cronkite and his friends knew it.

While Cronkite practically ignored him, Reasoner did not ignore Cronkite and, in fact, would entertain the CBS gang with imitations of Cronkite's lofty and almost self-important way of delivering the news.

When Cronkite was making $250,000 a year, Reasoner was making something like $100,000. This would have been enough to make a newspaperman dance in the streets but Reasoner could not be happy, his friends said, because he was always measuring himself against Cronkite.

When ABC offered him a job at $200,000 at the end of 1970, Reasoner was thrilled, especially since he felt that now, at last, he would be anchorman on a network.

But it didn't turn out quite the way Reasoner had hoped. First of all he was again part of a team—with Howard K. Smith—and their styles did not complement each other.

Then when he finally did become the sole anchorman in 1975, he was blamed for the wretched ratings ABC evening news quickly fell to within a half year—ten points behind Cronkite and seven points behind NBC's team.

But when ABC chose to boost its news ratings by hiring Barbara Walters as Reasoner's anchormate, it was as if Reasoner's whole world had collapsed around him and again he earned the pity and sympathy of his colleagues.

Even when ABC sought to soften the blow by raising Reasoner's salary to a half-million dollars a year—to be in the ball game with Barbara's million dollars a year—they still pitied him, and Reasoner seemed to feel a bit sorry for himself.

Now Reasoner's barbed wit was directed at Barbara, rather than at Cronkite, and even on the air it was clear that he felt a certain coolness, if not contempt for his co-anchor person.

Barbara Walters' fantastic career is evidence for every ambitious TV neophyte that it pays to play it humble and bide your time. Barbara did and the time it took seemed endless. You just don't hear about it, however.

You don't hear about the years she was trying to get into TV anywhere, and settled for a job in TV publicity at a small independent station. And the years on a local station in New York—WRCA-TV—as a behind-the-scenes writer. And the years writing for the CBS morning news program—the competitor to NBC's *Today Show*.

CBS must still be kicking itself because, though she was doing a great job writing interviews that on-camera people would conduct with famous people, she was fired during an economy drive in 1957.

The man who most must wish he had bitten his tongue was CBS's famous producer Don Hewitt, whose advice Barbara sought. She needed a little boost in confidence and she asked Don whether he thought she had the stuff for ever appearing on camera.

The answer Hewitt gave her is still quoted in Washington, New York, and wherever else TV executives and commentators meet. Hewitt looked at Barbara a little pityingly and said, "Barbara, you're a marvelous girl, but stay out of TV."

She almost did. She had studied to become a school teacher but decided that public relations or newswriting was much more exciting.

She went from job to job. The year 1961 changed her life and set her on the course she was to follow from then on. She got a job helping Dave Garroway, at NBC, put together his *Today Show*—thinking up interviews that women would like to hear early in the morning.

Barbara admits that she felt a little jealous as beautiful

women, cohosting with Garroway, mouthed the words she had written. Why couldn't she do her own talking?

When she had humbly made the suggestion enough times, she eventually got to appear for a few minutes, occasionally, with a little feature story she had written.

It wasn't much but it was enough to give her bosses confidence that she could cover a story with the rest of the TV journalists. And her first one was a blockbuster—Jackie Kennedy's trip to India as First Lady.

Babs did so well that she was given other assignments, and when Kennedy was assassinated in November 1963, NBC chose Barbara to go to Washington to cover the whole funeral, with all that it entailed.

She became a regular at the White House press room and is still well known to the Washington press. She has been accused so often of being an aggressive female that she is super sensitive on the subject.

Once she asked Helen Thomas of the White House UPI staff whether Helen was a pushy female.

Helen said, "I certainly hope so."

"Barbara looked stunned," Helen recalls.

Reporters cry into their beer at the Tap Room as they recall the days when newsmen really had power and newspapers were the only link between congressmen and their constituents.

Reporters were courted then. Now, if anyone is courted, it is a Walter Cronkite or a David Brinkley, who make it possible for a politician to be seen by millions of viewers of voting age with the snap of a finger.

So glamorous are TV newspeople these days that CBS gave a huge celebrity-filled party to mark the tenth anniversary of the *60 Minutes* show.

The superstars of the party—even among such names as Clifford Irving, Alex Butterfield, G. Gordon Liddy, CBS Chairman William S. Paley, Kurt Vonnegut, Beverly Sills and Mayor Ed Koch—were the top honchos of the program, Dan Rather, Mike Wallace and Morley Safer.

Don Hewitt, producer of *60 Minutes,* whose ex-wife, Frankie, is executive producer of Ford's Theater in Washington, explained that the appeal of the show amounts to the fact that three men on the tube are playing the roles of three reporters, just as on other shows the stars are doctors or cops or detectives.

With their new celebrity status, the public is fascinated to watch newsmen simply playing themselves.

282

What makes *60 Minutes* so appealing, Hewitt feels, is that these particular reporters do not seem to have developed swelled heads and seem to be enjoying themselves.

"My pet peeve in all the world," Don Hewitt said, "is news guys who think they belong to the priesthood." Chuckling, Hewitt vowed that he would "throw out anybody who takes himself too seriously."

But the *public* takes its TV heroes seriously. Especially Eric Sevareid, probably the most eloquent man ever produced by TV. When he retired in 1977, he made a farewell appearance in the National Press Club ballroom on November 16 and there were many misty eyes as he looked around the flag-festooned room.

Eric Sevareid lives the life of a country squire. At this writing he is not married. His life has been storm-tossed as his romances failed to lead to permanent happiness. Married several times, the surprise is that he has not been married more. Women— even twenty-year-olds—find him irresistible and conspire to bump into him, accidentally, wherever he goes. At political conventions, one of the problems of security was to keep eager females from storming the CBS barricades to get at Sevareid.

Martin Agronsky, with his enigmatic smile, is reported to have somewhat the same effect on women, though to a lesser extent. However—and this may assuage any feelings of jealousy on Agronsky's part—there is this eyewitness account of Agronsky's macho appeal.

A certain, otherwise sane, woman in Washington learned that a female acquaintance of hers knew Martin Agronsky. She offered cash on the barrel for an introduction, saying that he has, for years, been the true love of her life.

The poor soul lives from Sunday to Sunday, when she can share her living room with him and his friends during *Agronsky and Company.*

Still, to be too easily recognized means that pleasant things will happen as well as unpleasant things. For David Brinkley, all of it seems unpleasant—whether it's someone wanting his autograph or someone trying to be noticed.

Once, before he gave up on trying to look inconspicuous in a bar, a well-oiled loudmouth tried to get his attention. He started to throw peanuts at Brinkley when Brinkley refused to acknowledge his existence.

The more angry the jerk got, the more determined Brinkley was not to pay any attention to him. Brinkley finally gave up and hurried out without finishing his drink.

David Brinkley deserves much credit for bringing TV news commentators down from the clouds and letting them sound like ordinary people with ordinary regional speech differences and little funny phrases.

Before David Brinkley drawled his, "Good night, Chet," to Chet Huntley's, "Good night, David," every news commentator tried to sound as British as possible.

Brinkley recalls. Brinkley pauses to think. Brinkley makes funny comments if he feels like it, putting down anybody he chooses, or even an institution like television.

All of this has made him an innovator and one of the greatest stars of television news—and one of the most copied by young TV news hopefuls.

But getting back to putting down an institution... Brinkley has been known to say, "You could put a baboon on television and he'd become a celebrity if you kept him on long enough." If the person looks unconvinced, David will prove by citing the case of J. Fred Muggs, a young ape, who became a regular on the *Today Show* with Dave Garroway, and developed a great following of his own.

Brinkley's is the story of an average kid who makes it big in spite of being a high school dropout. Starting at a salary of around forty dollars a week, by the early 1970s he was earning around $300,000 annually, as the star of NBC's evening news.

The secret of Brinkley's success is that he was, from an early age, interested in everything—and practically lived in the library of his hometown, Wilmington, North Carolina.

A point of pride with Brinkley, which he will sometimes tell with a smile, is that he was the only person who ever read *Decline of the West,* by Oswald Spengler, and the librarian was so impressed with this that she let him keep the book. "I still have that book," chuckles Brinkley.

As for learning the news business, one of Brinkley's high school teachers had praised his writing style and thought he could become a newspaper reporter. With the courage this gave him, he applied at the *Wilmington Star-News* and got a job nights and weekends. By the time he quit high school, he was knowledgeable enough to become a regular reporter.

When the Army tapped him in 1940 he was stationed at Fort Jackson, South Carolina, still reading everything he could find, and when he was discharged he applied for a job at UP.

He became a one-man bureau, finding stories and sending them to New York. It taught him to be versatile and it taught him speed in getting a story on the wire before the competition, AP.

But the most important thing Brinkley carried away from those early days as a southern UP man is his air of skepticism. He learned to his surprise that men in authority in a community look out for number one, and he never let himself be surprised again.

The adventure that caused his eyebrows to lift took place when a local sheriff in Alabama arrested a Georgia bootlegger, who had a truckload of good Canadian Club whiskey.

The sheriff unloaded all the booze he had seized at the courthouse, and Brinkley, who was covering the case, was there to watch it be destroyed under orders of the judge of the court.

Brinkley became suspicious because, as the sheriff broke all the bottles with his sledgehammer and let the whiskey splash out, there was no strong odor. Brinkley surreptitiously leaned over and got a little of the contents to taste and discovered why there was no strong smell—the bottles had all been refilled with water.

As a good citizen, David went to see the judge and told him what had happened. The judge, who knew human nature much better than Brinkley did at that stage of his development, exclaimed, "Damn it. I told that fool sheriff to leave at least one bottle of whiskey in each case or this would happen."

Huntley and Brinkley were not an instant success as a team. As a matter of fact, for two years they lost money for NBC, until they suddenly caught on and shot to the top of the ratings.

Reuven Frank, the producer of their show on NBC, deserves the credit for convincing the network to let the team keep going in spite of a "huge deficit."

The crucial year was 1958. Suddenly the ratings climbed and kept going until NBC news was ahead of CBS.

It was just a fluke, Brinkley recalls, that brought Chet Huntley into his life to begin with. Walter Cronkite had become a great star in covering the presidential convention whirl of 1952 and had practically buried NBC's old-style commentator, Bill Henry.

NBC was desperate to come up with something new and different, especially since they were being kidded that Betty

Furness, who opened the refrigerator door for Westinghouse commercials during the convention, had stolen the show from the news.

When 1956 convention coverage came up for discussion, the NBC Washington office pushed for a new face, David Brinkley, to be the anchorman. A New York group wanted another young man, Chet Huntley, to try his hand at heading NBC convention coverage.

Somehow the thought popped into minds like Reuven Frank's that there might be nothing wrong with having two men cover the convention and share the anchor chair.

They fit together like pork and beans—Huntley was the hard news and Brinkley added the light commentary.

So well did they do in 1956 that the *New York Times* said that CBS could learn a thing or two from them about how to cheer up its news delivery.

Reuven Frank was determined to keep Huntley and Brinkley together and he started the nightly *Huntley-Brinkley Report*. But at first it was most depressing because for a whole thirteen-week season the show did not manage to get a single bit of commercial time sales, which meant that it had to be completely NBC "sustained."

Even worse, the "Good night, Chet"—"Good night, David" bit was the laughingstock of the nation. People, whose names were Horace or Doug, were suddenly saying, "Good night, Chet" and "Good night, David" to each other.

David Brinkley was less than thrilled with this signoff which Reuven foisted on them. David said, "It makes me sound like a damn fag."

But Reuven insisted that he knew what he was doing, and eventually the nation was using the signoff affectionately. The *Huntley-Brinkley Report* became the top-rated news show and its success was history making—due in no small measure to the breeziness of the Washington end of the anchor team.

David was always coming up with humorous solutions for political problems. When Congress was debating on whether to change the name of Boulder Dam to Hoover Dam, Brinkley eventually got tired of the issue and suggested that perhaps the former President could change his name to "Herbert Boulder," so he could be honored without Congress having to go to all that trouble.

As for our illustrious legislative body, Brinkley once commented that "it would take Congress thirty days to make instant coffee."

Walter Cronkite and David Brinkley have something in common—both formerly worked for United Press. But Cronkite worked much longer, spending about a dozen years in wire service before getting into TV news.

Cronkite's full name is Walter Leland Cronkite and his son is Walter Leland Cronkite III. Walter is both the son and grandson of dentists, but he at first thought he would be a mining engineer.

The family had moved from Missouri to Houston, Texas, where such a profession was considered the most noble calling for those seeking a fortune.

But Cronkite forgot about seeking his fortune when fate stepped in and he got a taste of the reporter's life as a part-time newspaper cub while attending the University of Texas.

So excited did he get about journalism that he quit college when he was offered a full-time job by the *Houston Press*. It was after a year on the *Press* that Cronkite switched to United Press.

He was such a live wire as a reporter that UP made him a war correspondent in 1942 and sent him overseas.

Cronkite might today be the head of the Washington bureau of UPI or in its New York headquarters if it had not been for Edward R. Murrow, who changed the course of his life.

Cronkite recalls with amusement how he first learned of the "big money" to be made in working for networks. Murrow had taken a liking to him and had offered him the astronomical figure of $125 a week to go into radio. At this point, Walter was making $67 a week and he immediately accepted.

But Cronkite admits, he did have a few twinges when UP bureau chief Harrison Salisbury tried to get him to stay by offering him a $25-a-week raise.

Such a big raise was not handed out at UP willy-nilly, and besides, he really loved the excitement and constant deadlines of wire service reporting. But Cronkite was a man of his word and he had shaken hands with Murrow to seal the deal, so he was ready to turn down the $92 weekly salary in favor of the $125.

Cronkite phoned Murrow to discuss it and Murrow was so peevish that anyone would want to work for a wire service when he could work for CBS radio, that Cronkite reacted emotionally, too, turning down Murrow and sticking with his beloved United Press.

CBS insiders say that Murrow never forgave Cronkite and never gave him full credit for his talents and achievements.

Cronkite eventually did make $125 a week at UP and also he had the adventure of going on bombing missions and covering the Allied invasion of Normandy, with his by-line a household word—heady rewards.

Cronkite eventually got into radio, but in his own way. He took the initiative and created his own job—that of Washington correspondent for radio stations of the Midwest.

As a result his salary jumped to $250 a week and that's where he was when Murrow tapped him a second time in 1950 and offered him a job covering the Korean conflict for CBS. This time he didn't hesitate and his name again became a household word when he covered MacArthur's firing by Truman for the new live TV.

Cronkite was so used to dictating UP stories over the telephone that describing something as he went along came very naturally to him.

His talent for talking off the cuff assured his success, and he was soon a CBS star of the news department, who, by 1970, would be making over a quarter million dollars a year. But Cronkite did not rely just on his gift of gab. He was and still is a stickler for detail.

When he heard that he was going to cover the political conventions of 1952, he studied everything he could lay hands on about convention folklore and parliamentary procedure, causing facts and anecdotes to bubble out of him in a fantastic manner during the first coast-to-coast TV convention broadcast.

He also was full of fascinating tidbits about the presidential candidates, Dwight D. Eisenhower and Adlai E. Stevenson, and their running mates, Richard M. Nixon and John J. Sparkman.

Even today those around Cronkite know that they are not to bother him if he is closeted away with a desk full of material relating to the background of the news of the day.

Only his producer, Don Hewitt, may enter his inner sanctum and discuss the evening news show coming up. This penchant for studying, plus his ability to sit for long hours in the CBS booth at political conventions, have earned Cronkite the nickname of "Old Iron Pants."

Some lesser lights around CBS also think that Cronkite

has a bit of an iron heart, because he does not socialize or take them to lunches, as Harry Reasoner used to when he was at CBS, before the ABC days.

But as long as Walter Cronkite remains in the top spot as dispenser of the six o'clock news, the CBS powers that be will go along with any office style Cronkite espouses—including locking everyone out if he wishes.

Walter Cronkite was the first electronic media person to receive the National Press Club's "4th Estate Award," in 1973.

Club members have always been interested in innovation. The late Cabell Phillips of the *New York Times* once recalled the first radio transmission into the Club during the administration of Warren G. Harding.

An elaborate hookup was made with the naval air station in Washington to receive a message from the *Detroit News*. President Harding, who was a dues-paying member of the Club, was present.

He cocked his ear to the receiver, but all he heard were clicks, buzzes, and squeaks. Suddenly, an angry voice poured forth in full volume: "This goddamned thing won't work."

According to the older members of the National Press Club, INS was the pioneer in radio copy—the first wire service to prepare copy especially for reading on the air.

Lou Brott, a NPC member and former radio man, has special reasons to remember that first INS radio service.

"When I came to Washington, D.C., from Portland," he chuckles, "I went to work for WINX, which was owned by the *Washington Post*.

"They called me assistant news editor and paid me eighty dollars a week. I shared an office with Bill Gold, who is still on the *Post* and writes a column on the funny page. Our office was one foot wider than a telephone booth. If we happened to meet, we had to pass each other sideways.

"That I could stand, but what I couldn't stand was that damn INS copy I had to read every day. Some of the sentences were almost six or seven lines.

"I would run out of breath in the middle of a sentence and I'd say on the air, 'I wish I knew who wrote this stupid stuff—I just ran out of air.'

"I finally got so disgusted that I called up the bureau chief of INS, whom I'd heard had a terrible temper and was called Hutch, short for Bill Hutchinson.

"I took the offensive and hit him with it right away. I

said, 'Hutch, who in hell is writing this terrible crap? I can't read it. Doesn't your writer know how to make a period? I'm embarrassed all the time. Every goddamn paragraph is six lines long.'

"Hutch could stand it no longer. 'Goddamn it,' he interrupted, 'you smart ass, *you* come and write it. Don't sit there telling me what's wrong.'

"And I did. For the next three years, I would go in every day and rewrite the radio copy that went out on the wire into short, clear sentences. Hutch paid me twenty- five dollars a day for the rewrite job, which was a princely income for me. Families were living on less.

"Hutch and I became the closest of friends for the rest of his life. And when he was buried in 1959 at Arlington National Cemetery, I was one of those present who truly mourned his passing."

Among the persons whom Lou Brott introduced on the air was the brother of Drew Pearson. Leon Pearson was the State Department correspondent for INS and did some special broadcasts on radio station WWDC.

Another famous person with whom Brott worked was Mark Evans, who eventually became Ambassador to Finland. "When I knew Mark, he was a soldier, stationed at Walter Reed and moonlighting at WWDC. In those days, one tailored a name to fit show biz and Mark Austad became Mark Evans."

When TV and radio media men are apt to be smug at the Press Club bar and say they don't drink like the newspaper gang, with the intimation that they are the elite of the media, one reporter had a perfect answer:

"Booze can't be all bad, after all, it gave your goddamn fabled Ed Murrow his start."

It's true. The story, confirmed by Gary Paul Gates in his book *Air Time,* is that Ed Murrow, who was merely on the fringes of radio as a beginner at CBS in 1935, got pixilated at a Christmas office party.

The booze gave him so much false courage that, according to Gates, he offered to do Robert Trout's evening news broadcast, "wresting the script away from him with the giddy explanation that Trout was in no condition to read the news. In truth, it was Murrow, and not Trout, who had taken on a load at the party."

The amazing thing was not that Murrow read the news smoothly, but that he was able to read it at all, considering his condition. He did so well, however, that he found himself on radio from then on.

But stage fright never left him and he always needed a bolt of white lightning before going on, even when he made his very successful transition to TV.

The man who probably had the greatest influence on TV news programs and the attitude of presidents toward the press was Lawrence Spivak, who started *Meet the Press* in 1945.

He is given credit for dragging presidents and other high public officials from behind their stifling curtain of "off the record" and "a high official said."

Spivak, for the first time in history, put presidents and kings in front of thousands of viewers and forced them to answer the piercing questions of a panel of reporters, to reveal where they stood on every sensitive issue.

Spivak had such a cold and relentless eye as he drilled each important guest that even presidents shook in their shoes when they were invited to go on the NBC program.

But though they dreaded it, they did go, because everyone who was anyone meekly accepted. It was *the* status symbol for several decades, and if a man or woman of importance had not been on, it was a clear sign he or she was not *that* important, just plain chicken, or bo-r-r-r-ing!

Even Lyndon Johnson dreaded Spivak's grilling but forced himself to sit on the griddle. Only one President refused to go on the show and that was Eisenhower, who did not take criticism kindly.

No news show since has had the impact of *Meet the Press*, including *Meet the Press* today, which is still carrying on in spite of Spivak's retirement. It shows the power that one reporter can have.

Like Spivak, Ruth Hagy—Now Ruth Hagy Brod and a literary agent in New York—was very important in the early days of Washington TV panel shows. Her program, *College News Conference,* which she moderated, captured such guests as Harry Truman and the young Kennedys.

As Ruth Brod tells it, "Many political, broadcasting, and journalistic careers and romances were born on *College News Conference.*

"Teddy Kennedy was a student at the University of Virginia Law School when we first invited him to be a panelist. He arrived with Joan [his future wife] and chaperoned by 'Aunt Ethel,' as he called his sister-in-law.

"Naturally, Teddy was very good, and we asked him if he would be willing to return sometime.

"'Aunt Ruth, I'll come back as often as you will have me. I have to learn to master television—this is the media of the future for politicians. I need the practice.'

"'And what are you practicing to be?' I kidded.

"But he was not kidding. He said, 'First a senator and then—who knows, after my two brothers ... well, who knows.'

"Young Teddy made many visits to *College News Conference* and he always brought Joan, whom he was dating, and was always chaperoned by 'Aunt Ethel.' I thought that was a quaint, old-fashioned touch."

Lyndon Johnson was practically a TV addict, keeping several stations on at the same time. Vera Glaser, columnist and Knight-Ridder reporter, recalls once when she was on the *Meet the Press* panel and Betty Furness, LBJ's consumer affairs adviser, was on the griddle.

"One of my questions was so tough that it tripped her up and LBJ was furious," Vera recalls. "Before we got out of the studio, he was on the phone telling her how she should have answered me. Betty and I are good friends now and we still chuckle over that one."

Some presidents loved TV, others did not. Ike liked to eat dinner on a tray watching it. Nixon could take it or leave it. He almost sweated blood when he had to appear on the tube.

Three men in Washington hold comparable jobs as news directors—Sandy Socolow for CBS, George Watson for ABC, and Don Meany for NBC.

All of them have to cope with an ever-increasing number of persons seeking to get into TV news, where the big journalistic bucks can be made.

As Don Meany points out, "There is a parade of youngsters coming into my office. For the past few years they have been drawn to TV journalism. They are cute and sound independent but they are confused and mostly they can't even identify what it is they want to do.

"They haven't been taught in school what it's all about

and what makes a good TV journalist. Gimmicks are not enough. My feeling is that a TV newswriter should be trained as a good solid all-round newswriter."

So a pretty face or a deep voice are no longer enough to get one hired in the big time. Meany advises youngsters to get all the experience on newspapers they can. As for schools of journalism, three that he mentions as being top-notch are the Columbia School of Journalism, Northwestern University, and the University of Missouri.

Those who go out to cover the stories for TV must be able to work as part of a group. Teams of four cover a story—a two-man camera crew, a field producer, and a correspondent. The field producer must also help do some writing. The correspondent appears before the camera telling the story. However, the field producer goes back to the studio and does the cutting. He or she puts it together, as the first stage. The final say belongs to the program producer.

Why are today's journalism students so eager to get into TV newscasting? It's the chance to be a local news anchor that is their immediate goal, with the job of national anchor person as the long-term ambition.

Local anchor persons are starting to push toward a quarter million dollars a year. Jim Hartz of WRC-NBC in Washington makes $200,000 and Jim Vance, with the same local station, makes $210,000 as estimated salaries, per year. In New York (WABC-ABC), Los Angeles (KNBC-NBC), and Chicago (WBBM-CBS), Roger Grimsby, Paul Moyer, and Bill Kurtis already are making a reported $250,000 or more.

Just a few years ago a local anchor person was very lucky to earn as much as $100,000, and it is still rare that any newsprint journalist can make this amount without writing a best-selling exposé book. No wonder they taunt each other with the names "motor mouth" and "pencil pusher." The inequity of the discrepancy causes deep resentment.

Washington has many TV news bureaus which supply special features to their clients.

Andy Cassels, bureau chief of the Cox Broadcasting Washington news bureau, does not take orders from the Cox Newspapers, even though the Cox family is the controlling stockholder of Cox Broadcasting. "They give us editorial control," he says. Andy's feature TV stories go to the five Cox TV stations in such diverse locations as Atlanta, Georgia; Dayton, Ohio; Charlotte, North Carolina; Pittsburgh and San Francisco, as well as many radio stations around the country.

Andy made history in the news media about six years ago when he was covering the steel negotiations, in which station WIIC-TV in Pittsburgh was especially interested. "The meetings were closed-door at one of Washington's big hotels and things were very tense because the steel contract was about to expire. A strike was imminent. All of us press and media people had been sitting on the story about a week and we were feeling pretty grim about being cooped up almost around the clock," he recalls.

"I don't know how many hours I had been there that session and I had to go to the men's room. I looked a mess—no jacket, tie hanging from open shirt—but I didn't care. While I was in the men's room four union guys rushed in from the meeting, looking about as disheveled as I did, and mistook me for one of them.

"'We've done it. We've done it!' they chortled to me and I beamed back, hoping they'd give me some hint of what was happening. 'We've just voted to approve the contract.'

"I told them that was great and rushed out myself, finding a quiet corner and broadcasting my story, saying that the strike had been averted and the contract approved. As it turned out I had a thirty-minute beat on that story before the negotiators came out and announced the agreement to all the reporters and TV men who had been waiting outside the door."

It is not unknown that radio or TV reporters occasionally hit the jackpot with a national scoop.

Such a time was June 22, 1968, when Malvina Stephenson was representing the Swanco Broadcasting Company, owned by the frozen food people, with radio stations in four Southwestern states.

It had been rumored that Chief Justice Earl Warren would resign in time for retiring President Johnson to appoint his successor. It was known that both men shared a long distaste for Republican candidate Richard Nixon, and anyone who would be chosen to the court by the next potential President.

According to the grapevine, Malvina recalls, "If elected, Republican Richard Nixon would be influenced by Senate Republican Leader Everett Dirksen of Illinois, a staunch foe of Warren. Warren had never forgiven Nixon and the Republican leaders for undercutting him in 1952 and getting Eisenhower to give Nixon the second spot on the national ticket instead of him.

"All this is background to the situation that existed when I went to attend the wedding of a friend in Georgetown, which involved a reception at the University Club.

"Little did I dream that before the social afternoon was over, I would have some confirmation of the plot, accidently, from Warren himself.

"I had thought it very fortunate, when I entered the University Club, to spot Chief Justice Warren folding his tall silver-haired figure into a phone booth at the rear. I had hoped to get some comment from Warren when he emerged from the booth.

"I told my friend to go ahead to the reception and I hung around, at a respectful distance from the phone booth. To my surprise Warren was talking excitedly for fifteen and then twenty minutes. Then as the booth became too stuffy and he became preoccupied, he slid the door open and I clearly heard his side of the conversation. I clearly heard him say, 'If Nixon is elected, Dirksen would get the appointment,' which I took to mean that the Republican senator would control the selection.

"I thought I had come to a wedding, not a press conference, so all I had in my purse for note taking was a lipstick and the wedding invitation, but I did the best I could.

"Among other things I jotted down was Warren's comment, 'Dirksen has already tried to ruin the Court,' referring to Dirksen's effort to amend the Constitution and nullify the Court rulings on legislative apportionment strictly by population. And also to nullify the Court's ruling banning school prayer.

"By the time Warren had crawled out of the phone booth, I had heard enough and instead of stopping to ask him anything, I raced to my radio microphone."

As soon as Malvina's broadcast hit the airwaves, the AP and UPI wires were picking up the story, and she soon found herself being interviewed on radio by a slightly hostile UPI reporter.

As Malvina recalls, "Jim Russell asked me if I thought it was entirely ethical to eavesdrop on the Chief Justice. I maintained that I had stopped there on a very legitimate purpose—to ask for comment—and that after phrases began to float out to me, I could not bring myself to move.

"I turned the tables by asking reporter Russell, 'Would you have run from that kind of big news?'

"He laughed and said, 'No.'"

Malvina points out that with all the publicity on her stunt, not one word of denial ever came from Earl Warren or Lyndon Johnson. They just kept mum.

And when Johnson tried to get his close friend Abe Fortas confirmed as Chief Justice, it became a dogfight, which ended with the first rejection of a Chief Justice nominee since 1795.

TV newsmen have exceptional problems on Capitol Hill and envy the pencil pushing newspaper media. "It's really unbelievable, what we have to go through to cover a congressman or a senator or some event on the Hill," says Andy Cassels, of Cox Broadcasting, which has some seventeen broadcasting properties in major cities throughout the United States.

"First of all you cannot set up a tripod anywhere on Capitol grounds without the permission of the architect of the Capitol, except for four specified locations—two on the House side and two on the Senate.

"As for the Capitol steps, which are so famous, most TV viewers don't know you cannot set a tripod on those steps at any time and have to hand-hold the camera. And another thing they don't know is that TV reporters are not permitted to interview an average man on the steps—only a member of the Congress. It's their home and they own it.

"Inside the Capitol itself there is only one place where you can set up—it's called a stand-up location. That's Statuary Hall. About the only freedom you have in there is that you can focus on a northern hero or a southern hero among the statuary for your background, or you can avoid a statue. Then there is a second place we TV people can set up, and that is in the old Russell Senate Office Building, outside the Caucus Room on the third floor.

"That's it. But even so there's a great change that has taken place in the last seven years, for the better. Broadcast media have gained greater freedom on the Hill, but it is still much too restricted."

If a senator is involved in a story he doesn't want to be questioned about he can refuse permission for TV cameras to station themselves outside his door. "In contrast to this," Andy Cassels points out, "the pencil press can wait for him outside his office and take notes on paper as they walk down the hall with him or behind him. We cannot do that. It is completely against the rules for a TV cameraman to follow a congressman or a senator and take pictures of him walking down a hall.

"If you can get permission to set up, you can have him walking toward you, but you must stand in one spot."

Among the many problems the TV media has is the handling of their equipment. They must park it at the radio and TV gallery and run like fury to get it when it is needed.

News coverage will improve with new techniques. I have seen a camera designed by an inventor in upstate New York, about the size of a paperback book, with a sound recorder as small as a pack of cigarettes. For all the shoddiness of TV, it is capable of greatness.

The news in public TV is that the House of Representatives has finally opened its doors to public radio and public TV. Though the filming and taping is done by the Capitol's own experts, the coverage is available to all broadcasting. However, most of it is used by public radio and TV, which can afford to be more leisurely since its funding does not depend on advertising.

Recently public TV got a shot in the arm when President Carter signed into law an act that extends federal support of public TV at an escalating rate through 1983. Thinking of George Orwell's tome, we'll be waiting to see what happens in 1984.

At this writing, one of the biggest names in public TV is Bill Moyers, who was headed for success in CBS programming before he decided his future lies in developing in-depth studies for public TV.

Why did he switch from network? As Moyers explained it, "The network correspondent's role is very limited. Here in public TV, I can get something moving in just a matter of days. It is very satisfying, in contrast to the frustration of trying to move something through the cumbersome process of network broadcasting, where so many people are involved in the decision making."

To indicate the comparative influence of public broadcasting, its popular evening news show, the *MacNeil-Lehrer Report*, draws about four million viewers over 243 out of 279 PBS stations, while the CBS evening news draws twelve million; NBC ten million; and ABC nine million.

What makes a good TV interviewee? Someone who understands that the ordinary TV story is forty-five seconds in length and knows how to speak concisely. Getting high marks for knowing the TV interviewer's problems, and how to tell a story in a nutshell is Senator Dick Schweiker of Pennsylvania, who is rated as one of the best TV interviewees by the media. Birch Bayh from Indiana is another. He, along with John Glenn of Ohio, of astronaut fame, are also rated high for being "nice persons" who will do almost anything to make it easy on the interviewer.

On the other end of the scale Hugh Scott of Pennsylvania was rated as the toughest, almost totally inaccessible to TV newsmen, except for the networks. He was used to newspapers and never did get used to TV coverage.

It's too bad the public can't see what goes on in the getting of a simple TV story.

Pencil-pushing reporters never know what to expect on a story, and neither do TV men. There was the time the Cox Broadcasting people were doing a special to show a senator's first one hundred days in office. They had chosen Senator Sam Nunn of Georgia, who was elected in 1972 to complete the unexpired term of the late Senator Richard B. Russell, and it was the end of the one hundred days. Ray Goddard, the TV cameraman, was, as a parting shot, filming the senator as he was heading for the airport on his way back to Georgia, on a visit to report to the voters.

Goddard was sitting in the back seat as Richard Ray, the senator's assistant, drove the car and listened to the senator's instructions on things he wanted done at the office. Goddard was filming the instructions, both men nicely in profile, and the moving scene outside the car windows.

As they crossed the Potomac River on the Fourteenth Street Bridge, the senator said, "What is that terrible odor?"

Goddard, who had stopped shooting for a while and laid his equipment down on the seat, preparing for the final shots in front of the airport, said, "Well, senator, it must be the pollution of the river, but I've never smelled it this bad before." Within a few minutes Goddard discovered it wasn't the river, but the back seat in flames. He had left the hot light on when he had put the portable TV light on the seat.

As Goddard tells the story to amused colleagues, "So Nunn, who was in office a mere three months, made a spectacular arrival at the airport, with a cloud of smoke and late for the plane. Everyone ran from the car—the senator and aide to the plane, and I to the coffee shop near the door. I yelled for a container of Coke because I didn't know how to get any liquid any other way, and service was slow. They must have thought I was crazy when they saw me toss the Coke into the water fountain, fill the container with water, and then run back and forth to the car until the smoldering fire in the seat was extinguished. That was one story I was glad not to see in the papers."

298

Knock on any TV reporter's door and you will get a sad story of the one that got away.

When John Kennedy was assassinated, CBS had a clear beat. In fact, Dan Rather was the first to flash the news that Kennedy was dead, on CBS radio, a half hour before the White House press secretary made the announcement at Parkland Hospital at Dallas.

Then came the moment, several days later, when Lee Harvey Oswald was going to be moved from the Dallas City Jail to the county jail for safety. Rather was again on the ball, ready to feed the story live, but the CBS New York office was more involved in the Kennedy funeral that was taking place in Washington, D.C.— they didn't want to break away from it.

They also worried about the delicacy of switching directly from a funeral service in a solemn church, with every world leader attending, to a seedy jail cellar, with the dead man's alleged killer marching along in handcuffs. So, in the interest of good taste, they had decided to have Harry Reasoner lead into the switch-in scene with a one-minute transition.

But fate does not wait, and when Jack Ruby came out of the crowd and gunned down Oswald with one crashing bullet, CBS was still getting ready to switch to Reasoner, for his intro.

NBC hadn't been worried about good taste and so had a ten-minute scoop until there could be the CBS playback. Writing of this disastrous bad luck in his book, *The Camera Never Blinks,* Rather said, "I felt physically sick. For the first time that entire nightmare of a weekend I just about threw up."

Some entrepreneurs make their own way in TV. Deena Clark, a member of the Washington Press Club, started out by taping five-minute interviews with social and political figures. It was her idea to do short profiles of people in the news as fillers between programs in non-prime time.

She would ask a few pertinent questions, needle the guest a little, and then let the guest talk about himself. The program was called, "A Moment With," and who could resist such a forum to talk about himself?

The idea caught on and eventually Deena expanded her independent venture to a fifteen-minute profile.

Having a program that everyone wants to be on helps a TV personality's social life, and one is forever reading in gossip columns that Deena Clark is in the Costa del Sol or flying to some weekend party in London or Izmir. At this writing Ymelda Dixon's gossip column reports that Deena and a merry group aboard an ocean-going sailboat owned by Turkish financier Rhami Koc are headed for Monaco to attend the International Red Cross Ball that is staged annually by Princess Grace.

When the former Iranian ambassador invited a hundred guests to Iran to meet Queen Farah Diba, Deena, Elizabeth Taylor, and my coauthor Frannie, were in the group. Top hosts and hostesses always invite at least one TV personage to insure visual coverage.

As an irreverent sort of person, I do not have many journalistic heroes but I believe that the future greatness of our country will depend more upon the men and women of radio and television, and those who follow them, than on any other group. They are the ones who reach the people first. They are the ones who can galvanize folks for action—hopefully for good, not evil.

19/The View from the Typewriter

"The trouble with reporting today is that writers are trying to turn every chicken-shit assignment they get into a case of investigative reporting." I don't know who said it first but that's the lament around the Press Club.

Some old-timers in news work maintain that any reporter who is any good is automatically an investigative reporter. Others are just as adamant that so-called investigative reporting is a lot of crap and the reporter's voice should be kept out of the story.

A good reporter, they say, is supposed to sit on the fence and just report what happens, without any little arrows pointing the reader in any particular direction, or editorializing.

They say the reader should not be led to believe that every congressman or senator who is being questioned by the Ethics Committee is automatically a son of a bitch.

Aldo Beckman, bureau chief of the *Chicago Tribune's* Washington office, goes along with this view.

Many beginning reporters come to him seeking jobs and advice. He seldom has a job to give but he does give this advice to young reporters:

"If you want to be a celebrity, choose another business. I think there are too many reporters in Washington today more interested in becoming names than they are interested in getting stories.

"I also would advise you or any young reporter to keep in mind that your principal job should be to inform readers and let them make up their own minds from the facts. Don't be a participant determined to sway public opinion."

There are several approaches to a story and we will get to that in a minute. I just want to say, with all due respect to his considerable writing talent, I differ with Aldo Beckman.

The highest aim of reporting, it seems to me, is to get results, to make things happen that otherwise would not have happened, or to stop things from happening. The top goal is to change history. It is seldom done.

Many a reporter has dug up news that has shaken a city hall or state house, put a wrongdoer in jail, lost a congressman his seat, or gotten an official fired. But few have changed the state of the nation. The main exception was the Watergate case, a chance missed by the top newsmen and won by a pair of youngsters through a fluke.

Reporters also deserve credit for first getting Egypt's Anwar Sadat and Israel's Menachim Begin on the road toward their first face-to-face meeting. Barbara Walters in a stroke of "TV diplomacy" helped goad Sadat into admitting on TV, in front of millions of viewers, that he was ready to talk with the Israeli chief and break the enmity of centuries between the Arab and Israeli worlds.

There are two kinds of journalism. Two viewpoints. One is *advocacy* journalism, in which the writer lets his bias show for or against something. The second, *objective* reporting, was the principle taught in journalism schools until recently.

Wire services try to practice objective journalism—that is, the telling of a story in which there is no hint of how the writer feels.

Some people—Ron Sarro formerly of the *Washington Star* included—claim there is no such thing as complete objectivity in journalism. "The trick," he says, "is refining one's subjectivity, always sticking to the elements of fairness and balance."

Somewhere in the middle, between advocacy journalism and objective writing is a kind of writing practiced by most columnists, *news analysis*. In such newswriting, a journalist will report the facts—tell what happened—then will tell why it happened and do a little forecasting, sometimes wishful thinking.

I've seen, from personal experience, what advocacy reporting can do. During World War II, the airlines were trying to sneak through a bill to keep their monopolies and bar the entry of new aviation enterprises, such as returning Air Force men were eager to try.

Being in the service, I could not work openly but wrote a scathing editorial for one of the aviation magazines. At a crucial moment, a reprint was sent to each congressman. Members came on to the House floor with copies in their hands, deeply disturbed.

"You sure raised hell," Congressman Jennings Randolph, now Senator, told my publisher. The bill was defeated.

Colonel Edgar Gorrell, the airline man who had worked day and night for its passage, died of a heart attack, to my regret. I was trying to kill the bill but not the colonel.

One of my near hits was that I almost got the Civil Aeronautics Act of 1938 passed a year early. It's a bizarre story which requires a little background.

I was half of a two-man lobby trying to get a bill passed to unfreeze the airlines. The bill was desperately needed because, under the grip of the Post Office interested only in mail, U.S. airline route mileage was limited by law while Hitler spread his wings over the world.

This sad state of affairs had resulted from a probe of airmail contracts by Hugo L. Black, a smart young senator eager for headlines. I knew him. He was a nice guy who had no intention of wrecking the airline industry. But he did.

Then Black was suddenly elevated from Congress when FDR named him to the Supreme Court.

There were rumors that Black had been a member of the Ku Klux Klan. The inside rumor was that Black tried to cover his tracks by withdrawing Alabama newspaper files from the Library of Congress. But Steve Walter, a friend of mine who did public relations for the electric utilities, hated Black for his "power trust" stand. He waited till Black went to the high bench, then struck, releasing the evidence that Black had been a part of the organization that baited Negroes, Catholics, and Jews.

Our aviation bill was being sponsored by Senator Patrick H. McCarran, a devout Catholic—and devout drinker. When I came to my office the morning the news broke about Black, I made the not-half-awake suggestion that if Pat said something nice about Black, Roosevelt might let our measure pass.

My partner, Bill Redding, who often seemed to snooze at his desk, had a way of rousing like a crocodile on a river bank. He called the White House. By noon, we had a commitment from FDR that if this came about, McCarran not only could have his bill, but could be chairman of a Senate committee on aviation.

This was great news but who was to tell the Honorable Pat? When that Irishman was in a dark mood, scarcely anyone dared face him.

At the moment he was flat on his back in the Naval Hospital, drying out, after rediscovering a bottle of wine he had hidden in his committee room—in spite of the close watch his staff had been keeping over him since his doctor had given him strict orders not to drink.

Since the senator had taken a liking to me, I was chosen to go the Naval Hospital. There he lay, his fierce aquiline face less ruddy than usual.

Things went well for a while. I sat and watched as McCarran started to put together his thoughts about Black and his membership in the hated KKK. "I belong to a religion that believes in forgiveness of sins," he wrote.

He didn't finish, saying he'd complete the statement later. Had he done so, it would have let him realize a great ambition—passage of his landmark bill and the committee chairmanship—but he didn't follow up. Possibly he talked to some high churchmen who were distressed at the naming of Black to the high court.

Anyhow, McCarran issued no statement and it took another year for the aviation bill to be passed and alleviate the distressed condition of the aviation industry.

The point I'm making is that any writer who keeps his eyes open and tries hard might change history.

According to Ron Sarro, the biggest compliment you can give a newspaper writer is to call him "a good reporter. Any other title is meaningless."

Only the more pompous writers and columnists want to be called journalists, even though that is their trade.

John Cosgrove, past president of the National Press Club, takes it one step further and says, "The only journalists are in the graveyard. When a reporter dies, they try to make his family feel better. It sounds grander in the obituaries to say, 'He was a journalist.'"

Washington is the Mecca of reporters and would-be reporters. Much advice is given by the seasoned reporters who earn very good livings. Anyone whose by-line appears regularly is looked to as a sage. Colleges are top-heavy with journalism students and have been since the Woodward and Bernstein movie *All the President's Men* gave the reporting profession pizzazz, and brought a new word into the English language, *Woodstein*.

As Ray E. Hiebert, dean of the College of Journalism at

the University of Maryland, reports, "Suddenly, reporters have become our darlings, our new folk heroes. And the journalism schools are clogged."

But among the most successful press people in Washington, there is no agreement on whether journalism schools help or hinder a fledgling reporter, whether they intimidate, and whether they force or encourage budding writers to imitate the style of the favorite instructor or the journalist whom some favorite instructor happens to like and holds up as the great example.

Neither of the authors of this book took a single journalism course, yet are earning good livings in the craft—and have for many years—so might be prejudiced.

Some old-time editors, such as William K. Hutchinson of INS, would not even hire someone who admitted to having gone to college for journalism.

The younger breed of reporter seems to agree with Hutch. Marilyn Millstone, whom we met before as a specialized reporter covering water—supply, pollution, and as a source of energy—says, "Most of what I know today my journalism school did not teach me—a statement with which most of my young colleagues agree.

"Unlike math, biology, art, or music, journalism does not fit neatly into the institutional framework of college. It can't be taught in a classroom, although newsrooms have been set up in many schools, usually providing only simulation, not real-world stimulation.

"Actually, my *high school biology teacher* taught me the best thing I ever needed to know about journalism. Before handing out his first exam, he told us, 'Don't BS me on these essay questions. I know bullshit when I see it.'

"My exam came back with 'Bullshit' stamped in red ink all over it. So I learned early to mentally stamp 'Bullshit.'"

No matter how hard a traveling correspondent may try to tell the reader back home the news of the world, some local murder or train wreck may preempt the space so his effort comes to naught.

Whenever reporters and public relations men get together, the question comes up, does truth pay? The answer is always "yes," and it is said that reporters are like Mother Nature and become furious when tricked.

As a good example, when AP thought it had been

promised wild animals at a press conference, and their photographer found only stuffed animals for children, they killed the whole story and said, in effect, to heck with the merit of it.

The important point here is that a fun human interest story which got good coverage by one wire service was chucked by the other major service because the subject had lost its credibility through PR oversell.

Do reporters pay for news leads or exclusives? Only if they have to. *Life* magazine found it couldn't get an exclusive story of the life and activities of the seven original astronauts unless it paid in the millions, and so it paid, and the original astronauts told how it felt to be astronauts and became wealthy.

Many sad stories are told over a whiskey glass about the bought news leak that didn't stay bought. Sometimes the stakes are very high. CBS was willing to pay somewhere between a reputed $10,000 and $25,000 for the first TV look at some home movies that had been taken of the JFK motorcade at the moment that President Kennedy was assassinated.

They did the leg work, located the man who had the film, arranged for it to be processed and did everything else they could think of to make sure they would be able to show the film first—film which might otherwise never have come to anyone's attention.

But suddenly the film's owner got carried away with the film's importance and hired a lawyer. And suddenly *Life* magazine was in the picture. And, what is more, had bought first rights for a reputed $50,000 to $100,000.

The average person would be amazed at how often a news source has his hand out, and how often newspapers do pay for exclusives. When the ghastly story broke of nine hundred victims of murder and suicide at the People's Temple in Guyana, some survivors were not above selling their stories on the spot to newsmen who converged on the cult camp.

Writer Fred Barbash, in his account to the *Washington Post,* told how publications around the world were paying cash on the barrelhead, including a reputed $10,000, for eyewitness accounts. Some American GIs who were preparing the bodies for transporting to the States, too, he reported, eagerly sold documents and information to reporters.

Some editors and reporters pay for hot stories with special treatment.

As every Washington reporter knows, there is a lot of

306

plea bargaining in journalism, just as there is in the courts of the land. In other words, reporters going easy on their sources.

Some refuse to do this but, make no mistake, they are in the minority. Tom Wicker of the *New York Times* says that when he was Washington bureau chief, one of the hardest problems he faced was deciding how easy to go on sources who spilled the beans to reporters in order to get gentler treatment for themselves than those they told about.

Wicker would advise his reporters to yield very little to the desire of sources. He talks about it in his book *On Press*.

"Be neither in nor out," Wicker advises, and he adds, "a reporter should not be so far 'in' with sources—particularly the high and the mighty—that he or she would be inhibited in writing honestly about them, or in letting the chips fall where they may."

The worst thing that can happen to a reporter in Washington, he says, is to become a judge on national security—as he feels did happen to a whole bevy of reporters in the Nixon administration, when reporters felt "elevated" into the inner circle of power.

Of such a reporter, Wicker says, "He becomes the ultimate insider; and the reporter's deadliest enemy—the desire to be an accepted part of the world of power all around him—has won its final victory."

Probably the reporters who have suffered the most as a result of Watergate are the White House regulars. It became obvious that they had sat on their butts, or even tried to shield Nixon, while Woodward and Bernstein, two comparative youngsters, and still-wet-behind the-ears reporters, scooped the pants off them.

But they were not alone. As a result of Watergate, Washington reporters have gone into a phase of trying to turn every romp in the hay or minor malfeasance, from Capitol Hill to the smallest government agency, into a major political scandal.

The yearning that is being nurtured in newspaper readers to read more and more sensational stories of congressional investigations into private lives of public figures, such as Senator Herman Talmadge or Bert Lance, is becoming known as the "Watergate syndrome" and the "Watergate mentality."

Someone has to dig away at stories on unemployment, civil rights, urban renewal, and energy, because the future strength of the nation rests on solutions to these problems.

As one reporter put it, "The country won't collapse

because one congressman is caught with his hand in the till, getting kickbacks from some employee, or in some girl's bra, getting his kicks, but it may fall if Carter vetoes important defense legislation and we cannot protect outselves."

Now we come to the question every journalism student visiting Washington or writing a Washington newspaper friend asks: How can a journalism graduate get a job in the nation's capital without working for years on a local paper in the boondocks?

Many beginning journalists come to Washington to be interns at newspaper offices or on Capitol Hill, where the news is made.

Jack Anderson currently has four interns in his office. Interns are usually among the brightest and the best of their colleges' graduates—Anderson's certainly are.

Sarah McClendon is a firm believer in the intern system. One of her interns was Francie Barnard, granddaughter of Dorrance Roderick, who was then owner of the *El Paso Times*.

"Roderick wanted me to take Francie and get her out of the Harvard atmosphere she was in and teach her to be a tough reporter," Sarah recalls. "She and I liked each other. She was sharp and already knew reporting.

"I put her to work at the Supreme Court and the law clerks found her fascinating."

But Francie Barnard ended up marrying Robert Woodward of the Woodward-and-Bernstein Watergate writing team.

At this writing they are the parents of a little daughter but are in the midst of a divorce.

Among other budding reporters Sarah McClendon has hired as interns is Jayne Miller, daughter of former U.S. Senator Jack Miller of Iowa.

Marilyn Millstone—who at twenty-two got her current job writing and editing the twelve-page newsletter *Water Information News Service*—still shudders as she remembers how hard it was to get her first job because of the competition of interns.

"No amount of preparation in college—not grades, contacts, or experience—unless it's full time—can guarantee a smooth transition from college to professional work.

"I would argue that my wealthier friends had the right idea—after four years of college most went on extended trips to Europe. But, unable to find anyone to support me ideologically or

KING OF THE COPS: Lou Brott, Washington public relations man without peer, can always come up with an angle. One of his accounts—Invest-in-America Council—has kept him exercising his imagination for eighteen years. One year, 1971, he arranged for J. Edgar Hoover to receive the "Gold Eagle Award" for "advancing the principles of the American democratic system." With FBI Chief J. Edgar Hoover, center, are importer George Beck; Elizabeth MacDonald Manning, member of the Board of Trustees of Invest-in-America, Vice-Chairman of the Washington Area Council Kenneth M. Crosby, President Zenon C. R. Hansen; and Lou Brott.

QUEEN OF ENGLAND: When Queen Elizabeth, mother of the present queen, visited with King George VI as guests of President Franklin D. Roosevelt in 1939, lucky Lou Brott got the PR assignment of arranging a great reception for her at the Statler Hilton (now the Capital Hilton), working with the British embassy and the White House. Brott came up with an eight-foot British crown made of yellow roses, and that is what the Queen is looking at with refined surprise. To the left is radio personality Ruth Crane of WMAL, now renamed WJLA.

KING FOR A DAY: Sometimes even a public relations man gets the royal treatment. Here Lou Brott receives the Silver Gavel Award of the American Bar Association for producing the best local TV program dealing with crime and punishment. On the same occasion, Raymond Burr also received a gavel for best national law series—the *Perry Mason* show. Left to right are Larry O'Brien; Joseph Goodfellow, vice-president of WRC-TV in charge of Washington NBC operations; Governor Adlai Stevenson; and Brott.

ON TO THE WHITE HOUSE: It takes clout to call the White House and get Harry Truman to meet you in the Rose Garden. That's just what Lou Brott did, bringing along this multitude who were in town to attend the annual National Conference of Christians and Jews. "Truman was a gracious host and everyone was very much impressed with his knowledge of their affairs and what they were trying to accomplish," says Lou, who is easily recognizable as the only casually dressed person in the group (far right).

CHURCHILL: It was a great moment for Paul Wooton, Washington correspondent for the *Times-Picayune*, when he played host to the great Winston Churchill and made the introductory address at a press luncheon in World War II days. The press conference that followed was off the record. Here, chatting before the luncheon is Churchill with Paul Wooton, right, and Eugene Meyer, publisher of the *Washington Post* and father of its current board chairman, Katharine Graham. Incidentally, I was a cub reporter under Paul Wooton, who also sponsored me for the National Press Club. (*Credit: Wide World Photos*)

KHRUSHCHEV: "I was giving Khrushchev hell at a reception in the Russian Embassy," says National Press Club member Ruth Gary Hagy Brod, a Washington TV personality, now turned literary agent. "Far from getting angry, he invited me to the Kremlin with my husband. We spoke in Russian. My family was from Kiev, the same as his!" (*Credit: Collection of Ruth Hagy Brod*)

ROOSEVELT: A rare picture showing **FDR** *standing* with cane and the support of the strong right arm of his son James, a painful exhibit of what passed for walking. Taken at the National Press Club, the faces of the reporters reflect their high regard of the wartime President.

TRUMAN: They didn't know he was great until Harry Truman was long gone from the White House. Then everyone sang his praises in books and speeches. This is the most famous photo of "Give-'em-hell Harry." It was taken at the Press Club when then-Vice-President Truman was entertaining troops and an enterprising public relations man hoisted movie starlet Lauren Bacall atop the piano to the delight of photographers—but the embarrassment of the surprised Truman. The piano is still at the Club—and so is this picture.

ELIZABETH: In Washington, Elizabeth means either Queen Elizabeth of England or movie queen and senator's wife Elizabeth Taylor, who tried her hand at American politics by helping her husband, John Warner, run for and win a Senate seat. The ubiquitous Ymelda Dixon is hobnobbing with her at a Washington party.

MARY MARTIN: NPC President Frank Aukofer clowns around with the fabled star of South Pacific. Far from washing that man right out of her hair, Mary held tightly to his hand all through the 1978 visit. "She may have thought she was saving me from stage fright," says Aukofer, "but she was giving me stage fright."

POPE JOHN PAUL II: Little did White House foreign ethnic correspondent John Szostak know, when he played host to Cardinal Karol Wojtyla in 1976, and the Cardinal extended his hands and gave a benediction for a happy home, that his Alexandria, Virginia, house was being blessed by a future Pope of the Roman Catholic world. The two have corresponded for half a dozen years. "You never know who you're hobnobbing with," says Szostak. "When I heard the news that Cardinal Wojtyla was Pope, I rushed out for a paper and read it, shaking like a leaf."

DUSTIN HOFFMAN, when he played investigative reporter Carl Bernstein in *All the President's Men*, was messier than any member of the Press Club when he came to call, but the women reporters and secretaries went wild over him anyway, and soon descended on him from all directions. Behind him is Club president Ken Scheibel. Recording the event for posterity is member Berny Krug at right, with camera. *(Credit: John Metelsky)*

INGRID BERGMAN: Press Club member John Metelsky, who took this picture of NPC president Warren Rogers with the internationally famous star, says, "Ingrid Bergman's pictures never do her justice. What a woman! She hypnotized me. I was almost ready to leave my wife and family and fly off with her. With her, you get that intimate feeling even surrounded by people." *(Credit: John Metelsky)*

KISSINGER AND THE ROCKEFELLERS: No Oysters Rockefeller were served when Happy and Nelson Rockefeller and Henry Kissinger came to the Press Club for lunch in October 1972. They were a lively crew and greeted dozens of reporters by first names. At right, looking at his watch is Robert Roth of the *Philadelphia Bulletin*, whose deadline kept him from fully enjoying the jovial bantering. *(Credit: John Metelsky)*

CONTRAST: It's an awesome thing to be at a presidential press conference in the Executive Office Building, and some reporters prefer not to speak up at all rather than have to ask a question before a critical audience of 200 to 250 of their peers. Here Ed Bradley of CBS is posing his question while President Carter listens and reporters make notes. *(Credit: The White House)*

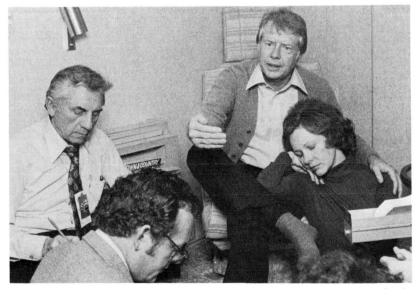

HOW SWEET IT IS, on the other hand, to be with Carter when he is relaxed and talking with reporters aboard his plane. As Ted Knap of Scripps-Howard (left) describes the scene, "We were on our way back from Europe in January 1978. Bob Schieffer of CBS [with glasses] and I were pool reporters, and it was like a cozy gathering in a living room as we interviewed Carter regarding his assessment of his first major overseas trip—throwing in a few other questions as well as they crossed our minds. The President had his shoes off. Mrs. Carter gave up her seat to the stenotypist and sat on the floor at Carter's feet. To show how relaxed it was, Rosalynn eventually fell asleep with her head in her husband's lap." *(Credit: The White House)*

RESURRECTION CITY: Ron Sarro of the *Washington Star* (taking notes at right) won the Washington Newspaper Guild's first prize for his reporting of the 1968 race riots and life in the makeshift Resurrection City which was set up at the foot of the Capitol after the assassination of Martin Luther King, Jr. Key figures, from left, are Walter E. Fauntroy, Washington representative of the Southern Christian Leadership (now delegate in Congress from the District of Columbia); Senator Hubert Humphrey (D—Minn.); New York Mayor John V. Lindsay, who came to consult with civil rights leaders and see conditions at the camp; Walter Washington, Commissioner and later Mayor of the District of Columbia; and Jim Bevil, civil rights activist.

IT ISN'T EASY to write a behind-the-scenes book about the star-studded and often outrageously cavalier Washington press corps. Here coauthors Ken Hoyt and Fran Leighton discuss some of the material from the hundreds of interviews and investigations conducted in order to pan the nuggets of golden anecdotes for this book.

AND CASTRO WORE A TIE: When Fidel Castro came to the National Press Club in 1959, not only did John Skelly interview him, but Castro wanted to hire Skelly to come back to Cuba with him. Skelly said no, thanks, but his Castro connection and the fact that he originally came from Cuba have been a millstone around Skelly's neck, careerwise. Since 1972, Skelly has been Washington correspondent for a San Juan newspaper, *El Nuevo Dia*. Incidentally, this picture is practically a collector's item because Castro is wearing a tie.

ANOTHER KIND OF PUBLIC RELATIONS MAN is William Gordon, who helps the foreign press at the International Communication Agency (ICA), and frequently travels around the country with them. Here he takes a group of journalists from sixteen different countries on an extensive tour to show them "The New South," one feature of which was a press conference with Governor George Wallace. (Gordon is the white-haired man closest to Wallace.)

LUCKY TEAM: Pat Munroe and his wife Mary are Washington correspondents for the *Daily News* of the Virgin Islands and are delighted when they are called to make an annual or semiannaul trip to the home office. "We always try to make it in winter," says Pat, "The foliage is so exciting and lush." *(Credit: Ariel Melchior, Sr., Daily News of The Virgin Islands)*

NOT SO LUCKY was Ruth Watson, who did a special stint in public information for HEW, starting in 1970, "to apprise the public of the importance of the welfare reform bill known as HR-1." After two years of work, she was transferred, and the bill, which would have made aid to dependent families uniform across the nation, was defeated. "I learned," says Ruth, "that I had been taken off the welfare assignment because President Nixon had decided to withdraw his support from HR-1 and had not wanted it passed after all."

FAREWELL TO A QUEEN BEE: When Mabel Cornett retired from "manning" the front desk as administrative assistant of the National Press Club, every past president of the Club rallied round at a gala farewell party in April 1976. Clockwise from top left, with their affiliation while president, are Don Larrabee, Larrabee News Bureau (now representative of the State of Maine); John Cosgrove, *Broadcasting* magazine; Ed Edstrom, *Louisville Courier-Journal*; Warren Rogers, *Chicago Tribune*; Clyde LaMotte, *Washington Energy Memo*; Mabel Cornett; Vernon Louviere, senior editor, *Nation's Business*; Dave LeRoy, correspondent, *U.S. News & World Report* (now executive director National Press Foundation); Bill Broom, chief of the Ritter Bureau (now with the *Philadelphia Inquirer)*; Frank Holeman, correspondent, *New York Daily News* (now director of the Tire Industry Safety Council); Michael Hudoba, *Field and Stream*; Felix Cotten, correspondent, International News Service (now U.S. Commerce Department editor in its Public Affairs Office); John D. Horner, *Washington Star* (now retired from ITT). *(Credit: Berny Krug)*

THE VELVET VOICES OF Senator Everett Dirksen and Frank Sinatra, Jr., fight the battle of the velvet voices at a National Press Club party, to the amusement of public relations Club member Don Curry, Representative Morris Udall, and Club member, lobbyist Michael Deane.

MACHO PRIME MINISTERS COME TO CALL, like Pierre Trudeau of Canada, who answers questions at a press conference held in the Club's mammoth ballroom. *(Credit: Stan Jennings)*

AND SO DO LADY PRIME MINISTERS, like Golda Meir of Israel, answering a question at a Press Club luncheon at which she was guest of honor, in 1973. The ritual is that members write out questions while they eat and pass them up to the Club president, who sorts through them and serves as moderator. Here Club President Don Larrabee does the honors. *(Credit: John Metelsky)*

KINGS ALSO COME TO CALL: King Hussein of Jordan, shown here chatting with member Don Curry, was one of many royal figures who have visited the National Press Club. *(Credit: John Metelsky)*

THE PRESS DOES HAVE ITS FUN WITH THE WHITE HOUSE
GANG! Seconds after this picture was taken, this ungrateful Georgia frog,
presented to Jody Powell, President Carter's press secretary, at a Press Club
Georgia Night shindig, disgraced itself and the Club by watering Jody
down. Jody took the assault in stride and said the frog was simply express-
ing its disgust at having been named "Lester Maddox." Laughing at right is
Bob Lewis, now correspondent for Newhouse News Service. *(Credit: Booth
Newspapers)*

PRESIDENTS OF THE UNITED
STATES: Every President since Teddy
Roosevelt has visited the National Press
Club in Washington, D.C., some to chat,
some to play cards, some to politic. Here
President Jimmy Carter signs the Club VIP
register for posterity. Club President Frank
Aukofer immediately locked up the book
for safekeeping, before some autograph
hound could thwart history. *(Credit: The
White House)*

AND ONE OF THEIR OWN: Warren Harding was the only member of the working press to become a President and so the National Press Club felt great pain when his tenure was marked by scandal that exploded after his mysterious death. But while he lived, he was a good Club member, coming in to play cards and kibitz and even to vote, as he did here in December 1921. Standing behind him is Club President Robert B. Armstrong, *Los Angeles Times*; seated are, from left, William J. Donaldson, House press gallery; Theodore Tiller, *New York Times*; Paul Mixter, *Detroit Free Press*; and Edward Coffin, American Red Cross.

LAYING THE CORNERSTONE—President Calvin Coolidge does the honors in front of radio hookup, reporters, and noted guests. The year was 1926, and it wasn't really the cornerstone, but the Club faked it and the grandstand stunt helped bring in investors to get the National Press Building built. Through the years this has become perhaps the National Press Club's most cherished photograph—in spite of, or maybe because of, the little chicanery.

FAREWELL PARTY: Felix Cotten and this book's coauthor, Fran Leighton, bid farewell to *New York Times'* correspondent Bill Blair, at right, at a Club party, and congratulate Bill on turning in his pencil in exchange for a fishing rod in Florida. As proud past presidents of the Club, Felix and Bill try to top each other on whose administration had the greatest disaster. *(Credit: Berny Krug)*

HISTORY MAKER: Arthur Wiese, Bureau chief of the *Houston Post*, made club history in January 1979 by becoming its youngest president in a half century at age 32. He compares heading the National Press Club gang with what Bob Strauss said about being chairman of the Democratic National Committee: "It's like making love to a gorilla. You don't stop when you get tired. You stop when the gorilla gets tired." *(Credit: Berny Krug)*

monetarily along those lines, I found myself—a cum laude journalism graduate of American University—job hunting in Washington during the city's notoriously muggy summer.

"Never look for a job in Washington in the summertime. People come here to work for *free*, for goodness sake, and others are happy with a pittance. I still cringe when I hear the word *intern*—zealous Ivy Leaguers happy to subsist on the sound of their employer's name—'Yes, I'm starving, but I'm writing press releases for my senator!'"

Millstone says that while job hunting for her first job in Washington she found herself enrolled in "Postgraduate course 101: Humility. In my case the course lasted three months, thirteen days, and nineteen hours."

"My big break finally came, " she says, "when I was offered the job of editorial assistant for a technical journal dealing with water pollution control. I quickly learned that 'editorial assistant' is used in the journalism world to mean anything from 'gofer' to all-around writer.

"What does not vary greatly is the salary, which is usually low—and, in my case, intolerably low—seventy-five hundred dollars."

"So after nearly a year of editing what scientists euphemistically term 'writing,' I began that most surreptitious of practices—looking for another job while still working.

"If one's present place of work is relaxed and pleasant, as mine was, the only problem with doing it was juggling the circus acts in my mind. The clanging guilt feelings: How can I leave these people after they elevated me from the ranks of the unemployed? The fear: What if my next employer turns out to be, perish the thought, a stickler for the rules? And the attendant feelings of insecurity: What if my new co-workers make my skin crawl?

"But for me, and most of my friends in similar situations, what usually wins out is resentment that the glut of journalists on the market make salaries for entry level positions abominable. And a healthy dose of resentment can carry one through that awkward period when interviews for a new job are known to one's employer as 'doctor's appointments.'

"Amazingly enough, one year's worth of full-time experience is magic. I averaged seven interviews for every ten resumés sent out; partly, I'm sure, because of my cover letters. In them, I was cocky and careful to point out how I would fit the position being offered as perfectly as a hand fits a glove. In my case the glove fit. I hope it fits some other hopeful reading this."

Something that bothers me is that among newswriters, few have passed critical judgment on their own profession. It has taken outsiders to do it for us.

A century and a half ago, Alexis de Tocqueville wrote of the American press that while each separate journal exercises little authority, their combined power is "second only to that of the people."

Now America's leading Russian, Aleksandr Solzhenitsyn, says the press is "the most powerful institution in our society—more than the legislature, the executive, and the judiciary." Then he scolds the media for their shortcomings. They misinform and do not correct errors. They make heroes of terrorists, give away national secrets, needlessly invade the privacy of public figures, and violate the public's "right not to know."

Despite their freedom to pursue all subjects, they cover a narrow band, he says. They follow "a common trend of preferences ... and accepted patterns of judgment."

In deference to the man, pundits of the press, such as the *Washington Post*'s Carl B. Seib, took issue mildly. He questioned whether anyone who spent so much time in Russian prisons and recently in a Vermont village could know so much about the American system. But it was in prison that Solzhenitsyn saw what happens in a land without a press free to expose wrongs. So why don't we make better use of ours?

It is left to a few off-beat papers, such as *Rolling Stone,* to spread awareness of press behavior and misbehavior. Also *The New Yorker.* The late and beloved humorist, Robert Benchley, wrote under the heading of "The Wayward Press." A. J. Liebling took over.

Liebling traced a good deal of the trouble to the dwindling number of newspapers, as the wealthier ones bought and scuttled their competitors or chains expanded to decrease competition and individual ideas.

We'll get back to that in a minute but first I want to point out other limiting factors, including the focus on the day's events rather than on long-term trends, lack of space as news is crowded out by trivia, and reliance on wire services rather than on independent digging. Pack journalism is a newspaper affliction. A mob of reporters will rush after the same story and miss others.

The most frightening example of missed news is what I call the Federal Management Conspiracy, whose plotters crept into control year by year. Their machinery was taken over and expanded by the Nixon conspirators. Since Nixon's fall, his people are still spread through the departments, biding their time.

It is an invisible government, unnamed and unknown, that would change the whole federal structure and does so bit by bit. Already they have divided the country into realms. Originally each federal agency set its own regional boundaries to fit its needs.

Then under Nixon, the Office of Management and Budget (OMB) got Congress to approve ten separate regions, each with its own capital. Office workers were uprooted and forced to move to their regional capital.

There was also a plan to regroup government agencies under super departments. One weekend in the Executive Office Building, next to the White House, offices were suddenly shifted around so people would be grouped with those of like function in the master plan—all unreported in the press.

Inside White House sources told me the offices were overstaffed so hundreds could be trained and screened to take over key posts throughout the government. Many are still there.

What was the purpose? Out of the millions of words in news and books on the Watergate scandal that brought Nixon down, the question not only is unanswered, it is unasked!

Jeb Magruder said Nixon wanted to pick his successors for a "perpetual presidency" in his mold. But what did the plotters intend to do with the government after they controlled it? Did they have a master plan? And, unwatched, are they still winning it in bits and pieces? They will win indeed for all the press is doing.

The only mention of the setting up of the "ten little Washingtons," incidentally, was a short report in the "Federal Diary" column of the *Washington Post*. That there could be any sinister connotation was completely overlooked.

The only major story I have seen on the unholy power of the budget system was in the *American Legion Magazine* of August 1965, complaining that funds Congress had voted for veterans' care were being held back, and quoting Lyndon Johnson as being alarmed that the Budget Bureau was a "czar."

OMB—the successor to the Bureau of the Budget—is closely tied with foundations staffed with experts in the structure of government. OMB is a proving ground for officials.

To my reporter's mind, what this state of affairs amounts to is that the invisible government makes decisions and gets Congress and the departments to carry them out. There is no single board of directors but several spheres of influence.

OMB's plan, under Nixon, was to reorganize the government into superdepartments, covering such functions as welfare, public works, and natural resources. Without waiting for Congress to approve, HEW Secretary Casper Weinberger was already beginning to act beyond his own department.

The conspiracy actually began after the Bureau of the Budget was created in 1921 as an agency of the White House to put a lid on annual spending and correct a flaw. Originally, bureaucrats would come in and ask for the moon with a ribbon around it and Congress would logroll the money. There was no ceiling.

Soon, beyond advising how much should be spent, the bureau schemed to work its will. They suckered President Truman into instituting a gag rule so that a bureaucrat could not go before Congress to complain he had not been given enough money.

Under this rule of *lese majesté*, a bureaucrat who dared say a budget amount was not enough was guilty of criticizing the President and could be fired.

Officials are still gagged. Not even a Cabinet officer can testify in Congress, consult about legislation, or answer congressional letters without approval by OMB.

It has been quietly gathering functions through the years, yet aside from the single day each January when Congress gets the budget message—now close to a half-trillion dollars—the press scarcely ever mentions this almighty agency.

The only recent exception was when President Carter's OMB director, Bert Lance, was hounded out of office for free-and-easy banking that had nothing to do with federal spending.

Still on the subject of missed stories, few reporters realize that there but for the grace of God went Nelson Rockefeller into the White House instead of Gerald Ford. I don't believe the political press realized how close it was.

I first saw Rocky when Roosevelt had sent him to South America, and he returned with a starry-eyed view of what could be done for that great continent. Thinking it a bit Utopian, I wrote a debunking report for the *New York Times Annalist* that was quoted in various newspapers. Little more was heard of Rocky's discovery of the Southern Hemisphere.

As governor of New York, Rocky still could not command a national following for president. He was ready to sneak into the back door of the White House when Agnew quit in disgrace as Vice-president and the job was open for a Nixon appointment. It was a good guess that he would somehow buy or elbow his way in.

It was a near thing. His speech writer in New York at the time was William B. Mellor, an old friend of mine. Bill told me that he and Rocky were packed to come to Washington till the last moment, when Nixon gave the nod to Ford. I saw no intimation in the press at the time that it had been so close.

Now to return to the earlier point, Liebling's concern over the dwindling number of newspapers. Today the newspaper profession stands at a crossroads. To be or not to be—gobbled up by conglomerates.

The future will see a new kind of star war—between those fast growing newspaper conglomerates.

What is bad is that people's minds will then be molded by only a few newspaper owners. Who will those owners be?

There is nothing that says the oil-rich sheiks of the Middle East cannot throw in a billion dollars to buy our newspapers and thus influence our thinking. Or crime barons of American vintage could buy control of newspaper conglomerates.

Even leaving out foreign influence or criminal elements, there is something unhealthy about one group having too great a control over the mind of a city. There is the story of Escanoba, Michigan, and a newspaper there owned by Pan Ex, which owns over fifty newspapers.

An editor was given two anti-Carter headlines to choose from for his front page, the order coming from higher management. The first headline accused Carter of sanctioning promiscuity. The second said Rosalynn was being groomed for the vice-presidency.

The editor refused to use either and was fired. Fired, even though, as he later reported, he had offered to make these merely feature stories elsewhere in the paper.

The Escanoba story was told with many others by Hughes Rudd, the CBS former anchorman, who is alarmed at what is happening to newspapers.

In a special hour show, he told how conglomerates are buying up newspapers of every size at an alarming rate and described what happens. In one city, for example, residents had to buy out-of-town papers to find out what was going on in their own town because the local paper refused to run a series on crime in the city. Why hadn't a competing newspaper in the city run the series?

Because there was no competing newspaper. It had been bought up and wiped out.

Newspaper advertising wars are taking place in many cities. For example, in Boston, the *Boston Globe* is getting most of the city's advertising and the Hearst paper, the *Boston Record American,* is having to beg for a slice of the advertising dollar of local business.

Hughes Rudd interviewed ad takers of the *Record American* who explained how they solicited ads only to be turned down. One said to him, "How would you like to be turned down sixty or seventy times a day?"

To which Rudd jokingly replied, "When I was young I was."

Three-quarters of newspaper revenue comes from advertising. So papers live and die by the ads they get. It is ridiculous to say that advertisers don't influence newspaper policy. Some newspapers are very brave in one area—say politics, but buckle under when it comes to printing something that might annoy ad buyers.

Ron Sarro is one onlooker who feels that competition between newspapers "helps keep both publications more honest and fair," and so is very necessary. "It requires them to cover things they could easily ignore if they knew the paper across town wasn't there."

Sarro also feels the second newspaper is important to the individual citizen. "The individual feels he has a second chance to be heard, an alternative if he feels he has been misquoted in a story done by the other newspaper. If there is only one newspaper, there is really nowhere for him to turn.

"One hears many horror stories of one-newspaper towns. The sole paper interprets events. There is much more slanting of the news where there is just one voice. With several perspectives on a story, the reader gets a clearer view of what is really going on in the city, and in the nation as well."

Congressman Mo Udall wants Congress to study the direction newspapers are taking: Is there something unhealthy about it? Do we need to expand antitrust laws?

As Udall points out, newspapering has changed more in the last ten years than in the previous hundred.

Unfortunately, it is no longer the purchase price of a newspaper that the owner-publishers are interested in—the fifteen cents or so per customer. The number of readers and the money from readers is only important as a way of increasing *advertising* circulation. Some publishers are getting rich beyond their wildest dreams. They are plowing in profits to buy up small papers as fast as they can, offering huge prices to the owners.

Now over 70 percent of all newspapers in the country are owned by chains. Some say there will be practically no independent small papers in another decade or two. There is no easy answer.

part four * * *

THE VIEW
FROM THE
ERASER

20/Life-styles and Private Lives

Ben Bradlee, most famous editor in Washington—executive editor of the *Washington Post*—works in a goldfish bowl and leads a private life in another goldfish bowl.

His glassed-in office—floor to ceiling—makes him an actor on stage to a tremendous newsroom audience. His love life, centered on one of his star employees, is also highly visible.

As a matter of fact, Bradlee finally married the girl after living openly with her. It took some kind of guts to do so, because as Lynn Rosellini, *Washington Star* staff writer, tells it, *Post* publisher, Katharine Graham was very upset when Bradlee fell in love with *Post* reporter Sally Quinn, and left his wife, Toni. But Ben did not turn back.

According to Rosellini, right after Bradlee moved out, publisher Graham was at a cocktail party and blurted to a casual acquaintance immediately following his greeting, "It's awful about Ben and Sally! How could they do that to Toni?"

Fran Leighton had the good fortune of catching Bradlee in a talkative mood while he was still defying convention with the classy news gal.

"Do you have any objection to my discussing your life-style with Sally Quinn in the book I am writing?" asked Frances Leighton during an interview with Bradlee in his comfortable and elegant office.

"Go right ahead," he said. "It's a fact of life. We've been living together without marriage for five years."

"Whose house do you live in? Your old house in Georgetown?"

"No, I live in Sally's house at Dupont Circle. I've been sharing her house for five years. We enjoy being together though not necessarily doing the same thing."

So why did Ben and Sally finally marry?

No big reason. As Sally Quinn told fellow reporters, "At

319

first there was no real reason to get married. But then, suddenly there seemed to be no reason for not getting married."

Bradlee and Quinn are only two of dozens of writers—including Carl Bernstein and Nora Ephron—who choose to live together openly first without benefit of clergy, proving that reporters are not a breed apart from the rest of society.

Discussing how he and Sally handled their social life, that is whether they led separate social lives, Bradlee said, "We go together. We are invited. Hostesses understand, and they invite us as a couple, of course."

When the interview took place, Ben had to shake hands with his left hand because he had a big gardening blister on his right hand, a reflection of their life style. "Every weekend we go to my mountain cabin in West Virginia," Bradlee said, looking wistful even as he thought of it. "I work in the woods. I chop wood, clear brush."

But Sally is not that kind of outdoor girl. "While I'm working she's reading or working on a story. Oh, we may go for walks together. That's the extent of her outdoor interest."

A much more interesting living arrangement is that of one writer in the Washington area, who is part of a ménage à trois. Though he divorced his wife and lives with his lady love, his wife continues to live with the couple and, in fact, still helps her ex-husband, serving as his unofficial research assistant.

Those who know them and love them accept them as they are and invite this lucky man with whichever partner he wishes to bring along.

Another interesting living arrangement is that of a technical writer, Bob Butler, senior editor of *Traffic World,* who moved into the fabulous, art-filled penthouse apartment of his "honorary Press Club member" friend, Tiger Farley of the National Association of Realtors.

They give elegant parties, are among the most popular couples at the National Press Club.

In contrast to Bob Butler, Ben Bradlee has severed his connection with the National Press Club. "I resigned from the Club—from everything," Bradlee said. "It's not my way of life anymore." Nor do he and Sally do much entertaining.

Bob and Tiger sat around the Press Club with Frannie discussing their life-style for purposes of this book. "We have nothing to hide. Times have changed and marriage isn't what it used to be anymore. We're happy. We don't want to tamper with our good luck." It is Bob speaking.

"That's true," adds Tiger. "Besides, we've both been married and know those miseries. This way is far more relaxed and tension-free. We're having a ball."

Anyone who sees them around the Club can attest to their happiness and good cheer. They are always the first to volunteer and get involved in Club projects—helping with staging and even acting, as the occasion demands.

"The marrieds are always rushing home and hardly have time for anything," says Tiger. At this writing, the couple is searching for an apartment that will be still larger and will hold more art than their present home.

According to Sam Fogg, former UPI and INS man and now with Jack Anderson's team, "The old clichés are gone. Like marriage. Now, in newspaper circles, if you're sleeping steady, you're generally considered loyal or basically married.

"Social Washington doesn't ostracize you anymore. The live-in couples get just as many invitations as the married folks, maybe more."

As for himself, Fogg says, "I've been married too long now to change my ways—I think thirty-six years give or take a few. As I recall, I married a nurse. Then she took graduate work in education and switched careers on me. I'm now married to a specialist at the Office of Education—same brainy lady."

Washington Post columnist Maxine Cheshire and her McGraw-Hill editor-husband, Herbert, are not living together anymore but, at this writing, they have no plans for a divorce, either. "We are the Claudine Longet and Andy Williams of the journalistic world," laughs Maxine. "I'm perfectly happy and the kids are happy." She lives in their Mount Vernon, Virginia, home and Herb has an apartment.

There are life stories around the Press Club that can make you laugh, but more stories can make you cry.

One of the saddest involves a writing couple who split up. The female of the team remarried very happily. The male, who had taken the breakup very hard, ended up standing outside her house on her wedding night crying and calling her name. Fellow Club members treat him with tenderness because it is said he still carries the torch.

Then there is the complicated story of the Club member who was "driven to drink by a woman."

Before the dramatic chapter in his life began, he was just your standard successful, well-paid reporter, with a nice Washington home, whose worst vice was burning the steaks in the backyard barbecue at the parties he and his very at-home wife held for his newspaper buddies.

Then suddenly everything changed. With his usual honesty, X announced to the fellows in the Tap Room that he was in love. It had an electrifying effect on him. He glowed. At least on the days he was rushing off to see her.

Eventually X brought his lady love to the bar, and though she was not a beauty, the committee of experts agreed that there was a certain sexy charm about her that could get under your skin.

Things went on from there, and the lady in question not only cast a roving eye but was abusing her "privileges of the Club" by turning it into a dating bureau.

At first our hero didn't see, and then he didn't want to see. When he had to see what was going on, because she was trying to get rid of him, he tried using the same technique she had, to hype her interest in him. He let her see him at the bar with a prettier and flashier girl.

It did renew her interest, especially when he mentioned that he would be spending the night with his new friend. In fact it caused her to fly into a fury and have hysterics. As a matter of record, the way the story came back to the Press Club, X was just entering the most important part of his *therapeutic* lovemaking when the phone rang.

Sex was impossible as his partner reached for the phone, fearful that it was her *steady*. But it wasn't her steady. It was his true love hysterically insisting that she must talk to X.

X listened and made soothing sounds and promised to be right over. "I'm sorry. I have to go," he said as he pulled on his pants. "She might do something desperate."

In the days that followed, X's friends had to exercise a lot of forebearance to put up with him, even with free drinks.

One day he glowed and the next day he glowered. What the lady had told him over the phone that famous night, was that she could not live without him and wanted him to get a divorce and live with her forever. He was delirious with joy. He hadn't mentioned it to his wife yet, but he knew she was a good sport and would go along.

Surprisingly, his wife was not a good sport and was paging him at the Club and threatening to ruin him if he didn't come home. He was spending a lot of time being paged because his true love was also paging him to say she couldn't make it—family problems and all that.

His bar bills got so out of hand that the Club threatened to revoke his membership. All his friends agreed that his problems at home were as nothing compared with the grave possibility of being thrown out of the Club.

His boss not only threatened but did sever his job connection and his wife did not know until it ran out, that she was living on severance pay.

Then came the cruelest blow of all. He discovered that his lady love had taken up residence with a more famous writer, whom she had met at the Club, thanks to him. Not only that, but she was madly and miserably in love with the SOB. And for added irony the noted writer treated her as shabbily as she had treated our hero. Worse.

Miss True Love poured all this out in a great reunion scene with our hero in the Club. The famous writer, she told our hero, abused her physically, treated her like a slave. She needed X's help to escape. But she was helpless and unable to control her actions because she was in love. If X could save her, she was still willing to marry him.

Our hero rose to the bait. He financed her psychiatrist. He promised to help her, even though at this point he needed help more than she did. Whenever the other reporter threw her out or slapped her around, she came rushing to X.

He gave her a good part of his severance pay so that she could afford to stay away from Svengali. Instead, she used the money to make herself more attractive so her new master would love her more and not throw her out.

It was an old-fashioned melodrama for a while, with the wife having no money to live on, the patsy reporter a broken man, crying into his not-paid-for drinks, and now being carefully avoided by his friends.

It had to end somehow, and it did. For months our hero was not seen around the Club. He was drying out, went the story. Some speculated that he had suffered a nervous breakdown.

Then suddenly he was back and a changed man. No longer does he mention Miss True Love. No longer does he drink at the bar. He has a new job and, it is said, is the most competent and conscientious writer on the staff. He's back with his wife.

"But damn it, the guy's no fun anymore," say the men at the bar who run into him now and then.

The not-always-gentler sex who invade the field of reporting seldom make spectacular marriages and seldom marry wealth, with the smashing exception of Marie Smith. Marie was a

Washington Post reporter with great gentleness who was the center of her colleagues' solicitude because they had beaten her to the altar. But when she finally married, she rocked them back in stunned shock by becoming the bride of the multi-millionaire oil distributor, Arnold Schwartz. Her erstwhile co-workers watched with ill-concealed yearning as Marie returned in triumph to Washington to earn kudos from HEW Secretary Joseph Califano upon the couple's funding of the $25,000,000 Arnold and Marie Schwartz Healing Arts Center. Marie and her guy had donated the whole thing themselves. *It was Marie's day.*

Do editors and reporters commingle? Do they ever! Verily they do. In one case, a married desk man had a long-term affair with a very attractive young reporter.

She freely admitted that she didn't love the editor but she was learning a lot, and besides, she was engaging in a little job insurance. But it didn't work that way.

One day he had a fight with his superiors and quit on the spot. He made no provision to protect her job. In a few days she was out on the street, looking for a new job, too.

It was the end of the romance. She was so angry that he hadn't looked out for her that she threw his shaving kit out on the street.

For Barbara Walters, who at times becomes a Washington commuter, life is not the happy-go-lucky whirl you would expect of a millionairess. It centers on her ten-year-old daughter, Jacqueline. So fearful of kidnappers is Barbara that photographers are never permitted to photograph the child.

After the news of the million-dollar-a-year contract came out, Barbara even added a private security officer at her apartment house.

So how do Barbara and her daughter amuse themselves? Mostly by visiting friends, especially those who have estates in the country, out of the public eye.

As for the huge New York apartment she lived in when she became ABC's million-dollar baby, those who saw it described how Barbara lived surrounded by the color red, making it one of the most cheerful pads one can imagine. Red was the color of the rugs and furniture and it was offset by stark white walls.

Most housewives would go ga-ga over the kitchen. The pots and pans were red. The formica counter tops were red. The ceiling was red.

"Red makes me feel happy," Barbara said. "I thought I would get tired of it, but I didn't."

Barbara was not a poor child but her life was full of uncertainties. Her father, Lou Walters, owner of the Latin Quarter, a New York night club, spent money lavishly when he had it but eventually went into bankruptcy.

Barbara has talked about doing school homework at the Latin Quarter while celebrities came and went, some stopping to pat her on the head. She admits that as a child she was lonely in the midst of crowds.

Having grown up surrounded by celebrities, she gravitated to people of power in politics as well and this bias helped her interview and get close to such men as Richard Nixon, Henry Kissinger, Fidel Castro, Gerald Ford, and dozens of others.

When Barbara Walters married, she chose a man quite like her father. Lee Guber was also an impresario involved in supper clubs and summer theater.

Theirs was a rocky romance but eventually Barbara said yes, even though she was also being courted by the well-known lawyer Roy Cohn, the Communist witch-hunter who had worked for Senator Joseph McCarthy's committee in Washington.

The story is told that on the night before Barbara was to marry Guber, Roy Cohn kept her on the phone for two hours trying to get her to promise to marry him instead.

Years later Guber produced a play in which Roy Cohn was a character. Barbara was most embarrassed, but not for long— the play flopped. Few remember the play's title—*Inquest: A Tale of Political Terror.*

The play, produced in 1970, was said to be one of the last straws in the marriage. But it had been hard-going all the way. The fact that they did not have children did not help.

After a third miscarriage Barbara decided to adopt a child. But Jacqueline, who was adopted as an infant in 1968, did not save the marriage. Lee and Barbara lived in different worlds. His world was the night world, just as her father's had been. Her day started at 4:30 A.M. As it was, friends said it was a miracle the marriage lasted the ten years that it did.

There was a time Sally Quinn was going to be the CBS star that challenged the luminous Barbara Walters in the TV constellation. Instead, she is the "star" of the *Washington Post* feature writers, which, some say is stardom enough for anyone's ego.

Quinn's penetrating profiles of newsworthy people appear on the front page of the Style section. Only she can get away with writing stories so long that they sometimes spill over to a third page, rather than just carry over to a second page. In any event, her stories seem to run considerably longer than any other feature writer's. And some detractors jeer, seem untouched by an editor's pencil. They may jeer, but her stories grab the emotions.

In the tumultuous summer of 1978, her touching story on the wife of the jailed Soviet dissident Anatoli Scharansky ran more than two complete half pages, under the intriguing heading "Avital Scharanskiy and the Politics of Sorrow" and the subhead, "The Hesitant Star of an International Morality Play, Traveling the Globe for Her Husband's Freedom."

Capturing the mood immediately, Sally Quinn's story begins, "You have seen her many times now, her soft sad doelike features are etched in memory.... Always you would hear the same plea, her feathery voice barely audible, her shoulders hunched over with the weight of her problems.

"'I am shouting for help. I am not a politician. I am not a diplomat. I am just living on hope. Hope that you will do something to help. All I want is for my husband to be saved.'"

There are some who say that Ben Bradlee must be helping Sally be this kind of writer. But Bradlee himself denies it.

"I don't help Sally with her writing. She does it all herself. We're different kinds of writers. She's not even in the newsroom. She's over in the women's section."

There still is a comparison one can make between Sally and Barbara Walters. In a way Sally Quinn is to the *Washington Post* what Barbara Walters is to ABC—representing glamour, talent, and comparative youth in a field dominated by older male figures.

And like Barbara Walters, Sally had a long apprenticeship first. She was hired back in 1969, even though she had no real journalistic experience. What she did have was verve and style and a certain brassiness she had acquired as an army brat.

Anything she needed to know, she learned in a hurry— the who, what, why of it. The main thing was she knew how to ingratiate herself during an interview and then write a story that could set off fireworks. She loved to shock, saying of Rudolf Nureyev, the Russian ballet dancer, for example, "He has a fabulous behind. Women follow him around and stare at his fanny as blatantly as some men would stare at a woman's bosom."

For one brief moment it certainly seemed that Sally Quinn might truly become another Barbara Walters, and CBS beat the drums heralding her appearance on its morning show. But the pressures and tensions almost broke her spirit.

She returned from New York like a wounded sparrow and poured out her heart in a book, then relaxed and went back to the feature writing she does so well.

It is not an easy thing for two high-pressured newspersons to be married to each other, and it hasn't been easy for Grant Dillman, UPI bureau chief, and his wife, Audrey, film syndication editor in NBC's Washington office.

Though they have been on the verge of splitting up in the past, as of this writing they have resolved their problems so smashingly well that it seems like a second honeymoon, and a third and fourth as they go flying off on many short and long trips together—New York, Cuba, the Iron Curtain countries, a luxurious cruise, doing the Rhine castle bit.

What holds Grant and Audrey together is an interest in news. In fact, they met when both were covering the Ohio legislature for the same newspaper, the *Columbus Dispatch*.

"Audrey covered the House and I covered the Senate," Grant recalls with a grin. "We used to pass each other in the halls going in different directions. It was the damndest romance on record.

"Even then, both of us had to write overnights, so we couldn't get together until around midnight. Finally, the legislature took a two-week recess or we'd never have gotten married."

Actually, in those days—1945—Grant was Audrey's boss and Audrey was just barely out of college.

As their friends say, Dillman's hobbies run from A to B—Audrey and boats. Weekends, before they took up travel as a hobby, would find Grant alone at Annapolis, Maryland, putt putting around in his twenty-two foot cabin cruiser. "Stink pot would be a better name for it," says Grant. In memory of the old days when Grant's B hobby spelled out booze, Grant named his boat the *Cutty Shark*.

Like many a frustrated organization man, Grant still dreams of writing the great American novel. It is somewhere in progress.

Another marriage of journalistic career equals was played out in the offices of the *New York Daily News* bureau. Doris Fleeson was a slick chick in her day, widely read as she wrote about big names in Washington. John O'Donnell was the Washington bureau chief.

They quarreled a good deal over his spending too much time in the Press Club bar and her spending too much time with Eleanor Roosevelt. She could swear like a fishwife when aroused.

I used to find them arguing on the stairs—he, barward-bound to the thirteenth floor—and give them a passing benediction, "Blessings on you, my children." Finally they were divorced.

For some years Doris kept an office, down the hall from mine with May Craig. May was long-noted for her tacky hats and her amusing press conference question directed at every President: "Is there anything happening that affects the state of Maine?"

Once the owner of her paper, Guy P. Gannett, came in to have lunch with me. "Let's see what the girls are doing," he said. Their door was unlocked so we went in.

"Ah, the *Waterville Sentinel*," he exclaimed. "I haven't seen a copy for years. I bought them a new printing press. Let's see how it looks." I could hardly believe my ears that the owner of a newspaper didn't bother to look at it from one year to the next—but truth is always stranger than fiction.

After sundry romances, Doris met her match in Dan Kimball, president of Aerojet Corporation, a former Secretary of the Navy. After she had interviewed him for a story, a romance blossomed and they eventually married. When Kimball died, Doris followed him a few days later. A heart can still break.

A most unlikely linking of newspaper ideologies by marriage—the arch conservative and the liberal—is that of Hearst columnist Marianne Means and *New York Times* Washington correspondent Warren Weaver, one of the most popular writing couples in Washington. Both have been married before and now seem idyllically happy, with each other, their cats, and children by his previous marriage.

They live in her house in Georgetown, where there is room enough for each to have a separate writing den. But that's not what is so unusual about this marriage. Lots of couples end up living in *her* house when divorce relieves him of his. What makes this arrangement a bit unusual is that Marianne is sticking to her name, Means, both in her private and professional life.

It hasn't been easy to do. "Even friends of many years think its cute to call me Mrs. Weaver. I have had to tell each one of them, sometimes rudely, that my name is Means and his name is Weaver.

"My professional name may not be as well-known as some others, but it is the only thing I have to show for twenty years in this business.

"I don't even use the name Weaver socially, because I think it's confusing to switch back and forth. More and more young women are keeping their own names after marriage, but older people still seem to resist the idea."

Marianne claims that as yet the double writing career in the family is not causing any trouble. "We don't have any basic conflicts in our profession because we have different time schedules. Warren deals with breaking news. I write a column that appears several days afterward, so I concentrate upon themes that are current but not urgent.

"Since we are both law school graduates, we share a curiosity about legal issues, but our approach is different. He has covered the Supreme Court for several years, interpreting its daily decisions; I weigh in with my opinions about various cases I feel are socially important."

Their paths will cross, however, at the next presidential campaign. "We have yet to cover a presidential campaign in tandem, because we've been married less than two years," Marianne says. "We will have to cover the upcoming campaign in our own separate ways and hope that our schedules cross now and then."

Reporters' romances have a way of maturing after both parties have known each other only vaguely for years. As Warren Weaver recalls it, "Marianne and I first met in 1967, when we were covering the first exploratory national trip of the Romney presidential campaign; we may well be its only long-range achievement.

"We were waiting for an elevator one morning in the Motel Utah in Salt Lake City. Her recollection is otherwise, but I am certain we were never properly introduced, that we just said, 'Good morning,' each knowing who the other was, as Washington reporters frequently do without the benefit of anything more formal."

Marianne was one of the lucky people to receive a puppy from the White House—LBJ gave her a beagle, daughter of Him. "But," says Marianne sadly, "my beagle died recently at the age of twelve so we now have two bossy cats.

"There is also plenty of drop-in company—Warren's four daughters, the youngest of whom is in college."

In the case of Helen Thomas, UPI White House correspondent, she found her future husband on her doorstep, so to speak—the White House newsroom. Helen Thomas is one of the few female Washington correspondents to be entertained by presidential families, including the Carters, as a personal friend.

In fact, in September 1971, First Lady Pat Nixon scooped Helen Thomas, herself, by announcing Helen's engagement to AP's retiring White House correspondent Douglas B. Cornell, at a White House party hosted by President Nixon.

As a matter of record, Pat Nixon also scooped the White House's own newsroom. Practically no one in the newsroom knew that Doug and Helen were even going together.

Both believed that a romance between the heads of the AP and the UPI White House contingents of reporters would make them the subject of much curiosity, and both were very private persons.

They even decided—because of the competitive nature of the two wire services—not to marry until one or the other retired. That's the kind of person Helen is—a very ethical one concerned with appearances as well as the substance.

Helen knew that she was not influenced in her White House reporting by the fact that she knew the top AP man, but she did not want even the suspicion that there could be collusion.

They had kept their romance a complete secret, or thought they did. However, a few reporters accidentally saw Helen and Doug now and then meeting at a street corner or some other spot enroute to dinner or to her apartment, but decided to keep her secret, not even telling Helen.

Evidence to the contrary, in the investigative reporting field and gossip-column writing, reporters are among the best people in the world at keeping secrets. What reporters know and don't tell could blow Washington, D.C., sky-high.

One of the classic Washington romances that survived through many years is that of columnist Robert Allen, who courted his wife, Ruth Finney, in the press gallery of the Senate.

She was a Scripps-Howard reporter covering the Teapot Dome investigation. He was the *Christian Science Monitor* bureau chief. The courtship continued on Herbert Hoover's campaign trail in 1928.

After they married, both continued their careers. Ruth Finney became a famous columnist.

"We didn't know how smart we were when we bought a

house in Georgetown with the money from one of my books," Allen reminisces. "It cost under ten thousand dollars and today it's worth many times what we paid for it."

Robert set up a writing den in its basement, where he could write the book exposés he became famous for, in collaboration with Drew Pearson. He still writes a column today for the North American Newspaper Alliance.

One writing team who were often invited to the private quarters of the White House by various presidents and first ladies, was Naomi Nover and her late husband, Barnet, of the *Denver Post*.

Together they covered all presidents and first ladies since the Truman administration. In fact, when their close friend John Gunther, author of *Inside Europe* and other *Inside* books attended a dinner at the Nover home, he wrote a story about meeting Harry Truman there, which appeared in the *Reader's Digest*.

Together they traveled the world on leading stories, Barnet writing the hard news and Naomi writing the human interest in her column "Washington Dateline."

Naomi is possibly the only female newswriter to have fan clubs. There are two Naomi Nover fan clubs, one in Colorado and one in Wyoming. To show the kind of adulation she inspired, the Colorado group sent her the Colorado state flower made from shells—a labor of love.

A different kind of team was that of Fay Gillis Wells and her foreign correspondent husband, Linton Wells. Together they covered the Italo-Ethiopian war for the *New York Herald Tribune*, as well as other trouble spots, such as riots in Syria.

Fay, who has covered the White House for years as a broadcaster for Storer Broadcasting Company, is honored as a founding member of the Overseas Press Club.

Everyone wonders about the life-style of Jack Anderson and how he manages to stay married.

Jack Anderson is a husband who spends much time on the road, yet his is one of the most successful marriages in a field that has an exacerbating effect on relationships. How does he do it? Simply by making his wife a part of his business, even as she works at home raising a brood of nine children. All through the years, Olivia, whom everyone calls Livvy, has handled the business end of the column.

Jack grew up with a tradition of husband-and-wife

teams. His father, of Swedish descent, was a postal clerk. His mother came to America from Denmark at the age of fifteen. When Jack, at the age of nineteen, wanted to become a Mormon missionary, his parents backed him up but didn't have the money to support him during the two-year stint during which, traditionally, Mormon missionaries must pay their own expenses.

To pay for Jack's tour of dedication, and still support his two younger brothers, Jack's mother became a taxi driver.

Jack's two younger brothers, incidentally, grew up to become a geologist stationed in Brazil and a real estate dealer based in the Salt Lake City area.

Jack and Livvy are continuing the tradition of the elder Andersons. Liv makes out the salary checks and the expense account checks. She balances the books and knows better than Jack just what the bottom line really is.

Livvy and Jack have been married since 1949, and the joke is that Jack is *indebted* to the FBI for her. Ironically, the agency he likes to berate has been very good to him in giving him a fingerprint expert, which was what Livvy was when she met Jack at a Mormon church function in 1948.

Their social life still centers on the church. Sometimes they go to church several times on a Sunday and Jack has the honor of being a Seventy. That is the highest rank a Mormon parishioner can attain without becoming a High Priest.

Livvy, who is considerably shorter than her husband and a pleasant-looking brunette, is just as relaxed about bringing up a large family as her husband is in dealing with his huge business operation.

She never worries about getting everyone to sit down to dinner. She simply places the food out buffet style and everyone takes care of himself.

All through the years she seldom had household help, preferring to do everything herself so that Jack's money could go toward building his column. The couple lived in a large nine-bedroom house in Bethesda, Maryland, on a quiet street safe for the children to play on.

Now three of the kids have married and the youngest is almost in his teens. And it's grandchildren who are playing in the yard today.

Jack and Livvy hope that their children, now ranging from about eleven to twenty-eight, are learning by example how to be happy life-mates. The youngsters have grown up seeing their father share his career with his wife. And they have seen their mother, day after day, spreading out the vouchers and the accounts on a table or bed to work on them.

Jack and Livvy hope the kids see that it's still possible in today's world to have a successful mom and pop kind of business, even in the newspaper game.

And what Jack preaches at home, as well as at the office, is that someone must be an investigative reporter to help the average taxpayer, the poor, and the powerless to fight the big government and its encroachment on private lives, and to make sure that business and government play fair, by holding the threat over their heads that wrongdoing and tyranny will not win out.

He assures his children that he does not set out to hurt people deliberately, but only to force government or business to make needed reforms—and sometimes, he adds, this results in high officials losing jobs or being castigated by their peers.

The children are free to bring friends home, and sometimes as many as twenty persons at a time have visited the sideboard, picking a ham or turkey clean.

Jack enjoys playing the host to his children's gang and treats them jovially, almost as if they were members of the family.

As a matter of fact, now and then, when his children's friends have troubles at home, they might stay overnight at the Andersons, where parents know they are safe from harm.

So far, strange to say, none of his children have attempted to join Jack in the writing business. But there are still many children to go—some in grade school, some in high school and college.

Though they may not be pushing to become reporters, all the kids know how to answer phones, how to keep secrets they might hear about some story their father is working on, how to take messages for their father.

Mornings, before Jack leaves for the office, he has already been at work in his den, banging a typewriter and making or receiving phone calls.

Jack laughs when guests suggest that his home telephone might be bugged. He says, "I don't think anybody wants to put up with listening to all these teenagers on the phone—it wouldn't be worth it."

Like Anderson, columnist-TV panelist Carl Rowan also

has a lovely large home, but in northwest Washington, D.C., in Forest Hills. His wife, a former government nurse, is known as an excellent hostess. The top people of government and news media are found at their dinner parties.

Even so, it isn't always easy to be a black person in a very wealthy white neighborhood. Carl tells the story of how he was out mowing the extensive lawns of his home one day when a woman in a big limousine called out of her window to ask how much he got for mowing the lawn.

Rowan thought a moment and called back, "It's not the money. The lady of the house lets me sleep with her." The limousine quickly moved on.

The life-style of the Washington press corps is as varied as the leaves of grass. I live on the edge of Lake Barcroft, Virginia, with my own seawall and clear view of a resident family of ducks.

My coauthor Frannie, opts to live in an apartment complex up the street from the White House, simply because every conceivable service is instantly available under the same roof— valet, dress shop, coffee shop, swimming pool, beauty parlor, deli, even the delivery of an aspirin by room service.

All her spare time is spent painting. Many journalists live a more rugged life. Columnist Walter Riley, who married a Korean woman who was working on her Master's degree in history at a local university, lives in a large house in Silver Spring, Maryland, but he seldom stays put.

He packs his wife and three kids into a motor home and tours the country. His excuse is that listening to people in small towns opens his mind to problems the nation faces, which insular Washington only dreams about. Many of the questions he is asked end up as subjects for his investigative reporting.

James Srodes may write what some consider stuffy financial news for his own wire service, but his private life is far from stuffy. He and his wife, who recently graduated from law school, are still at work renovating an old house in the Mt. Pleasant section of Washington, D.C. His home is a mecca for striving young talented writers, and he is, in fact, president of the Washington Independent Writers Association.

Vera Glaser, columnist and correspondent for Knights-Ridder newspapers, lives the good life in a large colonial-style house in the Palisades area, which is a veritable beehive of journalists, diplomats, and government officials.

Lyle Denniston, Supreme Court reporter for the *Star*, is a neighbor. So are Peter Chatenay, with the World Bank; Sid Levy, with the Kiplinger newsletters; Peter Hackes, NBC news—on the next block; John Finney of the *New York Times;* Maggie Hunter of the *New York Times*—a bicycle ride away; as is Fran Lewine, formerly AP White House correspondent and now PIO with the Department of Transportation.

Among senators who have lived near Vera are Jennings Randolph, James Eastland, and Richard Milhous Nixon. But Vera never remembers to mention the latter.

It's only natural that Vera's life-style involves a lot of small dinner parties with reporters from TV, radio, and newspapers, and also a lot of outdoor entertainment.

She teases her husband, Herbert, by saying that a fortune-teller once told her she would have three husbands, but she has had to make do with only one. Herbert, a genial host, is twice retired—once from the National Labor Relations Board and once from the Army. He was a Lieutenant Colonel in the Army Reserve.

There is nothing retired—or retiring—about Vera. She is a frustrated dancer, squeezes in tap dancing lessons when she can and formerly studied ballet.

Nelly Stone is the more unusual foreign correspondent. A news writer for Intermonde-Presse, she married an American attorney, changing her French name—Cauvin.

John and she live a happy life as "catters in dull suburbia—but to us it isn't dull."

The most unusual home and life-style of anyone in the Washington media is that of Deena Clark, who hosts the longest-running television interview show hosted by a female.

When she is not working on the next segment of CBS's *The Deena Clark Show* she is involved with seahorses. No, I'll take that back. Even her show is seahorse-ridden—the credits appear superimposed on a giant seahorse, and when she conducts her interviews Deena is sure to wear seahorse earrings, rings, or bracelets.

Every day she feeds an aquarium of seahorses with fresh brine shrimp. Every wall she looks at has some reference to seahorses, and seahorses are even a decoration on the outside of her stunning three-level home on fashionable Kalorama Road in northwest Washington, D.C., which was formerly owned by an executive of *National Geographic* magazine. The ironwork of a spiral staircase is in the design of seahorses. A plaster frieze around the living room ceiling is of seahorses. There are gold seahorse faucets in the bathroom, seahorse soap, seahorse artworks in glass and porcelain. There are seahorses on the dashboard of her Mercedes. On her dining room wall is a stunning, huge framed Belgian lacework of seahorses, which took two years to make.

How did this seahorse mania come about? "I was a schoolteacher in Honolulu and I took my class to the Waikiki Aquarium. I couldn't get over the darling little seahorses dancing around and even playing tug-of-war by linking their tails together.

"They had another little trick of sliding down grass like they were little firemen sliding down a pole."

Later, when she married and lived in Washington, she did so much research on seahorses that she eventually sold an article on them to *Reader's Digest.*

Her daughter, Niki, also became a seahorse addict and wrote and illustrated a book about them.

Though Deena, whose home my coauthor has enjoyed visiting, takes her seahorses seriously, she hasn't lost her sense of humor. She tells of the time former Secretary of State Bill Rogers was a guest and had gone through an evening of seahorses.

His place card had been decorated with a seahorse, the candles had been held by seahorse candlesticks and now he stood observing a pair of seahorses that predicted the weather by changing colors, as he sipped a drink from a seahorse-decorated glass.

"Bill turned to me and said, 'Deena, did it ever occur to you that you might already have enough seahorses?' I don't suppose it ever had—or will."

Both of Washington's top society writers live in sumptuous houses—Ymelda Dixon in Georgetown and Betty Beale on Garfield Street, across the way from Senator Birch Bayh and very near the Sheraton Park Hotel.

For years Betty Beale was a bachelor girl and proud of it. Then she amazed her friends by suddenly marrying George Graeber, the Washington representative of Union Carbide, who retired and went into a consultancy business of his own.

Betty swims in her outdoor pool every day, summer and winter, and leads a strenuous social life in the line of duty.

Ymelda, the widow of humor columnist George Dixon, does not go in for athletics. Her idea of fun is to fly to Madrid for a weekend.

The "Duchess"—Esther Van Wagoner Tufty—chief of the Tufty News Service, lives in George Washington's overseer's house, which sits directly on the Potomac River, and she is the envy of all her friends.

At Washington parties it is noticeable that newsmen and newswomen enjoy, and even search out, the limelight much more than TV newscasters who have grown weary of the bright lights.

David Brinkley is famous for avoiding attracting attention to himself. Newspeople who saw him walking his dog in Georgetown commented that even then he assumed an aloof air that discouraged others from stopping to talk to him.

Incidentally, Brinkley's life in the goldfish bowl is credited with having led to the breakdown of his long-term first marriage. His name had been linked with Barbara Howar and Lauren Bacall. Married a second time, he leads a very quiet life, as much out of the public eye as he can get.

Even when casual snapshots are being made with friends around his home, David usually grabs the camera and insists on taking the pictures to avoid being in them.

A story is told of the exact moment David discovered he had lost his privacy and didn't like it. It happened in 1960 when he was part of the press entourage traveling with presidential hopeful Hubert Humphrey.

David was following the candidate at a safe distance to observe just how the average voters were reacting to HHH. This was in West Virginia, prior to the primary there.

Suddenly he realized that the crowd was following him, not Humphrey. Instead of having his ego massaged, as others would have reacted, Brinkley was angered and depressed at the turn of events and started hugging the shadows in a crowd.

Though Brinkley's career didn't help his first marriage, it had a good effect on Chet Huntley's happiness. That is because Brinkley introduced his partner Chet, long distance, to the girl who would become Huntley's wife.

Brinkley, who operated from Washington, and Chet, who coanchored from New York, would frequently talk on the phone about their program. Huntley was not too happy in his life and one day David introduced him to the popular local Washington weather girl, Tippy Stringer.

Every day Tippy and Chet would chat over the wires and eventually they met and fell in love. When Chet retired, he and Tippy went out west to start a new life as ranchers, and after Chet's untimely death, Tippy ran for political office.

Brinkley is still around, but you need not try to find him in fancy restaurants, where autograph seekers are. Instead you are much more likely to find him at home working at his favorite hobby—furniture making.

Sometimes in the friendly village life of Washington's Georgetown, where many of the better-heeled news media people choose to live, a friendship of sorts will begin with the walking of dogs.

That's how Eric Ruff, correspondent with the Donrey chain of newspapers and TV and radio stations, happened to cross leashes with Dan Rather, who was his neighbor.

"I lived on P Street and he on Thirty-Third Street," Eric says. "His house is white with black shutters. I was walking my dog when Rather brought his tricolor Sheltie out of the house—a tiny dog like a miniature collie.

"As soon as Moose, my seventy-five-pound Labrador retriever, saw the Sheltie, he bolted to the little dog. We got them quieted down, and we fell to talking as the dogs got acquainted.

"We talked about journalism, naturally, and I even found myself sounding like a fan as I told him *60 Minutes* was an excellent program—but I meant it."

As a dog-walking neighbor, Eric would be aware, now and then, of Rather's misadventures. "He's got a Volvo car and the damn thing had the front end banged into. Then right after that was fixed, a week later, the side of it was banged into and had a turning light knocked out of it. Poor guy."

It's amusing to see how some reporters have gotten their kicks.

Drew Pearson loved huckstering. Maybe it was some memory of past money problems or humble beginnings that made him even seek to earn a little from his gentleman's farm in Maryland.

He was probably the only Washington writer who made money selling manure. And there were detractors who said that was his job full time.

People also came to his farm to pick farm products and pay for whatever they had picked.

Drew Pearson stories still abound at the Press Club. There was the time Pearson parked his car at the Mayflower Hotel and a hotel truck ran into it and bashed it.

Pearson, hating to waste money and fancying himself wise in the ways of the law, decided to act as his own lawyer. Somewhere along the line in court, Pearson smugly commented that the Mayflower was well-insured, whereupon the hotel lawyer moved for a dismissal, which the judge granted, on the grounds that such evidence is not admissible and that he had prejudiced the case.

After a week of living in the highest social strata of Washington society and covering the White House or following the President on state visits to foreign lands, as the case may be, UPI's Helen Thomas seeks the simple life.

She and her husband, Doug Cornell, head for their quiet lodge in Virginia, about eighty miles from Washington, where they are completely out of sight of houses and all things that remind them of their careers.

They walk in serenity beside a bubbling brook and watch the dancing of the leaves instead of the dancing keys of the typewriter. During the week, however, they also live as simply as possible, in an apartment, happy in the thought of what lies in their weekend ahead.

Water draws many reporters who claim it helps them rest their eyes. Joe Slevin of Knight-Ridder has a vacation home at Rehoboth Beach, Delaware, and George Embrey of the *Columbus Dispatch* is building one at Nag's Head, North Carolina.

Rowland Evans is seldom seen around the National Press Club. Instead he is to be found playing squash at the Metropolitan Club.

Several other well-heeled columnists and bureau chiefs are also members of the Metropolitan: Marquis Childs; Eric Sevareid; Scotty Reston; Ed Prina, head of the Copley Bureau; Pat Munroe of the Virgin Islands *Daily News;* and Austin Kiplinger.

Austin Kiplinger, who has done a superb job of taking over his father's newsletter, and building it into a still-larger empire, is also a member of the Potomac Hunt Club.

He lives the life of a country squire in the horse country of Maryland, raising horses on his estate, Montevideo, in

Poolesville. He rides to the hounds, and maybe his father turns over in his grave to see what has become of his son, who is "wasting" time that could be spent at the National Press Club. But then again he could be proud. Austin has also veered from his father's path in his interest in the National Symphony, of which, at this writing, he is about to become president.

Vacation spots for reporters follow fashion, and fashion usually ties in with the White House. When Nixon spent his vacations in Key Biscayne, the Florida Keys became the "in" vacation place. And when he moved to California's San Clemente, California was the place to be.

Lyndon Johnson sent them scurrying to Texas, where they discovered such delights, near the LBJ ranch, as a park with a genuine dinosaur footprint. And as a result of Lady Bird's interest, river rafts in the western rivers became the vacation mode of transportation, including shooting the rapids.

Jimmy Carter also gave a shot in the arm to rapids shooting in the West. Bob Boyd, bureau chief of Knight-Ridder, shot the Colorado River rapids with his whole family, for example.

Jack Kennedy's influence is still felt in that his old newspaper friends still choose the Cape Cod area for their holidays.

Martha's Vineyard is and was the place long before Jackie Kennedy followed the trail by buying three hundred acres there. Art Buchwald, of the funny column, publisher Katharine Graham of the *Washington Post,* and Scotty Reston, the political columnist, can be found there every summer. In fact, last summer Reston landed in the local hospital when his bicycle had a slight altercation with a vacation van—making the hospital the new social center. Scotty Reston, incidentally, owns the local newspaper, the *Vineyard Gazette.*

Some chose more northernly spots. Walter Ridder of the Ridder family spent his summer sailing in the environs of Nova Scotia.

Walter Cronkite, too, has a special feeling for the far north—the rugged coast of Maine. Not too long ago he became part-owner of the small weekly coastal newspaper the *Camden Herald.*

Many reporters talk of their plans to retire to far-off places, and a few do.

Sam Fogg, of Jack Anderson's staff, after many years on

340

wire services, is actually buying a place in Corsica for retirement about four years hence.

"It was the damndest thing," he says, "but my wife and I got carried away with a postcard picture. The way it happened was my wife had a hairdresser who had once been married to a Corsican. They had a daughter and so the hairdresser was taking their daughter back to see where mama had once lived.

"When we saw the pictures of what Corsica looked like, we took a trip and bought a little villa. It was purely impulse buying. It's all there waiting—the mountains and the sea, the little clay-colored house with tiled floors and timber roof. There is a balcony and terrace and flowers growing riotously everywhere."

It's hard to believe that the rough, tough newshound has succumbed to the lure of a riot of flowers, but Sam insists that he couldn't be more serious and offers as proof of his intention the fact that he is now taking courses in French and has advanced to the point where he can give a friendly, "Ça va?"

"However," he adds gruffly, "we're going to hang on to our Dupont Circle apartment so we can sort of go back and forth."

To talk of life we must also talk of death.

Philip Graham was not the only Washington newspaperman to die by his own hand. There have been far too many who could not stand the strain of deadlines, poor pay, firings for drunkenness or other misdemeanors, and even the devastating knowledge that they would never write the Great American Novel.

Jim Cullinaine knew that he would never write it, although he won the Newspaper Guild award for a story about a Washington lawyer whom he called "the Sixth Street Cicero." Having worked and been fired from various Washington newspapers, he ended up in another city, blowing his brains out with a shotgun.

Merriman Smith was another reporter who took his own life. A fine newspaperman, he was for many years head of the UPI White House staff. Then he took to bringing a jug along with him to the White House and having a few snifters to see him through the day. This eventually led to his being transferred to another beat, but he was not too happy, and when he seemed to have licked the habit he was reassigned to the White House. But his seniority was gone. The man who had for years been the one to say, "Thank you, Mr. President," was suddenly low man on the totem pole. It hurt, but worse was to come. Tragedy struck when he lost his son in the Vietnam War. For a time he seemed to have pepped up and became enthusiastic about raising rare dogs. He was going to make a lot of money at it, he told my coauthor.

And then inexplicably came the news that Merriman had died at his own hand. The White House flag flew at half-mast that day, something never done before at the death of a newspaperman.

As we are writing, comes word of the death by suicide of one of the finest investigative reporters in the country—George Bliss, three-time Pulitzer Prize winner of the *Chicago Tribune*.

Writers can try too hard and it can break them down. As Bliss's editor, Clayton Kirkpatrick, said, "Bliss was a perfectionist ... in effect, a victim of his own intense devotion to journalism."

21/Have Press Pass, Will Travel

Having a press pass has helped more than one news hen or hound see the world. Famed Helen Thomas, wearing her White House press pass around her neck, has circled the globe several times with presidents—flying high with LBJ, Nixon, Ford, and Carter.

Possibly her most exciting trip was to China with Nixon in 1972, when the American President made history by opening communications with the previously hostile country.

Usually reporters just grab a suitcase and go but Helen recalls the extreme measures the reporters on the press plane took to be ready for China. "I had never before seen reporters, including myself, so immersed in piles of books and abstaining from booze."

After her return from the China adventure—on which there were only three women representing the news media, she, Barbara Walters of NBC, and Fay Wells of Storer Broadcasting—the Washington Press Club had a party at which Helen and others told what it was like in China.

"Life in China was a cultural shock to us," Helen said. First of all, there was such cleanliness in the streets of Peking that she carried tangerine peelings around in her purse for days so that she wouldn't be a litterbug.

Then there was the matter of the hotel rooms to which the press had been assigned. They could only be labeled, she said, as YWCA-style.

Instead of the ever-present Cokes and Pepsis of American life, each room had a thermos of hot water and a little cannister of tea.

The wastefulness of the Americans was definitely not understood by the Chinese. Every time one reporter tried to throw away his old underwear in the wastebasket in his hotel room, they kept reappearing on his bed washed and pressed.

When reporters talk of traveling with presidents, the mere mention of the name Jerry Ford brings an automatic smile.

343

One incident is told by Vernon Guidry, Jr., of the *Washington Star*, about the time Ford "literally stumbled into Austria in 1975."

The way Vern Guidry tells it, the American interpreter, Harry Obst, a German language specialist, had been stationed thirty feet from the stairs of *Air Force One* to report the grand arrival at Salzburg.

The reason he was so far away, he later explained to Guidry, was that the previous President, Richard Nixon, had been very sensitive about outsiders, like interpreters, horning in on the camera. And the old rules were still adhered to. One of Nixon's cameramen had been banished for appearing in the background of his inaugural picture on Capitol Hill.

But to get back to the scene at Salzburg, not only was Obst out in left field, but it was raining, a noisy rain.

As Ford came down the stairs, he fell. But Obst could see nothing. Then Ford was making his arrival speech and among Obst's many troubles, like the rain washing away his inked notes, he was having trouble hearing over the patter of the raindrops.

Suddenly Obst thought he heard the President apologizing about something. It made absolutely no sense to him that the President would be apologizing, because he hadn't been in the country that long. He hadn't had time to do anything. But Obst used his brain to make a safe guess and stated that the President apologized for bringing the rain.

It was not till the next day that Obst learned from the local papers that Ford had apologized for taking a tumble.

You never know what to expect next when you are traveling with a President. It can be funny or dramatic. Frank Holeman of the *New York Daily News* Washington bureau was one of the White House corps traveling with Ike to Denver for a summer vacation, which turned into a nightmare.

As Holeman's headline said, "Ike Suffers Heart Attack—Taken to Army Hospital Near Denver, Put in Oxygen Tent."

The date was September 25, 1955. Making it harder to cover the President, Jim Hagerty, the presidential press secretary, was not around on this dramatic day. He was off on his own vacation.

Instead of having a slight vacation themselves, Holeman and the others ended up working around the clock. "Somehow you get adjusted to no sleep—the adrenalin keeps flowing."

Traveling with the President can be hazardous. There is

the danger of getting in the way of crackpots who are after the President.

And then there are dangers to one's health. When Jimmy Carter traveled to South America and Africa, the 150 reporters and other media persons who went along were given so many horrendous warnings, that it almost kept them sober so they could stay alert. Recently Carter himself, in Mexico, spoke of suffering from "Montezuma's revenge."

But it wasn't just the usual ice-cubes-should-be-avoided and don't-drink-the-water warnings. In Brasilia, for example, the gentlest-looking animals were to be avoided because of a rabies epidemic. And around Caracas cars were in danger of falling down cliffs at sharp curves. And Rio de Janeiro beaches were famous for sunstroke and undertow. And if the Rio noonday to two P.M. sun didn't get you, the pickpocket geniuses would.

The reporters who had thought that Africa would be a pleasant relief from all this hassle found that they were warned that in Liberia mamba snakes were prevalent and poisonous. They were told to avoid the shorelines' beautiful vegetation where the mamba lay in wait.

Many a sad tale is told of how reporters have been robbed when in their cups traveling on a story or political campaign. But UPI Washington bureau chief Grant Dillman brags about the time he entered the infamous Casbah of Tunis with eight hundred dollars cash and came out with his money intact, thwarting every pickpocket. It happened in 1957 when Dillman was a UPI reporter accompanying Vice-President Nixon to Africa. When he tells of this feat, other reporters always want to know how he carried his money—in a money belt?

"Nope," he says, "I used an old Ohio trick. The money was in my shoe."

The National Press Club keeps its Travel Committee chairman William Whyte busy dreaming up junkets to far-off lands.

The Club has sponsored trips to Russia, Bermuda, London, India, and all the places between. The problem now is to find someplace different. "Maybe the moons of Jupiter," Bill says.

Government public relations people are also circling the globe. Once Priscilla Baker of the National Park Service found herself at the village of Beaver, near the Arctic Circle.

"I arrived in a Cessna 185, flown by a bush pilot,"

Priscilla recalls, "just after the monthly mail plane had been there. The only mail that had come for the month was a Dear Occupant letter from American Express.

"When I got there, the chief of the village was trying to read it, of course, and asked me to help him. We spent quite a while going over the advantages of little green plastic cards as described by American Express. The chief was utterly delighted, even though there was virtually no currency in the village.

"I do believe he was about ready to sign up."

One of the exciting things about being a government public relations person is that one can be "detailed" to another agency to meet a short-term need. In 1977, Priscilla was detailed to the National Commission for the Observance of International Women's Year to help run the press operation for the National Women's Conference.

Her roommate was Fran Lewine, formerly AP White House correspondent, and now PIO for the Department of Transportation.

Even though Baker worked full tilt "about twenty hours each day for ten days, to try to keep the thing afloat, presswise," she admitted, "I have many fond memories of irreverent events.

"My favorite is of Bella Abzug sitting in her suite at the Hyatt Regency in Houston a few hours after the conference, doing imitations of Congresswoman Barbara Jordan playing God while Gloria Steinem, Fran, and I doubled up laughing."

Vera Glaser recalls with high glee how she and Malvina Stephenson made life hell for the first Chinese Communist delegation to the UN, in order to get a good story for their off-beat column.

"That was back in 1969," Vera recalls, "and Malvina and I flew up to New York and managed to occupy the suite at the Roosevelt Hotel directly over that of the Chinese delegation chief. We chased those people from morning to night, monitoring what they ate and drank and said.

"We interviewed some of them. We smoked their cigarettes. We even drank their tea. When we were through with them, they were through with us—but we had a really great column about what the Chinese were all about."

Triumphs of travel, as far as the press is concerned, involves getting some extra story, above and beyond the one you are assigned to get.

Vera Glaser was not satisfied with an assignment to go to India and interview Prime Minister Indira Gandhi. She got that story without any trouble. But what she did have trouble getting was her self-assigned story.

"I had made up my mind before going that I wanted to interview an untouchable," she relates. "I finally found one in a village outside Jaipur, but he was amazed that I wanted to interview him, and the interpreter I found, who had to speak Hindustani— they have fourteen different languages in India—was most upset about it.

"The man had a job working for the city, cleaning streets which, I learned, was several steps up from his earlier status. The biggest improvement in his life, the untouchable told me, was that he was now sending his children to school.

"This untouchable had progressed far beyond some other untouchables I sought out. I recall one who cleaned bath-rooms at the Lake Palace in Udaipur. Poor creature—he was afraid to look anyone straight in the eye."

Of course there are sad moments for journalists who go adventuring or travel to report the more dismal facts of life.

Wars have always taken their toll of reporters as well as foot, sea, and air soldiers. Ernie Pyle, one of the most beloved columnists, did not return from covering World War II. Ray Richards, columnist of the Washington Hearst bureau, died of bullet wounds in a lonely ditch during the Korean conflict.

And reporters who didn't even go to war sometimes got killed just trying to see what preparations were being made for fighting the war.

Felix Cotten of INS was with a group of reporters touring war plants when a whole planeload of his colleagues crashed to the ground, killing all aboard, including a *Baltimore Sun* reporter, with whom Felix had been teamed up.

Felix would have been dead, too, except that he had contracted an illness and was sick in Detroit.

"We had gone to Manitowoc, where they were building subs and pitching them into the Mississippi River at a forty-five degree angle, and floating them down to the Gulf of Mexico where they joined the sub fleet.

"It was mid May and I had gone without a topcoat only to get caught in some freezing rain at thirty-eight degree tempera-ture. By the time I got to Detroit I was in bed with fever while the

347

others went to Kansas to see gliders launched. The cause of the air accident was pilot error due to drink. It was a very sobering experience for me."

One of the saddest travel stories concerned those reporters who hopped aboard with Representative Leo Ryan when he went to investigate reports that cult members were being held against their will and lived in fear at the People's Temple compound, run by the self-appointed prophet, the Reverend Jim Jones, in Guyana.

When the chilling news came to the Press Building that three newsmen—NBC news correspondent Don Harris, *San Francisco Examiner* photographer Greg Robinson, and NBC cameraman Robert Brown—lay dead in Guyana, the victims of an ambush by Jones' cultists, voices became hushed. Word was that several other reporters around the Press Building had almost joined Ryan on this "great investigative story opportunity." There but by the grace of their editors went they.

Ryan's personal exploits, such as moving in with a black family under an assumed name after the Watts riots in the summer of 1965, and posing as an inmate at Folsom Prison, had become a bit old hat. But of course, with his death, the world would reassess and realize the great bravery of the adventurous congressman.

Especially mourned in Washington was Don Harris who had formerly worked for WTOP-TV in the nation's capital. He had even won an Emmy for his reporting of the Washington riots that followed the murder of Martin Luther King, Jr., in 1968.

In past years, press groups often flew free of charge in military aircraft, a privilege later frowned upon by meanies who wanted to take the fun out of life. I was long active in the Aviation Writers Association, whose nationwide membership was assembled for annual meetings by pickup from east to west and points between.

One of the most adventuresome of these tours was in 1944, when the Air Force lent a pair of troop carrier C-47s, the military version of the old workhorse Douglas DC-3. These olive-drab craft had bucket seats—wooden benches with hollowed posterior fittings that hinged to the wall. Bags and parachutes were stacked in the aisle. Overhead a steel cable ran for hand-over-hand locomotion in turbulent weather. Little round windows shed dim light.

The wing-weary planes took our brethren and a few

sisters from New York and Washington to Dayton where the Air Materiel Command displayed its wonders. The great innovation was an experimental jet whose snout, without propeller, caused the irreverent to call it the "Flying Hard-on."

From Dayton, en route to Dallas, our next inspection point, our brave young pilots flew into a thunderstorm. Whump, whump we went as gusts tore at the wings. One lassie failed to get under her seat belt and clung white-faced to the wall. A row of seats collapsed, to be righted with Herculean effort. Caught in a fierce downdraft, we plunged in roaring darkness until we broke through the bottom of the clouds and skimmed the treetops.

Revived with bourbon on the ground, we shuttled about to see planes in the making, including a wooden mock-up of what was to be the controversial B-36, as big inside as a railroad tunnel. As we were about to take off for our next inspection stop, another Texas storm came tall and black. As the deluge broke, we taxied back to the hangar, where a bomber with its bays open made a handy screen for several to stand and take turns at a bottle.

As the rain beat on the roof and hope faded for a takeoff before morning, the Navy offered two buses. Whiskey was loaded and off we went into the dusk. Not far from town, we were surrounded by water where a stream had gone over its banks. The drivers could only guess, from the cottonwoods on both sides, where to find the road.

The front bus coughed and stopped. Knock-knock at the door. A delegate from the rear bus had waded to demand whiskey as the price of a shove. The ransom was paid, the rear bus pushed, slam-bang; and all cheered as the front bus started. This was repeated a time or two till high ground was reached.

Now the problem of rest stops was acute. A chivalrous sailor came to the aid of a suffering girl reporter by holding an umbrella, his back discreetly turned. "He said the cutest thing," she later confided. "He said, 'My, that must have been a relief, ma'am!'"

At midnight, still in high spirits, though hungry, the caravan did it again—made a wrong turn and bogged axle-deep in mud. I don't know how we all survived.

Not always do press travelers receive a warm greeting. It happened that a valiant band of "explorers" were being flown to see a new kind of housing development in the Chicago urban area.

They were taken by helicopter right to the housing site. In fact, they landed on the parking lot of the recreation center, where new sod had just been laid, to present a perfect picture from the air.

The way *Chicago Tribune's* Jim Sloan recalls it, as the helicopter came down, the sod came up. The workmen shook their fists and yelled, "You lousy so-and-sos" at the descending chopper, but by the time the men had climbed out, they realized that they were talking to the press and changed their tone to jovial as they said, "Oh well, we'll put it back in place."

So the reporters went to extended cocktails and lunch and a tour of the project and returned to the helicopter. As the scribes, with tummies full of good cheer, apologized to the workers who were still there, the workers were all smiles and graciousness. Their leader beamed, "See, we got it all fixed up. We staked it down. Everything's okay."

And they had indeed done what seemed like a good job of laying the sod a second time.

But unfortunately, as the helicopter took off, the sod took off, too, because the workers had staked it at only one end. The reporters looked down and the sod was waving at them and so were the workers—but their hands were clenched fists.

As the men at the bar comment, "Sometimes working for the press is like being an actor in a Mack Sennett comedy."

I recall in the early sixties, the Federal Aviation Agency was under White House pressure to get on with supersonic transport development and wanted to show the press that the job was under way.

One of the problems was the sonic boom that an SST makes as the shock waves of its passing hits the ground. To gauge the effects, the FAA had built a little village in the military testing area at White Sands, New Mexico.

Several dozen of the Washington press were flown to the site by FAA to be briefed on sonic booms and to see their effect. Air Force fighter planes were to be flown over the experimental area. After each sonic boom, effects on the houses, such as cracks in the walls, were to be carefully recorded.

Stealing a march, a photographer asked a pilot to make a low pass so he could get a better picture. We were all indoors at the briefing when, WHAM! like thunder the pilot broke the sound barrier at low altitude. An ashtray jumped from a table and smashed to smithereens. Plaster dust fell.

We rushed outside to find the experiment wrecked.

Windows were shattered and walls cracked in one mighty sonic boom, rather than by slow stages as had been planned, so that the effect at various levels of sound could be seen.

When we got to the air base, our plane had flown to El Paso and was not due to return for several hours. I pleaded that we be given buses to go to Juarez, across the border, have a Mexican meal and board the plane at El Paso. Nyet.

So there we all were in the officers' club. It was Happy Hour—drinks at half price—with the inevitable results. Rather than letting us get some sleep and leave in the morning, the FAAers insisted on our taking off late at night.

We had not eaten and the drinks were wearing off. A load of peevish reporters enplaned. Then the final disaster. When the plane was up a few thousand feet, the air pressure seal broke with an ear-popping outrush of air.

So back we limped to the base to eat our box lunches at midnight on the ground. A weary and bedraggled lot arrived at Washington National Airport at dawn.

So devastating was the experience, that the FAA has hardly dared have a press flight since.

Tales are legion about George Haddaway, the "Texas typhoon," who long published *Flight Magazine*. They don't make pranksters like Haddaway more than once in a century. I remember well his stunt at the Cleveland Air Races. Jackie Cochran, famed aviatrix, was in the perfume business and wanted to advertise her scent by having the grandstands sprayed with it from a crop-dusting plane.

She should have kept her eye on Haddaway and Warren Smith of Fairchild Aircraft. Before the flight, when the pilot's back was turned, they mounted a ladder, unzipped, and left an additive in the tank—a touch of Texas and a bit of Maryland.

After a bogus press release was circulated with spoofing interviews about the perfume, Madame Jackie, very much the prima donna, went into a rage. She talked of lawsuits and mayhem. It was years before she forgave. But such charm does Haddaway exude, still today, that women *always* forgive him.

The best travel stories never hit the wire. Take the strange malady of Pat Nixon, when she traveled with her husband, then President, to China. Out of the blue she came down with a mysterious circular rash in a delicate place.

The Chinese were upset. Their doctors were upset.

351

Everything had been done to make the Nixon visit a thing of beauty. Perfection was carried to such an extent that even the toilet seats had been lacquered to become works of art. And now this.

Photographs of the mysterious malady were sent to military doctors in Washington from the Chinese doctors. The diagnosis was idiotically simple—the First Lady was allergic to lacquer. Cover the toilet seats. Not a word of the incident got into the papers. But an "investigative" reporter managed to get a copy of the photo and it was shown, with discretion, to a few faithfuls in the National Press Club bar, all of whom complimented the subject highly.

But times have changed. When a travel story involving a Jacqueline Kennedy Onassis bathroom adventure came to the attention of the press, the event ended up on the pages of the *Washington Post*. It began innocently enough in February 1979, when Jackie was on her way to attend the wedding of her nephew, Joseph P. Kennedy II, in Pennsylvania. Needing a rest room desperately before she could get to the church, she stopped at the gas station of Ray Utz, in Gladwyne, Pennsylvania.

Unfortunately, her limousine did not go undetected. The gas station owner and an amateur historian who happened to be present decided the event should be recorded for posterity. Surely, a commemorative plaque was in order. It was promptly installed:

"This room was honored by the presence of Jacqueline Bouvier Kennedy Onassis on the occasion of the wedding of Joseph P. Kennedy II and Sheila B. Rauch, February 3, 1979. Merion Square Historical Society."

22/Campaigning We Will Go

You never know what kind of expenses you are going to run up when traveling with the presidential candidates. For those who followed candidate Jimmy Carter to Plains, Georgia, during the campaign and transition period, and ended up playing softball with him and his brother, Billy, a big expense item was medical.

The campaign crowd around Carter was tough, and so were the newsmen—but not tough enough. Jim Wooten of the *New York Times* once kept count and logged seventeen injuries for one series of games.

Jim had time to reflect because he broke his wrist and was walking around with a cast and sling which hung from his shoulder.

Jim McCartney of Knight-Ridder's Washington bureau, pulled a leg muscle and ended up limping around in an Ace bandage for two weeks.

And then there is the expense you might just label "keeping up with the candidate." A classic campaign travel expense account story along that line dates back to the golden days of journalism when Harry Truman presided in the White House.

Art Hermann was covering the White House for INS in 1948 and went out with Truman to Kansas City, during the campaign, where he stayed at the Muehlbach Hotel with the rest of the reporters, and commuted to Independence, Missouri, Truman's hometown.

One night when Truman was traveling by train, he sent back to the press post to ask for a poker player—his game was short one player. Proudly, Art Hermann rose and joined Truman and some of his famous poker-playing cronies.

Art was still proud as he made out his expense account on which he listed an item of "$250, lost playing poker with the President," and he showed it around.

The expense account went to the INS New York business office, which was not particularly proud of Art's playing cards with the President and in any event thought $250 was a high price to pay for the privilege. The item was disallowed.

Art Hermann fought back, demanding to know what he should have done when asked to play poker with a president.

Back came the answer: "You should have played better poker."

Porter on the *Philadelphia Record* knew how to handle a situation like that. When someone lifted his coat somewhere along the trail, he naturally had to rush out and buy another one immediately or risk pneumonia, and he put the item on his expense account—"one coat: $65."

The editors not only disallowed the coat, informing the reporter the newspaper was not responsible for carelessness, but they sent none of the money coming to him, ordering him to send a proper voucher.

If it was *carelessness* they were against, the reporter would show them. With the greatest of care, he reworked the expense account, sending it in again.

The total was exactly the same but nowhere was there the word *coat*.

The expense account was paid without a murmur.

Expense accounts reporters can handle but wives are a different matter, and a few marriages have fallen by the wayside when weary reporters have returned to their homes from long trips vastly hung over and with the wrong clothing in their suitcases.

One wife, trying to save her marriage, coyly pleaded with her husband to refuse to go back on the campaign because "I'm afraid to be alone in the house, honey."

When this swinger reported this back to his buddies, they said, "Why don't you get her a gun?"

"And risk getting shot?" he retorted.

Those who travel with presidents and presidential candidates learn tidbits which seldom are exposed.

Those who traveled with Hubert Humphrey learned how he kept up his amazing energy with a combination of handfuls of vitamin pills and a glass of booze.

Booze is the continuing expense—bar bills are a big cost item—and a candidate who helps along by setting up a bar here and there for the press is a real sweetheart.

But if you traveled with the world's richest candidate, Jack Kennedy, you might have gotten stuck with a lunch check. It was Jack's point of pride that he didn't carry money, didn't need money.

Jerry terHorst, the newsman and former presidential press secretary who flashed to prominence when he quit President Ford over the pardoning of Nixon, covered every presidential campaign since Ike's second term.

One of his memories is riding with candidate Jack Kennedy in his private family plane, the *Caroline,* in 1960. As he remembers it, there were just a few reporters along, including Phil Potter of the *Baltimore Sun,* and no secret service men.

"We sat around in a little lounge in the forward part of the cabin and we took off from National swinging over the Pentagon before turning toward the Midwest. As the Pentagon slid by us below, Kennedy looked down at it and said, 'There's one thing I'd like to do—close that damned doughnut up.'

"Having said it, he wouldn't elaborate. He would let his hair down now and then but he didn't that time. At least not enough to tell what he'd really like to do with the military."

During a presidential campaign, Washington pundits find it is easy to lose perspective without frequent junkets around the country. Merely reading or talking to visitors from Bugtussle, Oklahoma, or Thompson Ledges, Ohio, is not enough. One must go see "who's on first," so to speak.

But the forays by Washington political writers who follow candidates across the country or presidents across the world can be almost as confining as the White House itself; it is a view mostly from the inside of airplanes, buses, and hotels. And most of the things seen and heard are controlled by the stage managers.

Until after Truman's whistle-stop campaign in 1948, reporters went forth by train. Now they follow the President's plane. *Air Force One* is no particular single aircraft, like Truman's *Independence.* It is now simply the name given any plane that the President boards.

Right behind *Air Force One* is a jetliner chartered for press people at their own expense. On the campaign trail there must also be an extra plane for TV technicians and their equipment and odds and ends of reporters. On arrival at the hustings, reporters are packed into buses, still a captive audience.

As growing numbers have joined the candidate followers, scores of reporters cover the same events, read the same press releases, and hear the same briefings. It results in staged reporting, stacked to give the manipulators of public opinion their own way despite what stout old pros of the press corps may try to do.

Carter, in the tradition of other recent candidates and presidents, has scored by herding the press around. When his ratings slipped in the polls, he could and did arrange a foreign tour or two so television audiences would see him getting the cheers of crowds that he was not earning in Washington.

The fun place to be on any political campaign is the "Zoo plane." That's where the wild ones are—the TV crew and those incidental reporters who don't have the clout to ride in the number one plane with the candidate or the crowded press plane.

Why is it called the Zoo plane? Because the elite feel the camera crew are merely animals, subhuman and hardly fit for polite company. There is much more sex on the Zoo plane. It is expected.

Females are more predatory in the Zoo plane. There is more need for medication. During the Nixon-McGovern campaign several Zoo passengers came down with a social disease known as a "cold."

Those who were on a particular Zoo plane during the 1972 McGovern-Nixon race, remember with affection one female reporter who, well oiled with booze, talked a bunch of male reporters and photographers into holding down a handsome member of the plane's crew while she stripped off his clothes. He helped land the plane in just his shorts. Had the landing been even a hundred yards further away, he might not have been that well covered.

If one has to cover a campaign but needs not take it too seriously, the Zoo plane is the one to take.

Of course, the prestige in presidential campaign travel lies in being a part of the pool of four or five reporters—two from the wire services, one from newsmagazines such as *Time* and *Newsweek,* and one or two from newspapers such as the *New York Times,* the *Washington Post* and maybe another paper or two—who travel in the same plane as the presidential candidate to record, for history, anything that happens to him or bits of wisdom he wishes to dispense en route.

The vast array of reporters of course are in the press plane.

But the Zoo plane always has the most going for it.

356

The gang on the Zoo plane that followed McGovern's *Dakota Queen II* probably had the most fun of all. It had been nicely decorated with unflattering photographs and posters. A dandruff ad had been generously augmented with dandruff and mocked up to show George McGovern as the sufferer.

Skeletons and other Halloween decorations attested to the fact that it was always Halloween on the Zoo plane. The bar was open from the moment of the first opened eye in the ghastly mornings.

But what really made the hotshot correspondents and network stars halfway yearn to give up their seats of prestige and get on the Zoo plane were the stories of the wild nights they kept hearing about. Anything went—under a blanket. And there were plenty of blankets.

For some reason Joseph Alsop is the reporter the campaign press gang of years past voted they would least want to be shipwrecked with on a desert island.

Every group has to have a patsy and the press flights had Joe Alsop for theirs. But not matter how they gnashed their teeth, Joe Alsop always came out on top.

For example, the press was as usual having a terrible time getting close to the vice-presidential candidate, Spiro Agnew. They were being kept behind certain imaginary lines. Secret Service men had the audacity to put down tape to show the exact line they were to stand behind.

Then came Joe Alsop. And lo! He was ushered into the vice-presidential plane instead of the press plane by Vic Gold. The regular press cursed under their breaths and bided their time.

They shouted approval and felt a lot better when they heard that Joe had then gone to the McGovern plane and had been assigned to ride in the Zoo plane with the minor reporters and TV crew. The story is told by Timothy Crouse, author of *The Boys on the Bus,* about how Joe Alsop showed up wanting to travel with the political reporters on Senator George McGovern's plane.

Frank Mankiewicz, who was McGovern's top press aide, is quoted saying, "Put him on the Zoo plane. I don't want to see him on the senator's plane. I don't want him anywhere near there."

According to Crouse, when press aide Polly Hackett wanted to know why he didn't want him on McGovern's plane, Frank said, "Because I'm liable to punch him in the nose, that's why."

One of the stories told about Joseph Alsop by his political reporting colleagues concerns how he insisted on highest standards in his life-style, no matter where the political campaign took him. One night, exhausted reporters, checking in late at a typical hotel on the hustings, encountered Alsop, who had already examined his room and was protesting to the room clerk.

He was, in fact, demanding fresh accommodations because there was dust on his windowsill. They didn't wait around long enough to find out if he got them.

It is true that when the press travels with the President or any other politician, they are known to drink a little to relax after the illustrious one has gone to bed, and can surprise them with no more news till morning.

The story is told that on one such trip with Jerry Ford, two Washington correspondents relaxed so thoroughly that they forgot what time it was and reeled out of the hotel in the wee hours for fear that they would miss their early-morning bus.

As they stood outside looking around they were still perplexed and they buttonholed a fellow to ask, "Say, is that the sun or the moon?"

The fellow, who was a correspondent from another part of the country and in about the same condition as they, studied the sky in the direction they were pointing and replied, "I'm the wrong one to ask, fellows, I've never been here before."

Of course reporting is not always that cooperative or we'd only need one newspaper.

The greatest show of loyalty happened a few campaigns back when a colleague stayed zonkered for three or four days in a row while his buddies rose above competitiveness and coordinated his story-filing among them.

One guy would volunteer to cover the candidate's morning activities and someone else would do the afternoon, and still a third would do a small overnight. Or on a slow day they'd all do it together.

Sometimes the styles of writing varied greatly, but his friends were doing the best they could. There was one clever drunk, however, who bragged that he never needed anyone to fill in for him.

His standard procedure was to get a local newspaper his editor never saw, clip the article on the subject he was "covering"

358

and take it to Western Union. He would remember to change the by-line to his own before sending the story collect.

But one day during the Truman campaign, he got so drunk, he outsmarted himself. He wheeled into the Western Union office with his precious clipping and signed the wrong side of the story, becoming annoyed when the Western Union clerk dared ask him if that was indeed what he wanted to send.

He told the clerk off in no uncertain terms, telling him that "when I need help from a smart-ass clerk, I'll ask for it."

Having stated his piece, his only-slightly-more-steady buddies helped steer him righteously out of the Western Union office and back to the local press club.

An hour later the fellow was being paged, and his angry editor was demanding to know, "What the hell's the idea of sending me a list of stock quotations?"

Reporters who suffered the most during Nixon's 1972 campaign were those who had to cover the activities of Vice-President Agnew, who was substituting for the man in the White House and was throwing the campaign barbs against the opponents for him.

They became so desperate that two men on the Agnew press plane—Lou Cannon and Jim Wooten, both of the *Washington Post*—started amusing the gang with writings of a different sort.

Wooten's contributions were in the form of the "Barry Goldwater Memorial Intelligence Test." Lou Cannon did a special straight reporting job for the *"Transylvania Newspaper* under the by-line of Irving Doppelgänger," giving a rat's eye view of the events of the campaign to date.

Agnew, everyone agreed, had gotten the notion that he was President running for reelection, which annoyed the press considerably. They were kept at arm's length from him.

Further adding to their annoyance was Agnew's press secretary, Vic Gold, who screamed and cursed a lot, even at passing motorists getting in the way of the Agnew press bus.

When the campaign was over, the press gang gave Vic a gift—a straitjacket.

Sometimes those who travel with presidents still feel a little sorry for them when the presidents find out they are not as well loved by the public as they delude themselves into thinking.

Ron Sarro, who was with Nixon in 1970 and covered

sixteen states while the President tried to swell the number of Republicans in office during a congressional election year, says, "I'll never forget Tennessee. Poor Nixon. Instead of signs for him there were signs for the star the people really came to see: WELCOME DAN RATHER.

George McGovern's campaign was in a class of its own. Everything went in an opposite direction than it should have, including the voting that gave the poor man only one state and the District of Columbia—some kind of record in the pits.

It is still the most talked-about campaign in the annals of the Press Club bar. Looking back, the incident that would most go down in history was a real sleeper.

You could slug the story "Custer's Last Stand,"—but this was Custer, South Dakota. It was here that George McGovern was hopelessly outflanked by Big Chief Eagleton.

Big stories evolve in their own sneaky way, without fanfare, and that's the way it was with the famous Eagleton revelation, which still excites heated arguments over what is ethical and who did in whom.

Perhaps no one will ever know the true story, but this is the way reporters piece it together.

It was on a Tuesday, July 25, 1972, in the "spring" season of the Nixon-McGovern campaign, when it looked like McGovern had a chance.

The situation in Washington was that Nixon was hiding in the White House, doing as little campaigning as possible and acting "presidential." McGovern had been working his tail off but at this point was taking a rest.

And while he rested, the reporters took it easy, too, just writing enough copy so that editors knew they were still alive and sober.

McGovern's running mate, Tom Eagleton, was scheduled to drop in at Custer, in the Black Hills, to pay his respects to his leader.

None of the reporters was too excited about this small scheduled visit, but they gathered round, out of habit. After Eagleton was introduced by McGovern, Eagleton announced, out of the blue, that he had been hospitalized for "nervous exhaustion and fatigue" not once but three times.

Yes, he admitted, he had had psychiatric help. McGovern was not perturbed, and said he would not have any interest in dumping Eagleton.

360

Afterward, most newspaper and wire reporters didn't seem to make too much of the revelation, but TV's Harry Reasoner differed and gave Eagleton one week before he'd be off the ticket.

Isolated as they were, the reporters eventually got the feedback that some people were demanding that McGovern drop Eagleton.

One reporter—Carl Leubsdorf of AP—managed to get to McGovern and filed a story that McGovern would "wait and see" what to do. The others screamed that it was unfair for McGovern to give one man a statement when the others weren't there. They beefed to Dick Dougherty, McGovern's press man.

Now the story gets a little tricky and reporters still are not sure if McGovern himself ever made a statement that he was 1,000 percent behind Tom Eagleton.

What happened is that Dougherty phoned a statement to an assistant, who pinned it to the press room door. It attacked the wait-and-see AP story of Carl Leubsdorf and said the candidate was 1,000 percent behind Eagleton.

The note did not give a direct quote from McGovern on this exaggerated show of loyalty.

That was Wednesday. Two days later, on Friday, McGovern not only dumped Eagleton but he didn't tell him in person that he was dumped. Instead McGovern did it through the press, leaking the story through various reporters, each of whom thought he had an exclusive.

It was a lousy way to run a campaign and the press was wary of trusting McGovern again.

But the question still hangs in the air: Did McGovern himself say that he was with his running mate 1,000 percent or was that just a colorful way that press aides stated it?

Maybe we'll never know but—it's hardly the kind of question one would torture a former candidate with by asking him about it today. But what this certainly shows is that a candidate must be very careful about delegating authority, and the rule is "When in doubt, don't." This is just one of many sidelights of the most screwed-up campaign in history that reporters mull over at the Press Club bar.

At the end of McGovern's campaign, McGovern's nerves were frayed—understandably. He actually snarled at a heckler in Jackson, Michigan, as he heard one hoot of derision too many from the small airport crowd. Reporters could scarcely believe it. From those prim lips, as he hissed, venting the anger probably inspired by reporter Richard Stout, they heard the words, "Kiss my ass."

What really had McGovern upset was Stout's *Newsweek* story, which said two things that cut to the quick—that McGovern's voice sounds "like grace at a Rotary luncheon," and that McGovern was resorting to "the harshest rhetoric of any campaign in memory."

Stout had said, rather sanctimoniously, in the *Newsweek* story that came out the week before the election, "To charge that the Vietnam War is racist or genocidal is to impute guilt not only to the President but to the nation...."

Even so, McGovern made a tactical mistake getting angry. McGovern had tried to give Stout an out, asking him if the editors had done the hatchet job. The diplomatic answer would have been yes.

But Stout, whose nerves were also frayed, said no indeed, everything had been his own idea. And to rub it in, he added he had okayed the final version. Then he innocently asked why the candidate was asking.

"Because," said McGovern, flushing with anger himself for a change, "it was just a bunch of shit."

In the heat of the campaign, very sane and sober reporters have been known to do some pretty wild things. In 1960, when Kennedy made it and Nixon didn't, Murray J. Gart, who is now editor of the *Washington Star* but was then with *Time*, was covering the platform deliberations just before the Republican convention in Chicago, with his *Time* colleague Neil McNeil.

As Frank Aukofer of the *Milwaukee Journal* recalls it. "In those days, the platform was a tightly guarded secret, but *Time* insisted on the story anyway.

"Gart and McNeil discovered a false ceiling over the meeting room. Then, on a pretext of interviewing the kitchen helpers about their reaction to an upcoming visit by President Eisenhower, McNeil slipped through a storage room and into the ceiling while Gart went through the motions of getting quotes from the employees.

"McNeil stayed up in the ceiling for five hours and got the whole story. *Time* never ran a word of it."

One of the most momentous near-happenings of modern times was at the Republican convention of 1940 in Philadelphia, when I was publicity director for Senator Taft. If his political managers had done as well as his press handlers, he would have won the nomination.

But against this isolationist, as Hitler's war machine took Europe, international interests had secretly waged a ruthless pressure campaign to swing delegates to Wendell L. Willkie, a utility magnate. With phony admission tickets, the galleries of the convention hall were packed with gas and electric company employees to din "We Want Willkie" into the ears of the milling delegates.

Newsmen from across the country seemed deaf and blind. I had the facts and free access to press and radio eager for news. I did not act, partly because it was hard to find our campaign chairman in the confusion; partly because our people expected to win without a fight that might be disruptive.

The swing to Willkie was hairline close. To the last, his floor managers were offering our delegates fantastic prices to switch. Bold action could have made the difference. It was a failure of which in the long run I am glad. Taft later told me he would have harassed Roosevelt on interventionist acts. This could have meant the fall of Britain. It would be presumptious to say the good Lord held me back. Who knows?

Press guys have been known to go to great lengths to amuse themselves—and supposedly the candidate. There was, for example, the time Jim Naughton, *New York Times* reporter and later to become national editor of the *Philadelphia Enquirer,* put on a huge chicken costume at a party for presidential candidate Gerald Ford.

There was the time when the McGovern press gang, in a great show of sentimentality, had helped the McGoverns celebrate their wedding anniversary along the campaign trail.

They had even gone so far as to get a silver bowl and have it engraved with the words that McGovern had bravely shouted after his bomber was hit in World War II, words that could, if McGovern won, become as famous as Kennedy's coconut message. They were: "Resume your stations. We're bringing her home."

Unfortunately, at the tenderest moment of the presentation, somebody—undoubtedly thinking of McGovern's ghastly rating at the polls—shouted, "What do you want him to do? Bleed in it."

Well! It was the end of a magic moment.

The absolute pits of campaign trail parties, however, was the one given for Edmund Muskie during the Wisconsin primary of 1972.

The excuse was that the candidate was having his fifty-eighth birthday. Muskie was running an uptight, tense campaign, so what could be nicer than helping him relax a little. Especially since his wife, Jane, was there to share it with him.

And for a while it looked as if the senator would relax, as he sat pulling on a bourbon, trying to lose the cares of the day. But the reporters were four or five drinks up on him and ready for anything.

Then it happened. *Newsweek's* Dick Stout stood up and called for silence and in the hush that followed gave a perfect imitation of Muskie giving a speech.

It was so funny and wooden that reporters fell down laughing. The only trouble was that Muskie was too sober to appreciate it and his fixed smile looked like a death mask. Jane, at his side, also gave a good imitation of a smile.

Then, as if they weren't in trouble enough, the exuberant reporters presented Muskie with a gift they had thought, in their happy condition, was the only perfect thing they could have possibly found—a T-shirt emblazoned POLISH POWER. He obviously found it offensive.

After that came a huge cake, iced and decorated with a sketch of the White House. The senator was hardly smiling as he cut the cake and reporters stepped up one by one to receive a piece of it.

The whole fiasco seemed endless and the press gang were sobering up enough to realize this thing could drag on endlessly. But suddenly, in a wild climax to the party, Jane Muskie, still smiling that little smile, walked over to Stout with a big piece of cake in her hand.

"I have something for you," she said sweetly.

"Oh..." said Dick, relieved at this show of friendliness and about to say something more.

"Yes. This," and suddenly she mashed the cake right into Stout's face.

Now she was laughing raucously, *her* tensions were relieved.

Poor Muskie was not that lucky. He looked more tense and uptight than ever at this signal that the party was over.

As I said, it was the pits of campaign parties.

23/The Press and Presidents—Prisoners of Love

There always has been a love-hate relationship between the President and the press. Presidents learn to handle the press like a keg of snakes, cautiously dropping in food and trying to stay out of fang's reach. It can't be done. And presidents get bitten by the ungrateful reporters they are trying to feed choice morsels.

Richard Nixon seldom was gentle with the press. As an animal "handler" he acted menacingly and there was a veiled threat, hinted by his press secretary, that the misbehaving reporter would be cut off from the vital flow of White House news.

As an example of spite by the Nixon White House, the *Washington Post*'s society reporter, Dorothy McCardle, was barred from covering White House social functions—not because of anything she had done but because Nixon was miffed at the *Post* for its coverage of Watergate.

All the other women of the press, my coauthor among them, would leave Dorothy McCardle sitting in the White House press room while they covered something in the East Room or other formal reception room, and then hurry back to brief Dorothy on everything they had learned.

This could have been taken by the *Washington Star* as a signal that it was the teacher's pet, as long as the *Star* minded its p's and q's. But the *Star*, realizing that it might be next on the shit list printed an editorial that it would not cover White House social affairs, either, until the ban was lifted. It soon was.

More sinister was the comment one of the White House gang, Charles Colson, made to a *Star* staffer. Probably thinking he would make the *Star* man rejoice, Colson was reported to have said, "We will shove it to the *Post* as soon as the election is over."

However, the *Star* reporter, being concerned for the freedom of the press under the Nixon White House, repeated this comment to Carl Bernstein, who was already working on the

Watergate investigation before Nixon's reelection. It was secret no more.

Jack Anderson truly made the White House "handler," RMN, uncomfortable, long before Watergate. After certain of Anderson's exposes implicated the White House in power plays or financial dealings, everyone who might have been the source of leaks to Anderson or his men would be given lie detector tests.

Anderson's sources have told him that in the Nixon days the fury unleashed against him was so great that State Department Xerox machines were placed under guard.

Covering the White House might seem one of the most glamorous spots in journalism. Surely it is one of the most prestigious. The White House press gang are the heavies of the press corps, by-lined and seen on television. But this spot also can be one of the most frustrating and both sides have, at times, felt imprisoned by the other.

To some White Housers, it looks as if the President is the captive of the White House reporters and to others that the reporters are the captives of the President—"We're stuck with each other—we're prisoners of love."

Just once Carter managed to sneak away to the Kennedy Center without the press catching wise and there was hell to pay until the reporters had tracked him down and gotten him within sight at the Center.

The regulars for the wire services and major papers are penned in little cubicles. Other accredited correspondents who come and go are also in a limited area, not free to roam.

The aim of the White House staff is to tell only what they want told, to the greater glory of the President. The job of the press is to find out what really is happening, like the inmates of a jail keeping tabs on the warden's office.

Inevitably it is an adversary relationship. If the President is to be a leader, he must set plans and seek public backing. Naturally he peddles all the pluses and none of the minuses. Manipulating the press to sell the official view, right or wrong, has become an intricate game with national and world issues at stake.

Helen Thomas is one reporter who deplores that the White House press corps doesn't get to see more of the President. She feels there should be more contact than "just at press conferences where everything is hand-fed to the press."

Still worse, is the fact that she must stick to her White House cubbyhole, within reach of her UPI phone and the Presidential press secretary's office. The President might take a notion to go to the Kennedy Center or make an earthshaking announcement and she must be there.

Frank Cormier, who covers the White House for AP, puts it this way, "We're like firemen waiting for the bell to ring. When it rings we hop to it and slide down the pole."

Pack journalism is possible because reporters are afraid to leave the group on any excuse. Something could happen at just that minute. One reporter was in the rest room answering a call of nature when Arthur Bremmer shot presidential candidate Governor George Wallace at Laurel, Maryland, in the early days of the presidential campaign.

The worst thing that happens to White House reporters is that they get the notion that any handout is important just because it says White House on it. They forget that the average person around the country is no longer thrilled with the mere mention of the word *President*, or *White House*. Those days died with the Nixon era.

Do presidents have teacher's pets among the press? They sure do. LBJ promised more than one reporter he would leak to him "like a dog leaks on a fire hydrant." And he did, punishing one or another reporter for an unfavorable story by leaking to his worst competitor.

Dan Rather was one of the most independent reporters LBJ had to contend with. And in his book Rather admits Lyndon Johnson once said to him, "Rather, are you trying to fuck me?"

LBJ once sought out Holmes Alexander, whose column appears in more than a hundred papers, and shook a column at him, livid with rage. "What the hell is this bullshit?" he demanded.

Holmes, who had come to the White House in all innocence, was caught off guard and tried to explain. Lyndon would have none of it. He raised his hand to stop him and said, "Holmes, the trouble with you is that you talk to too many Republicans." Then he led Alexander around to some of his aides, telling them to give the columnist any information he wanted.

"I'll never forget the way he actually said, 'Anybody who works for me, works for you,'" Holmes Alexander recalls, shaking his head. "And then, sometime later, after I'd interviewed him, I wondered if there was anything he wanted to add. I said, 'I've been asking all the questions, Mr. President. Is there anything else you'd like to volunteer?'

"Johnson put a big heavy arm around my shoulder and said, in his deepest Texas drawl, 'Just that ah love you!'"

Back in the days of Andrew Johnson one presidential friend, a reporter by the name of J. B. McCullagh, got an exclusive interview with quotes from the President, and it appeared in the *Cincinnati Commerical.*

This history-making precedent raised the prestige of the paper but it lowered the prestige of the President, who was reprimanded by every newspaper that didn't have a reporter who could march into the Oval Office.

One paper went so far as to say interviewing a President made journalism "an offense, a thing of ill savor in all decent nostrils."

But soon all reporters were clamoring to interview presidents.

In the early days of newspapering, partisan politics was the rule. Newspapers lined themselves up on one side of the political fence or the other and did not even try to be even-handed.

Sometimes a newspaper got special treatment because of its publisher. Grover Cleveland favored the *Daily Post,* the forerunner of the *Washington Post,* because it was frankly Democratic.

Kennedy had many favorites—Ben Bradlee, which gave Bradlee a leg up at *Newsweek,* was possibly tops. Then came Bill Lawrence, whose star burned even more brightly at the *New York Times* because of JFK.

By now it should come as no surprise that a President can turn a reporter into a superstar even if he hates him—simply by focusing attention.

In the case of Bradlee, thanks to a friendship that began when JFK and he were neighbors in Georgetown, we have invaluable insights into the personal life and character of Kennedy that would otherwise be impossible to know. Even small things that don't seem very important might have influence on a man's performance as President.

At any rate, because of Bradlee, we know that JFK was slightly embarrassed because his breasts were a little larger than is normal for an average man—a trait he attributed to his mother's side of the family.

Through his good friend Bradlee, we know that Kennedy, in a personal conversation, denied that he had been married to one Durie Malcolm, as had been reported in a genealogy book. According to Bradlee's report, Durie was a friend of his brother Joe, and JFK had merely dated her a few times.

Again, we have Bradlee to thank for the information that Kennedy was privately complaining that it was costing him as much out of his own pocket to live at the White House as it had cost at his Georgetown house. And for JFK's wonderful punch line when Bradlee's wife asked what a certain butler did to earn a living around the White House— "He leads in the guy who brings breakfast."

The friendship between Ben Bradlee and Jack Kennedy began in 1958, when JFK was already toying with the notion of running for the presidency and was still smarting from having failed to get the vice-presidential nomination in 1956, as Adlai Stevenson's running mate.

Senator Kennedy's wife, Jackie, and Bradlee's wife, Toni, became moderately friendly, too, which helped make this a business and friendship foursome.

Bradlee, as a *Newsweek* man, was able to introduce Kennedy to various political writers he should know, and many of them ended up participating in bull sessions with JFK and his advisers in the Kennedy's Georgetown backyard.

Stories on Jackie Kennedy that female reporters could never get out of the White House have also come to us from Bradlee, who shares these examples of her vanity as well as her gallantry in his book *Conversations with Kennedy.*

The case of vanity was illustrated on at least one occasion, when the First Lady took paintbrush in hand to restructure her dress in a photograph.

The gallantry was demonstrated when a pixilated guest at the White House fell into and ruined a very expensive old engraving that Jackie had just paid one thousand dollars for and brought home in triumph to the White House for the President's birthday.

Instead of showing her emotions, which were understandably fury and disgust at such clumsiness, she gallantly assured the man that she could get it fixed.

Reporters' insights on the presidents are often shared at the National Press Club.

Whose ego was greatest among recent presidents? Hard to say. It could be Johnson. He kept asking questions that elicited praise. Because he was sensitive about his jug ears, he gave orders that the lectern and teleprompters be placed so that he never exactly faced the camera, thereby preventing his ears from being viewed in full relief.

Nixon was rather pleased with the way he looked and he knew he did a good job on TV. To be ready for TV at all times, he took to wearing pancake makeup almost regularly, which caused some people to raise their eyebrows a bit—especially visitors who did not know how often he was on TV.

Truman won respect by knowing his stuff. Even tough budget briefings, which presidents traditionally turn over to budget officials to answer the questions of the press, the little man handled himself. He had done his homework, staying up much of the night to study the fat budget document and he pulled figures from the top of his head.

But just because a man is President and can explain finance, doesn't mean he knows everything. Felix Cotten remembers the time he was sorry he had assumed too much when he was covering Truman at the White House.

Felix had missed out on a walk that Truman had taken through Rock Creek Park with some reporters, during which Truman had held forth on the subject of snakes.

"So at his next press conference, I was standing right beside him at his desk and I thought I'd be sociable during the badinage that always preceded those stand-up conferences," Felix recalls.

"I said, 'Mr. President, I understand you are interested in herpetology.'

"Truman looked at me and said, 'What the hell is that?' I didn't think it would be politic for me to be teaching a President terminology, and the conference was ready to begin, so I just kind of shrank away."

In those days, Cotten recalls, a press conference would begin when Bill Donaldson, a Hill employee on loan to the White House because he recognized the faces of political reporters, would yell, "All in."

As Felix remembers the flow of presidential press conferences, reporters always stood in the presence of a President until Dwight Eisenhower changed the rule and let them sit.

Truman didn't care what anyone said about him politically and even joked among friends that "They could call me a son of a bitch if they want, just as long as *I* know I'm doing the right thing."

In view of that, Washington newsmen were truly amazed when he sent a most profane letter of abuse to the *Washington Post* music critic, Paul Hume, who had dared to criticize the singing voice of Truman's one and only child, Margaret, the apple of his eye.

Truman told Hume, in effect, that he would cut off his balls if he ever got near him.

Kennedy gave press conferences a new dimension when he permitted open questions, thrown at him with TV cameras grinding—a great innovation. Kennedy, of all Presidents, could parry a question so skillfully that he kept from looking ridiculous.

What he didn't like he turned to humor, about the question or the questioner or the newspaper he represented. There was an intimate or familial feeling about it, which gave the reporters the warm sense of belonging.

Johnson blew hot and cold. Sometimes he cursed and sometimes he flattered. When he was acting most country boy, he was being most clever.

As reporters later learned from an LBJ intimate, the doorkeeper of the House, who wrote about it in the book *Fishbait*, Johnson's act of opening his pajamas to show his gall-bladder scar, was really to pull the wool over the press's eyes. He was cleverly trying to show that the operation was not for something worse— cancer.

Nixon answered reporters with exaggerated courtesy that hid the fact that he loathed the press. He would go to great lengths to avoid the press and his attitude rubbed off on his Vice-President, Spiro Agnew, who took to doing Nixon's dirty work by needling and insulting the press for him.

Ford let his press conferences get out of hand at first, because he was trying so hard to be a regular guy and show that he was not at all like Richard Nixon. Reporters shouted whatever they wanted to get his attention and it sounded like a labor union meeting.

Carter came on smooth and glib. His voice, a little high-pitched and reverential, was just a tad too sincere for the taste of tough reporters. As the White House regulars commented, "He sounds like a goddamn missionary. I'm not buying."

Eisenhower tried to give the press straight answers

without dramatics but he was forever getting tangled in endless sentences which could not be resolved. Some people collected Eisenhower answers to press questions.

At one of the mountain parties that some of us Press Club members used to hold near my place in the Blue Ridge, we had a spoof on an Ike press conference. Questions were asked by reporters from imaginary papers and were answered by excerpts from an actual Eisenhower tape.

This was during the Korean conflict. One squeaky-voiced questioner asked, "Mr. President, is it true that you are planning to send female gorillas and baboons to Korea to comfort the troops?"

The presidential voice boomed, "As a soldier, I think that would be a good thing to do."

Though Jack Kennedy won the prize among presidents for wittiness and off-the-cuff punch lines, Jerry Ford won the prize for all-around good fellowship and good-guy speeches, which had more jokes and quips in them than other presidents'.

And he frequently singled out reporters to help his humor along. Sarah McClendon, the famed thorn in the side of presidents, was included in one speech in which he said, "I saw my very good friend Sarah McClendon. Sarah is very outspoken—but not by anybody I know."

David Kennerly, who was his official photographer, now writer-photographer, recalls when he had taken an underwater White House pool picture, using an underwater camera, of course, showing President Ford and Dick Swanson of *People* magazine swimming together.

The President liked it and sent a copy to Swanson inscribed, "To Dick Swanson, we've got to stop meeting like this. Jerry Ford."

Kennerly says that Ford had to have a good sense of humor to withstand all the little fiascos that were always happening, involving him.

For example, once Kennerly was present when the President's driver was unaware that the President was standing on the roof of his car talking to a crowd and started to drive away. The Secret Service men yelled to the chauffeur to "Stop very, very slowly."

Another time the President was entertaining Queen Elizabeth and Prince Philip. Secretary of State Kissinger and his wife were with the presidential party, and they had all gone into the East Room to see the entertainment.

"As Kissinger sat down he leaned back in the wooden-back chair and it broke with a loud noise. The Queen and the President laughed. Kissinger was only slightly embarrassed, but I'll never forget Nancy Kissinger's look of shocked surprise."

Kennerly talked with my coauthor while he was putting together his memories of Ford and the White House into a photo-crammed book entitled *Shooter*. David was undoubtedly the first and only White House photographer to be able to move freely around the White House and in and out of the Oval Office taking pictures of a President, no matter what the President was doing.

For this, of course, some not-so-fortunate White House aides and employees hated Kennerly's guts. But that was the quaint arrangement Kennerly had with the President.

"It was almost as if I had diplomatic immunity," David recalled. "I could do whatever I wanted to do whenever I wanted to do it and nobody could lay a hand on me." Some said that Kennerly was as close to the President as his own sons—or closer.

Kennerly confesses that once in a while the President would complain because Kennerly was riding in the press chartered plane instead of on *Air Force One* with him. "I kept telling the President," he said, "if you'd put stewardesses on, I'd ride it all the time." *Air Force One* has only stewards.

Ford surely wasn't the only fellow in the White House to be the "victim" of goofs, over which he had no control. Carter's White House has also racked up a few. When Prime Minister Takeo Fukuda of Japan quietly arrived for some conferences with President Carter in May last year, first there was the misspelling of the Prime Minister's name and the grinning reporters gathered round the bulletin board to draw each other's attention to the misspelling—Fuckuda—in a release about the new arrival's activities.

Then after lunch he became the first head of state to be baptized in water by the born-again Christian administration of President Jimmy Carter. As he took an impromptu walk on the South grounds, the sprinklers went on without any warning and there was a sudden cry for help.

The press was sure somebody must have goofed on another day when all visitors were thrown together in the Oval Office in one big smorgasbord.

As White House correspondent John Szostak tells it,

"The routine at the White House is, of course, for any visiting dignitary to be received separately by the President in the Oval Office. They have a few private words with the President, they usually have their picture made with the President, and they go away feeling happy.

"Not so on April 5, 1978. It was what one could consider to be a delayed April Fools' joke. Among the visitors were the Prince and Princess Hitachi of Japan, waiting to meet President Carter and present him with a vase, some people waiting to make the annual Cancer Award presentation, some military personnel, and someone doing public relations for a potential Democratic office seeker.

"Suddenly, instead of one at a time, everybody was herded into the Oval Office like cattle. The photographers and reporters among them. It was like Grand Central Station.

"When the royal couple started to present the gift, a reporter yelled out that the gift would be a 'Sony hi-fi.' The President was not amused.

"In all the confusion, the press had difficulty finding out who was who. Seeing the princess look confused, a reporter commented in a low voice that now they could go back and say they had experienced Georgia-style hospitality."

Reporters hear many stories and get many insights. Sometimes years go by before they're able to ascertain whether a particular story is true.

One story that made the rounds at the Press Club after presidential nominee Jimmy Carter picked Fritz Mondale as his running mate was why he hadn't picked Senator John Glenn, the former astronaut, whom he had seemed to lean toward. The way the story goes, when each potential vice-presidential couple came to visit and get acquainted with the Carters, Rosalynn Carter had become alarmed because John Glenn's wife, Annie, had a stammer.

The story went that Rosalynn Carter had felt that the speech impediment might cause the couple to be less effective as campaigners.

An easy story to confirm was that of President Jack Kennedy's womanizing. Stories were frequently told in newspaper circles about the President's eye for the ladies, but in those days reporters tended to protect the private lives and foibles of the presidents—except among themselves.

One reporter who covered Kennedy's activities fairly closely comments, "Jack Kennedy was the damndest woman chaser

I've ever known—but I'd rather not be quoted. Christ, a lot of other newspaper guys knew what was going on. He was notorious. He had assigned one guy, a Secret Service man, to spot good-looking gals among the people who would come to hear him.

"And I believe a staffer as well would go around and ask some particularly attractive girl if she would like to meet the President. This would be even on the streets of different cities—California, New York, They knew his tastes.

"Many were so honored. And make no mistake about it, the girls did feel honored. It was said one of these girls even got a job at the White House and others were fitted in at other spots around Washington.

"They might never see him again. If a president says, 'Help this little girl get a job,' they find her a job. Others didn't want a job—it was strictly for the emotional binge and the honor of it. After all, how many girls even get to meet a president, let alone get a private audience?

"But some disappointed honorees came away saying they had had better."

How times have changed. Now anything of a sexy nature is happily reported in the newspapers, if it will make the White House look ridiculous.

When a young woman in a popular D.C. bar, Sarsfield's, accused presidential aide Hamilton Jordan of spitting his drink down her dress front because she wouldn't pay attention to him, it made the front page of more than one newspaper.

A few years back if such a thing had happened, it would have been hushed up. Only if the police became involved, as in the case when LBJ's top aide Walter Jenkins was picked up in the men's room of the YMCA, did such stories make the newspapers.

Also on the subject of reporters' insights, Vera Glaser reveals that when she traveled with and interviewed Rosalynn Carter, "I found her not at all knowledgeable politically.

"I went with the First Lady to Orlando and Tampa, where she was raising funds for ERA," Vera recalled in an interview with my coauthor, "and I interviewed her in depth when she got back to the White House.

"It was at this time that Carter was in such deep trouble with Congress that Congressman John Moss of California had called him the 'least effective president I have ever known in my twenty-six years in Congress.'

"I asked Rosalynn, who had been in the White House

over a year, 'How do you explain your husband's poor relations with Congress and how would you suggest he improve them?'

"The First Lady looked at me as if I didn't know what I was talking about and said, 'Why his relations with Congress are great.'"

Vera was also astounded at the First Lady's comments about Larry Flynt, publisher of *Hustler*. This was before the shooting which made an invalid of Flynt. Ruth Stapleton, the President's evangelist sister, had befriended the porno publisher and Vera was asking Rosalynn Carter what she thought of the friendship.

Vera asked if the First Lady would invite Larry Flynt to stay at the White House and Rosalynn said she would. Vera told the First Lady, "You know he hasn't given up porno. He has just turned the magazine over to his wife.

"'Yes, I know,' Rosalynn said.

"I said, 'And yet you would invite this pornographer to stay at the White House? How would you justify it?'

"The First Lady said, 'Of course, I would. Jesus said you help those who need help.'

"That never was in print. The desk just didn't want to get into it and they said the story didn't need it. But I was really surprised at such reasoning."

The world would be a duller place if reporters did not penetrate the inner circles of the White House and Cabinet and record the irreverent goings-on for posterity.

It was Jack Anderson, the investigative reporter, who inadvertently learned the names top presidential advisers Hamilton Jordan and Zbigniew Brzezinski call each other behind each other's back. Jordan, Anderson reported, called Brzezinski "Woody Woodpecker" for his disheveled hair, and Brzezinski returned the compliment by referring to the President's chubby top assistant as "Porky Pig."

Helen Thomas's irreverent humor is well known around the White House—in fact, around the world.

Jerry Ford hit the nail right on the head when he said about Helen, "I'm firmly convinced that if the good Lord had made the world today, He would have spent six days creating the heavens and earth and the living creatures upon it. But on the seventh day, He would not have rested; He would have had to justify it to Helen Thomas."

Helen Thomas was one of the few women who didn't mind correcting a president. Whenever Lyndon Johnson would refer to "the boys"—meaning the White House press corps—she would pipe up with "Some of us are *not* boys, Mr. President."

Female reporters have not been shy with presidents. Once President Nixon was completely taken aback when Kandy Stroud of *Women's Wear Daily* yelled out at him, while he was putting Golda Meir into her car after a state dinner at the White House.

"Did you give her the jets?" Kandy yelled. It was at a time when Israel was badly in need of planes and this was rumored to be the purpose of her visit—to convince Nixon to sell jets to Israel.

At first Nixon looked disgusted at this question and threw up his hands. He started into the White House, then as if compelled to answer Kandy, came back and said, "She makes quite a case." It was obvious to all the reporters, thanks to Kandy, that Mrs. Meir would get her jets.

Nixon didn't seem to care who knew about his feelings toward the press. Even as far away as China, Premier Chou En-Lai knew how bitterly Nixon felt.

Helen Thomas relates how once when Chou was being friendly in asking reporters if they were having a good time, Nixon had muttered, "More than they deserve."

Another time, Helen relates, when the photographers were taking a lot of pictures of the Premier, Chou told them to shoot some pictures of Nixon. According to Helen Thomas, Nixon said, "with a bitter smile," that if they did, " 'they would only burn them.' "

Every president has had painful questions thrown at him. But it's the tough question that makes the news. Dan Rather of CBS developed a tough attitude which helped make news in recent administrations. In Nixon's he was the first reporter who dared ask Nixon point-blank what went through his mind when he heard people say that perhaps he should resign or be impeached.

Nixon's feeling about the press corps came out in his historic reply: "Well I'm glad we don't take the vote of this room."

Jim Hagerty was the press secretary who most completely could talk for the President—Ike. It was the word among reporters that Hagerty *was* the President much of the time and that Ike wanted it that way as he putted golf balls on his private putting green outside the White House.

The closest any press secretary has come to having that degree of a president's confidence since is Carter's Jody Powell.

Jody, however, did not capture the affection of the press as Hagerty did, and has shown his bitterness to them. When he spoke to the White House Correspondents Association, filling in for the President, who broke an eighty-year tradition with a no show in 1978, top Washington reporters could hardly believe their ears. Was this a White House spokesman insulting them so roundly?

Jody said, "President Carter wanted very much to be here tonight—after all, he seldom has the occasion to dine with an institution held in lower esteem than—." He did not finish that sentence but let it dangle in the air, then added, "Unfortunately, time does not permit me to say all the things that are regrettable about the White House correspondents."

The press is not intimidated by presidents, let alone mere presidential press secretaries, and Aldo Beckman, Washington bureau chief for the *Chicago Tribune,* and president of the National Press Club, gave back as good as he got.

"Good taste forbids me from reminding Jody," Aldo said, "who the last President was who wouldn't have dinner with us.

"One year he flew to Honolulu to avoid us and another year he scheduled a presidential press conference the evening of our dinner—in Phoenix, Arizona." He paused as a ripple went around the room of reporters reminding each other this had been Lyndon Johnson before he retired.

Aldo continued, "But this is the first time we have lost a president because he was exhausted by an SEC report."

Uneasy laughter exploded in the room.

But Aldo Beckman wasn't finished with Powell yet. "The President has been in office for fifteen months and has already scheduled his fourth overseas trip," he began innocently enough. "Since presidents traditionally increase foreign travel when their popularity slips at home, the American people may never see him again."

It did tend to clear the air. At this writing, there is a happier relationship between the press and their chief *warden,* Jody Powell.

Powell is still leaning on humor, for which the *inmates* are duly grateful. For example, reporters at Camp David during the Sadat-Begin high-level conference were to see that the American

President was using a bicycle for his "shuttle diplomacy" between the Egyptian and the Israeli leaders.

Jody Powell turned aside the reporters' snide remarks about the dignity of the mode of transportation. Commenting on a photograph of the President on a bicycle, he said, "You'll notice the photograph has been carefully cropped so it is not possible to tell there are trainer wheels."

The White House connection has not hurt presidential press secretaries. George Reedy, who left LBJ, became a college dean of journalism at Marquette University.

Another LBJ protégé, Bill Moyers was first rumored to be the heir apparent to *Newsday,* of which he was editor. The story, according to John Davis, who wrote about the Guggenheims as well as the Bouviers, is that Harry Guggenheim, owner of the newspaper changed his will after Moyers opposed the sale of *Newsday* to the Los Angeles Times Mirror Co.

According to Davis, Moyers wanted to sell it to a liberal publisher, which annoyed his benefactor.

Pierre Salinger started a new life in Paris, after his Kennedy years, complete with a new French wife—the life around JFK was credited with competing with his previous marriage. Press Club members frequently see Pierre as he travels back and forth between Paris and the States.

George Christian went back to Texas with LBJ and stayed with the LBJ school and library, where he is today.

Jim Hagerty, Club members were happy to see, did very well for himself in becoming a vice-president at ABC in New York.

Ron Nessen—Jerry Ford's man who tried to help him back for a second term, turned to columning.

Jerry terHorst, his predecessor, is back in the writing game, writing a column which appears in his old alma mater, the *Detroit News.*

William Safire, President Nixon's former speech writer, has now added the luster of a Pultizer Prize for his reportage on Bert Lance, Carter's budget director, and Lance's personal financial problems.

Vice-presidential press aides do pretty well too, sometimes even better than presidential ones. Vic Gold, for example, who helped Spiro Agnew make up all those nasties, such as "the effete press," has made his fortune as a fiction writer.

Many a reporter has made a good living on the juicy

subject of Jacqueline Bouvier Kennedy Onassis, including my own coauthor, Fran Leighton, who even got mileage on a book on Jackie's "little dressmaker," Mini Rhea. But the current big money-maker is Kitty Kelly, a former newspaper and magazine reporter, who acknowledged her debt to Frannie's coauthored books in her own book and in person at a National Press Club party—*I Was Jacqueline Kennedy's Dressmaker* with Rhea and *My Life With Jacqueline Kennedy* with Mary Barelli Gallagher.

When a *Washington Post* reporter asked Kitty what the most exciting thing was that had happened to her at the party, she said, "I've just met Frances Leighton at last."

Jackie Kennedy herself has not yet written her own memoir but she has gravitated to the written word, as an editor, first for Viking and then for Doubleday, actually helping to bring out several books.

Gloria Steinem, who went to interview her for *Ms.*, was startled to find Jackie happily crawling around the floor to work out a picture layout for one of the books!

Nixon has proven more valuable out of the White House than in. In addition to making a fortune for Woodward and Bernstein, elevating the *Washington Post* to a superpower, elevating his speech writer William Safire to a *New York Times* columnist, enabling his aides to recycle their transgressions and tribulations into best-selling books and movies, Nixon himself is still trying to be the leader of the pack.

His book cost more and was heralded as "the ultimate truth." So carefully was this treasure handled that the manuscript was delivered to the publisher with greatest security measures. Reporters had a field day at the Club pub when it leaked out that even a letter of instructions concerning the manuscript was cut in half and could not be deciphered until a courier had delivered the second half.

But in spite of all the trumpeting and beating of drums, Nixon's book was upstaged by leaks from his aides, whose books were best-sellers overshadowing his own.

24/Walking Around With Reporters

Looming on its wooded slope, the Capitol is the real center of power, unlike presidents, who come and go. Against the eastern sky, the ornate dome gleams in the sun like a huge wedding cake.

The statue at the top stands with her back toward the city that was supposed to have been on high ground beyond, rather than in the lowlands to the west.

North of the dome is the Senate and to the south the House, each topped with a flagpole where flies Old Glory when the respective chamber is in session. The Capitol has become a mighty bureaucracy.

Two Senate office buildings are packed with people and a third is under construction. On the House side, three office buildings are filled and spilling into two annexes. Across the plaza is the Library of Congress, reaching for more space. The library finally got a stunning new building—some say the best architectural structure on the Hill. It was almost gobbled up by the House of Representatives, demanding it be converted to more offices.

One thing is in common throughout this beehive of humanity. In a roundabout way, the job of everyone on Capitol Hill is dependent on public good will in that every one of the 435 congressmen must run for reelection every two years and each of the 100 senators every six years. In turn every employee's job is dependent on the goodwill of some legislator. If he goes, a dozen or more staffers go.

So for most, every day is part of a never-ending popularity contest that each member and his staff are out to win. Of course, some of the old hard-shells, whose seats are uncontested through the years, may tend to get crotchety. Here and there an aide may become self-important. But the eager wish of most is to please all comers. One never knows by looking who may be important. So everybody is important.

That is why Capitol Hill is the friendliest place in the world. Walk across the Capitol plaza and a cop waves you through a red light. Show your briefcase at the guard desk in the entrance hall and you are passed with a cheery good morning. Go to a congressman's office and the receptionist lights up like a neon sign.

The great man himself gives you a hearty handshake. So much is routine but the feeling is real and the friendships you make are lasting.

For reporters the Hill is a happy hunting ground. Usually they come not as adversaries, as in the White House, but as working partners. Every congressman lives by publicity. He pays heavily for it in campaign years and between times is grateful for every favorable mention he can get to keep his name before the voters.

As a source of news, Congress not only encompasses every branch of government through legislative and money bills but its staffers are in close touch with the federal agencies they oversee. More inside news originates here than from any other place.

Capitol Hill has its own rules for reporters. Just as women in Congress may not wear their hats on the floor, so must female reporters take off their headgear when they are watching the proceedings from the press gallery.

Though congressmen may take a little snooze on the floor of the House or Senate, no one is permitted to fall asleep in the galleries. This is considered disrespectful to the often-sleeping lawmakers below. The press room off the press gallery is not as jovial as it used to be. You seldom see a card game anymore. Now that reporters are being paid a living wage and more, editors, perhaps unreasonably, expect them to rush around and follow a story wherever it takes them, it is not enough to just sit in the gallery taking notes.

Top Hill reporters cover Congress like a city hall. Early in the morning they make the rounds, stopping in the offices of congressmen in their newspapers' area, congressional leaders, no matter what part of the country they are from, and the offices of staff members of congressional committees. Here and there they share coffee, sometimes laced with a little booze to get the blood flowing.

As many Hill reporters attest, if you don't make the rounds and show you are interested on a day-to-day basis, you are not the one who will be called when something important happens, or, better yet, *before* it happens. That kind of marching around results in a reporter becoming known as an investigative reporter.

The phrase, "a nose for news" is a good one; a good reporter learns to sniff out trouble. He should be able to walk through a room and sense news through his pores.

Reporters are luckier than lobbyists on Capitol Hill. They can grab a congressman as he comes from the House floor, but a lobbyist must stand at a certain distance from the door so that a congressman has the option of whether or not to be bothered with him. Now and then senators and congressmen refuse to talk to a reporter who has been writing unfavorable stories about them, but most legislators learn to grit their teeth and still smile and answer questions.

Every once in a while, a reporter inadvertently does a good deed. Eric Ruff was going to do a story on the mood in the office of a defeated congressman.

An Oklahoma congressman had just lost in the primaries and had suddenly become a lame duck. "I walked into the congressman's office about ten o'clock the morning after his defeat and it was like a morgue. I had it from three different people that the congressman had threatened his staff before the primary that if he lost he would fire everybody.

"He had called long distance just before I had arrived and had talked to each person on the staff and told them they were through, they told me. But, they said they could not be quoted because they needed to find new jobs and did not want to arouse the boss's ire and get a bad job recommendation.

"I promised that I would not mention them but would seek confirmation elsewhere."

Eric could not reach the congressman at the district headquarters but he did locate a relative who said flatly, "There's no truth to the rumor."

"Have you talked to the congressman today?" Eric pursued.

The relative admitted he hadn't but said he was sure there could not be any truth to such a rumor.

Eric was in the press room on Capitol Hill when his office called saying the congressman wanted to talk to him.

"I called the Hilton Inn in Tulsa," Ruff recalls, "and after a couple of minutes on hold he came on and I told him what I had. He said there had been a mistake. I said, 'The information I have is that you will keep one girl to answer phones and everyone else is out of the office by September first.'

"The congressman assured me that he had no intention

of firing anyone, he was not pushing anyone out, and he had only meant that they were free to start looking for other jobs since he would be out as of January first."

Grinning about it, Ruff says, "All I know is I had calls from the staff thanking me and I told them no thanks were necessary, I was just doing my job."

Some reporters on Capitol Hill switch and become public relations men for congressmen and senators. Malvina Stephenson, an Oklahoma reporter, worked for a while on the staff of the late Senator Robert S. Kerr of Oklahoma.

She helped him develop a weekly newsletter for printing in the home state papers. It was one of the first such newsletters and one that many Hill press aides credit with having started a trend.

The newsletter Malvina and Kerr turned out ran heavily to humor. For example, after being invited to a White House luncheon by the new President, Eisenhower, Kerr's column started with, "I climbed the social ladder, but fell off my diet."

A little later the humor turned to sharp barbs against Republicans in strategic positions. As Malvina Stephenson reveals, "Finally, the then-New Hampshire Senator Styles Bridges advised Senator Kerr that if he wanted to get appropriations for his prized water projects, he had better tone down his jibes at Ike and the Republicans in general.

"Kerr wanted to be able to deliver the water projects he had promised his constituents. Hence, our column lost much of its spice for me, and we were reduced to more prosaic reports of the senator's accomplishments for the home folks."

Malvina eventually went back to newspaper writing but in looking back on her years with Kerr, she is proud to have coedited the senator's book on the development of natural resources, titled with his campaign slogan, *Land, Wood and Water*.

Reporters who cover Capitol Hill sometimes are let in on the wild things that go on. One reporter recalls when it was Senator Goldwater's birthday. Barry Goldwater was on the Floor and a page came down the aisle to tell him there was a call for him from the President.

President Ford was in office at the time so it was right and fitting that he, a Republican, should acknowledge the older man's seniority. Goldwater ambled back to the Republican cloakroom and picked up a phone.

"Hello, Mr. President," he boomed. A strange voice said, "Senator Goldwater, you are a motherfucker," and the phone was abruptly hung up. Goldwater went stumbling back to his seat, his expression best described as "stormy."

Reporters who got the whole story later from a staff member rolled in their gallery seats with laughter, especially as they learned the mystery voice had been that of Goldwater's friend Senator John Tower of Texas, the jokester of the Senate.

I do not believe a reporter can really understand the workings of Congress without having been intimate—verbally or otherwise—with Hill secretaries. In years past, their numbers were fewer but liaisons were easier. As staffs were small, offices were unoccupied after hours. And there were leather couches.

The tall doors in the Senate Office Building had locks that worked in three positions. On the open setting, one could enter by turning the knob; on the second with a key; and on the third no intrusions.

Big electric clocks on the wall went a minute at a time. A newsman I know was deployed on a senator's couch with a redhead, apprehensive about interruptions. The clock gave an extra loud tick that startled him so they were uncoiled. The redhead soon corrected this. They were up and away before the senator returned.

The Hill, never a hotbed of chastity, has become a lively place since the sexual revolution. The great increase in personnel and the accent on women in responsible jobs brings hordes of above-average career girls who crave more action than they can get from jaded congressmen and staff men who go home to their wives.

Girls looking for dates and to be taken home are plentiful at after-hours parties held in Committee rooms, such as the Friday meeting of POETS—Piss on Everything, Tomorrow's Saturday.

One of my friends was pursued by an eager chick as he left to call home. She burst into the phone booth, unzipped him, and performed an unladylike act before he could protest.

Another staff man was sent to the Democratic Club to get salads for lunch and was gobbled in the cloakroom while the greens wilted. Such goings-on are a passing fad, I trust.

Anyhow the Hill is a more fruitful place for news than the Press Club bar. Waxing lyrical, I wrote the following to be sung to a Gilbert and Sullivan tune at a meeting of the Bull Elephants Club of Republican aides.

> *Three little girls from the Hill are we*
> *Ready to say that we will, all three.*
> *We can perform with skill, you'll see,*
> *Three little girls from the Hill*
>
> *We can't type and we can't spell*
> *We don't answer phones so well,*
> *But we kiss and seldom tell,*
> *Three little girls from the Hill.*
>
> *Three little girls who quite unwary*
> *Took to the trade of secretary;*
> *Found what it meant was secret—tarry,*
> *Three little girls from the Hill.*
>
> *Three little girls from the Hill, that's us.*
> *We make love without a fuss,*
> *Even in manners curious,*
> *Three little girls from the Hill.*
>
> *Just as long as we draw pay,*
> *We will never say nay-nay.*
> *Love will always find a way.*
> *Three little girls from the Hill.*
>
> *We are ready, willing, able,*
> *On a desk or on a table;*
> *Ready, willing, that's our label,*
> *Three little girls from the Hill.*

And from yonder Hill, I hear a hearty Amen.

The gang who cover the Pentagon are perhaps the most reserved, even antisocial. They do not have a club like the White House gang, which meets once a year for a banquet, and they do not play poker as they wait for a newsbreak.

Each keeps to himself. Yet they are not totally without a sense of humor. The story is told about the *Baltimore Sun's* defense reporter, Mark Watson, who became angry at how the press corps was being treated by Robert McNamara, then Secretary of Defense.

When he could take it no longer, Watson rose at a press conference and yelled, "Mr. Secretary, this means war!"

Probably the hardest beat in all of Washington is the

Supreme Court. In that august edifice reporters get no advance releases on how a decision will go.

They must be ready to jump two ways. They must be able to glance at a decision and race to dictate a story, making it exciting, in contrast to the dry-as-bones legal style in which the decisions are usually written.

But even that is an oversimplification. There are decisions and dissents. Take the Bakke Decision of August 1978, which ordered a California medical school to admit a white student, Allan Bakke, on grounds they had discriminated against him because of his color.

When that decision was handed down, reporters were faced with six separate opinions, some of them covering 150 pages. The decisions were handed out just after 10:00 A.M. and at 10:05 the first wire service bulletin was flashed around the world. Such speed-writing takes a sharp mind and steady nerves.

It wasn't always that frantic. In the days of Charles Evans Hughes, justices read their opinions and no reporter was permitted to leave the chamber until the justice was finished.

Finally they rebelled, but now they have the opposite extreme and suffer in a different way. The great hope of reporters who must cover the Supreme Court is that some compromise could be reached, such as giving the reporters one hour to scan the decisions before the release hour.

Charlotte Moulton of UPI knows what it's like on the toughest beat because she covered the Supreme Court for many years, starting back in the forties, when she was "a tube stuffer" for the United Press. This meant that she waited in the chamber at noon each Monday until each decision was handed down and quickly popped it into a pneumatic tube to be sped to the UPI senior reporter waiting in the press room. It was a lowly job equivalent to copy girl.

The case Charlotte remembers most vividly was the 1954 School Desegregation Decision which the world had been waiting for.

By this time Charlotte was no longer stuffing tubes but dictating the stories herself over the direct line to the UPI office.

"As Chief Justice Earl Warren announced '*Brown* versus *Board of Education*,'" Moulton recalls, "no pages came through the tube. Of all times, the Chief Justice had decided to read the whole decision aloud.

"Fortunately UPI reporter Ruth Gmeiner Frandsen was

helping me that day up in the chamber. She began madly taking notes and shoving cylinders down the tube but it was not until Warren had virtually finished reading that it could be said with certainty that a radically dual system was unconstitutional.

"Apparently Warren believed the dignity of the occasion required reading the entire opinion before copies were distributed. We reporters would certainly have preferred it otherwise.

"Supreme Court routine is different now. There are no reporters' desks in the chamber, no pneumatic tubes, no five-foot booths. All opinions are released through the press office and wire service reporters file their stories by computer terminal.

"Chief Justice Warren Burger has given the press an assist by ordering the official head notes added prior to the initial release of each opinion. This makes it easier to grasp the import quickly.

"Time has marched on. But those tube-stuffing days remain a nightmare."

As we go to press, Charlotte is looking toward retirement. She'll be hard to replace since even the justices have a special regard for her expertise.

As Justice Lewis Powell said at a reception for her at the Supreme Court, "She's been here longer than any justice on the Court and I suspect she knows as much as anyone on the Court."

Walking around with Warren Weaver is a special treat. He is one of the most popular newspapermen in Washington, has covered politics for many years and currently covers the Supreme Court.

Weaver is a thirty-year man with the *New York Times,* a fact he calls "some kind of record for mutual tolerance." He remembers his first day with the *New York Times* very well.

"On my first day, voters were choosing between Dewey and Truman, but I was assigned to cover a Manhattan delicatessen opening where the owner's report of rioting among eager customers proved without basis.

"The next day, my first real story, was a fare increase hearing for Fifth Avenue buses, populated by Dewey civil servants on the State Public Service Commission and corporation lawyers; when a boy stuck his head in the door shortly after eleven A.M. and said, 'Truman won,' *all* faces fell."

Warren has seen a lot of history made in the thirty years

since then but the particular scene he cannot erase from his mind was one horrible night in 1968.

"Probably my most dramatic story was the Bob Kennedy assassination," he recalls. "I was one of four or five *Times* reporters on the scene at the time for the California primary, and I dictated about two-thirds of our story by telephone to New York with much assistance from my colleagues. I guess the highlight was dictating a description of Sirhan—we had no identification until considerably later—as a knot of police carried him past me; it was the only time I ever felt that I was beating television on a story.

"One of the few comforting aspects was to realize, afterward, that you could carry on with your own job under the severest kind of emotional and time pressure; until it happens, you never know."

Warren Weaver's most embarrassing moment dates back to 1962. "As a newcomer to Washington, I boarded an elevator at the -Justice Department and said, 'Four, please' to the stocky black-suited man standing at the control panel.

"He pushed my button, and when I got off, I discovered to my dismay that he was J. Edgar Hoover."

What is fame? Some reporters are remembered for a particular story—but Warren Weaver has a most unusual niche in the reporters' unofficial hall of fame.

Warren says, "I will probably be best remembered as the author of the Weaver Rule: When reporters are traveling together in a taxi on an out-of-town story, the one in the front seat pays—or the outside one in front if you're really crowded.

"It was developed purely for convenience, then developed into a fairly hazardous sport involving speed, body blocks, and agility. With some regularity, all over the country, I discover reporters disembarking from cabs with those in the back joyfully shouting, "Weaver Rule!"

"A *Times* colleague of mine swears it was invoked on him in Lebanon. I occasionally arbitrate domestic disputes involving the Rule that are called to my attention, but I have no overseas jurisdiction."

But seriously, Weaver has had impact on government in his time. His book, *Both Your Houses,* was required reading for the staff of Senator Humphrey's office.

"Among the reform recommendations proposed in the

book which Congress has since adopted," Warren says with pride, are, "a considerable relaxation, if not abolition, of the seniority system, better Senate filibuster controls, open committee hearings and markups, codes of ethics for members, the new congressional budget system, a strengthened congressional foreign policy role (some now say too strong), public financing of presidential campaigns—but so far not congressional ones.

"My book was obviously only one factor in achieving these advances, but I take satisfaction in the possibility that it had some influence, particularly on budget reform."

It's an intimidating experience for a reporter going to the White House for the first time. It's intimidating in fact, the first hundred times.

If one doesn't have a special press pass hanging from one's neck, as the regulars do, one is subjected to the humiliating experience of standing outside the little gatehouse at the entrance, in full earshot of one's colleagues, and having to give one's age and other identifying data in a good loud voice into the microphone.

Even when this data is on file—as it is for those who come more than once—the charade must be played out. Reporters must stand and wait in the rain until all the points have been verified—and it is seldom done quickly.

Worst of all is the intimidating, stony expressions of the gatehouse guards, who feel that friendliness would be *declassé*.

But once past their scrutiny, a buzzer rings, releasing a small gate, which enables the reporter to enter the White House grounds. As the reporter passes the gatehouse door, he or she is handed a temporary pass to clip to his or her clothing.

But the grounds are beautiful. The White House looms ahead, pillared and beautifully proportioned, and a certain joy and pride wells up in one's chest.

It's worth it after all!

Unfortunately, reporters do not go up to that pillared entrance, but to a small, inconspicuous entrance between the West Wing and the mansion, proper.

Enter and you are standing where the old White House swimming pool used to be. Nixon had it covered over and made into the press quarters, far from his own. Before Nixon, reporters used to be stationed in the West Wing, where they could watch every visitor coming and going to the Oval Office.

Reporters are not happy about losing their access to the President's visitors.

They blame Nixon's hostility toward the press for this step backward. Nixon didn't want nosey reporters sizing up and buttonholing his guests. And so presidents present and future will be influenced by this quirk of Nixon's—and, of course, so will reporters.

The public seldom gets to see the byplay and the many funny or touching little things that happen when the President receives visitors. But the White House press corps see and sometimes even become participants.

One day last year when President and Mrs. Carter were receiving the Democratic Women's Club in the East Room, one of the guests, a little elderly, nervous lady with a small camera, planted herself among the press and cameramen to take pictures and insisted that one of them was in her way.

She had chosen as the object of her ire John M. Szostak, one of the feistiest reporters, who had even sued a newspaper when he didn't like their treatment of him. Pow! She hit Szostak over the head with her camera so hard that it fell apart and exposed her film.

Now the little lady resorted to tears, and John, who in his pain didn't know whether to laugh at her misfortune or cry with her, settled for, "You see, God punishes little ladies who hit correspondents over the head."

But when his pain stopped and the lady's tears didn't, John found himself offering to send her a set of pictures to replace her loss—which he did.

After getting his own pictures of the President and Rosalynn greeting the club bigwigs, Szostak realized that the little old lady had made him late to the press briefing in the West Wing, and all the other press had left.

Since reporters are not permitted to wander around the White House alone, a Secret Service agent escorted John down and around a complicated route that took them outside to get from one wing to the other.

Szostak was feeling a little used and abused and pressured when something happened that changed his day. As he strode outside on the south portico and prepared to enter the

White House via the diplomatic entrance, he realized that he was being given the "Hail to the Chief" ovation from a group of high school band students.

They were from Georgia, and it was obvious that they had mistaken John for the President. There is a slight resemblance in size and sunny smile but to top it off, both Carter and Szostak were wearing almost identical blue pin-striped suits and ties that day.

Everyone laughed as the band leader and those who signal that the President is approaching realized the mistake and stopped the music.

John Szostak, for his part, laughed as he played the role of President Carter for a few moments, holding up his hand and saying, "No speech today," and then, on inspiration adding, "I shall not run—for a second term."

Among the regulars who cover the White House there are specialists. Some always ask questions about foreign policy. Some specialize in the President's economic policy. Some gauge the President's popularity from week to week and some concentrate on First Ladies.

Malvina Stephenson, who has her own bureau, specializes in presidential hometowns.

Such a hometown buff is she, that she even visits and studies the hometowns of the losing candidates in a presidential election. Because of this hobby, when a man finally becomes president, Malvina knows his character perhaps better than anyone else in the White House press room.

This penchant of hers for rooting around among the people who know a candidate best, makes her a delightful dinner companion when the conversation veers—as it always does—to what a presidential family is really like.

At this writing Malvina's sparkling chatter centers on Plains: for example, "President Carter's little village may be the seediest-looking of all hometowns, but the people there are the most colorful and entertaining. I have always said, if the President loses out in politics next election, *The Carter Family* would be an all-time hit on TV. All they have to do is play themselves."

Malvina, who is acknowledged to be the greatest expert on Plains among the press corp, first spotted the news potential of the town very early in 1976, when Carter had barely begun his race.

How did she go about becoming intimate with the town when she was in Washington and it was in Georgia? "I subscribed to the local *Americus Times-Recorder.* I became conversant about the local news and the personalities who carried weight. Eventually I went there.

"I think I had the first story on 'Miss Allie' Smith, Rosalynn Carter's mother."

There comes a time in a campaign when relatives and candidates' immediate families suddenly stop talking, because they eventually get gun-shy. Malvina, knowing this inevitable occurrence in every campaign, probed each Carter family member while they were still telling what was on their minds.

Jeff Carter, the candidate's son, told her, "I am going to live at the White House. I'm never going back to Plains."

Malvina stepped up her stories on his family and friends.

"During one rainy day in suburban Virginia," she recalls, "I interviewed Rosalynn in the back seat between campaign stops. There I first became acquainted with her then-chauffeur, a well-tailored Englishman who was their Washington representative. His name, was, of course, Peter Bourne, still comparatively anonymous and never dreaming that all this effort to help the Carters would ultimately lead him to a White House job as expert on drugs and then a front-page ouster with all sorts of embarrassment professionally and politically when he helped a White House staffer buy drugs using a fictitious name for the patient.

"I remember I began to talk to Bourne about Admiral Hyman Rickover—I had read in Jimmy's book *Why Not the Best* that Rickover gave him this slogan—Mrs. Carter made a wry face and turned to primp herself. She was combing her hair and powdering her nose. It was a little incident that stuck in my memory. She had a certain look. I always wondered if she was a bit annoyed—had Rickover been given too much credit for the book's title—or with the usual feminine vanity, was it just that she wanted to look her best for the next stop?"

What a contrast that scene was to the scene in the summer of 1978, when Malvina was in the presidential press party that went to Plains, hoping to get a look at the wedding of Billy's daughter. Now the press were definitely out and unwelcome, and Malvina laughs as she recalls, "It was amusing to see some of the

Washington TV stars dusting their heels at the roadside while the elite of Plains and environs were shuttled in style to the mansion and the wedding. But, finally, the last laugh was on the guests.

"The rains came. In torrents. All fifteen hundred guests were standing on a red clay tract the size of a football field. Only a few in front had seen anything that was happening.

"As the torrents fell, the intimate wedding group rushed to the house, leaving the hundreds of guests stranded. They had to wait until the buses could shuttle them to their cars and those that did any walking were soon dragging five pounds of clay on each shoe."

Malvina, being clever and having made all her contacts in advance, got an exclusive story about the wedding fiasco because she had prearranged to interview Brenda Jennings, who was one of the guests.

"She is a natural raconteur," Malvina says, "with a candid sense of humor and tongue loose at both ends when she gets started. So I got the true story from her. She said the guests tried to huddle for protection at the refreshment tables, but the chicken-wire roofs laced with leaves leaked like sieves. The food was swimming in water and inedible.

"By the time the women guests got to their cars, they could wring out their dresses. Her account still makes me chuckle, whenever I think of it."

Even before Malvina had tried to get a look at the wedding party from a distance, she had been given a special tour by the postmaster, Robert McGarrah, "the seventy-year-old bachelor whom the town has tried to match up with Rosalynn's mother all these years. Mrs. Allie Smith, a widow, had worked for him in the post office until retiring when she reached seventy.

"McGarrah showed me Billy's previous home, before he moved to his present mansion—a rambling frame house, dilapidated and peeling. Apparently vacant now.

"On an adjoining tract owned by Billy, with weeds and grass growing wild, stood a mobile trailer home. This was to be the residence of the couple who were getting married that afternoon—Billy's daughter and a neighbor boy, both nineteen I think."

It's not the biggest stories that White House press correspondents relate when good friends get together. Aldo Beckman, who was White House correspondent for seven years, traveling in all fifty states and making numerous foreign trips, including Nixon's China trip, turns to just a tiny nugget among his souvenirs:

"The one story I got the biggest kick out of writing, and it was hardly a blockbuster," he says, "was one that told how Ford had pounded his desk, demanding that his aides stop leaking to the press.

"The reason for my amusement was that it had been an earlier story of mine about staff dissension and White House feuds that had caused him to make his pounding demand."

Aldo, incidentally, won the 1976 Merriman Smith Award for his deadline coverage of the San Francisco assassination attempt against Ford.

Walk with Bill Hill and you start to get a feeling for White House history. William Hill, who was for forty-three years writer, editor, and managing editor of the *Washington Star*, remembers the time he first went on the desk as an assistant editor and, being green, broke the release date on a White House story.

It was the story of the day, President Herbert Hoover okaying the Reconstruction Finance program, for which FDR would later take credit.

The word came from the White House that the President was furious and wanted to see the man who broke the release date. Hill was to come to the Oval Office at 8:00 A.M.

Poor Bill suffered through the rest of the day and hardly slept that night, almost feeling the axe on his neck. Not only had he broken a release date, but for beginner's luck it had to be one that affected the President of the United States.

Long before light the next morning Bill was at the White House, standing with quaking knees, waiting for doom. When he was ushered into Hoover's presence in the Oval Office, the *Star's* White House correspondent, who had come along, introduced him in a way that made it no easier. "This is Bill Hill, who broke the release date on Reconstruction Finance, Mr. President."

As Hill, now representative of *Editor and Publisher*, tells the story today, with a little smile, "Hoover turned in his chair and looked out the window for what felt like five minutes, but must have been only a few seconds, while I stood with awe and fear on legs that had turned to jelly.

"Then Hoover turned and said in a tired small voice, 'It doesn't matter.'

"And that was it. I walked out with brisk steps. Reprieve."

How different FDR was from Herbert Hoover was evident the day that the *Washington Post* made a *little* mistake in a headline. The President had gotten sick and the *Post* headline said, "FDR in Bed with Coed."

It was the bulldog edition. Barry Sullivan was the reporter who happened to pick up the phone at the city desk to find FDR himself on the phone.

He was sure he was in for a dressing down. Instead the famous voice asked jovially, "Can I get a hundred copies of the bulldog edition? I plan to send them to all my friends."

Reporters who remember covering Harding at the White House are very few.

John Draper Erwin, the dean of the National Press Club, who, at ninety-six, still comes to the Club every day for dinner and a chat with "the boys," well remembers the days of wine, roses, and Harding. "I covered the Harding scandal," he likes to reminisce as Club members a third his age gather round.

"I just ran across a letter from the managing editor of the *New York Evening World* saying my coverage of the Teapot Dome scandal was by far the best."

Reporters who care about such things can get Erwin, whom they call Ambassador, because he was named the Ambassador to Honduras in FDR's administration after his newspaper days, to go through all the ins and outs of that old predecessor to Watergate—how Gifford Pinchot's office boy, Harry, was really an undercover man, keeping the boss informed on all kinds of shady doings, and how Senator Albert B. Fall lived high, wide, and handsome.

But what the "boys" in the Club like best is hearing about the life of a White House reporter back in the Harding and Coolidge days, and when, they ask Erwin, did he become a member of the Club?

The Ambassador does not exactly recall the date of his joining. "I'd say it must have been about 1910."

As for the Harding days, Erwin remembers how one ambitious reporter waited hidden across the street from Ned McLean's home, where Harding liked to drink and play poker, and saw him come out at 5:00 A.M. after a night of carousing.

"For Harding's press conferences, we always stood

around his desk at the White House, popping questions. I would just call out whatever question I thought of," Erwin recalls. "We never sat down. It was not considered respectful to sit in the presence of a President. I remember Frank Kent, the *Baltimore Sun* reporter, said he never asked a question of Harding. It made him nervous."

Erwin was there when Harding was sworn into office on the specially built platform outside the U.S. Capitol, and remembers Mrs. Harding, especially.

"She had eyes sharp enough to see a woman faint way in the audience down below. She kept motioning to a guard to go to that woman, because she was going to fall."

Did Erwin know that President Harding and his wife were not happy together? "I never saw her crack a smile," the dean of the Press Club says. "Harding was a henpecked husband. We all knew that. And Mrs. Harding knew the kind of husband she had.

"She knew he gambled and had dealings with fast women. Among the press he had a bad reputation. She was trying to protect him."

Erwin recalls that after Harding was taken sick in Alaska, his secretary, George Christian, tried to keep it out of the press. The press fellows knew Harding was sick because of what happened one day when they were playing dice on shipboard. As Erwin tells it, "Harding walked by and one fellow said, 'Mr. President, do you want to join the game?'

"Harding said, 'No, I'm not feeling at all well, It's my stomach.' If Harding didn't want to play cards, he was really sick.

"A telegram was sent to the Palace Hotel at San Francisco to have lodging ready for the President. They put him to bed and he never got up again.

"An AP man had a tip about how bad off the President was. He tied up the line to Washington so no one else could use the phone. He was lucky because he had a brother who worked for the telephone company. So AP had a newsbreak hours before anyone could get through that Harding was very sick."

One question that reporters asked Erwin was whether the rumor was true that Harding had Negro blood. "I remember that. There was a story that his grandfather was black or had some black blood. One day a political reporter asked Harding right out, 'Is it true about you having black blood in your family?'

"Harding answered crossly, 'How would I know if one of

my ancestors crossed the line?' And that's all that was said at the time. The reporter did not pursue it." As Erwin recalls, this particular reporter called Harding by his first name, Warren. Harding was the kind of President whose friends could call him by his first name."

When Coolidge inherited the presidency, after Harding's death, there were all kinds of stories about how cheap Cal was, Erwin says, recalling, "He had rented a house in the suburbs for twenty-seven dollars a month. He liked to squeeze the dollar."

Coolidge was not much use to the reporters, according to the old correspondent of the *New York Evening World*. "I don't recall that Coolidge ever said a memorable thing at a press conference. We called him Silent Cal, and it wasn't meant as a compliment. He never helped the press. He was not a mixer. Only two reporters got his ear—both were with Boston papers."

As Erwin recalls it, "The only exciting thing that happened in the Coolidge administration was the exposure of the scandals of the Harding administration."

In White House reportorial lore, President Grover Cleveland became the first president to talk to a reporter on the phone. It happened accidentally. An enterprising journalist, excited by the installation of telephones, phoned the White House and was amazed to have it answered by the President himself.

It's too bad there weren't tape recorders to record the whole conversation but, as the story goes, the startled reporter had the presence of mind to ask if the President had any news to report.

Talk with White House reporters and you are rewarded with vignettes of history.

Reporters could come in and out of the White House freely in the old, easy days before tight security. The first President to give them their own quarters there was Theodore Roosevelt.

The ebullient Teddy would talk to newsmen while in the barber chair being shaved. Never pretending to be impartial, he deplored muckrakers and fed news to his own pet reporters known around town as "Teddy's fair-haired boys."

Styles of dealing with the press varied with personalities of the Presidents. Once when Woodrow Wilson was pursued on the golf course by the press pack, the Secret Service men told them that they could go in a toolshed and watch or shoot their pictures by holding their cameras up to knotholes. Once inside they were locked in, and there were no knotholes.

It's pleasant to look back and see how press and presidents have fussed and feuded with each other and to realize it isn't necessary for them to love each other to have an effective government. Joe Alsop said it best when he told Joy Billington of the *Washington Star*:

"It seems to me ridiculous to judge presidents the way we appear now to judge them. Presidents are like plumbing fixtures. What matters is that they flush. I don't give a goddamn whether the plumbing fixtures are orchid color, white, or black as long as they do flush. And, as a president, Nixon was quite effective. He was also half crazy. [However], if the fixture flushes, it's a perfectly satisfactory plumbing fixture."

Reporters knew but never told how certain presidents felt about the churches they attended. FDR, for example, was an Episcopalian but was mad at the hierarchy of the church and so he stayed away from the famed Washington Cathedral. Instead, he found an excuse to go to the little Episcopal church in Alexandria. One day FDR was there squirming a little as the preacher felt called upon to lecture the President on what he considered his Christian attitude should be.

The press sat squirming too, for other reasons, and taking a few notes in their seats right behind the President. Suddenly Fred Pasley of the *New York Daily News*, who wasn't the soberest of men, could take it no longer and stood up and shouted one word, "Bullshit!"

The next day Steve Early, the presidential press secretary, who had been hearing all the versions of the story, which was the talk of the press room, went in to see the President.

"Well, I suppose we should take away his credentials," he commented.

"Certainly not," FDR exclaimed. "It *was* bullshit."

An Afterword From
Your Native Guides

Our tour of Washington pressdom ends here. As your native guides, we two writers did not introduce ourselves at the outset but simply invited you to come with us and see for yourself. Now let us add a few words about our own experiences.

Between us we have engaged in almost every phase of reporting. I, Kendall King Hoyt, have written for newspapers, magazines, newsletters, and house organs; was a columnist and commentator. Aside from news work, I did publicity, sales promotion, political campaigns, and lobbying; managed national associations; served in the Air Force; traveled as an organizer; was a civil engineer; dug ditches; and once was assistant to a buzz saw operator.

Frances Spatz Leighton covers the Washington scene for Sunday supplements reaching many millions. She has a flock of books to her credit, including some that set the dogs barking for having exposed the private lives of the great. She writes features about celebrities for women's magazines; did television shows; is a talented artist, decorator, and gourmet cook. She knows more than I about the White House and other essentials to our story.

Fran is a human-interest writer, dealing with the lives and involvements of people. I am more concerned with the flow of events toward some line of action. There is not much of that in our book; so little can be done to change the press corps. One can only try to understand it.

If you want to know how people get into such work, there is no set way. The best start is a desire to write. When still in baby dresses, I was eager to learn the alphabet and scrawled words in childish print as my mother spelled them. The first money I made was from a prize essay about how I invented a toy cannon that made a big bang.

In high school, a poem I wrote attracted girls who thought I must be soulful, one of the hazards of authorship. In college, I wanted to be editor of the school magazine but was business manager.

Since my dad was an engineer, that is what I was trained to be, stifling any creative urge until, by chance, I became a writer after all. From there I went to publicity and promotion, moving easily from one role to another.

Press people are supposed to write objectively, not to be swayed in heart or mind by any feelings of their own. But I think those who have been participants in life can see with more depth than mere onlookers.

My exposure to Washington was early; I was born four blocks from the Capitol. Most people here seem to be from other parts of the country. I do not know what became of the hundreds of natives in school with me.

My father was a bureaucrat who supervised the measurement of river flow and traveled among his district offices. Our house was on the crest of a rise overlooking the city. I could see the Capitol and Washington Monument from my window. We were on a street of scientists, remote from the comings and goings of those transient officials who pretended to run the country.

My only visit to the White House as a child was at a reception by President Taft. As he took my tiny hand, he loomed like an elephant. I could not have imagined that thirty-odd years later I would direct publicity for his son's presidential campaign.

Outside on the lawn each Easter Monday, children came to the fertility rite known as egg-rolling. We brought baskets of boiled eggs we had dyed in bright colors. We knocked them together and forfeited those that broke. One boy cheated with a china egg. Nothing as dishonest since has happened at the White House, of course.

My only trip to the Capitol was with the daughter of a congressman. We viewed his bald head as he came to the Floor. I was not there again till I sat in the press gallery.

Before the First World War, New York was still the center of power and Washington was a sleepy village. It was surrounded by woods that could be reached in minutes. With other lads I camped on a Potomac island. We hunted with rifles and ran naked as little Indians.

It is hard to believe that such great change has come in one lifetime. My dad took me to see Wilbur Wright fly. The plane was a noisy contraption of fabric and wires. A horse reared and a lady fainted as horses and ladies did in those days.

The city then had gone from horse cars to electric trolleys but private transportation was mostly horse-drawn. The

402

small town where I spent my summers, out of the Washington heat, was almost wholly so.

My folks were from upstate New York. I am a tenth-generation American of English stock except for an Irish great-grandmother, whose heritage might explain why I try to write liltingly now and then. Several of my ancestors marched in George Washington's Army instead of sensibly staying home.

My father's forebears were carriage makers. Grandpa went to California to look for gold. I have a bottle of black sand with yellow specks, probably all he found. On my mother's side were land speculators who owned farms and built big white houses.

My great-grandfather was a doctor who had a jar of leeches and concocted his own patent medicine. After he went to deliver a baby or set a broken leg, his old horse brought him home. I have his diploma saying after his sixty-day course he was a doctor of medicine.

My great-uncle rang the church bell and was the village painter. He had an enlarged thumbnail he used as a scraper. So much for professionalism.

The point in telling this is that if you are to evaluate my account, you need to know my viewpoint and my biases. It means something to think back to simpler times when the work ethic prevailed. God was ever present. He looked, I thought, like white-whiskered Senator Frank Hiscock who married my great-aunt.

As for drink, all in my family were teetotalers except Great-uncle Lucius. His wife often had to lead him home. Mother taught me that saloons were degrading. In what I have written about the Press Club bar, this prejudice may show where Fran has not edited it out.

Also my grandmother thought wasting money was not merely foolish; it was wicked. When I can mix a drink from my office fridge for 30 cents or so, why pay $1.45 plus tip at the Club?

Father made his start running a peanut stand at a lake resort in summer and studied civil engineering at Cornell, where I followed. After healthy outdoor work dangling on cables over rivers to measure the flow, I unexpectedly returned to Washington to write for the McGraw-Hill magazines.

Under the tutelage of the famed Paul Wooten, I was told that a news item was "like a spear with a solid shaft of facts headed by a glittering point." Given a typewriter, swivel chair, and Paul's old rolltop desk, I was supposed to become an expert in such fields as aviation, chemicals, electric street cars, food, mining, textiles, and general business. I had to judge what was news and know what was old stuff.

One of my first assignments concerned a hurricane. Like a cub reporter at his first fire, I wrote a lurid account of which building materials failed in the devastating winds. It was not printed for fear of offending advertisers of these products.

At hearings and debates in Congress, I learned that it is not always easy to find "spear points" and one must make inside contacts. Once after a closed meeting, I found a congressman who had been there and, guessing, told him I understood thus-and-so had happened. Rather surprised, he said, "Well, since you seem to know, I might as well tell you the rest."

Once when a federal agency would not give me facts I thought should be known, I got a Senate resolution passed to make the information public.

Top figures were not hard to meet in those days. I could talk with such Democrats as "Cactus" Jack Garner, soon to be Vice-President, and Cordell Hull, to be Secretary of State, then unheeded by the arrogant Republican majority. Hull, that fine gentleman, lectured me on how laws are made in smoke-filled rooms and invited me to come and see him anytime.

In the tariff hearings I saw the trade of the world pass in review and took time out to visit abroad—Europe, China, and Japan. Nothing much happened except on my Atlantic crossing the ship struck an iceberg and on the Pacific a typhoon raised sixty-foot waves.

It was easy for a young reporter to get ideas about his importance, quickly deflated when jobless. In the Depression years, I was hired to promote industrial employment measures for President Hoover's Unemployment Commission and saw the kind of incompetence that does too little. In Roosevelt's New Deal, I saw the kind that does too much.

In 1936 I worked in Chicago on the Republican National Committee staff. Some will remember how the *Literary Digest,* then a major magazine, folded after its poll predicted a Landon victory when Roosevelt was headed for a landslide.

Now I began to succeed as a reporter with a weekly tabloid-size page in the scholarly *New York Times Annalist* and a daily front-page column in the *New York Journal of Commerce*. I was rated as somewhat of an oracle but to me it was shallow. No one man can know that much.

Having to meet so many deadlines was not the way I wanted to live my life. To this day, when the phone rings at suppertime I fear it is the *Journal of Commerce* wanting another item. I was lured by the challenge of campaigns where writing was a means rather than an end in itself.

I helped Congressman Everett Dirksen, later Senate leader, in his pioneer attempt to encourage the use of alcohol in motor fuel—gasahol—still to be fully realized. As half of the two-man lobby for the Civil Aeronautics Act of 1938, to save the airlines from bankruptcy, I wrote statements for an unknown Senator named Harry S Truman. I was publicity director for the 1940 presidential campaign of Senator Robert A. Taft, one of the world's brainiest men, who would rather be wrong than President. His autographed picture hangs on my wall. I speak aloud to him and get some of the damndest answers.

A youthful dream of mine was to be beating my typewriter with a rhythm that turned into the clatter of a printing press and then to the tramp of marching feet. This came to pass. After working as manager of the National Aeronautic Association, I volunteered for the Air Force at the outset of World War II and served in the headquarters of its Civil Air Patrol, whose cadet corps I set in motion with a one-page memo. It was a proud sight to watch those wonderful youngsters marching behind the flag.

After the war, I specialized mostly in aviation. There were more bills to pass; more groups to organize; more papers to write for. I commanded an air reserve squadron, ran for the Virginia assembly, and otherwise digested samples of life.

So here I still am writing, organizing, flying out to give talks, trying to get congressmen and officials to do more for aviation, and wearing no man's collar. I work in my snug little Press Building office, go home to my house on a peninsula jutting into a residential lake, and spend weekends at my hillside place on the Blue Ridge.

I have kept all my hair, once brown and now graying; have twenty-twenty vision without glasses and stand fairly straight despite all the years bent over a typewriter.

Like so many other newspeople, I always intended to write a book but never finished one until I teamed up with Fran Leighton. It is my good fortune that she usually writes with a coauthor, though she might do better on her own.

Frannie has large green eyes, long reddish hair that

curls over her shoulders, and incredible energy. I have thought of getting her patented as a perpetual-motion machine.

She wears pantsuits and big floppy hats in vivid colors that make her recognizable from afar. Though she looks about as timid as a Bengal tiger, she has an underlying shyness and does not want much said about her here, though much could be said to her renown.

She was born on an Ohio farm, still in the family, complete with beaver pond. On her own since a teenager, she won a scholarship to Ohio State University; then joined the Hearst empire, first as a dictation girl at International News Service, then promoted to Washington correspondent of *American Weekly*, the Sunday supplement of the Hearst newspapers. She since has represented other Sunday magazines, such as *This Week*, and still writes for *Family Weekly* with multi-million circulation.

Her chief fame is from books. She was among the first to discover that the public is keenly interested in the "little people" of government as well as the biggies. Her first best-seller was *My 30 Years Backstairs at the White House*, the memoirs of a maid, recently filmed in Hollywood as a miniseries for NBC.

Another best-seller was *My Life with Jacqueline Kennedy*, with the First Lady's secretary. Others were *Dog Days at the White House*, with the President's dog keeper, and *Fishbait*, with the doorkeeper of the House. A recent book was *Cousin Beedie and Cousin Hot*, a Carter family saga with Hugh Carter, the President's cousin.

To sum up our collaboration, the book is less critical of the press than if I had written it alone. Not from any envy of these people, since I would not trade my way of life for theirs. I feel the news system needs to function better if our nation is to be well enough informed to meet the problems I fear are ahead.

Otherwise, I have reason to be glad of their failings.... Someone could have written a book like ours long before now and it would not have been left for us to do.

I am reminded of the time when I was with some fifty reporters in a big naval boat. The sailor steering it seemed to be just off the farm. I could see that he was about to bang into the dock and braced myself for the shock, while all the others stood looking the other way and had a pratfall. And there I leave them. Hah!

Bibliography

Behrens, John C. *The Typewriter Guerillas*. Chicago: Nelson-Hall Company, 1977.

Brayman, Harold. *The President Speaks Off the Record*. Princeton, N.J.: Dow Jones Books, 1976.

Chenery, William L. *Freedom of the Press*. New York: Harcourt Brace and Company, 1955.

Cheshire, Maxine, with John Greenya. *Maxine Cheshire, Reporter*. Boston: Houghton Mifflin Company, 1976.

Hoyt, Kendall K. *Ink & Avgas*. Aviation Writers Association, 1963.

Kay, Ellen. *Barbara Walters*. New York: Manor Books Inc., 1976.

Liebling, A. J. *The Press*. New York: Ballantine Books, 1961.

Means, Gaston B. as told to May Dixon Thacker. *The Strange Death of President Harding*. Washington, D.C.: Guild Press Ltd., 1930.

Moore, William T. *Dateline Chicago*. New York: Taplinger Publishing Co., Inc., 1973.

National Press Club. *shrdlu*. Washington, D.C.: Colortone Press, 1958.

Phillips, Cabell. *Dateline Washington*. Garden City, N.Y.: Doubleday & Company, Inc. 1949.

Rather, Dan, with Mickey Herskowitz. *The Camera Never Blinks*. New York: William Morrow & Co., Inc., 1977.

Roberts, Chalmers M. *The Washington Post: The First 100 Years*. Boston: Houghton Mifflin Company, 1977.

Rosten, Leo C. *The Washington Correspondents*. New York: Harcourt Brace and Company, 1937.

Stealey, O. O. *Twenty Years in the Press Gallery*. Published by author, 1906.

Steffens, Lincoln. *The Autobiography of Lincoln Steffens*. New York: Harcourt Brace and Company, 1931.

Wicker, Tom. *On Press*. New York: The Viking Press, Inc., 1978.

INDEX

Prina, Ed, 339
Prohibition, 19, 20
Project Max, 179
PR (public relations), 259–77
Pulitzer, Joseph, 93, 96, 97, 115
Pure & Simple (Burros), 153
Pyle, Ernie, 223–24, 347

Quinn, Sally, 319–20, 325–27

RCA, 276–77
Radziwill, Prince and Princess, 185
Rafshoon, Gerald, 262
Randolph, Jennings, 335
Rather, Dan, 40, 279–80, 282, 299,
    338, 360, 367, 377
Rauch, Sheila B., 352
Ray, Richard, 298
Rayburn, Sam, 16–17, 49, 50, 135
Reasoner, Harry, 278, 279, 280–81,
    289, 299, 361
Rebozo, Bebe, 77
Redding, Bill, 303
Redford, Robert, 166
Reed, Jack, 45
Reedy, George, 238, 239, 379
Regeimbal, Neil, 14–16
Reiner, Julius, 19
Reporters Committee on Freedom of
    the Press, 177
Reston, James (Scotty), 133, 146, 182,
    186, 216–17, 219, 339–40
Reuss, Henry S., 55
Rhea, Mini, 380
Richards, Ray, 347
Richardson, Elliott, 55, 266
Rickover, Hyman, 179, 393
Ridder, Walter, 340
Rigby, Cora, 72
Riley, Walter, 35, 154–58, 183, 334
Riordan, Emmet, 197
Robb, Chuck, 245
Robb, Linda Bird, 245
Robinson, Greg, 348
Rockefeller, John D., 27, 259
Rockefeller, Nelson (Rocky), 75, 312–13
Roderick, Dorrance, 308
Rogers, Bill, 336
Rogers, Warren, 40, 52–53
Rogers, Will, 60
Rolle, Bill, 137
Ronstadt, Linda, 200
Roosevelt, Eleanor, 61, 72, 88, 121, 248,
    328
Roosevelt, Franklin D., 12, 25, 44, 48,
    58, 88, 121, 122, 303, 312, 363,
    395, 396, 399
Roosevelt, Franklin D., Jr., 261–62
Roosevelt, Theodore, 6, 58, 60–61, 77,
    94, 111, 117, 398
Roots (Haley), 11
Rosellini, Lynn, 319
Rosenthal, A. M., 176–77, 216–17
Ross, Sherwood, 274

Rosten, Leo, 180
Rowan, Carl, 212–13, 334
Royster, Vermont, 146
Ruby, Jack, 299
Rudd, Hughes, 313–14
Ruff, Eric, 160–61, 215–16, 338, 383
Rum Row, 83
Rumsfeld, Donald, 160
Russell, Jim, 295–96
Russell, Richard B., 298
Rutherfurd, Lucy Mercer, 122
Ryan, Eddie, 98
Ryan, Leo, 348

Sadat, Anwar, 46, 302
Sadat-Begin conference, 379
Sadler, Christine, 72
Safer, Morley, 282
Safire, William, 379, 380
St. John, Jill, 75
Salinger, Pierre, 53–54, 379
Salisbury, Harrison, 287
San Clemente, California, 217
San Simeon, 94
Sans Souci (restaurant), 182
Sarnoff, Robert, Jr., 276–77
Sarro, Ron, 74, 105, 112, 167, 278, 302,
    304, 314, 359–60
Sauer, Marie, 139, 140
Scali, John, 232
Scharanskiy, Avital, 326
Scharanskiy, Anatoli, 326
Scheibel, Ken, 146, 206
Schlesinger, Arthur, Jr., 199
Schlesinger, James, 249
Schmidt, Helmut, 39
Schultz, George, 229
Schwartz, Arnold, 324
Schwartz (Arnold and Marie) Healing
    Arts Center, 324
Schweiker, Dick, 297
Scott, Hugh, 298
Scripps, E. W., 87
Seay, Tom, 256
Seib, Carl B., 310
Sevareid, Eric, 63–64, 283, 339
Sexism in newspapers, 131–47
Shanahan, Eileen, 78–79
Shepard, Lily Lykes, 72, 74
Shepherd, Alexander R., 109
Sheppard, Pratt, 120
Shield laws, 176, 177
Shooter (Kennerly), 373
Short, Robert, 156, 157
Sidey, Hugh, 217
Sigma Alpha Epsilon, 31
Sills, Beverly, 282
Simon, Bill, 229
Simpson, Kirke L., 87
Sinatra, Frank, 272
Sirhan, Sirhan, 389
60 Minutes (TV show), 282–83
Skelly, John, 231–32
Slevin, Joe, 339

416

417